Vigtok Islands
The Rimy Islands
Alba Sea
Wunlu
Anilsaatok
Albanian Seaterras
Inp...
Bay
...gas Passage
Laban
The Hoeden Mountains
Borealis Sea
The Ollaoise Forest
Flei
...ndfather Waters
Betmeer Lake
Perman
Pealagus Sea
Lacuserra
Seaterras of Yús
...rigas
The Grandiesse Mountains
The Purana Mountains
Bahyasi Grasslands
The Alidima Mountains
...ry ...ains
The Openlands
The Jum'nebona Forest
Mapane
Pavdee
Monsoon Sea
The Twins
Baninchi
The Kawaitu Forest
Gaznah
The Mirrad Basin
Mteale
Panpole
The Imperium Cantons
The Koyoran Basin
Sebpixan
Suquwas
Diverge
...rge
The Manduka Forest
...e Everglades
Atoll Sea
The Pachaku Mountains
Iguacu
Latana Seaterras
Blue Reef Sea
...s Sea
The Malana Forest
The Machida Mountains
Penguin Channel
Seaterras of Fire and Ice
...a
Great Alimendia Sea
...n Islands
Sealion Bay

# BIRTH
## OF THE
# ANIMA

ANCIENT LANGUAGE OF THE EARTH

BOOK ONE

ANCIENT LANGUAGE OF THE EARTH

BOOK ONE

# BIRTH OF THE ANIMA

KELSEY K. SATHER

THEIA BOOKS

THEIA BOOKS
P.O. Box 6151
Bozeman, Montana 59771
theiapublishing.com



Printed on 100% post-consumer recycled paper in Canada.

First Edition
ISBN 978-1-7355205-0-6
LCCN 2020916240
FICTION / Fantasy / General
FICTION / Nature & the Environment

Book cover design by Sarah Whittaker
Typesetting by Lorna Reid
Proofreading by Lauren Humphries-Brooks
Maps by Kelsey K. Sather

kelseyksather.com

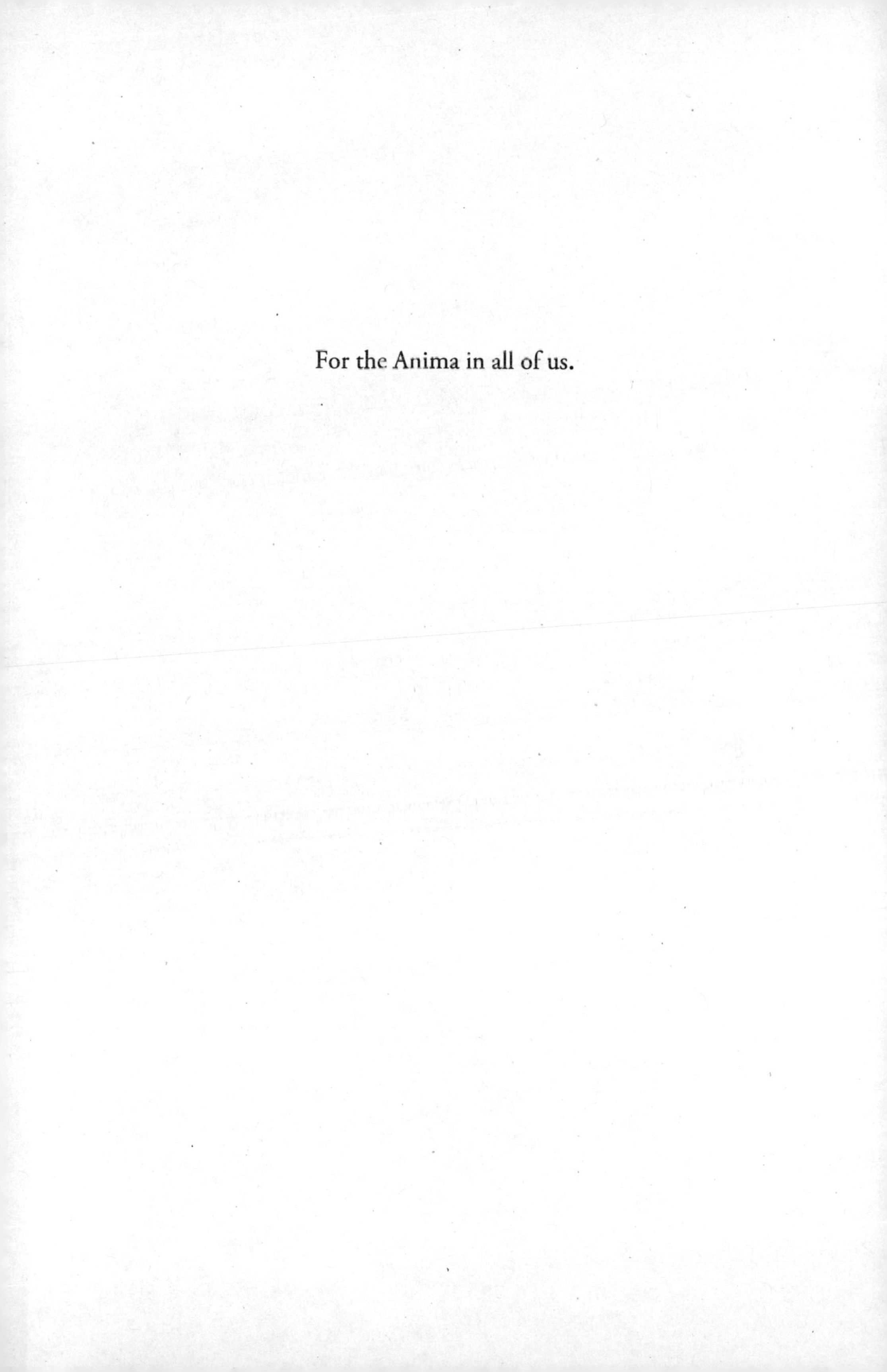

For the Anima in all of us.

CONTENTS

# I

# DISORDER IN THE EAST

*Man rules over all others: women, animals, and plants.*

- Second Proverb of the Power

# AVNI

## 2,210 YEARS BEFORE PRESENT

### PRAJATUYA, OLD MAKALON

Her master interpreted the stars and wrote his constructs in the foreigners' language. Though he had been born an Alidiman, the Yiúsians had acknowledged his gifts and afforded him prestige. Prestige—not freedom. No Alidiman, Avni figured, would ever live free again.

Master Saket pretended to be free like a lord. He barked orders at Avni and her older brother, demanding more wine, more ink. When she would set food and drink on his desk, she hovered as long as he allowed, trying to read what he wrote. Though she understood Yiúsian words aloud, the pitch scratches upon the vellum appeared as meaningful as lines left in dirt by ants.

Back when he had been simply Saket, he would share his interpretations with the village every full moon. If one knew within what moon she had been born, she could hear, through Saket, what the stars said about her future. Avni had never been such a person. She knew not what day her life had begun.

She ground burned bones for his ink. The smell of rock against charred fragments of ribs and vertebrae reminded Avni of the mine in the mountain. She wondered if her dad still swung his axe, or if he, too, had died in last week's collapse. Not that it mattered. She had grieved the death of her father a hundred times over. In any way it mattered, she lived as a parentless child, neither daughter nor girl. Only slave.

The bones a gray powder, she added the tar and pitch. She stirred the masi into Saket's desired thickness, relishing the rare solitude she had found in the courtyard today. The birch trees hinted to fall in leaves lined with gold. Rows of flowering shrubs, flowerless for near a moon now, grew beneath the trees. Avni didn't know the names of these plants. The Yiúsians had brought their seeds along with their army.

She worked on the graveled walkway between the planted rows. Pebbles pushed into her bare knees. The sun, hot with summer's end, bore down from the rectangle of sky the courtyard permitted. The courtyard was all she saw of the outside world. The mountains—the gods of her people—stayed hidden behind the walls of stone. She took as much time as she dared making the masi. These sips of the outdoors helped her endure the white and black walls waiting for her underground.

When she stood, the pebbles left little craters in her knees. She wondered, with no fat beneath her skin, if her bones, too, had little indents. She dusted off her chiton, dyed slave-red with lac resin, and shook out her hair. They kept her thick hair chin length and curled. All the female slaves living in the palace received daily beautification. When Avni had last returned from the courtyard, a single leaf's defile of the beauticians' work had earned her nothing short of three whippings. She hadn't seen her reflection in years, but she imagined her back looked a lot like the vellum etched with those foreign words.

Her sandaled feet pitter-pattered down the stone hallway. She passed a pair of Yiúsian lords, their chitons a deep purple achieved only through dye made from a snail they shipped here from their homeland. She kept her eyes to the ground as taught. They swept by, speaking with harsh tones about an overdue shipment from Spítheo.

Avni skipped down the stone steps leading to the basement where they housed the exceptional Alidiman. It was a dungeon by all but name. Only a few small torches lit the dirt hallway, and rats the size of small dogs were often found ravaging cow legs they had stolen from the kitchen. Sometimes Avni imagined the rats feasting on her sleeping body. She also sometimes imagined being buried alive, should, or when, this underworld cave in on itself.

Saket sat hunched over the desk, muttering to himself in Alidiman. Avni slipped into his room. He startled upright and cursed her sudden appearance.

"Sorry, master," Avni said, bowing her head. "I didn't mean to scare you."

He slouched back over the vellum. "They said they'd cut my tongue out should I speak again in that language," he whispered in Yiúsian. "It's just—I think in it."

She set the bowl on his desk. He sniffed at the masi and stirred it with his needle. When he returned to his fevered writing without another word, she knew she had done her job well. Judging by the salted stubble of his usually clean-shaven head and jaw, Avni figured he hadn't left the room in over three days. She wondered what the stars could have possibly said to demand such continuous work.

In their quarters next door, Ved rolled a scroll. Avni sat on her cot and watched him unfurl the scroll, again and again, until it wrapped flush around the wooden rod. He secured his work with a cut of white linen and set it in the pile of scrolls next to his cot.

"Well done," she whispered.

"We'll see," he replied, shifting to lie down. He had outgrown the boy-sized length of his bed, and his feet, still sandaled, dangled off the end. He told Avni a moon ago that his sixteenth year had arrived. She doubted the sureness of such a statement but had congratulated him nonetheless. Sixteen for an Alidiman male was considered old. Most died their first year in the mine.

The Yiúsians had yet to pull Ved from the palace for pickaxing. When they had come for him shortly after a gesture of muscle formed on his arms, Saket had protested. It was the first and only time Avni had seen her master stand up to the Yiúsians. He had argued that training another boy to perform Ved's duties would put his work too far behind the ever-moving skies. Saket probably had spoken the truth. More so, though, Avni knew their master had grown fond of Ved for reasons beyond his expedient handiwork. In either case, the Yiúsians, in an extraordinary act of assent, had permitted Ved to stay.

Avni had thanked their gods, should the mountains still care to listen.

Ved had cursed them. *I would trade a day out there for a lifetime down here*, he had said.

She lay down on her cot and stared up at the ceiling vaulted by stone, waiting for Saket's next command in silence. Running a hand along the bumps of flesh emerging on her chest, she felt the day near when the Yiúsians would come to make the trade for her.

☾

Avni leaned against the marbled surface of a kitchen counter as she waited for the cooks to finish preparing dinner. She could now almost sit on the counter after her most recent growth spurt. The cooks added leftovers from the Yiúsians' dinner to the stew. They scraped the half-eaten lamb chops and wilted piles of greens into the pot. Avni smelled hints of garlic and sage. Even she would eat like a lord tonight.

A robust woman spooned the stew into three bowls and set them on a platter for Avni. Her red chiton, cut low in the front, revealed engrossed bosoms. Avni wondered if she was one of the nursing-slaves rumored to breastfeed Yiúsian infants. She opened her mouth to ask, but the woman shooed her away.

"Off you go now," the woman said. "Git."

Avni took the platter and sulked out of the kitchen. She needed to know her secret. She needed to know any secret for how an Alidiman woman managed to stay in the palace. She held her breath with each step down the stairs. Even a drop of spilled soup could be reason enough to send her away.

She reached Saket's quarters victorious. The platter remained as clean as when she had left the kitchen, and yet steam still rose from the stew. When she walked into his room, she nearly dropped the whole platter on the ground. Entire slurps splashed out of the bowls.

He had her brother bent over. When they noticed her, Saket withdrew with a curse, and Ved pulled his chiton down. Her brother's face matched the color of his clothes. Avni stared at the platter, demanding the tears to wait. Mumbling an apology, she set the bowls down and walked from the room without her dinner. She ran back down the hallway and indulged in a moment of crying beneath the stairs. She knew Saket took her brother in this fashion, so why had seeing it caused her to stumble?

"Stupid girl," she whispered. "Stupid, stupid girl." She dried her face and wiped the platter off as best she could on the stone of a stair's underside. In the light above, she saw the stone had done nothing to hide her mistake.

The woman in the kitchen took the platter from Avni and gave her a disgusted look. The woman glanced behind her. The other cooks were busy prepping for breakfast. She quickly poured water over the platter and took a wet rag to Avni's face.

"Never again," the woman said. "If they saw I wasted water on the likes of you..."

Avni bit against the trembling of her lip and nodded. She strode from the kitchen, resisting the urge to run, and returned underground. When she at last reached her cot, a drop of blood leaked down her chin.

Ved had his back turned to her. She wanted to do something for him. How did one comfort another? She wanted to know if it hurt—partly because she cared for him, and partly because she wondered for her future self. Should she touch him? She remembered a time, in the courtyard, when a little Yiúsian boy had tripped and scraped his knee. His older sister had hugged him and that had seemed to make his hurt go away. Maybe her brother had held her in such a way when she was a baby. They had never touched in her remembered life. To do so would merit whippings beyond Avni's imagination.

And yet, darkness hid them now. She slipped her feet off the cot and took one soundless step after another. She had never moved so slowly in all her life. When she reached Ved's cot, his eyes were closed. He must not have heard her. Her heart beat frantically as she reached a hand closer, closer, closer to his shoulder. When her fingertips brushed his skin, his eyelids whipped open. He crunched her fingers with his hand. She swallowed the gasp of pain.

*Never,* he mouthed in Alidiman. He released her hand and returned to stillness. Avni drifted back to her cot. She lay with her back to his and held her fingers, wondering if they were broken.

A shake to Avni's shoulder woke her. She blinked up at the face of a stranger. He wore the yellow chiton of a guard.

"Come. Now," he said, twirling the whip's handle.

She scrambled upright and fumbled with her sandal's strappings. Her brother wasn't in the room. Sleepiness caved into reality, and panic gripped her throat. She followed the guard out of the room. She had known this day would come sooner than later, and yet here she was, struggling to breathe.

When they passed Saket's room, she stopped. "Please," she said. "Please, I won't say anything. I won't!"

Saket continued writing, his eyes remaining on the vellum. "You speak nonsense."

The lash on her arm silenced any response. The guard raised the whip again. "If you arrive with too many scars, you will be deemed fit only for dog food."

She looked once more at Saket bent over his work. The palace slaves said he had been the village Wiseman. They had whispered rumors of his powers. He had lived on a hill overlooking Demá Peak, where he could study the stars above any light cast by candles in the homes below. And now look at him, Avni thought. He had no love for her. Why should he? He was neither Yiúsian nor Alidiman, but a mole living out his sunless days.

She followed the guard, holding the whip's cut with fingers still throbbing from her brother's grasp. She didn't look around for Ved as they walked up the steps and down the path lined by white stone columns. The guards manning the entrance lifted the crossbar. When they opened the doors, Avni walked out of the palace and onto what, she had once heard, was called a street. Her eyes blinked against the sun's fullness.

"This way," the guard barked, and she followed his voice. The bursts of light subsided, revealing patches of her surroundings. Giant piles of dung littered the wide dirt road. Wood houses and buildings staggered the larger structures made of stone. Avni marveled at the wooden planks, neatly stacked one on top of the other. The palace slaves had said Alidimans had built their homes from pine, but Avni hadn't been able to imagine walls made of trees rather than rock.

A rumbling noise grew behind her. The guard growled, "Watch out," and pushed Avni closer to the buildings. She cowered against the wall. Creatures ten times larger than any dog she had seen in the palace thundered past. They had long noses and round, glistening eyes. The way they led with their muscled chests reminded Avni of how the Yiúsian guards walked. Their feet made clunking noises as they trotted down the dirt, spraying up dust and dung.

The two animals pulled behind them a man riding a strange table on wheels. He wore the purple chiton of a lord and a golden headband atop his black curls. The guard bowed as he passed, and the lord acknowledged him with a single nod of a head held high. Avni thought he looked serene, like the painting of the Yiúsian king hanging in the palace dining room.

Yet the man raised his whip, and any serenity on his face twisted into severity as he yelled, "Git! Go on, now, git!"

When the whip met the creatures' golden backs, Avni could feel her own scars throbbing. The guard yanked her away from the wall, and they continued down the street. They passed Yiúsian commoners dressed in white chitons. The men and women, half a head taller than the average Alidiman, walked between buildings with importance.

Avni snuck glances at the women. Their hair grew to the small of their backs in silky black waves. Some of the women wore elaborate braids, and some had the curls twisted up into coils that reminded Avni of a beehive she once saw in the courtyard. Alidiman women weren't allowed hair longer than their chins. She wondered if her hair could even grow as long as the women's around her.

The occasional woman in red shook out rugs from balconies and raked dung into piles. She saw no men in red. She assumed they all worked and slept up at the mine.

The mine! The mountains! She looked over her shoulder and nearly fell to her knees. The guard, still holding her wrist, tugged on her arm. "Watch your step."

She continued to walk forward while stealing looks over her shoulder. The palace slaves old enough to remember had said the mountains were gods, bigger than any human, bigger than any building. They had said they wore crowns more brilliant than any headpiece a king could don. They had said they gave water—they gave life. And for the first time in Avni's life, she could see her people had spoken the truth.

The guard pulled her toward a two-story stone building. Avni gaped once more at the massive pinnacles cloaked in a purple deeper than even the lords' chitons. She reached a hand out as if she could touch the gleaming mountaintops. The guard opened the door, and the walls once more swallowed her gods from view.

☾

"How does it work?" Avni asked.

Pam pulled the last rod from Avni's hair and fluffed up the curls. "You lay on the bed and wait for him to come in."

Avni couldn't tell if Pam sounded tired or annoyed. She knew she pressed her luck either way, but the fear of it outweighed the fear of her new master. "I mean—the act of it. How does it *work*?"

"It's perfect you don't know." Pam stepped back to admire her handiwork. Her red chiton hung loose on her thin frame. She was almost skinnier than Avni.

"But won't he need me to know?"

Pam leaned in and brushed a charcoal powder atop Avni's eyelids. She painted a berry-stained beeswax on Avni's lips. Avni fantasized eating the entire tin of lip tint. She had a fresh berry once in the palace, and its sweetness still haunted her.

"The lord requested a virgin," Pam said, putting the lid back on the tin. "If you knew what you were doing, he'd question the authenticity of your—girlhood."

Avni swallowed the familiar taste of panic. "But does he know I'm no girl? My moon-blood came this spring."

Pam smiled and cupped Avni's jaw. Her hands felt as cold as her smile looked. "Oh child, it takes more than blood to make a girl a woman." She released Avni's face and motioned for her to follow. "It's time," she said, walking out of the room and down the hallway.

Avni could hear moaning on the other side of the doors. So it did hurt. She tried to relax her body: this had helped make the whippings less painful. Pam held a door open for her. A window allowed sunlight in, and the stone-white room glowed. Avni stared at the window, fighting the desire to run to it and look once more at the gods. A large bed dressed in white centered the room. Long strips of white fabric hanging from the ceiling surrounded the bed.

The bed reminded Avni of a cloud. She, too, wore white. She had never seen fabric other than red against her brown skin. When she sat on the bed, she thought her bare arms and legs resembled fallen birch branches atop snow.

Pam told her to lie down in the middle. She adjusted Avni's legs so one was straight and the other was bent. She told her to prop up on one arm and place the other so her hand rested between her thighs. Pam fluffed Avni's hair once more. She smoothed the sheets and stepped back.

"You're a vision." She almost sounded motherly.

Avni tried to smile.

"Don't move," Pam said, any maternal tone dead in her voice. "If I hear there is so much of a *wrinkle* in this sheet before he arrives, you can kiss your life goodbye." She closed the door behind her. Avni felt sweat beads bubble up on her forehead. Would she ruin the makeup? A cramp began to form in the calf of her bent leg. She closed her eyes and begged her body to relax.

Just when her entire leg threatened to seize up, her eyes now wet, the door opened. She prayed the single tear dripping off her nose fell clean of charcoal. The man, not as tall as Avni had expected, studied her as he closed the door. A belt of braided leather wrapped around his waist over a purple chiton. A branch of leaves and berries, painted gold and wound into a circle, topped his long, brown curls. He kept his beard trimmed close to his face, as was typical of Yiúsian lords.

Yet his eyes were nothing close to typical. Neither the dark brown of Alidimans, nor the golden brown of Yiúsians, they were white. Or were they blue? They gazed at Avni as two spheres of ice, though not unkindly. He looked more curious than cruel. Avni wondered if this was how all men approached a virgin.

Was she supposed to smile? She glanced down to make sure her hand hadn't slipped away from her groin. He sat on the bed, still looking at Avni with those cool, calculating eyes. She managed to slip the corners of her mouth up. The sweat had begun to drip. She could taste its salt.

"Please," he said. Was that—Alidiman he spoke? This position must be cutting off circulation to her head.

But he spoke again, and sure enough the words clicked and rolled in her native tongue. "Please, relax." He patted the corner of the bed next to him. "Come, sit with me."

When she moved to obey, her entire leg seized at last, and she dragged it like a dead weight.

"Are you okay?" he asked, watching her crawl across the bed.

"Fine, fine, my lord," she said in Yiúsian, coming to a sit. Thank the gods, her muscles relaxed.

He traced a rib poking against her chiton. "Clearly you are not." He continued to look at her with an expression Avni couldn't place. Was it sadness? Maybe the color of his eyes clouded her ability to name it. "You have been a slave your whole life?"

Avni couldn't tell if it was a question or a statement. Was he expecting someone different? A free woman, perhaps? She wondered if there had been a mistake. She remembered Ved bent over the desk, the white knuckles of his hands grabbing the edge. Saket's hips had moved back and forth. It seemed the act of it didn't require words.

"You have been a slave your whole life," he repeated. He unthreaded a leather pouch from his belt. "I found this at last."

He opened the pouch and withdrew a mushroom. The cap was the same color as the stain on her lips. Little white dots punctuated the red. Its stem, white and striated like a stone column, still had flecks of earth on it. The way he held it in his palm told Avni that he cared for this mushroom more than she had cared for anything in all her life.

So when he asked her to take it, she didn't at first. She shook her head and said, "I can't, my lord. I'm not worthy of your treasure."

His smile was unmistakably sad. "But Anima," he said. "It belongs to you."

Confused, she continued to shake her head. "I'm sorry, my lord. You have been misled. My name is Avni, not Anima."

He tore a piece off the mushroom's cap and folded the fragment into Avni's hand. He then tore off another piece, held it to his mouth, and gestured for her to do the same. She did as told, and when he began to chew the mushroom, she did as well. Swallowing took effort. The mushroom tasted the way fall smells, of sweet decay. When the white canopy overhead spun and spun, she felt like the sky had yawned open and the cloud they rode took them into the sun.

☾

Water dripped, dripped, dripped from the stalactites. Wax stubs littered the ground. Avni and her war council gathered around three candles and a map of Prajatuya. Thousands of Shapeshifters had amassed. Dozens sat in caverns and leaned against the cave's mossy walls. Hundreds more stood outside in the mountain air, waiting.

Hamia placed a finger on the palace. "Avni says the kings' quarters are in this wing."

"Lords," Avni said. "They are but lords. The king lives in Spítheo."

"Kings, lords, whatever the name. They are the men in power here. If we kill them first, chaos will be our ally."

A few dozen Shapeshifters murmured their agreements. A few, though, whispered concerns.

"What of the guards?" Sabaa asked. She sat poised in her human form next to Gaagi. The other Shapeshifters often said she and Avni looked like sisters. They both were Alidiman. Like all Shapeshifters, Sabaa had been born millennia earlier than Avni, even though they appeared similar in age.

"When I flew over the town yesterday," Sabaa continued, "I saw at least twenty manning each of the four entrances. And for every twenty manning an entrance, a hundred more guard sections where the wall is incomplete."

"And that is why we attack now," Hamia said. "Before the wall is done."

"How many in total, would you say?" Avni asked.

"At least five hundred," Sabaa said, looking at Gaagi.

Gaagi confirmed Sabaa's estimate with a nod. As a Salvager, he already knew the exact number of guards. He hardly resembled the man who had come to Avni in the whorehouse two years ago. His hair had grown back to its natural white color. Avni couldn't believe she had fallen for his impersonation of a Yiúsian. He could speak and dress like one, but as he sat now in quiet, preferring, as usual, to listen rather than talk, he was anything but Yiúsian.

"Making the odds two to one," Hamia said, smiling. Her white teeth gleamed in sharp contrast to the silky black of her skin. She kept her long hair in hundreds of tiny braids.

Avni rose to her feet. "We are the ones able to stop this Disorder spreading," she called out loud enough for the Shapeshifters gathered outside the cave to hear. "The Anima and her Shapeshifters are enough to bring the Sacred Balance back to this land." She flexed the muscles of her chest and arms, feeling them swell with their power. The scars on her back thinned as they stretched across the expanse of her strength.

The Shapeshifters exploded into their preferred form. Sabaa stripped into her silk animal underskin and morphed: her arms grew black and red feathers, and her skull curved forward into the scythe shape of her eagle head. Her golden eyes alone didn't change. Half of the Shapeshifters remained human, and half turned into animal. The snow leopard hissed. Hamia, still human, growled as if she had morphed into her cheetah form.

All the Shapeshifters joined in a cacophony of roars, howls, and yelling. When they ran down the mountain, the earth quaked, the evergreens shook, and they trampled grasses under paw and foot. They charged through the town's outskirts, slaying men dressed in white. The Yiúsian women and children were gathered into a cow corral. Avni put the dead men's weapons in the hands of humans dressed in red. They held the swords and spears with limp grips, blinking at Avni and the half-dozen Shapeshifters who stayed to help stand guard over the prisoners.

"If they try to escape, injure, don't kill," Avni commanded.

She sprinted away to join the flood of fur, feathers, and skin descending on the white walls enclosing Prajatuya. The guards scrambled to form lines. Some guards yelled and others screamed as they angled their spears at the strange wave of creatures galloping at them. Their beards did little to hide their fear.

Avni's long hair whipped as she launched at a Yiúsian, stabbing him with her daggers. She landed on her feet in a form remarkably similar to the snow leopard next to her. Shapeshifters weaved through sweeps of iron. The boar ran between a guard's legs and pierced the man's groin with his tusks. The tiger killed another Yiúsian with a massive claw to his head.

The guards, their yellow chitons stained red, littered the ground. For every four Yiúsians killed, one Shapeshifter fell lifeless to the earth. Avni and the Shapeshifters rushed through the gate and continued their attack within the walls. Alidimans ran past, some crying, some whooping and hollering. Horses stampeded out of the town and into the open. Some of the Alidiman women pulled weapons from dead hands and sought their own revenge.

Avni moved through the chaos with her head bent toward the palace. She slipped her daggers back into her boots and withdrew a whip from a man dead beneath his chariot. When a sword or spear tried to stop her, she wrapped the whip around the weapon and flung it into the sky. She let the Shapeshifters trailing behind her take care of the weaponless men left in her wake.

Her footsteps echoed in the empty palace. No guards manned the doors; no lords strutted down the stone paths. Avni found the cooks hiding in the kitchen. She paused, seeing the woman who had cleaned her tear-streaked face a lifetime ago. She went to the water basin and filled a jug. Standing before her people, Avni poured the water over her own head. It washed the salt and blood off her face.

She went back to the basin, filled the jug again, and helped the woman she remembered to her feet. She poured the water over the woman's head and said, "We are worthy."

Setting the jug back down, she left the kitchen. Hamia, Sabaa, and a few others followed behind as she walked downstairs. She could smell the lingering smoke of the extinguished torches. The lack of light mattered little: she and the Shapeshifters saw through the dark. They found the Alidimans in the last room, her old quarters.

The children screamed. Avni couldn't hear them over blood pounding against her eardrums. She walked to her old cot, and the children sitting on it scurried to the opposite side of the room. One of them was a girl not much older than Avni had been when she last slept here. Avni watched the girl stumble to Ved's old cot, and Avni raised a hand as if to touch her. She instead ran her fingers along the hard surface of the cot. She lay down on it and stared up at the stones above.

They all shared in the silence. The Shapeshifters stood quiet with a knowing reverence. The children, unaware of their freedom, held their tongues as they had been taught. Avni returned her feet to the ground. The children bit their lips, and tears welled in their eyes. She resisted the urge to tell them they could cry; it would take moons of freedom for them to understand.

"Where are the men you call masters?" Avni asked in Alidiman. The children exchanged looks of terror. Again, she resisted an urge to place a reassuring hand upon them. Touch, like emotion, would take time to understand. Instead, she placed the whip on her lap and asked the same question in Yiúsian.

A little boy, his hands stained black with masi, whispered, "They are hiding beneath a lord's bed." Shaking from the effort, the boy lost control and broke out in sobs.

Hamia moved to hold him, but Avni told her no, not yet. She asked the Shapeshifters to watch over the children until the fighting was done overhead. On her way out of the basement, she stepped into Saket's room. He had spilled a bowl of masi across a cut of vellum, obscuring the entirety of what he had last written. Avni studied the sea of black liquid across the stretch of skin. If Saket had seen their coming, he hadn't warned the Yiúsians.

She returned above and found the hallway she had never been permitted to walk down as a slave. She opened the large wooden doors, carved with ornate patterns, and stepped into a circular room with four more doors. Behind each one was a dead lord. The last door revealed the Alidimans who had lived downstairs. A pair of Shapeshifters watched over them. One of the Alidimans lay in a pool of his own blood. Avni recognized him as the woodworker.

The fox Shapeshifter, standing in his human form, frowned at the corpse. "He fought back."

Avni nodded. He chose prestige over freedom. So be it.

"Avni?" Saket's voice was a whisper.

She walked to where he was sitting on the bed, his knees pulled into his chest. He seemed even bonier than she remembered. His sunken cheeks and ashen skin told Avni he was weeks away from death. She twirled the whip's handle in her hand as she examined the wrinkles falling from his eyes and mouth.

When she imagined this moment in the moons leading up to the attack, she thought she would find him and exact the pain he had inflicted on her. But now, more than his cruel dismissal of her, and even more than his twisted taking of her brother, she remembered the image of him bent over his work, a mole among men. She set the whip between them. He flinched when she touched his shoulder.

"Where is my brother?" she asked.

Saket looked at the floor and mumbled, "The mine."

She thanked him, although she had already figured as much. She stopped in the courtyard on her way out of the palace. The birch trees, full with summer's bounty, trembled in a breeze. The flowers of the foreign plants blossomed with yellow and red petals. Avni crouched on the pathway and gathered the pebbles within her hand. She had once believed these pebbles were fragments of the gods. Now she couldn't say one way or the other.

The Yiúsians guarding the mine hadn't heard or seen them coming. The Shapeshifters swept over the men in yellow as quick and complete as a mudslide. The Alidimans walked out of the holes in the mountainside. They covered their eyes and moaned with the pain of light. Avni remembered the first time she walked onto a street, how the sun had overwhelmed everything else.

When all the freed men had walked out of the mines, and Ved did not appear, Avni rested a hand on the cliff and breathed into the hole where her hope had lived. The Alidimans sat on the ground, still covering their eyes. There weren't even a hundred of them.

The Shapeshifters piled the bodies of the guards. Some of the Alidimans had begun to peek out through slits in their fingers. Many of them coughed persistently. Dust particles drifted out of the mines. Avni could feel a thin layer of grime forming on her sweaty limbs.

She spoke quietly. "I am Avni, the Anima," she began. "And you are no longer slaves, but Alidimans once again."

The men tilted their chins up. Some managed to open their eyes completely. One began to laugh. His cackling digressed into a rattling cough. Another began to cry. The men around him moved away as if he had a contagious disease.

Avni asked them to follow her back to Prajatuya. They hesitated to stand up, stealing glances at the pile of their former whip-bearers as if the evidence of their freedom would suddenly evaporate. The Shapeshifters stayed behind as Avni and the men trudged down the mountainside. When the men staggered across the farmland leading to their town, more than one of them began to cry. By the time they reached the wall, a wall half-done, Avni was crying as well. They walked into their town and were greeted by a couple hundred people dressed in red.

Only a few recognized a spouse or child. These sobbing reunions, though, were enough to help the rest of them remember that they, too, had been loved by someone at some point, even if it was but the moment their mother saw them enter the world.

One person, then another, turned to Avni. The crowd all looked at her and waited. How did they begin again? She returned their stare as she struggled to find words.

The woman from the kitchen knelt. Another did the same, and another, until all the Alidimans were bowing. A prayer moved through her people, and she heard them call her goddess. The whisper grew from a question to a proclamation. They called her a beast, saying she ran like the fox and killed like the tiger. They agreed she was a child of the gods.

Avni shook her head with horror. "No," she said. "No, no. I am no goddess. Please, stand."

They didn't seem to hear her. They continued to kiss the earth, murmuring words of gratitude and thanks to the gods for their daughter, the emancipator.

She stepped back. "No, that's not the point. I'm not the point. Stand up," she yelled. "Stand up!" Gaagi's hand came to her shoulder. She hadn't seen him approach and hugged him with relief.

"Remember how you had to learn to be free," he said. "Let their beliefs serve as stepping stones to the truth."

"But they think I'm a deity. I am no goddess. I am no queen."

Gaagi turned Avni back to face her people. They were still bent low to the ground. Blood from the battle had stained their knees red. "For now, you will be what they need," he said.

"And what is that?"

"A bridge between their hopeless past and their new reality."

☾

On her deathbed, Avni remembered these words Gaagi spoke. He had died a decade ago, shortly after celebrating over three thousand and five hundred years of life. He had hoped for Avni to bring all of Lacuserra under the banner of Order, starting with the Yiúsians, then the Flüschen further north. Alongside Shapeshifters and Alidimans, she had driven the Yiúsians back to their homeland and restored Order to the liberated people of the Socok Desert and Samnotama Steppes. Yet while the Yiúsians had been defeated in Makalon, Disorder continued to fester in Lacuserra.

The medicine man said Avni was dying of old age. She figured she was dying from caring too much for too long. Her heartbeat waned. The Task remained far from complete—it was now a charge for future Animas.

The Salvager born in Gaagi's place, a woman named Laurel, held Avni's head and kept her face cool with a wet rag. The entire village prayed for her death to be a beginning. They had gathered in the streets with candles and song. Even as she died in this very moment, her mortality circling in like an owl on a mouse, they still thanked their gods for the gift of their child, the goddess, the Anima.

*A bridge*, Gaagi had said. "He made it sound temporary," Avni muttered.

Laurel, her eyes like his, white and blue at once, looked upon Avni with love. "Everything is temporary," she said, running her cool fingers along Avni's jaw.

Avni smiled at this, and, lying in the courtyard beneath a sky made starlit with darkness, she felt her life run free from her body. But before she released into nothing—everything—she whispered, "The next will be born where animal became human."

# II

## FREDA OF THE CANTONS

*"She perverted all I thought I knew of the world and my role in it."*

- Adalbern Hertz, The Wolfwoman of Taléria

# SCROLL

## 105 YBP

TWIN RIVERS, PROMINENCE DISTRICT

Freda excavated the earth, removing pottery shards and obsidian flakes with her long tweezers. Yarrow Peak stood as witness to her, just as it had witnessed a woman's burial here millennia earlier. Wind teased the wild grasses, sending silver ripples across the green. Freda brought the fragments of history to her eyes with gloved hands. The petite features of her face were smooth and sun kissed. Though she was twenty-four years old, someone in passing might have thought Freda a young boy, playing in the dirt, cropped hair matted with sweat and soil.

Her probing came to a hard surface. She brushed away dirt to reveal the top of a wooden box. "Hey," she called out. "Come look at this." No one responded. She looked around and saw her cohorts and the Imperial government officials eating lunch under a tent across the field. "Thanks for the invitation," she mumbled.

She wiggled the box free from the earth and cleaned it of soil. Each stroke of the brush revealed a creature carved into the wood: mouse, muskrat, swallow, skunk, deer, raccoon, fox, bear, cougar, wolf, pika. She figured the carvings represented some of the Bilawáxan deities. It would have been impossible to fit the entire pantheon on this box; every vertebrate in the regional ecology had a spiritual archetype in Bilawáxan cosmology. Every vertebrate, that was, save humans.

Freda found the lid's seam and gently pried it open. Inside, rolled up, a scroll lay within an otherwise empty and unlined container. She unfurled the vellum with great care. Small letters were etched into the hide, not of the Bilawáxan alphabet, nor any of the common languages. "Setú," she whispered.

A singular thought overcame her—she must not share this scroll with her superiors, much less her cohort.

This demand, seemingly spoken by the scroll itself, silenced the risks. She could be kicked out of her doctorate program for stealing artifacts. She could be fined thousands of dollars. She could be imprisoned. Getting caught was not an option for these obvious reasons.

Yet a much larger consequence shadowed these potential ramifications, just as Yarrow Peak dwarfed the tent where the crew finished lunch. Was it intuition telling her this? Freda didn't know. She also didn't know what this monumental consequence could possibly be. She could only *feel* it as devastation she wouldn't be able to endure.

One thing she knew for sure: the scroll and box were meant for her. She found them. Alone. They belonged to her. And although a voice, quiet like a distant echo, told Freda these thoughts were irrational—*insane*, even—she couldn't hear it. Or rather, she refused to listen. It was as if the scroll unearthed an absolute truth within her, rather than the other way around.

She reasoned her talent as an archeologist already surpassed that of her professors. She figured that's why her cohort always left her out. They envied her, were intimidated by her, felt alienated by her brilliance. It didn't help she was a woman, the only in the program and one of ten in all the university. With more and more men being drafted to the Imperial Army, the university had begun admitting the most promising women scholars. Having a father as a professor may have sealed her admission, but she alone earned the top grades in her class.

Excellence and exception came at a cost, and she had paid her dues ten times in solitude. Now it was her time to cash in on her skill. She glanced at the government officials talking to one another under the tent. The Imperial watchdogs, as she called them, were allegedly there to ensure no one stole from the dig. She found their presence off-putting. Freda had done many digs on behalf of Twin Rivers University, and yet this was the first one the government deemed worthy of protection from theft. She placed the scroll back in the box, wrapped the box in her sweater, and slid it into her backpack as the crew sauntered back.

She continued to dig, in silence, unfazed by the flints of bone and cracked stone bowls emerging beneath brush and trowel. As a crew, they sought clues to why the death of a woman held significance to the ancient people of the Crazy Mountains. Freda figured she had the answer to this question in her backpack.

What *was* a scroll presumably made in Old Makalon doing in a box buried in Prominence? The box and scroll sat on Freda's kitchen table as she paced the studio apartment, turning this question over and over.

The relics had to relate to the woman buried nearby. A couple of teenagers had found her remains deep within a cave. Freda thought of the woman's bones on the steel table in the lab on campus. The skull appeared more feline than human, with unnaturally high cheekbones and large eye sockets. Her skull wasn't the only deviation from the skeletons of her contemporaries; her toes were much longer, and the density of her bones was heavier. The forensic anthropologists all agreed she had been strong and fast—much stronger and faster than her male companions.

This abnormal skeleton was most likely the reason the Imperial government guarded the dig. The Bilawáxan specialists figured she was a manifestation of some rare genetic mutation. They hypothesized her physique would have demanded respect. She could have even held power in a social system that had been exceptionally egalitarian. Her burial was the only of its kind yet discovered in the region. Bilawáxan skeletons were rarely found near remnants of campsites. Most of their bones were discovered at random, encountered as haphazardly as one came upon the remains of a cougar kill. If a Bilawáxan was going to die, it appeared as if he would walk off into the folds of forest, alone.

Freda sat at the table and examined the box once again. It looked to be made of yew. Someone had crafted it long after the woman's death; even a layman could see the box was less than five hundred years old. Yet she couldn't guess the scroll's age. The leather remained largely intact, having been buried in the box. She unfurled the scroll, feeling anew the desire to *own* the parchment. This returning need of possession confused her. Wasn't it hers now?

She stood and poured more wine into her mug. It was past midnight, and she had yet to eat dinner. She pulled leftover fried chicken from the refrigerator and warmed it up in the oven. The couple in the apartment above was having sex again. Dust rained down from the ceiling fan. Freda leaned against the window frame and looked out on the road below. A sedan puttered down Main Street, but otherwise Twin Rivers' downtown had been deserted. Beyond the flickering lights of the Pizza Parlor's sign, a crescent moon hung above the black silhouette of the Crazy Mountains.

The timer binged, and she sat back down at the table with her dinner. She ate without looking away from the scroll, wondering what it said and why it had chosen her. What story did she now hold in her possession—and how did this story possess her?

Freda rolled out of bed, hungover and bloated. She had slept through her first class and would miss the second. After a shower and a slice of toast, she walked to campus. Light rain pattered on her trench coat. Sedans splashed through puddles while the occasional horse-pulled buggy clunked down the slow lane. A rancher drove a few sheep down the slow lane as well. His leather jacket was dark with wet, and a grimace pulled his face tight beneath a cowboy hat.

She thought of the report on yesterday's excavation that was due Friday. There was no point in writing about obsidian flakes and pottery shards again, but she would do it anyway. Her professors needed something. They always needed something, having publications to achieve, tenure to acquire. Freda knew she was but a cog in their careers.

She strode up the library steps with her head down. Inside, she kept her hood up and walked to the pay phone. "Hi, yes, this is Freda Johansson." She forced a hoarse voice. "I'm sick and won't be able to"—a couple of coughs—"teach my anthropology class today. Please let my students know they have the day off."

A few words of well wishes later, Freda hung up the phone. She walked to the library's filing cabinet. The books she needed were on the seventh floor, in the dim, musty back corner of the building's highest level. She rented the books and stepped outside. Lightning spread across the sky in white branches. Thunder rolled over the valley and echoed off the mountains. Freda marched through the pummeling rain back home. She locked the apartment door behind her.

The storm continued to rampage as hours passed. She hunched over the scroll with a magnifying glass, transcribing the faded caricatures onto a sheet of paper. Long after the storm had blown through, she finished jotting down the Setú words. She looked up to the clock. How was it nine already? She opened the window, and the after-rain smell filled her apartment. A group of university students, maybe a couple years younger than she was, laughed and drank beer around a bonfire below.

Freda slipped on her coat and walked to the corner store. She bought some more fried chicken, potato salad, and another bottle of wine. Back at the kitchen table, she unbuttoned her jeans. The pants had fit her well last year. She shifted in the chair and bit into a chicken leg. With a refilled mug of wine, she reopened the Setú dictionary and began working through all the possible translations. The words resembled Alidimanic Setú more than Grahanyanis.

Voices from the bonfire faded. Midnight slunk in, then out. Moonlight funneled through the open window, shining on Freda's pen moving back and forth, book pages turning, dust from sepia paper swirling up. She had translated ancient languages before, yet this scroll eluded concrete rendering. The words felt slippery. Their meaning posed a riddle dependent on context, the context subject to interpretation. Was *kamanara* sorcery or magic? Did *jagmayanan* mean a mysterious world, or the mystery of the world?

Two, three, four o'clock passed. The wine bottle emptied. As dawn broke with gray light, Freda rewrote the translation she found most coherent, most settling. She cleared the sleepless night from her throat and breathed life into the words with her voice.

☾

Freda knew nothing existed apart from cause and effect. Isolation wasn't real. It was a closed system, after all, this planet. The flap of a butterfly wing and everything. Yet she couldn't think of any possible reasons for why a scroll presumably written in northeast Baninchi had been buried in Owl Creek Canyon. She still assumed the scroll's story somehow included the Bilawáxan woman; its burial next to hers was too coincidental to be chalked up to chaos.

If her translation was correct, the woman could have possibly talked to animals. Not literally, of course. The words *magic* and *language* were loose interpretations. Freda mistrusted her translation, but she couldn't speak to any of the Makalonian specialists on campus. She couldn't speak to any specialists in all the Cantons for that matter, not without committing career suicide.

She had slipped further and further away these past two months as the scroll continued to consume her. It demanded her attention when teaching, taking notes in class, reading, writing. She continued her work at the excavation site, but none of the emerging artifacts seemed important. Nothing else mattered but the scroll and the box. They alone could answer why the woman had been buried in the cave.

And while the scroll had absorbed Freda into its mystery, the guilt had faded, though the first few weeks following her discovery proved torturous. Her awkwardness around her peers had increased to borderline anxiety attacks anytime cohort meetings required her to interact. The burial site crew was banging their heads against the wall, and Freda knew she held the sledgehammer in her hands. She feared she would reveal her secret by some slip of the tongue.

So she didn't talk. Her peers asked her questions, probing her for guidance as they always did. Her quiet non-brilliance clashed with her usual outspoken, clever self. Her peers found the change infuriating; her professors were alarmed. Freda's advisor pulled her aside after class one day, asking if she was okay. She assured him she was fine.

The semester ended, and Freda packed her bags. Not for some holiday family gathering, as she wouldn't need to pack to visit family. Twin Rivers was her hometown, but her father had died a year into her university studies, and her mother lay comatose on life support after a stroke last spring. Freda swung into the hospice before leaving, telling the void of her mother she would be using some of the inheritance to take a trip. She hadn't touched the money her father had left for them until now; it had felt too wrapped up in loss.

But the scroll had changed this, too. Freda knew her father would have disapproved of her transgression, the blatant sabotage to the university. The doctorate had been his idea. He had worked for three decades as a professor of journalism before his death. None of that mattered anymore—his hopes and needs for her as a parent, and the sacrifices made to open doors for her, a woman. The scroll had chosen her. It was the guiding force in her life now. Freda hadn't known she held her own hopes and needs for something like the scroll until it was birthed to her from the earth.

Mushroom. That was the only word on the scroll Freda felt confident about in her translation. It was the key, she believed, to unlocking where the scroll had been crafted. That word, *mushroom*, had brought to mind a lesson from her undergraduate studies, something about a sacred talisman in the goddess-worshipping religion of the Alidimans, an ancient people indigenous to Old Makalon's Purana Mountains. Since the scroll was written in Alidimanic Setú, she had returned to the library and found a textbook on the theory discussed in class.

The textbook examined a collection of ancient parchments found in the Purana Mountains. The parchments mentioned a sacred plant. The textbook's author, an obscure archeologist with the pen name of R.R.M., proposed it was the Fly Agaric mushroom. While the theory had provoked severe backlash in the anthropology community, it held possibility for Freda. If the plant mentioned in the ancient Old Makalonian texts *was* a mushroom, then the scroll could have originated in a similar culture, maybe even the same region.

Freda had checked out all the books on the Fly Agaric. The mushroom proved influential in the places it grew. For centuries, shamans, healers, and witches throughout the world used the red-capped, white-dotted mushroom to induce psychological visions. The ancient Flüschen tribes of Grahimland had called the mushroom "Raven's Call," though scholars had yet to discern why. The Sypayos witch doctors of the Manduka Forest were known to use the fungus for spiritual trances, as were the now-extinct Talhüman shamans of the Lug Steppes.

Lore and fact blurred together. After yet another weekend holed up in the apartment, pouring through books, one thing was clear to Freda: the Fly Agaric held spiritual significance in many cultures throughout time and space. The mushroom mentioned on the scroll *could* be that mysterious plant referred to in the Old Makalonian texts; given the texts and scroll were both written in Alidimanic Setú, the likelihood existed, if slim.

It was this margin of possibility, this keyhole emerging from the mist of myth and history, bringing Freda to Makalon on a one-way ticket now.

☾

When she stepped off the plane, humidity pressed against her body. The smell of trash mingled with body odor and an unnamable sweetness. She had her canvas backpack and nothing more. Outside the airport, little buggies honked, and people swished by in long pants and skirts. Men on bike taxis pedaled with passengers sitting in the rickety carriages. A man approached her with no teeth and hands stretched out, asking for money. She placed a copper coin in his upturned palm and waved down a bike taxi. One swerved over, and she slid into the carriage.

Fumbling with the pages of her Makalonian dictionary, she said, "Please—take—me—hostel."

"It's okay," the biker replied. "I speak a small Imperial. I know of a hostel."

He started to pedal. Freda was impressed with his speed. Shops lined the street, little bakeries and shoe stores. Women knitted on the sidewalk next to peddlers clinking cans of coins.

"Why you in Makalon?" the biker asked.

"I'm here for a study."

"Are you stay in Svayah?"

Freda shook her head. "I'm leaving as soon as I can find a translator."

"How long? Where you go?"

A crowd of people crossed the street. The biker looked at Freda over his shoulder as he rested a foot on the ground. He appeared to be in his late teens.

"I'll be gone as long as it takes. I'm heading northeast, to the Pavarmaya Temple."

"Old Makalon, huh?" He frowned. "Imperials—they no go there much. What you pay translator?" He began to pedal again.

"Ten coppers a day, plus food, travel, and lodging."

The street opened to a market square, and he biked to a small building. *The Palace*, a sign read in Imperial. He parked the taxi and helped Freda out of the cab.

"We can leave in morning," he said.

Freda gave him a once-over. It felt too easy. She hesitated, her jaw clenched. But whom, really, had she planned to hire?

"Pack warm clothes and good shoes," she said. "We'll most likely end up in the mountains."

"Amil." He stuck out his hand.

She shook it. "Freda."

Amil was waiting in The Palace lobby when Freda walked down the stairs for breakfast. They ate a quick meal of flatbread and chutney. He told her how excited his parents were about this trip, how he'd make more in their time together than a year taxiing.

"Enough to find bride," he said, giving Freda a wink.

Freda softened. He seemed like a nice young man looking for work. She told herself to be grateful she had found someone so quickly.

They boarded the first train for Old Makalon. The city gave way to green and yellow fields. Freda could see people squatted down in the expanse of crops. The growth was a stark contrast to the white winter back in Prominence. They passed women dressed in bright wraps, holding large, woven-grass bowls atop their heads. The train crested a hill and descended into a wide valley. A river meandered through the lush green. Freda fell asleep. She woke with a start and grabbed at her bag. Amil slept, his mouth parted and black hair covering his eyes.

The train pulled into Bandmak, and Freda nudged Amil awake. They would only stay the night in the city. Over dinner Freda explained that she didn't really know where they were going, only the general region.

"I want to get into the Purana Mountains as soon as possible," she said. "We're not going to find what I'm looking for in any city, much less one at this elevation."

"What you look for?" Amil asked.

Freda glanced at her pack next to her. Her fingers twitched, feeling the letters etched into the vellum. "I'm not sure yet," she answered, clutching her fists. "Tell me more about this bride."

The next day they boarded the train to Parapte. The railway moved through the Purana foothills, dipping into tunnels and slinking across narrow bridges. Freda couldn't imagine how they managed to construct the railway nearly a hundred years ago. She found herself holding her breath as the train pummeled through the greenery of the foothills, over bridges built on arches with vines crawling up the masonry. One tunnel left them in darkness for a few minutes, and Freda hugged her pack to her chest until the train rolled back into light. Amil pretended not to notice. Freda blushed as she relaxed her grip.

The train gained elevation, and eucalyptus trees gave way to pine and juniper dusted with snow. They arrived in Parapte and stepped out into the midday. Amil pulled a cotton shift from his pack while Freda slipped into her fur-trimmed wool jacket.

"Is that the warmest layer you have?" Freda asked.

Amil nodded.

Freda asked Amil to get directions to the temple. On their way to the bus station, Freda bought Amil a wool coat and a pair of boots. Macaques populated the streets, walking among the people as if they were also going to the store or work. Freda stared at one perched on a railing as she walked by. A hood of fur framed his red face, and his eyes darted between Freda and her pack. Freda quickened her steps. They reached the bus station and waited in the cold.

"I never have see snow," Amil said, picking up a handful. He sniffed it.

"Beautiful, isn't it?"

He marveled at the world around him. "Yes, beautiful."

The bus slipped and snaked up a large hill. With each violent fishtail, Freda thought they were bound to roll down the mountain. But they made it to the temple, alive though carsick. She and Amil stood on the side of the road, taking in the view of the town woven throughout the forested foothills. Snow covered the red roofs and evergreen treetops. The Purana Mountains towered above it all as blue and white pinnacles. Red and yellow flags flapped in front of the white temple with a pointed red roof and yellow trim. A large bell rang while smaller ones tinkled. People clicking and clacking in Makalonian moseyed around the temple.

Freda walked up the steps with Amil close behind. They stepped inside. Myrrh incense filled the damp darkness, and murmurs of prayers threaded with the tinkling bells. Pilgrims knelt in front of an altar for the goddess. Amil joined the people praying. Freda studied the mural of Avni hanging above the altar. The goddess hovered over the mountains with arms stretched wide. Blackness encompassed her radiating body, and a full moon shined as a silver orb in the sky above her. Freda waited for a while before touching Amil on the shoulder. She motioned with her hand for him to follow her back outside. They blinked their eyes against the bright light.

"We need to find someone who has been here a while," Freda said. "Someone who takes care of the temple."

They sat and waited. The day faded. People came and went. Amil went back into the temple for a while.

He returned to Freda and asked, "What is in your pack? I do not steal. No one here steal. What thing made you so scared of people?

His intense forthrightness unsettled Freda. She licked her lips. "I—well, there's this thing I found. Or these things..."

She knew she would need to reveal the scroll and box eventually. As her translator, he would need to be present when she showed the scroll to people who may have answers. But would the scroll demand his obsession in the same way it demanded hers? Would he want to take it from her? He was a little taller than she was, but she was thicker in the arms, more robust. She could protect her ownership if needed.

"Come," she said, standing. They found a secluded spot, and she removed the box from her backpack. In her other hand, beneath the backpack, she gripped her knife.

Amil blinked at the scroll. "That's—it?"

His eyebrows pulled together as he watched Freda stroke the deteriorating vellum with her free hand. She assumed he had expected something gold or silver, embezzled with shining jewels. But an old piece of leather? The thing visibly disgusted him.

"Can't you see? It's—it's *extraordinary*," she whispered.

Amil picked the box up and examined the rough etches of foreign animals. "This is nice," he offered.

Freda pointed to a monkey in a tree nearby and slipped the knife back in her pack when Amil turned to look. She wondered if he faked his indifference, but his eyes revealed no greed. She carefully set the scroll back in the box and the box back in her pack.

"Did a loved one give those things to you?" he asked.

Freda looked out at the sun melting behind the snow-capped mountains. She thought of the Crazy Mountains, the way Yarrow Peak had watched her bring forth the box from the earth. "You could say that," she answered.

The last bus back into the village would be coming soon. They walked through the temple and around the premises with no luck finding an attendant. Dusk fell in slivers of black.

A woman, dressed in a white and silver wrap, swept the stairways. She worked in a solemn quiet. Her black hair, threaded with red, cascaded down past her breasts. Her face radiated as if a light shined behind the skin, and her eyes gleamed a golden orange. Freda's gut tightened. This was the person with answers.

The woman's gaze met Freda's, and they exchanged an unspoken awareness of Freda's need. The woman walked to them, the glow of her absolute against the settling darkness. When the woman stood before them, Freda could see red dots tattooed across her brow. She spoke. Freda had forgotten about Amil until he translated the woman's words. His voice felt harsh in contrast to the woman's soft tone. She had asked them to follow her into the temple.

Only a few people remained inside. The woman said something, and the people left. Alone now, Amil, Freda, and the woman sat on the ground in a pool of candlelight. Freda retrieved the box from her backpack, her movements strangely slow and calm. She placed the scroll into the woman's upturned hands. Every flicker of a flame, each call of a bird singing its goodnights resounded in the quiet as the woman read and reread the scroll. For the first time since receiving the box from the earth, Freda felt safe. At least in this moment, she relinquished the hold of the scroll to another.

The woman finally spoke.

"She said the answers you need be in a cave to the west. Few who go return," Amil said.

The woman's eyes found Amil. She said something to him that he didn't translate for Freda. He seemed horrified. They exchanged a brief conversation. Amil's face dissolved from fear to passive resolve. Freda felt annoyed with her exclusion and cleared her throat.

"I do not go with you," he told Freda. "She said the scroll chose you alone, and that I be killed if I go into the cave with you."

Freda opened and shut her mouth a few times. She looked from Amil to the woman and back again. "But how will I get there without your language?"

The woman startled Freda with her answer, spoken in Imperial. "The language you need is not our own."

Amil and Freda took a bus to the village of Prajatuya and slept in one of four rooms in the town's hotel. Old Makalon's ancient capital didn't see many tourists, if any. The town was made entirely of wooden homes and buildings except for the stone temple to the goddess Avni in the center. Freda had read the two books the university library contained on Old Makalon. The great temple of Prajatuya was believed to be a Yiúsian palace before the mysterious departure of the Yiúsians from the region over two thousand years earlier.

As she and Amil walked out of the city limits early the next morning, they passed by remnants of a stone wall the Yiúsians had left behind. Amil helped her rent a donkey from a farmer. The farmer spoke rapidly, pointing to the mountains and back to Freda. He insisted Freda pay the donkey's full worth as a deposit. Freda did so with the promise she would receive most of the money back upon the donkey's safe return.

The farmer returned to his field, and Amil handed Freda the reins. She raised an eyebrow, still confused by the exchange.

"He thinks you not return," Amil explained.

They continued toward the mountains. The sun began to rise. He reiterated the rough directions the woman at the temple had given. Freda was to follow the dirt road to the base of Demá Peak. The road would end, and a footpath would begin. Freda would take this trail, and when it forked, she was to turn left and continue eastward.

"That's really all she said?" Freda asked again, strapping a bag of rice and beans to the donkey.

Amil fastened a pot to the donkey's other side. "Yes."

They finished, and a long pause stretched between them. They both knew they most likely wouldn't see each other again. Freda feared for her life. It was winter, after all, and a white cloud obscured the mountains.

Amil braced her shoulders and said, "Trust your path."

Freda thanked him and gave him a hug. She couldn't remember the last time she had hugged someone. His warmth and hay-smell relaxed her body, if only for the few moments they embraced. She paid him her promised rate plus a generous tip. He tried to refuse the extra money, but she said it was a wedding present.

When Amil was but a black speck on the northern horizon, Freda mounted the donkey and began plodding down the road. Farmers watched the Imperial pass with gaping mouths. Freda offered smiles and nods. She would wave but felt like she might fall if she released a hand from the harness. It was her first time riding a donkey since being on her grandfather's farm as a little girl, and the going felt insecure.

As promised, the dirt road ended, and a path began. When she ascended into the cloud, a light snow encompassed her. The path remained clear for a few meters in front. And this was how the miles passed: three paces at a time. She stopped the donkey at one point to pull the hood around her face. She was but a pair of eyes in the mist and swirling flakes.

A fork appeared, again as promised. She steered the donkey east. The dirt path dwindled into a rocky, steep, ambiguous route. The donkey slipped, nearly throwing Freda to the ground. She dismounted and led the donkey on foot. There were no signs, no footprints in the thin layer of snow.

Amil's last words became Freda's mantra. *Trust your path. Trust your path.*

She began to shiver. The donkey's breathing became a haunting. Her thoughts catapulted back and forth between trust and fear. This was her path. Was she going crazy? This was the way. The way to her death?

She could no longer hear or see the donkey in the whiteout. Her whistles turned into frantic calls. What was the Makalonian word for *come*? The donkey carried the dictionary, not to mention her food and warm layers. It had been hours since a breakfast of duck eggs and rice at the hotel. Was that this morning? It felt like days ago.

A root caught her foot, and she catapulted forward. She wiped snow and tears from her face. The donkey stood a yard away. She couldn't help but laugh at his deadpan expression. *Fool,* he seemed to say. A breeze swayed the clouds, revealing a small grove of juniper trees beyond the donkey.

Freda stopped to make lunch. Or was it dinner? Her father had taught her how to create a cone of twigs to start a fire. She remembered camping with him the weekend before she started university. She saw his hands in her own as she lit one match after another, each flame dying in the damp wood. With only a few matches remaining, she realized she wouldn't be eating. Why had she only packed rice and beans? She needed to find shelter. She should have sought this cave in the safety of spring

As she put the matches back in the donkey pack, a glimmer of light caught her eye. She realized the donkey was staring at the cave. It wasn't but twenty feet away.

Fear prickled down her back. Though inside awaited the answers she needed, she didn't feel ready. *Few who go return,* they had said. She figured she would die anyway if she tried to navigate her way back to town in a snowstorm in the dark. How silly. She had come all this way, and now that she had found what she sought, she felt frozen by apprehension. The scroll had chosen her. Even the woman at the temple had said as much. Surely it wouldn't lead her to her death.

The donkey started walking into the cave, and Freda followed behind him. Like a grand palace, a long hallway led Freda to where the cave widened into a large, multi-roomed cavern. Candles guttered in hundreds of crevices, and a thin stream trickled down the middle of the cave. She gasped. In the cavern's center, surrounded by candles, were twelve humans sitting in a circle, eating soup.

They all looked at Freda. Their expressions made her wonder if they knew she would be coming. No one acted surprised. Some even smiled.

Beyond them, sitting in a throne made of juniper branches and jewels, a skeleton, bones fastened together, stared at Freda with eyeless eyes. She almost fell over.

It looked exactly like the skeleton extracted from the Yarrow Peak cave. Yet now the woman's eye sockets looked down at Freda from a throne, rather than up at Freda from an examination table. They both had catlike skulls and large bones. Freda knew their existences—though hundreds of miles apart—were inlaid as the scroll and box resting along her spine.

A woman dressed in a white fur cloak and pants made of hide motioned for Freda to sit down. She had lilac hair and white-blue eyes, and many piercings adorned her face and ears. Tattoos reminiscent of ferns curled up her chest and throat. She handed Freda a bowl. Freda nodded her thanks and downed the soup. The woman asked if she wanted more. Freda startled. Did she just speak Imperial? The woman asked again, and Freda realized that, yes, this woman spoke her language. Freda looked closer at her. She had light skin, not as white as Freda's own, but not the coloring of a Makalonian, either.

"I'll explain as much as I can," the woman said, refilling the bowl. "But first, let's get you fed."

As Freda ate, everyone had a turn looking at the scroll and box. As it was with the woman at the temple, Freda didn't feel possessive as these strangers beheld the vellum.

"We heard of your coming from Sabaa," the woman began. "She's the caretaker of Pavarmaya. She told us of what you bring. Now, here you are, with the scroll I crafted. Thank you for making the journey here."

Freda felt twenty-four eyes crawling over her skin. She sat taller. Had the woman said she created it? The scroll had to be at least a hundred years old. This woman seemed but a decade older than Freda, if that.

"I'm Laurel," the woman said. She gestured to the circle. "All gathered here are Keepers."

Freda looked around the cavern. Keepers of what—mold and bones? The last person to examine the scroll and box set both in the middle of the circle.

"Will you say what is written on the scroll?" Freda asked. "I tried my best to translate…"

Laurel spoke the words without hesitation. Freda smiled as a flush of ego ran through her. Only a couple minor words differed from her translation and Laurel's oral reiteration.

"You've received the scroll because it deemed you worthy of its secrets, of *our* secrets," Laurel said. "The Keepers here protect Avni's remains from those who wish to erase the Anima's history from the earth."

"Anima?"

Laurel tilted her head toward the skeleton upon the juniper throne. "The Animal Woman. Avni was the fifth of eleven come and gone. If the masses oppressed by the World Forces knew about the Anima's history and her imminent return, an uprising would follow. The impoverished would gather behind their hope, their leader. We, the Keepers, protect the Anima's history in order to preserve this potential."

The woman's words tangled into a thorny mass. "But I don't understand," Freda murmured. "These women, they have come and gone. What good is a dead leader?"

"Don't you understand the words, if nothing else? *Its timing following a golden spiral.* The mushroom resurfaces in a cycle determined by the golden ratio. The Anima will return. I believe you—as the one the scroll has chosen—to be destined to find the next mushroom. This mushroom will bring forth the twelfth and final Anima."

Freda remembered the illogical influence the scroll had on her the moment she found it; the way she took it home as if it were a baby she needed to protect from a predator. Even then, in Owl Creek Canyon, Freda knew something beyond reason had been exhumed. Yet she was a scientist. There had to be a rational explanation for all of this.

Her mouth had gone dry. "I need water," she said. "May I please have some water?"

The man next to them retrieved a canteen. Laurel asked everyone to leave so she and Freda could speak alone, and the others disappeared into caverns. Freda thanked Laurel; the onslaught of eyes had only served to quicken the swirling sensation in her head. Smiling, Laurel moved closer to Freda and set a hand on Freda's thigh. Freda opened her mouth to ask one of a dozen questions, but Laurel spoke over her.

"You are most comfortable in solitude. You live alone." Laurel closed her eyes and tightened her grip on Freda's thigh. "I see you found this scroll in the mountains of your home, where the first Anima was buried." Her voice dropped a few octaves, and Freda had to lean in to hear her above the water trickling around them. "You came to us as soon as you could."

Laurel's eyes snapped open. They shined bright white, like sunlight reflecting off snow. Freda gaped at her.

"How do you—"

"You, Freda of the Cantons, will go to a Haven outside Nafáit when you leave tomorrow. You will learn all you can of the Anima while you are there. Once you discover where the last mushroom will grow, you will leave for that place, telling no one where you are going. It's *imperative* no one knows where you go—and I mean *no one*."

Freda frowned at Laurel's hand, still gripping her thigh. "But *why?* Why must I find this mushroom? Why can't anyone know?"

Laurel stood and brought the scroll back to where they sat. When she gave it to Freda, she held Freda's hands around the scroll. Freda felt a strange warmth spread up her arms and down her trunk. The feeling of ownership and belonging—*belonging at last*—circulated through her body with the warmth. She struggled against unexpected tears.

"Your secrecy ensures survival of hope," Laurel whispered. Her eyes engrossed Freda with their searing radiance. "You are capable. This scroll chose you, of all people, to come here. The world *needs* the Anima more than ever. The world needs you to find the mushroom, alone, in secret, before the forces oppressing both human and animal find it."

Laurel lifted her hands and the warmth diminished. Freda clutched the scroll to her chest.

# HAVEN

## 105 YBP

### NAFÁIT, TALÉRIA

She traveled by train to Taléria. It took ten times as long to arrive than it would have by plane, but Freda saw parts of the world she had only read about in school. She chose a nonlinear route, opting to trek for a couple days in the Kazurg Desert of northwestern Baninchi, where she saw a pack of golden jackals take down a gazelle fawn. Once in Lacuserra, she spent a couple days touring the streets of Marélle, eating the Sangerrain capital's famed pastries and touring its renowned museums. The train skirted the Sientado Mountains, affording a day in Hermida. She drank Solerian wine until she threw up, and she spent a day nursing a hangover along the busy Orua River.

Once in Desnord, she veered the farthest yet from her route, a day's train ride east, to the border of Desnord and Bosveld. Here, her father had once said, was the home her relatives had left after the Imperium had established the Cantons. The place proved underwhelming. Many small villages scattered across the rolling hills. The locals, distant relatives for all she knew, gaped at her, a foreigner, presumably their first in years. She offered waves and hellos, and they jutted their chins at her and resumed lives working the land. Freda hurried onward, to Braedun, deciding home wasn't the place one came from, but the place one lived.

Nonetheless, the alienation disturbed her. She had never felt comfortable calling Prominence her own. Not as an Imperial. History classes taught her the violence inflicted upon the Montane indigenous when the Imperium spread west. She saw them on occasion, the Bilawáxan and Tatankoy native to Prominence. They eyed her with mistrust, loathing even, and she couldn't blame them. She felt particularly hate-worthy, digging up their ancestors' valuables in her work as an archeologist.

She *dug* up the valuables, Freda reminded herself. Dug, as in something she did, not does. The spring semester had begun last week, when she had been sipping cappuccinos in Marélle cafés. No one in Twin Rivers would be able to explain her mysterious and abrupt absence. Freda took comfort in this, and she sunk deeper into her train seat, watching the velvet green land of southern Taléria speed past her window.

The train rode up and down, flying over the hills. Sheep dotted the verdancy like white spots upon a skin of grass. As they traveled north, the green gave way to a snowy landscape. She ate lunch at a homely restaurant near the shores of Diaberraige Lake. The placid waters reflected the stone galleries of Doroch Castle and the surrounding pine trees nuanced with snow. The final train in her travels left later that day, and two weeks after leaving the dilapidated boarding station in Prajatuya, she arrived to Nafáit in the dusk. She walked from the small station onto a dirt road lined with wattle and daub buildings.

A slight panic stirred as the dozen other people on the train scattered back to their homes. They left boot prints in the snow and an engrossing quiet. A few windows shined beneath the thatched roofs. Had it been morning, with a day's light ahead of her to figure out what she was doing, Freda would have found the village charming. But in the moment, she felt stranded in a strange place.

Laurel had said the Haven would be north of Nafáit, in the forests below the Hoeden Mountains. If she reached Hellörf she had gone too far. When Laurel had said these things, Freda hadn't thought to question their nebulosity. After all, she had been in an ancient cave, in ancient mountains, with a woman who had knowledge Freda didn't understand. The novelty of the experience had intoxicated her, and now Freda berated herself for not demanding more information from the woman. Had her logical, inquisitive mind been firing as it always did, Freda would have at least asked if her travels began on a particular road in Nafáit.

She walked toward the larger buildings. A distant hint of music lightened her steps. Ahead, beyond the quickening dark of the street, the music poured out of an open door. Laughter grew louder alongside the trill of a flute, the jumping of a fiddle. A wooden sign announced she had arrived at the Four Inn. When she stepped into the pub, she stalled in the doorway.

Men in wool pants and tweed vests clapped their hands to the beat as women twirled in front of the musicians. The women tapped their heels in unison on the wooden floor, emphasizing the music's fast-changing pace. They wore white dresses with green corsets woven over the front. Their hair, long and curly, fanned behind them like scarves of brilliant red and raven black. The corsets pushed their breasts up toward smooth clavicles. Freda flushed at the heat growing in her root as she watched the women stomp and whirl.

No one noticed her, the stranger standing at the entrance, until the music crescendoed to its end, and the fiddler stuck his bow in her direction.

"Eoin," he said, "you've got a visitor."

Everyone turned to face her. Their eyes lingered on her pants. She wished she had packed at least a skirt, with pants being still a novelty on women, even back home where life was seemingly twenty years ahead. Would these people, like those in rural Desnord, treat her with mistrust? As if she had spoken this question aloud, the bartender clapped his hands.

"The Four as witness you speak the truth. Come, come," he said, motioning for Freda to sit on a stool. "Bryna! Bryna, heat up a spot of stew. We've got a weary one."

Freda felt her blush grow deeper. The men and women erupted back into boisterous conversation. They spoke Imperial, yet their accents, lyrical and thick, made it hard for Freda to understand all of what they said. Eoin poured her a dark beer from the tap and set it before her with a wink. The beer reminded her of buttered mushrooms. She drank deep; she was thirstier than she had realized.

Eoin laughed. "A woman who holds her own. I like it," he boomed, taking the empty and pouring another.

He was a portly man, much chubbier than the weathered men sitting on stools around her, sipping pints of their own. His black, curly hair and dark beard reminded Freda of her father. Bryna bustled out of the kitchen with a giant bowl of stew in one hand and a basket of rolls in the other. Large like Eoin, she had deep red hair and cheeks pink with her hustle. She put the soup and rolls in front of Freda, and Eoin placed a slab of butter beside the rolls. Freda thanked them over the music.

She enjoyed a couple more beers and just as many songs. People smiled at her and clunked their pint glasses against her own, but no one asked her where she had come from or why she was there. Freda found herself relaxing. She even set her backpack on the ground to give her shoulders a break, though in front of her and in plain sight, of course. At one point she was clapping along with the men as the dancers twirled around. The women mesmerized her with their nimbleness and beauty.

When the fatigue of her travels set in, Freda asked Eoin for a room. He led her up the stairs with a lantern in one hand. He opened a door to a room with white walls and a twin bed. It smelled like her grandmother's attic. The lantern's light scintillated across cobwebs.

"My apologies," he said, fanning his arm along the wall to gather the cobwebs on his sleeve. "We don't see your like much."

"My like?" Freda asked. Her voice was defensive, and she wished she wouldn't have asked.

He set the lantern on the bedside table. "Imperials," he said, not unkindly. "Travelers. We haven't had any in years."

Freda nodded as if this made sense.

"We sleep out back, in the cottage. If you need anything, don't hesitate to knock. We'll have breakfast ready by six."

"Six is perfect," Freda said. "I intend to leave in the morning."

"Figured as much." Eoin smiled. "Sleep tight, then." He closed the door behind him.

Freda slipped off her pack and set it behind the pillow. The wool blankets scratched her neck and chin, and the mattress's hay compressed beneath her weight. This place, though homey, unsettled Freda in its archaic details, like the lantern flickering beside her bed in lieu of a lamp.

She also found it strange that Eoin had called her an Imperial as if he was something other. Taléria had been part of the Imperium since its conception. Major battles leading to the Three Kingdoms Union had been fought not far from this town. Freda blew out the candle within the lantern. She figured she would learn more about this place, including reasons for its evident isolation from the rest of the Imperium, in due time. After all, she would be living in the neighboring woods for as long as it took to gather answers to questions. But first she had to figure out what questions she needed to ask.

Eoin and Bryna insisted she take a knapsack stuffed with rolls, a slab of butter, a few apples, and a generous hunk of cured ham. When she tried to pay for the food and lodging, she offered Imperial dollars. Apart from the train ride out of Old Makalon, she had paid for everything up to this point with dollars. They looked affronted by the money, as if she held out a snake.

"Please, put it away," Bryna said, wincing.

Freda looked at the five dollars in her hand. Was it too much or too little? She wanted to repay them for their cheer and generosity. She hadn't encountered much of either yet on this trip.

"It's the least I can give you," she said. "You've been kind."

"Then do us a kindness, dear, and put your money away." Though Eoin gave her a patient smile, there was something cold in his tone, telling her it was best not to argue.

"But how can I repay you for the night?"

Eoin and Bryna exchanged glances. "Life has a funny way of working these things out," Bryna said. Her face lit up. "I almost forgot!" She spun back into the kitchen, moving with dexterity surprising for one so large. She returned holding a muffin topped with streusel.

Freda suppressed a groan. Why did they spoil her and refuse her the chance to reciprocate? She accepted the muffin with a resigned bow of her head. "Thank you." She stuffed the money back into her pocket. "Both of you."

Eoin showed her to the door. "Good luck."

Freda thanked him again and began her travels anew. She tore off bites from the muffin as she walked north, back up the dirt road. The day was overcast, cold, with a suggestion of more snow. She passed the train station and a few dozen wattle and daub homes. The road forked, and Freda again asked herself why she hadn't demanded more thorough instructions from

Laurel. She chose the left road, randomly, and walked along a cobblestone fence.

A man strutted across the field beyond the fence, carrying a bucket to pigs in a pen. He waved as she passed. The road ended where the forest began. Freda finished the muffin and hesitated before stepping into the trees. At first it was mostly deciduous growth. Winter had stripped bare the oak, ash, and birch branches, allowing the overcast day to light her way. Vines, silver with frost, wound up the tree trunks. Boot prints in the snow told of people coming and going.

Eventually the boot prints grew fewer and fewer until only Freda's tracks, alongside that of stoat and deer, imprinted the white ground. The deciduous trees transitioned into pine, and her surroundings turned gray and cold. She figured she had walked a few miles by now. How big was this forest anyway? Should she continue straight or veer east? She opted to eat an apple and some ham.

Straight, she decided, zipping her pack up. There seemed to be more of a parting between trees this way. It wasn't a large parting, and her wool jacket and pants grew damp as she rubbed up against the snow-laden boughs. She remembered how the cave had materialized when all hope had been lost back in the Purana Mountains. For now the temperatures allowed for damp clothes. The winters here were much milder than back home. Night, though, could bring a different story.

She began to murmur the mantra Amil had gifted her: *trust your path*. Her voice sounded crazy in the quiet. Freda yelped in surprise when a snowy owl swooped through the trees ahead. She laughed at herself and stopped to eat again. When Bryna had wrapped an entire roll of butter into the knapsack, Freda had wondered who could possibly eat that much butter alone. Now, though, she cut a large chunk and made a butter sandwich with a roll. She ate it and made another. The fat, she realized, may prove key to her survival, should she get lost in this wilderness. She wondered if Bryna had figured the same.

Onward. The pines only grew thicker. Snow cascaded down as she disturbed the trees. She felt herself sweating and said her mantra louder. She spoke so loudly she almost didn't hear the stream ahead. She halted. It wasn't just a stream she could hear. Someone, or something, splashed in the waters. Freda moved as slowly as possible, which wasn't hard to do considering how heavy her clothes felt. She stopped when the trees thinned enough for her to see the stream.

The waters ran silver between rocks covered in bright green moss. The forest continued on the other side of the stream, just beyond a pair of women. A small fire flickered beneath a metal bucket. One woman dunked a shirt into the bucket while the other ran a pair of pants over a washing board. The woman washing the shirt had bright red hair. It was curly and wild and nearly reached her belly button. The other woman had equally long and tousled hair, though it wasn't much darker than the snow around her. They both wore fur coats, leather pants, and boots lined with fur. They both, Freda noted despite herself, were stunning.

The redheaded woman lifted her chin to Freda, and the blonde did the same. Freda opened and closed her mouth. She felt like a child who had been caught doing something wrong. The women looked at each other, and the blonde rolled her eyes.

"You can come out now, Freda of the Cantons," she said. Though her northern accent made it hard to tell for sure, her tone sounded bored, maybe even condescending.

Freda felt even more the child. How long had they known she was there? She stepped from the forest and, as if on cue, began shivering.

The redhead looked concerned. "She's freezing," she said. Her accent sounded similar to the blonde's.

"Well she's wearing a wool coat in snow," the blonde said. There was no mistaking the condescending tone now. "What did she expect?"

Freda stiffened, forcing the shivering to quell. "*She* is right here," she said, mimicking the blonde's tone. "You can speak to me directly."

The women lifted their eyebrows at each other, and Freda grimaced. Great introduction. Why did she always have to run her mouth? Freda cleared her throat. "My apologies. I'm tired, and yes, you're right. Wool seems to have been a poor choice. I lack—fur, I suppose."

The blonde woman shook her head and gathered her washing board and a pile of clothes. "You deal with this," she said.

She turned to walk away and Freda met eyes with the redhead. When Freda glanced back at the blonde, she startled to see that she was already gone. She must have walked back into the forest, and yet her boot prints—

"Come over here," the woman called. "I'll lead you to the Haven."

Freda frowned at the moss on the rocks. "But how?"

The woman looked at Freda and then the rocks. "Oh," was all she said, and she picked up the bucket and her clothes and skipped across the river, lithely moving from one rock to the next. The moss must be slippery, and yet she moved with fluidity reminiscent of last night's dancers. The woman continued on, walking purposely, and Freda followed.

The woman spun around. "I'm Tillie." She stuck out her hand.

Freda shook it. "Freda—I mean, obviously."

Tillie held the handshake longer than Freda found appropriate. Freda tried to release the grip but Tillie held on.

"This way," Tillie said, and she pulled Freda a few steps ahead.

Freda blinked and shook her head. A cottage stood where it hadn't a moment earlier. Vines, silver with frost like those in the forest, grew up the cobblestoned walls. A watermill spun in the slow-flowing stream, and smoke snaked up from a chimney. Tillie released her hand.

"The Haven," she said, gesturing to the cottage. "Let's get you warm and then answer questions."

Still blinking, untrusting her senses, Freda followed Tillie up stone steps and into a warm kitchen. Pots and pans hung from a light fixture. Many herbs, garlic, and some dried meats also hung above the wooden island centering the kitchen. A fire burned in a stone hearth, and a wooden table with six chairs stood adjacent to the cooking space. Beyond the table was a room enclosed by windows. A woman and man sat on wicker chairs in this room, their heads facing away.

Freda placed a hand on a cobblestone. It was solid. She touched her face and wiggled her fingers before her eyes. Had she just not seen the cottage? She must be more exhausted than she knew. Tillie grinned as she watched her. She had bright blue eyes and a pale complexion covered in light freckles. Freda figured they were around the same age.

"I know, you're confused," Tillie said. "Do you have dry clothes?"

"I only brought the one set. I thought my travels were going to be—shorter."

"We look similar in size. Come, let's get you changed before you meet the others."

She led Freda down a hallway of seven closed doors: three on each side and one glass door facing the front of the house. Plants pushed up against the glass door. Freda wondered if the other residents knew she had arrived. Tillie opened the second door on the right. Her room was small, with a double bed dressed in white sheets and a gray wool blanket. Shelves lined with books and plants hung on the wooden walls painted lavender. A circular window within the cobblestone revealed the pine trees and a gray sky.

Tillie withdrew a simple shift and a pair of wool leggings from the dresser. "Your room's this way," she said, signaling for Freda to follow her back down the hall.

She opened the last door on the left. The room shared a wall with what looked to be a greenhouse. Plants grew thick against the other side of the glass, protecting her privacy. Drapes on either side of the glass wall hung as an option for further privacy. Her bed, identical to Tillie's, sat across from the glass beneath a wall painted sage. Out of the window Freda could see the stream, goats, sheep, a chicken coop, and a fallow garden. Like Tillie's room, plants and books lined shelves, and a dresser and desk accompanied the bed. Freda found the simplicity inviting. Her apartment back home had been cramped and cluttered, but she had always been too busy to care.

Tillie set the clothes on the bed. "We'll meet you in the veranda when you're dressed and ready. She closed the door behind her.

Freda slipped out of her wet clothes and pulled on the shift and leggings. Tillie's clothes fit snug and hung long. Freda pinched at fat pushing into the shift. She wished she could check her reflection. Tillie had looked both groomed and wild in a way Freda found alarmingly attractive. She wished the thoughts away as she ran her fingers through her hair and picked at her teeth. She had forgotten her toothbrush at the hostel in Braedun. Exhaling into her hand, she wondered if Tillie thought her breath smelled bad.

She swished some water from her canteen around her mouth and put her pack back on. As she walked down the hall, she wondered if she should reveal the scroll to these strangers. Laurel's instructions hadn't said one way or the other. When she turned the corner, three more people, including Tillie and the blonde from earlier, had joined the man and woman sitting on the wicker furniture. She stepped in and all gathered faced her. Tillie alone offered a smile, though it was strained.

The blonde gave her the same bored, disdainful look as before. A man with shoulder-length black hair watched her with his fingers steepled below a handsome face. Judging based on her education, Freda assumed he was either Tuttuán or Nukopa. The third woman seemed to be at least partially Solerian. She had a hooked nose, olive skin, and eyes dark with makeup. The man sitting next to her had tan skin, gray eyes, and hair pulled back into a low bun. Freda figured most women would find him sexy. She found his scowl disturbing.

"Go on then. Take a seat." The woman's accent confirmed she was from Soleria.

Freda sat on the open chair between Tillie and the blonde. She set her backpack in her lap. The blonde visibly leaned away from her, as if she smelled. She probably did.

"We expected you days earlier," the Solerian woman said. She sounded annoyed. Freda wondered why Laurel had sent her to hostile people. Had this—had this been a trap the entire time?

"I took my time." Freda tried to hide the panic rising. She hugged her backpack closer to her chest. They all noticed and looked at the backpack. She forced herself to relax her grip.

"I've never been to Lacuserra," she continued. "I chose to visit cities along the way."

No one found this worthy of response. The blonde began cleaning dirt from her nails with her teeth.

"Well I suppose we start with introductions. Right?" the Solerian woman said. "I'm Javiera and this is Damari." She touched the man's arm next to her. His scowl remained unflinching as he nodded once at Freda.

"Orvik," the other man said.

The blonde didn't look at her when she said, "Brigid."

"And you've met Tillie," Javiera said.

Tillie pulled her lips taut.

"Laurel sent word of your intent to stay at the Haven."

"*My* intent?" Freda asked.

Brigid sat up in her chair, and Orvik lifted his eyebrows. Though Freda thought it impossible, Damari's scowl deepened.

Javiera lowered her chin. "So you believe yourself helpless, as if your life is not your own? You believe you can't make decisions for yourself?"

Freda wasn't sure if these were questions or statements. She shook her head. "It's not like that…" And yet Javiera hinted at the truth. Laurel hadn't escorted her here with a knife to her throat. Freda shifted in her seat.

"You're fine," Javiera said, swatting the air with the back of her hand. "Laurel's envoy mentioned you have proof of your—*nomination*—to be here."

They all looked again at the backpack. Freda closed her eyes and tried to determine whether she felt safe revealing the scroll or not. The feeling of security had been so clear at the temple and in the cave. Though she couldn't discern the same security, she figured the scroll would clarify why she was here. Laurel trusted these people enough to send her, caretaker of the scroll, to them. Besides, Damari looked lethal. Freda needed some way to curve the hostility.

She zipped open the pack and withdrew the box. Everyone leaned closer. Her fingers shook as she removed the lid and lifted the scroll up.

Javiera placed a hand over her chest. "Whoa," she breathed. "I can feel it from here."

The others nodded in agreement.

"Feel what?" Freda asked.

"The magic," Tillie said. "It's radiating from it."

Javiera reached out her hands. "Can I?" she asked softly.

Freda brought the scroll closer to her chest. Magic?

"It's okay," Javiera continued. "It's yours. That's clear to all of us."

Tillie placed a hand on Freda's shoulder. "She speaks truly," she said.

Freda grimaced as she held out the scroll. Javiera took it as if receiving a newborn. She brought the scroll to her face and sniffed it a few times. She then licked it. Freda grunted, incredulous.

Javiera unfurled it and ran her fingers along the vellum with closed eyes. "Ah, yes, of course," she murmured. Only then did she examine the words etched into the scroll. "While I don't speak Setú, I am fluent in the language of Florávo," she said at last. "And this, my dear ones, is powerful magic. Extraordinarily so."

She handed the scroll to Damari. He conducted the same strange behavior upon the scroll, smelling, licking, and feeling it. Freda no longer hid her disgust. She frowned at Damari and crinkled her nose.

Tillie laughed. "Can you imagine how weird this is for her, a Commoner?" she asked the others.

"Commoner?" Freda asked.

Javiera nodded at Tillie. "Very weird," she said, also sounding bemused. She looked to Freda. "A Commoner, yes. One ignorant to the existence of magic."

What did they mean by *magic*? Magic was how people described natural phenomenon before the advent of science. It was catchall reasoning consequential to ignorance. Yet—how else *would* she describe the scroll's hold on her? What to make of Laurel's uncanny insight into her life? And the cottage, it had seemingly materialized out of nowhere.

"I detected three binding agents," Javiera said. "The flowers of snakeroots, of course. More commonly known as milkwort. Though the flower nectar soaked into this vellum was from a different species of milkwort than the one that grows in northern Lacuserra. Regardless, I assume the properties are similar: hope for the miserable, or transformation into self authority—or, quite possibly, both."

Javiera paused as she regarded Freda with renewed curiosity. Freda squirmed.

"Was that yew I smelled?" Brigid asked. She leaned across Freda to pass the scroll to Tillie. Freda resisted the urge to snatch it back.

"Yes, but again, it's a different species than the yew of our home. And again, I imagine its properties are similar."

"Protection or rebirth?" Tillie asked. Though she sniffed at the scroll, Freda could tell she was unsure of her actions.

"Both, most likely," Javiera said, smiling. "Very good, Tillie. I can see your studies are paying off."

Tillie blushed as she handed the scroll to Orvik. Freda smiled at her despite it all.

"And the third?" Damari asked. His accent was unmistakably Torerran.

"Yes, the third. The rarest of the three. I only know of it from my time with Laurel. The nectar of a pygmy water lily endemic to the swamps of Old Makalon. Typically the nectar of lilies also offer rebirth, often experienced as an opening of sexual energy."

Freda felt her face burning. She stared at Javiera in fear her eyes might find Tillie.

"Yet the plant used in this binding agent came from the still and tannic waters of Old Makalon's secluded swamps," Javiera continued. "I assume both the flower nectar and a tincture of its roots went into the potion. Laurel explained how one of these lilies, when found with twelve petals, offers more energy than even a nine-petaled lotus."

Orvik whistled. The others also appeared to be amazed.

"What are you even saying?"

"What I'm saying, Freda, is that this vellum was soaked in a binding decoction. For a full moon, I'd guess. Judging by its potency, and knowing Laurel's—*knack*—for thoroughness, the moon turned both blue and red. Meaning, it was the thirteenth full moon in a year with a lunar eclipse at some point in the moon's cycle."

"In other words, a rare moon," Brigid said, as if talking to a child.

Freda rolled her eyes. She could deduce this much, even if everything else Javiera had said didn't make sense.

"Rare being an absurd understatement," Javiera said. "Laurel created this scroll for it to find a particular person. And by find, I mean *bind* to a particular person. Why, though, we can only guess."

Damari scoffed. "Typical Salvager work," he said.

"Yeah," Brigid said. "How can she think it's *appropriate* to get an Imperial involved?"

"I'm not sure," Javiera sighed. "But here she is."

Everyone looked at Freda. She wiped her palms on her pants. "Aren't most of you Imperials?" she asked. Apart from Orvik, they all seemed to be from Lacuserra, the birthplace of the Imperium.

Javiera alone didn't look as if Freda had slapped her in the face. The others, even Tillie, exchanged affronted expressions.

"Born Imperials, raised as Mages," Javiera said. "Laurel found us all as orphaned children and brought us to this Haven. She trained me at the Prajatuya Palace to be the High Mage."

Freda remembered the giant stone building in Old Makalon. "I thought that was a temple for the goddess Avni."

"It is, in a way."

Freda wasn't sure what that meant. She picked the scroll up from the table centering the chairs. Running her fingers over the etched words, she asked, "Do you know what it says?"

They shook their heads. Freda recited the words. Each person's jaws dropped, but no one responded. Freda clenched her teeth. What had she said?

At once, they all talked.

"*What?*"

"Knowing about the Keepers is one thing—but the *Anima?*"

"Who does Laurel think she is?"

"Fucking Salvagers!"

"Shit."

They continued to talk over one another.

"Enough," Javiera shouted. "Enough."

They quieted.

"So." Javiera folded her hands into her lap. "You know about Animas."

Freda could tell the calm in her voice was feigned. "A little," she admitted. "Laurel called them Animal Women and said they were leaders of the oppressed. She said the last would return. And she said"—Freda paused, looking at the faces of disbelief around her—"she said I would be the one to find the mushroom."

Awe slackened Tillie's face. Incredulity, though, tightened that of the others.

Damari scoffed again. "She can see the past—but the future? This is Salvager hubris, plain and simple."

Brigid and Orvik obviously agreed.

Javiera, though, looked thoughtful. "Perhaps," she said. "But I alone have worked with Laurel. She is more powerful than any Keeper I've ever met, Shapeshifters included. Her work with Florávo is—unmatched. Mugwort divination is an imperfect art, but not impossible."

"But an Imperial? Killer of Animas past?" Orvik was clearly livid. "How could she even—*think* this was a good idea?"

"Calm yourself," Javiera said.

Orvik plopped back in his chair.

"Need I remind you all that we were Imperials once as well," Javiera said.

"But we were raised as Keepers," Brigid said. "Laurel always said Mages had to be children—"

"Do you know Freda's heart?" Javiera asked. Though she spoke quietly, each word cut as a sharp blade.

The flush of Brigid's face deepened to crimson.

"Then I recommend you hold your ignorant mistrusts. Laurel has been serving the Anima *millennia* before you were even born."

A silence stretched. Though Freda understood very little of what they said, she felt gratitude for Javiera's defense.

"You're right," Orvik said. "Laurel gave each of our lives a greater purpose. We owe it to her to trust her reasons for bringing an Imperial into the Haven."

Freda heard the reluctance in his voice but relaxed a little nonetheless.

"Agreed," Tillie said. "I say we give her a chance."

"You're just saying that 'cause she's your type," Brigid snapped. "I'll go with what the group agrees, but I will never, ever, *ever* trust a born and raised Imperial. And you all would be wise to do the same. Need I remind you—"

"No," Damari said. Freda barely heard him. He glowered at Brigid and then at Freda. "No, Brigid, you do not."

The tension of old drama settled into a shared silence. Freda saw a hint of pity in the look Javiera gave Damari.

"It's decided then," Javiera said. "Freda of the Cantons will be staying in our Haven until—when, exactly?"

"Laurel said I was to learn all I could of the Anima before—*becoming* it."

"Becoming *her*," Javiera corrected. "We'll also teach you Florávo, because an Anima learned in plant magic will be an awesome force." She looked to Tillie. "You can teach her what you know, Tillie. It'll be good reinforcement for your knowledge."

Tillie smiled at Freda. Freda wondered how red her face was becoming.

Had Brigid really said she was Tillie's *type?* Did that mean Tillie was like—like her? She tried to keep her smile casual.

"Magic," Javiera began, "is the belief that there is more than meets the eye in life. Everything is animate, full of energy. Terrific, beautiful, latent energy." She paused and looked at Freda over half-moon glasses before continuing. "It's the belief that there is a true yet nameless, formidable yet loving energy within everything, and that we, as humans, can enter into this supernatural life force. One needs to *believe* in this energy first before she may wield it."

Javiera wore a white dress that accentuated her large breasts and butt. A silver butterfly clip held her hair atop her head in a messy bun. She wore the same dark eye shadow of yesterday and red lipstick. Freda wondered why she bothered dressing up in a cottage out in the middle of nowhere.

Freda and Tillie sat at the worktable in the greenhouse. Freda had changed back into her regular clothes. She felt the wool grow damp with sweat. Though the dead of winter outside, the greenhouse remained warm enough for hundreds of different plants to flourish.

Javiera turned to a sage plant growing in a pot on the table. "Sage. Simple sage. A staple in many gardens," she said, running a finger across a leaf, as if petting it. She smelled it. "Tell me, Tillie. Besides seasoning turkey"—Tillie giggled and Javiera smirked—"besides this, what Florávian properties does sage offer?"

"A tincture of its leaves, when consumed bi-moonly, can increase one's lifespan by ten percent. The potency increases by a factor of three if leaves are harvested from a juvenile plant during a blue moon."

"And a decoction of its roots?"

Tillie chewed her lower lip in thought. Freda looked away in fear she might be goggling her outright.

"Heals damaged tissue?" Tillie asked tentatively.

"Precisely." Javiera moved to another potted herb. "Ah, thyme. The warrior's best friend. Do you remember, Tillie, how to prepare a valor decoction?"

"First you harvest the leaves—"

"First *one* harvests the leaves," Javiera corrected. "Remember to use the language of Florávian science."

Freda snorted. Did she just say science? Both Javiera and Tillie frowned at her.

"Did I say something funny?" Javiera asked.

"Nope." Freda pursed her lips and shook her head. "Nothing at all. Please, continue explaining your *science.*"

Tillie's hurt expression alone made Freda regret her sarcasm.

"It's okay, Tillie," Javiera said. "This is a good time to invite Freda's skepticism into the open."

Freda readjusted her seat and scratched at her neck.

"Why wait?" Javiera continued, talking to Tillie.

Tillie didn't like whatever idea Javiera was suggesting. Her heels began moving up and down.

"Here. I'll go first," Javiera said. She walked to the shelves behind her, plucked three white flowers from a bramble branch, and turned back to them with the blooms cupped in her hands. She closed her eyes and stood there, unmoving, for a long moment. When she opened her hands, Freda gasped. The blooms glowed a dazzling white.

Freda gripped the worktable in fear she would topple over.

"I've evoked the flowers. They can now be used as a charm, or be preserved for future use as a sere. The bramble bloom's unique elicitation offers fertility."

The casual tone of Javiera's voice juxtaposed the chaos exploding in Freda's mind. She knew she gaped openly at Javiera, but any facade she had maintained up to this point had been stripped away.

"Anyone can learn plant magic," Javiera continued. "There were once many magic practitioners. Laurel created Florávo from her study of plant magic practices across the world. This was, of course, before the Imperium repressed the existence of magic. One trained in the science and art of Florávo is called a Mage. Starting one's study as a child, of course, offers a large advantage. Children more easily access magic. They're less—*resistant* to its existence."

Javiera placed the flowers on the table and walked over to a jasmine plant. Freda stared at the bramble blooms. A part of her mind still grasped for a rational explanation for what she had just witnessed. She picked a flower up and slowly turned it in her hand. Holding it brought a curious awareness to her lower stomach.

Javiera held out a jasmine flower to Tillie. Tillie accepted it with hesitant hands.

"Remember to work from your root," Javiera said.

Tillie cupped the delicate bloom and closed her eyes. She took much longer than Javiera had, but when she opened her hands, the flower radiated.

Javiera beamed. "Well done."

Tillie slumped, exhausted.

Javiera filled a glass of water and handed it to Tillie, saying, "You'll need at least five of these today."

Tillie nodded and drank deeply. She looked like she had just run up a mountain.

Javiera poured a glass for Freda as well. "Tillie is our baby," she said. "She's been with us, what has it been, three years now? She's still new to her powers."

There were many things to question, many faults and fissures in the reality surrounding Freda. "How many Mages *are* there?" she breathed.

Javiera hesitated. "Thousands. Spread across three other Havens and the Prajatuya Palace. We keep this Haven small because of its proximity to the Imperium's nexus."

Freda shook her head. Thousands—all this time? "Why doesn't anyone *know* about magic?"

"The Imperium," Javiera said. "It erased magic's presence in common knowledge when its army appropriated plant evocation for its own ends. Thousands of practitioners were murdered."

Tillie seemed to be regaining energy. She gave Freda a sideways glance, embarrassed almost.

Javiera set a hand on Tillie's shoulder and said, "Mages have historically been some of the Anima's greatest allies. Our powers, no matter how nascent, are to be celebrated."

Tillie sat up taller. The two women looked expectantly at Freda, as if they waited for her to bust out in applause or something. Freda felt like bugs crawled beneath her shirt. She shimmied her shoulders a little.

"So," Freda said. "Magic is real."

Javiera clapped her hands. "Exactly. And you have the ability to learn it."

Tillie grinned at Freda as she handed her the jasmine flower. Though twenty years of training in rational thought continued to gnaw at the edges of Freda's mind, she grinned back at Tillie. Freda felt like she should kiss her right here and now. Looking down at the star-shaped bloom glowing in her hand, she wondered if it was possible Tillie had intended for her to feel this way.

☾

Lapwings trilled within the canopy of budding leaves. Sunlight, full and golden as sap, fell uninterrupted upon the meadow Tillie and Freda picnicked within. Food spread across the quilt between them: a jar of serviceberry jam, a loaf of sourdough bread, baked this morning, and cuts of ham from the pig they butchered last week. Tillie refilled their glasses with the rosehip mead Javiera had crafted from the fall harvest.

"What do rosehips offer again?" Freda asked.

Tillie swirled the pink liquid around in her glass and sniffed. "Their properties are similar to rose, I believe." She sipped the mead. "Thanks for joining me today." She leaned forward and kissed Freda's cheek.

Freda stiffened but tried to hide the reaction with a smile. She didn't want Tillie to not kiss her, even though it felt strange—it felt *wrong,* somehow. Tillie leaned back and adjusted the collar of her yellow sundress. She gave Freda a calculating look.

"What?" Freda asked.

"You're still not comfortable with this—or the possibility of it."

"This?"

"Us."

Freda looked into the evergreens. She felt like she couldn't hide anything from Tillie, or anyone at the Haven for that matter. It was a battle of relief and discomfort, to be *seen* for the first time in her life. "It's not you," she said.

"I know." Tillie sipped her mead. "Homophobia's a disease of the Imperium. It almost killed me."

Freda gulped. “How?”

Darkness dimmed Tillie’s eyes. “It was my father. He caught me kissing the neighbor girl and…” She shook her head. “I ran away the next day. Javiera found me a month later, fighting for my life in the alleys of Nordung.”

“Is that why you take clove maceration?” Freda asked, her voice hesitant.

Tillie shrugged. “Partly, I’m sure. But sometimes I think I was born depressed.”

Freda willed her hand to touch Tillie’s thigh. It was as soft as she always imagined it to be. Tillie ran a finger on the scar across the top of Freda’s wrist from when she had cut herself on a barbed wire fence as a child.

“Did your parents know?” Tillie asked.

Freda frowned. Her mother—was she still alive?

“I’m sorry,” Tillie whispered. She leaned back. “I don’t mean to pry.”

“It’s not that.” Freda sipped her mead. “No, they didn’t. I couldn’t bring myself to tell them. It didn’t seem to matter, anyways. I lost both of them before I was old enough to marry.”

“I’m sorry,” Tillie said again. “My mother’s dead as well.”

Her mother was dead in any way it mattered, Freda reminded herself. Nonetheless, the guilt of leaving her alone all these months pressed against Freda’s chest. She took a deeper drink from her glass.

“Similar to rose, huh?” Freda said, forcing her voice bright. “It seems you’re downright trying to seduce me, Tillie.”

“Javiera gave it to me. She said—it would help.” While Tillie’s grin slanted to one side, her voice was serious.

Freda crossed her legs. “With what?” she asked, though she knew.

“You can’t work from your root if it’s blocked.”

Freda felt her face redden. “I’ve only been practicing Florávo for four months.”

“I get it. I was scared in the beginning as well. It still feels vulnerable to me.”

“But you’re a natural.”

“It’s impossible to be a natural when you carry shame from abuse.” Tillie set her empty glass down and tore off a chunk of bread. “You weren’t here for the first year. I was blocked as well." She spread jam across the bread and ate it.

A flock of lapwings swooped overhead. Freda lay back and watched cumulus clouds drift across the sky. Summer felt a day away. She could smell it in the marsh marigolds, newly blossomed across the meadow. The mead made her feel light-headed and relaxed. She wondered if Javiera had evoked the rosehips to attract romantic love or to heal emotional trauma. Both, Freda figured, knowing their High Mage was capable of evoking all aspects of a plant. Would she ever be as talented as Javiera? Apparently not, if a block prevented her from even the most fundamental practices.

"How did you break through your block?" Freda asked.

"It's less of a break, and more of a release." Tillie lay down as well, and they looked up at the sky side by side.

Freda could feel the heat of her. She let her foot relax to the side so their toes were touching.

"You have to want to let it go," Tillie continued. "Trying to break it, or fight it, only makes it bigger."

"I don't want to feel shame."

"Maybe the better question, then, is what do you *want* to feel."

Freda watched the clouds disappear beyond the forest, leaving the circle of sky above them clear. She thought of how her parents had groomed her for a normal life in the Imperium. From buying a dress for her for the school dance, even though she didn't have a date, to paying for her university tuition, she had always lived between the lines they drew.

"Free," Freda said.

Tillie shifted to her hip and propped her head on a hand. Her red hair spilled across the quilt around her. "Is that all?" She ran her finger along Freda's bicep, causing goose bumps to flush down Freda's arm. "What about joy? Pleasure?"

The whole meadow seemed to quiet, leaving Freda's heartbeat alone in its clamor. "Those would be nice," she managed.

Tillie's finger traced Freda's collarbone. "You have to want to let it go," Tillie said again. "The shame, that is."

Freda wondered if her swallow was as loud as it felt. "I think I'm ready."

"Think, or know?"

Freda paused. She could wait—but for when? And why? Her parents couldn't disown her anymore. The Mages wouldn't care; apparently Javiera encouraged their attraction, given the empty bottle of mead beside them. Freda turned onto her hip to face Tillie. She moved closer, so their noses were almost touching, and placed an arm around her.

"I know I am," Freda said.

Freda wasn't sure if she'd know how to kiss, but when they did, something ravenous within her took over. They kissed until Tillie pulled back and slid her hands down Freda's torso, to her pants buckle. When Tillie came back up to rest beside Freda, she brought a plucked marigold.

Freda caught her breath as the world returned to her body. "I can't even…"

"Then don't," Tillie said. She gave Freda the marigold. "Try."

"Right now? I can barely speak."

Tillie nodded. "Right now."

Freda sat up and pulled her pants back on. She cradled the flower between her hands and moved her energy from her root to the plant, as Javiera had taught her. She felt the flower glowing before she even opened her hands. When she did part her palms, the petals radiated an amber light. Though she was more exhausted and thirsty than she had ever been in her life, Freda almost cried with elation. She and Tillie smiled at each other.

"Marsh marigold," Tillie said, taking the flower from Freda to examine the light of its evocation. "A flower for the dead." She handed the flower back to Freda. "Seems fitting to me. Goodbye, shameful Freda."

Freda held the flower close to her chest, beaming. "And good riddance."

☾

The moon's light cast her room in silver. Today Freda turned twenty-six, two years older than the day she had arrived at the Haven. She spread her birthday gifts across her bed. Orvik had given her a thin flute and a box, both made of cedar. Carved into the instrument were many birds in flight: large hawks and small songbirds, eagles and herons. She lifted the flute from the box and played a crescendo of low notes.

A thud on the window startled her. Outside, a giant barn owl beat its wings, cooing in reply to the flute's music. Freda lifted up the window and let the owl fly in. He perched on Freda's shoulder and rubbed his head against her ear. Delighted, Freda laughed and stroked the owl before he flew back out the window.

She unfolded the blanket Javiera had crafted. Bright wool threads wove into an image of a cougar in a tree. Freda remembered watching Javiera shave the sheep a few months earlier. She sniffed and licked a corner of the blanket. Though still a neophyte in her Florávo studies, she could detect dyes of blackberry, lichen, oak bark, and madder root. Vinegar nearly overwhelmed the Florávian herbs infused into the dyes, but Freda could also identify the unmistakable presence of senna and lemon balm. Both offered the warmth of love.

Freda wrapped the blanket around her and, sure enough, she felt heat flooding into her body from the blanket. She began to tear up a little. Javiera's generosity and kindness almost made up for the fact Damari and Brigid still refused to speak to Freda. Orvik had begun talking to her a few months after she first arrived. He told her stories from his childhood spent on the Tuttuán seaterra of Anilsatok. The anthropologist forever inside her relished his memories of hunting whales in boats made of seals' skin and intestines.

Tillie had asked Freda to open her present in private, after dinner and cake. Inside the small box was a leather satchel strung to a chain. Freda unfastened the satchel's tiny wooden button to reveal a collection of apricot flowers. Their white petals were dyed pink with Tillie's blood. Tingles leaped through Freda's body. She placed a flower in her palm and evoked it. Sure enough, minutes later Freda heard a soft knock on her door. When she opened it, Tillie stole into the room.

Tillie sat on the bed, naked, and grinned. "I was hoping you would call for me," she whispered.

Freda sat beside her and touched Tillie's jaw. "I'll always be calling for you."

When Freda woke, Tillie still slept. Her hair was a mess of red upon the white sheets. Freda figured it was four in the morning. Midsummer had passed two moons earlier, and the dawn came with greater ease each day. She lit a lantern and tiptoed down the hall. After preparing a cup of tea, she walked into the veranda. The light revealed her reflection in the dark glass. Her hair, grown now to her chin, stuck out at odd angles. She had lost all of her Imperial fat, as she called it now, and then some. Homesteading had carved muscle into her arms and legs. She smiled at her reflection. It looked as healthy and happy as she felt.

Freda set the lantern on a side table and picked up the bundle of dried willow branches sitting on the windowsill. Working from her root, she evoked the branches until they glowed a bright apricot color. She held the tip of the branches into the lantern's flame until smoke puffed up from the bundle. When she moved the smoking bundle across the veranda's only wooden wall, a hidden door creaked open, revealing a bookcase.

The bundle hissed as she dunked it in a pitcher of water. She skimmed the shelves, looking for any books she may not have read since Javiera showed her the library two years earlier. The Mages had debated for months whether or not Freda should be permitted access to their collection of books on the Anima. Ultimately, on a vote of three to two, they had determined Freda, as the assumed Anima-in-waiting, should know as much about her predecessors as their library afforded.

The books offered many details, much knowledge, but no answer to the question Laurel had sent her here with: where would the next mushroom grow? When Freda had read about the Anima's Death Revelation in a book written by a Salvager named Rua, she thought it strange Laurel didn't already know where the last mushroom would grow. If Animas revealed, when dying, where the next mushroom would surface, wouldn't a Salvager like Laurel, with the ability to see all things past, have heard the last Anima's Death Revelation?

She had asked Javiera this question last winter, after reading Rua's book. Salvagers, Javiera had said, need to know when *and* where to look for an answer. The last Anima had disappeared after the Imperial Army burned her home to the ground—no one knew where she went or when she died. Freda shivered as she ran a finger along the spine of Rua's book. *Disappeared.* If the last Anima had died a death similar to Erie, the Anima who lived in this very Haven four centuries ago, she had died in pain.

Freda had read about Erie in a book written by a Commoner named Adalbern. *The Wolfwoman of Taléria* told the story of Adalbern's quest to bring Erie's ashes back to the Haven. Beyond these books, Freda had read a dozen others. She knew the white dots atop the mushroom's red cap would be arranged in the Flower of Life pattern:

She also knew it would grow on a new moon among deciduous trees on the summer solstice, and it would be the smallest mushroom in a ring of twelve. Yet all this knowledge was useless if she couldn't find out what the last Anima had said in her Death Revelation. She withdrew Rua's book for the hundredth time and sat on the wicker couch. Sipping her tea, she scanned the pages yet again, looking for any details she may have missed. She set down the tea and massaged her temples.

Javiera had said the last Anima had lived on the Alimendia seterra, near the shores of Meadowland Lake. Freda closed Rua's book and set it back on the shelf. She shuffled the books around, looking for anything, *anything* she might have missed. Dawn began to give shape to the forest outside. She stilled, her hand upon a shelf, and slumped. She knew it. She had for months now, but she had been avoiding the truth.

Laurel's instructions had been clear: Freda needed to find the mushroom, alone and in secret. The books on these shelves revealed a history of the Anima's Task to fight against the harm inflicted by the World Forces. Her education within the Imperium had told her its expansion across five of the seven seterras had been a righteous campaign—a spread of knowledge and light throughout a primitive, barbaric world. The history of the Anima revealed an alternative story, one where both humans and the natural world suffered for millennia under the oppression of greed.

Freda had done as Laurel asked. She had learned all of the Anima she could here in the emerald forests of northern Taléria. The truth, clear and cold, remained: knowledge of where the last mushroom would grow did not exist on these shelves or anywhere in this Haven. She assumed her best chance—maybe her only chance—for the answer she sought was hidden somewhere in the remains of the last Anima's home.

Her submission to the inevitable wrung the air from her lungs. The Haven—this homey cottage, with its bountiful garden and fresh goat cheese. Her studies in Florávo—the promise of her skill, the power still waiting for her. Javiera, Orvik—the kind of friends she had always wanted. And Tillie.

Tillie. Her love. A love she had thought her life would never hold.

She returned to her room where Tillie still slept. Freda traced Tillie's cheekbone with a finger. Tillie slowly opened her eyes and frowned.

"What's wrong, love?" Freda asked.

Tillie sat up in the bed. "When do you intend to leave?" she whispered.

Freda's breath caught. How could she have possibly known?

"What do you mean?"

"Don't play dumb, Freda."

Freda quelled a cringe. "I still don't know where the next mushroom will grow," she replied, maintaining a placid face.

Tillie stood and slipped a tunic over her head. She sat back on the bed and met Freda's eyes. "I can feel you drifting away," she said, touching Freda's shoulder. "You've spent a lot of time in the library, alone. I can't help but feel like you're going somewhere I can't go."

Freda already hated herself for what she needed to say. "I'm not going anywhere soon," she lied. "I love you, Tillie, and I love my life here." These last two things were true, and Freda felt as if she would rip in half. She pulled Tillie into her arms and held her tight, but not too tight.

Over a breakfast of eggs and greens, they sipped tea and talked about the things that needed to be done before winter. It was a chilly fall day, and Brigid started a fire in the hearth. Tillie eyed Freda over her teacup. Freda could feel her gaze but pretended not to notice.

The warmth of this kitchen, melody of voices, nourishment of the food they cultivated: even her childhood house hadn't felt as home as this place.

Freda fought against tears, looking anywhere but across the table. Tillie slammed down her teacup and announced she didn't feel well and would be spending the day in solitude. Javiera raised an eyebrow but said nothing as Tillie strutted back into her room. Brigid scowled at Freda as if she knew Freda was to blame for Tillie's sullen mood.

When Tillie walked back out of the room, she turned her chin toward Freda and offered the tiniest tilt of her head. Freda nodded in return, though she wouldn't follow just yet. There was too much to be done before leaving. The front door clanged shut behind Tillie.

Between butchering meat chickens and harvesting the last of the kale, Freda squirreled bread and cheese into her room. While everyone took their midday break, Freda moved frantically around the greenhouse. She brewed a concentrated tincture of valerian, poppy, and magnolia bark and slipped the bottle into her pocket. She managed to steal a couple of books from the library before the others emerged rested from their bedrooms. When she arranged the box and scroll, books, and birthday presents in her backpack, she wept soundlessly.

Freda could still feel the sear of Laurel's white-blue eyes. *It's imperative no one knows where you go,* she had said.

By dinnertime Tillie was still gone. Javiera announced they wouldn't eat until she was brought back home. Freda fingered the bottle in her pocket. There would be no need for sleeping potion after all. She wondered if Tillie had planned to create a diversion for her to escape, though she quickly dismissed the thought as fantasy. Her head began to throb with the competing pressures of anxiety, guilt, and despair. Javiera gave each person a cardinal direction. She would stay behind in case Tillie returned home, and everyone was to come back within the hour.

When everyone stood, Javiera said, "Freda, please wait."

Freda sat back down. Her palms felt slick. She tried to slow her breathing. The Mages pulled on cloaks and boots and trudged outside. Brigid and Damari shot her loathing glances on their way out. Orvik gave her a shrug as he closed the door behind him.

Javiera took Tillie's seat. "Did something happen between you two?"

"No. I think she's having another—episode." Freda's head pounded harder. She hated herself already, but using Tillie's depression for her own lies? This was a new low. Her chin quivered with the effort not to sob.

"I figured," Javiera said, though her face didn't agree with her words.

Freda considered telling Javiera the truth. She had been her teacher, her friend, a mother, even, for two years now. She knew Freda would need to leave eventually. Freda could hear Laurel's chilling tone saying *no one*. Laurel's plan, Freda knew, was bigger than her. It was bigger, even, than the love she had for Tillie and her life here.

Freda also knew Javiera trusted Laurel. She figured when she returned to this Haven as the Anima, Javiera would forgive her. Tillie, though, may never understand. She couldn't be sure of either assumption. Only time would tell—time made longer with her hesitations.

She stood. "I'm going to join the search now."

Javiera nodded. As Freda walked back to her room, she thought she heard her whisper, "May you find what you seek."

Freda's hands shook as she pulled on her backpack over the fur coat she and Tillie had crafted together from hare skins. She bowed to the room as a goodbye and left the Haven out the greenhouse door. Javiera had told Freda to look south, and south she ran. She craved to see Tillie standing in the trees, her red hair and red cloak hot against the evergreen. But only twilight's shadows accompanied Freda. The tears streamed out behind her as she pushed through the will to stop, running faster than she ever dreamed possible for her body.

*Your secrecy ensures survival of hope,* Laurel had said. *The world needs you. The world needs you.*

Her wool undergarments had grown wet with sweat, but she couldn't fit the fur coat in her backpack, and she refused to leave it behind. She continued south, reaching the road to Nafáit by midnight. The moon, a day waning from full, revealed little, if anything, had changed since she was last there. Pigs still populated the farm west of the road, and the town hadn't erected any new buildings.

She decided against staying at the Four Inn. Though a bed would be ideal after hours on the run, she didn't want anyone knowing she was there. She curled up in a patch of withered yarrow behind the train station. Grasping the satchel hanging around her neck, her face contorted as she tried to stifle the sobs.

# HOMESTEAD

## 102 YBP

### Alimendia Seaterra

Freda spread a map of Alimendia across a tray on an airplane flying over the Yellow Sea. The Wildwood Mountains contrasted sharply with the seaterra's Colossal Desert. She knew the protectorate wasn't renowned for its red dunes and cow carcasses; that would be bad for its nascent tourist industry.

Alimendia grew as a favorite vacation destination since the seaterra's absorption into the Imperium nearly two decades ago. From the airplane window, Freda could see why. Giant peaks rose above an aquamarine inlet. The city of Kingsburg populated the hills surrounding the water. Walking through the airport's halls, Freda saw advertisements of bright green fields and teal lakes.

It was nearly midnight. She took a cab to the city center and rented a bed in a cheap hostel. The next morning she walked down streets wet from a rainstorm. The sky remained gray and dark. She followed signs to the bus station, passing shops opening for the day. After yet another restless night and a few days of travel, Freda felt half-asleep.

The bus to New Paddock left in a half hour. She bought a bun and coffee from a newsstand and ate her breakfast on a bench overlooking the inlet. White and bright pink flowers blossomed in the trees, the opposite of Taléria's golden autumn three days ago. The smell of eggs cooking nearby brought to mind her last morning at the Haven. She clutched the satchel yet again.

The Imperium had established a fleet port in Kingsburg. Commercial boats and freights were harbored away from the aircraft carriers and frigates. Freda found the hustle and bustle among the navy ships unsettling. She had heard whispers of war on her travels here. Newspaper headlines and passengers on the trains and planes had spoken of rising tensions between the Imperium and Republic. Freda knew she needed to get off Alimendia as soon as possible. The last thing she wanted if war came to the world once more was to be stuck on a seaterra in the middle of the action.

She took a seat in the back of the bus, a few rows behind the half dozen other travelers. As they bumped their way out of the city, she removed the scroll from the box. She stroked the carved letters and recited the words again and again. An onlooker would have assumed she was crazy. She felt crazy. Maybe she had gone crazy somewhere along the way and had yet to realize it. Crying, she prayed that she was in the right place. She prayed she had made the right choices, that there was such a thing as destiny, that leaving her education, a safe future, her dying mother, a true home, her love—maybe *the* love—had been the right things to do. Hugging the scroll to her chest, she whispered these prayers over and over.

Half a day later, the bus stopped at her destination. She walked into a sunny afternoon. The advertisements at the airport hadn't embellished reality. Even the town's bus stop boasted a surreal view of Meadowland Lake, the world's largest body of freshwater. The lake shimmied with light dancing across the green-blue waters of glacial melt. On the west side of the lake, giant mountains penetrated the sky. Hundreds of people swam and sunbathed on a sandy beach. She walked to the closest restaurant and ordered a generous portion of rice and vegetables. In between bites, she reexamined the map. The mushroom had most likely grown somewhere in the mountains.

She followed a path along the lake's shore. The beach faded into forest, and the crowds faded away as well. She passed only a few other hikers. One couple, stopped alongside the trail on a water break, asked Freda where she was going.

"To the top of Mount Wildwood," she lied.

"This late?" the woman said. Her drawl revealed they came from Cattleland Canton. "But you don't have any camping gear."

"Oh," the man said, drawing out the o, "are you staying at the commune?"

"Commune?" Freda asked. Though his tone sounded derogatory, Freda refrained from telling him it was none of his business.

"Haven't you heard of the Freepeople?" the woman asked. "They live up there. A bunch of—well, they're making a statement."

The man nodded. "They're anti-modernity, from my understanding. They set up shop a few miles back. You'll see the trail a mile or two up this main one."

"How interesting," Freda said. "But no, I'm not heading there."

They bid her farewell, and she continued up. If Freda had learned anything by now, it was not to dismiss clues for coincidence. She decided to see if these Freepeople offered any leads to her search.

She reached the commune as dusk descended. Fires burned in pits between tiny wooden shacks. A couple dozen people gathered around the fires, talking and eating out of bowls. Freda's stomach turned. Was she hungry or scared? She pressed on toward the first group of people. They turned to watch her approach. Both the men and women had dreadlocks, some falling all the way to their bottoms.

They smiled and welcomed her. One woman stepped in for a hug. Freda lurched back, the woman's pungent smell repelling her.

The woman closed her eyes and left her arms wide open. "Welcome," she said. "Welcome."

Freda could tell she had also come from the Cantons, the northeast by the sounds of it.

The others nodded. A man set a hand on the woman's shoulder. He stood more than a head taller than her. His red dreadlocks reached his belly button. "It's okay, Sunshine," he said. "She will enter when she is ready."

Freda furrowed her brow. Enter? There was something off about these people, but Freda willed away her judgments and stuck a hand out. "I'm—Diana," she lied. "I've come to—learn more about your ways."

Everyone looked at her hand as if she held out a claw. Sunshine dropped her arms and took a step back.

"We don't shake hands," the man said. "We, the Freepeople, view the handshake as one of the many forms Imperial oppression takes to make humans less human."

Again, the others nodded in unison. Freda withdrew her hand.

"I'm Firehorse," he continued. "That's Mountaindew, Riverdance, Starlight, and this is Sunshine. Come, join us by the fire. Are you hungry?"

"I am," Freda said, following him to the fire.

More people at neighboring fires waved at her. She could see, even in the dim light, their torn clothing and dirty faces. Riverdance returned with a bowl of soup, and Freda ate it with vigor. The warm food helped settle her nerves.

"What brings you, fellow wanderer?" Mountaindew asked.

"I'm here—on a research project," she said. "I'm an archeologist studying the use of psychedelics in small communities."

The lie came to her fast, and she smiled at herself. But then again, it wasn't really a lie. She would always be an archaeologist, even if she may never be employed as one. The rest was truth wrapped in a veil of vagueness. The psychedelics bit could serve as an opening to questions about the Fly Agaric.

No one spoke and an uncomfortable energy spread across the camp.

Firehorse's face turned scarlet. "That's presumptuous of you, don't you think? To just walk right into this camp and accuse us of drug use."

The others nodded. Freda wondered how their heads moved up and down in such startling synchronicity. Her mind backpedaled frantically. How quickly these Freepeople shifted from open arms to slanted eyes.

"I'm sorry," Freda stammered. "I must be lost. I'm looking for a mushroom called the Fly Agaric and anyone who may use it."

The people glanced at one another. Surprise flickered across Firehorse's red face. In the corner of Freda's eye, she saw a man's hand move to the dagger on his belt.

"I see," Firehorse said. "You are aware of the Imperium's drug policies, of course. We, the Freepeople, would no longer remain free if the government were to discover any illicit drugs. We do not need drugs to feel alive. The forest brings us to life, and we live off what we find and grow, and that alone."

Freda feigned happiness. "That's wonderful, just wonderful," she said, bringing her hands together. "I just love to hear that. As an independent scientist, I don't involve the government in my research. But alas, you don't have the data I seek. So it goes. I'm just thrilled to hear of your self-sufficiency, and it seems you all are living your—your dreams." She felt exhausted by her own inauthenticity.

"I'm glad you understand," Firehorse said. The red had drained from his face, but Freda wasn't oblivious to the fact his smile didn't extend to his eyes.

"If it's okay with everyone here, I would spend the night and leave in the morning. Circumstances being what they were, I left ill-equipped for the journey." Freda winked at Mountaindew. The woman's smile was as unconvincing as the one on Firehorse's face.

"Of course," he said, motioning for Freda to follow him. He grabbed a torch lamp burning nearby and led her down a dark path intermitted with light from candles burning within the shacks.

The Freepeople watched her pass. Freda walked with shoulders back, meeting their stares with her own unwavering gaze. Her hand rested on the weapon she had attached to her own belt: a pouch of dried belladonna berries. They stopped at a tiny shack at the edge of the development. The lamp revealed a cot with a deer hide on it. Nothing else would have fit in the space.

"Let any one of us know if you need anything. My family and I sleep in that house over there." Firehorse pointed at a shack, not much larger than this one.

Two small girls with bright red hair peeked out from the open doorframe. Children lived here? Their eyes glowed white against faces dark with dirt. Freda waved at them, and they disappeared back into the shack.

"Thank you, Firehorse. This should be fine. More than fine. I appreciate it."

They said their goodnights with forced cheer, and Freda sat on the cot. The hide smelled even worse than Firehorse. She wondered who the hell these Freepeople really were and why they had reacted so violently to an admittedly forward but seemingly benign question.

Maybe the Freepeople had already dealt with reprimands from drug use in the past. If this commune was anything like the ones in the Cantons, psychedelics were a part of everyday life. Judging by the surprise on Firehorse's face when she mentioned the Fly Agaric, the mushroom must serve some sort of role in their lives. She remembered seeing Sunlight or Starrynight or whatever his name was reaching for his dagger. Violence also seemed to serve some sort of role here.

The warmth of the spring day faded into the chill of a mountain night. Freda kicked off her boots and opened her backpack. She took out the blanket Javiera had made for her and wrapped it around her shoulders. The shivers melted away. Lying down on the ground, she used her backpack for a pillow. She rested her head atop the box and imagined the scroll whispering its words to her.

The sounds of twigs breaking grew louder. Freda's eyes snapped open. Someone approached. She pushed away a strange dream and stuffed the blanket into her backpack. Coming into a squat, she unlatched the belladonna bomb from her belt.

A man stood in the doorframe, leaning against a wooden stick taller than he was. Though he had a white beard and white hair, his face looked young, his body strong. His eyes, white-blue and luminescent, reminded her of someone. He stood self-possessed, knowing, looking back at her with impatience. Laurel. His eyes were like Laurel's, and Freda realized she was looking at the Salvager named Rua.

He motioned for her to follow. She slung on her backpack and hurried after him, careful not to make any noise as well. The white tail of his cloak led her through the darkness. She would think she had lost him, and then *whoosh*, there his cloak swayed again. Freda heard voices and slowed. A strange light radiated ahead. She could no longer see Rua.

The people spoke in Imperial. She moved from tree to tree until the voices grew into seeable things. Two men stood in front of a giant greenhouse. They stopped talking and swiveled toward her. She froze. They swung the guns on their backs into their hands.

She didn't think they could see her, but they walked right at her. A hand grabbed her wrist. Her free hand found the pouch in counterattack. With a finger to his lips, Rua released her wrist and waved for her to follow. She ran as fast as she could to keep up. He stopped in front of a tree and bent down to the ground. The men with guns neared. Rua held up a trapdoor and pushed her toward the revealed stairway. She all but fell down the steps, and he closed the trapdoor behind him without a sound. Freda held her breath as she listened to the men's pounding feet pass by overhead.

Candles lit a small living space below ground. She ducked inside. The burrow had a bed and a few ceramic bowls on the floor. Along the walls to her right and left were hundreds of jars, bowls, and vessels of dried flowers, roots, and leaves. Herb bunches hung from the ceiling alongside branches and boughs. It reminded her of the greenhouse back at the Haven, only darker, danker, and without living plants.

Rua walked down the stairs and past Freda, beckoning for her to come deeper into the room. She saw where he led her and halted with shock. There, atop a cut of canvas on the ground, in various stages of dehydration, were a hundred Fly Agarics. She picked up the freshest looking mushroom. Little white dots spotted the blood red cap. She half expected the dots to be arranged in the Flower of Life pattern. But of course now was not the time, here was not the place.

Freda startled when Rua placed a hand on her shoulder. "Laurel sent word of your coming," he said.

"I—"

He waved a hand. "I know, I know. You're seeking *where*. I'm glad I found you before they killed you. What were you thinking? Marching in there and asking about the Fly Agaric like you're asking for a potato."

Freda leaned back. "Who *were* they?"

"Some of your enemies. That's all you need to know for now." He took off his cloak. A sleeveless tunic underneath revealed a large, circular scar on his right shoulder. He took a box down from a shelf and handed it to her.

Freda gasped. Cradled in a cut of cloth within the box was the skull of an Anima.

"We managed to retrieve some of her remains," he explained. "I—well—I am to blame for the last Anima's murder." Freda could hear a deep pain in his voice. His eyes grew wet, and he swallowed. "Laurel believes it's best if Keepers don't orchestrate the final birth. For once, I have the wisdom to agree with her."

Freda lifted the skull to her eyes. A line cut the top of the head in half. Someone, or something, maybe time or mishandling of her remains, had halved her skull into two.

"Her name was Flo," he continued. "We aren't able to hear her last words. I believe the Imperial Army killed her in a facility blocking our Hindsight."

He sat beside Freda and looked at the mushrooms arranged on the ground. Freda set the skull between them.

His mouth drew down in a grim and determined expression. "To access the Fourth Dimension is to enter death." He talked in a low whisper, as if to himself. "I most likely will not return."

"Then don't—"

"You are to leave as soon as you learn what you need to. Don't wait to see if I wake or not. Don't wait for daylight. *Don't wait.* Just go. Should I wake, I won't remember what was said. It's—best this way."

She could hear the hesitation in his voice, and she wanted to argue with his decision. Was she capable of bearing his death on top of the burden she had already collected? She preferred not to find out. And yet it seemed she didn't have a choice. He studied the mushrooms, murmuring to himself.

Plucking one seemingly at random, he put it in his mouth and chewed it. He closed his eyes as he chewed and chewed. Freda watched helplessly as he moved forward with his decision. It felt as if an hour had passed before he finally swallowed. He repeated this two more times, eating three mushrooms total.

He cupped the skull within his hands. Bowing his head and closing his eyes, he chanted in a low hum. Freda strained to hear him, but the noises streaming from his mouth made no sense to her. His noises sounded like wind rushing through a tunnel at one moment, chipmunk calls another. He would occasionally crescendo into cawing, roaring, or bugling before plunging back into the white noise of wind.

Time had no place. The candles burned on. Freda lost feeling in her legs. The skull remained forceful in its presence. An hour, maybe five, flowed by. Rua grew quiet. The absence of noise shattered the moment, and time flooded through the cracks.

His body began to twitch. The twitching grew into convulsing, and his voice returned as a frantic cacophony of noises. Freda panicked. Was he having a seizure? She scrambled to brace him. He quit moving. His body grew still as stone, and he opened his eyes. Freda leaned back and stared into the wild glow of his irises.

He didn't look like a man. He barely looked human. When he spoke, the words escaped between gasps of agony from a twisted mouth. "The—last—will be—born—where the—first—was buried. Spine"—he gagged, the last words caught in gurgles—"of——the——Earth."

Freda opened her mouth but nothing came out. The luminance faded from Rua's eyes, and his warped face relaxed. He crumpled to the ground. She brought her fingers to his wrist and found a pulse—quiet, but there. He felt rigid and cold, as if his body had already experienced rigor mortis. Freda trembled as she wrapped Javiera's blanket around him.

She lay in a fetal position on the bed. The last Anima had clearly died in agony. Freda covered her eyes with her hands. Who had killed her—and *how*? When she removed her hands from her eyes, she could see slivers of light streaming through gaps between the trapdoor and earth. Her body began to calm. She tried to lift Rua onto his bed, but he was too heavy. She put Javiera's blanket back in her pack and wrapped the stretch of fur from the bed around him. His lips were blue and his face a disturbing white. It didn't look like he would live much longer.

She put her backpack on and walked toward the cracks of light. After three years of seeking, the journey to find her destination had come to an end. Freda of the Cantons would return to where her quest had begun.

☾

The alders in the graveyard reached with naked limbs into a white sky. Freda stood in her fur coat and wool pants. It felt warm out, like it always did in Prominence before it snowed. Her mother's tombstone looked fresh next to that of her father's. They had made it identical to his, with her name over the years of her life and the seventh proverb of the Power carved above it all: *Death consumes lovers and foes alike.*

Freda hated it. And she hated this hate. How could she even have an opinion about her mother's tombstone? They had done what they could in her absence. The people at the nursing home hadn't hid their disdain for Freda when she had walked in, looking for her mother. When Freda hadn't responded to the dozens of letters and calls, imploring her to take care of her mother's deceased body, they had buried her. A nurse had handed Freda the bill, and Freda had paid it with inheritance money set aside for her funeral. She gave the rest of the funeral fund to the nursing home as an anonymous donation, though the gesture did little to pacify her guilt.

"I'm sorry," she whispered to the graves. "I've failed you—both."

She knew they would have been disappointed in her. *Disappointed* wasn't a big enough word. *Heartbroken*? *Disgusted*? Those felt more fitting. She had let her mother die alone. She had left the position her father had secured for her at the risk of his reputation. The university had taken pity on him, a sonless father. And above all, she had, at last, expressed her deviant sexuality. She figured if they could look down on her in an afterlife, her mother would be crying, and her father would be furious.

Freda touched a thorn on the rose she held. It was a white rose, her mother's favorite, probably trained in from Soleria. She remembered the way Tillie had helped her undress the shame she wore from a childhood suppressing her sexual desires. Tillie had called homophobia a disease of the Imperium.

"It is, you know, a disease," Freda said to the tombstones. "I'm not blaming either of you, but, well." She stopped. Was she really lecturing the memory of her parents? She squatted down and set the rose on her mother's grave. "I *am* sorry," she repeated. "For you both, I mean. For the failure you must feel, given the circumstances of your lives. But I'm not sorry for what I've done, or what I am."

She began to cry. "I'm sorry you died alone," she whispered. "I just hope—I hope you'll see why, someday, and forgive me." As she walked away, the year's first snow began to drift down. She walked under the cemetery gate, down Twenty-fourth Avenue, back to Twin Rivers' Main Street, and straight into a bar.

The bar bustled with the after-work crowd. Freda looked around before approaching the counter. Alongside letters from her mother's nursing home, letters from her university professors and even some students had filled her post office box. At first, her superiors had been concerned. When an investigation revealed she had bought a one-way ticket to Makalon, they had terminated her fellowship. It wasn't uncommon for archeologists to go rogue.

Thankfully, she recognized no one in the bar. Twin Rivers had grown in the three years she was away. She felt eyes following her as she walked to the counter. It was the fur coat, she assumed, though she also suspected she was attractive to these men. Her hair now reached her shoulders, and her body was trim and fit from the Haven.

She ordered a whisky, neat, shot it back, and asked for another. The bartender filled the glass again and pushed it toward her. "What brings a beauty like you to the Susie Blue?" he asked. He was tall, muscular, with a mess of brown hair and a dimpled grin. He reminded Freda of Damari.

She tilted the whisky down her throat and gestured for another. "I came for the booze," she said. "And the men." She gave him a wink and shot the whisky back.

Hugging the toilet, Freda threw up again. She stood and cringed at her ghastly reflection in the bathroom mirror. The woman looking back at her was a corpse. She remembered Rua on the ground, his face the color of larvae, and dry heaved into the sink.

The bartender still slept as Freda pulled on her pants, shirt, and backpack. She closed the apartment door behind her without a sound. At a shop down the street, she bought a bun and coffee. She vomited the bun up in an alleyway garbage can. The coffee burned her throat, but she drank it anyway as she waited for the bank to open.

When the teller unlocked the door, she marched up to the counter and asked for her account in cash. He eyed her dirty coat as if it were roadkill.

"All of it?" he asked for the second time.

"All of it."

Freda glanced sideways at the people around her. The teller asked her to follow him into a back room. She signed paper after paper before he retrieved her lockbox. Freda opened it to find over fifty thousand dollars, her mother's wedding ring and diamond earrings, her father's pistol, and her birth certificate. A large fortune, all things considered. The box wouldn't fit in her backpack—not with *the* box already inside it—so she carried it to the Army Surplus store.

She bought a larger backpack and placed the smaller one in the trash bin outside the store. She paused, looking at the pack in the garbage, remembering the plane to Makalon, the trains across Baninchi and Lacuserra, the bus to Meadowland Lake. The pack had served her well. She thanked it and continued south, toward the next town.

She would need to live close enough to the mountains to conduct her search but far enough from Twin Rivers to avoid contact with her old life. She had learned upon returning to Prominence that the excavation site at the base of Yarrow Peak had been terminated a year earlier, freeing the land for her hunt. Laurel had said the mushroom would grow again soon. Freda need but settle into a new home and scan the burial site for the mushroom every summer solstice until she found it. Simple enough.

A light layer of snow covered the dead grasses alongside the dirt road leading into Middle Fork. Last night, she decided, had been a purge. She touched the rawness she felt from the sex and decided she'd never do that again. She had needed to prove to herself, to her parents, maybe, that she was what she was and wanted what she wanted. Should his seed, well—she knew of a couple herbs.

A man on horseback trotted by with his herding dog. She gave him a wave, and he tipped his wide-brim hat in reply. Though still hung over, she began to walk quicker down the road. Each step brought her closer to being the Anima, and she felt reinvigorated with the promise of her path. She imagined herself finding the mushroom this very summer and taking it to the Haven. She would arrive, give Tillie the biggest kiss of their lives, and take a bite. When she woke again, she'd be in Tillie's arms, reborn as a hope for the world. Tillie would understand and forgive her. Sure, life as the Anima would be dangerous and difficult, but it would be more meaningful than any other life Freda might have lived.

She arrived to Middle Fork around noon. The town was a fraction the size of Twin Rivers, with a bank, general store, café, school, and three bars. Mostly ranchers and farmers populated the surrounding area, though a couple neighborhoods had sprouted up along the Crazy Mountain foothills west of town. Stepping into the general store, she hoped to discover one of these houses was for sale.

The woman at the cashier frowned at Freda's coat as she approached the counter. She wore red lipstick, and her bob was perfectly curled. The lipstick stained the filter of the cigarette she held to the side in her gloved hand.

Freda slapped her hands on the counter, and the woman jumped. "I'm looking to buy a house."

The woman took a drag of the cigarette as she shuffled through the newspaper next to the cashier. "Have at it," she drawled, placing the classifieds between them.

Freda thanked her and took a seat on a couch in the store's lobby. The pickings proved slim. A ranching home on ten acres some twenty miles east. Too far away. Another ranch east of town, in the small mining community of Culbright. Again, she wanted to be as close to Yarrow Peak as possible. The only suitable option seemed to be a modern home, built in Desnordian fashion with brick and oak. It sat on half an acre on the third of Middle Fork's three streets.

She walked to the listed property. A *For Sale* sign sat in front of a whitewashed fence. The property was smaller than Freda would have liked. She planned to cultivate as much of her own food as possible, and the backyard looked barely large enough to host a proper garden, much less chickens and goats. The house, she reminded herself, would only be home for a short period. She didn't need a Haven when she had one waiting for her already.

Freda opened the gate and walked up to the door. People talked on the other side. She knocked, and the door opened to reveal two men. One stood a little taller than Freda, with white hair and glasses reminiscent of Javiera's half-moon spectacles. The other was a huge man. He towered over them both, with broad shoulders and a long, black braid. He looked Bilawáxan, though blue eyes spoke of mixed blood.

"Can I help you, Miss?" the shorter man asked.

"I, yes, I hope. I'm looking to buy this house."

The taller man grimaced. He held up the papers in his hand. "I may have beaten you to it," he said. He looked genuinely concerned.

Freda's stomach dropped. But this was the only suitable option in twenty miles. She tried not to let her panic show. "Oh," she managed.

"Sorry," the old homeowner said. He held out his hand to the other man. "Nice doing business with ya. We'll have your keys ready by the end of the week."

Freda stood awkwardly as the men shook hands. The former

homeowner shrugged at her as he closed the door. Freda walked back down the pathway with the new homeowner. He seemed to be assessing her. She doubled her efforts to repress the mounting anxiety.

He stopped. "You really want this house, don't you?"

She glanced back at it. The brick and oak was no ivy-clad cobblestone, and the yard looked dead and blasé. She would have to work hard to get the land in tillable shape, just in case the mushroom hunt took longer than a year or two. *Want* wasn't really the word.

"I need a home, yes," she said. "But you beat me to it, fair and square."

He sighed as he looked beyond the house, to the Crazy Mountains. "I just need a place to store my stuff, while I'm—well, when the war begins."

Freda felt her face grow red. If the rumors were true, he would be leaving for war sooner than later. And here she was, a woman safe from the draft, feeling sorry for herself because she'd need to look harder for a home.

"I'll find another," she said. The bright tone of her voice sounded unnatural.

"Not around these parts." He shook his head. "I barely got my hands on this one. Everyone's buckling down. Just in case."

He kept looking at the mountains, and she turned to look as well. The peaks stood the same as always: snow-capped, royal blue, huge against the belt of sky.

"I've got a home, technically," he said. "It's, well—inconveniently located." He shook his head and began walking back to the brick house. "Come on. Let's get you your home."

"Wait. What do you mean, *inconveniently located*?"

"Oh. It's just my grandma. A Bilawáxan through and through."

Freda lifted an eyebrow.

"I inherited this place from her. Back there," he pointed to the peaks. "I mean, *back* there."

Her heart began to flutter. "Like, Owl Creek Canyon back there?"

He smiled, surprised. "You know your Crazies. Try Badger Creek Canyon back there."

Freda began to laugh. She blinked up at the sky. Really? This easy? "I, just, wow. Just wow," she said, still laughing.

"What?"

"Can you show me this place? I have a feeling it's just what I'm looking for. I mean, if you're selling."

"Oh, I'm selling. Been trying to for years. I don't think you get it, though." He waved his hand. "It's back there. Like, nobody's around. It's not exactly a woman's home."

Freda lifted her chin. "We'll see about that. Will you show it to me or not?"

He studied her with renewed interest. "It's too late today. I mean it's a hike. There ain't a single road back there, I'll tell you that. And we'll have to stay the night, unless we want to hike back in the dark. It's more than twenty miles one way."

"When can we leave?" She would go right now.

He shook his head, smiling. "You're not from around here, are you?"

"Yes and no." She put her hands on her hips. "I can go whenever."

He paused, still looking at her with curiosity. "How 'bout six we meet at the café? We can eat up and hit the trail from there."

"Perfect."

"Name's Todd," he said, offering his hand.

She shook it with gusto. "Di—Freda," she said. "I'm Freda. I'll see you in the morning."

"Okay," he said, drawing out the o.

He walked back to town with a wave, and she turned to the forest creeping down the foothills. Yesterday's snow had already melted, and there didn't look to be more coming tonight. She found a large pine with a nook beneath its boughs. The new pack, with padding on its straps and back, worked better as a pillow than the old one. Wrapped in the blanket from Javiera, Freda's hand found the satchel hung around her neck, and she fell asleep with ease.

Over coffee, eggs, ham, and potatoes, Todd told Freda about joining the Army's Infantry right after boarding school. He'd be serving as a second lieutenant in the war.

"So it's happening," Freda said. She sipped her coffee.

He shrugged. "I don't see any way around it. The Republic and Imperium have fought these little battles over the protectorates since the first war in Suqwas. It's been over two centuries. One big push, and it could all be done at last."

Freda set down her coffee. "Yes, well—shall we?"

He motioned for the check and began to take his wallet out.

"I insist," she said, placing a dollar on the table. "You're going out of your way, on a whim."

Todd looked uncomfortable. "The man usually pays."

"Well this isn't a date and no one saw," she said, standing. "Besides, you can probably tell by now that I'm not a woman to follow *usually*."

He laughed. "Ain't that the truth."

He pulled on a daypack, army issued, and Freda put her pack on as well. They walked west down Middle Fork's main street. The road continued all the way to the mountains. Ranches lined either side. They passed a wolf, shot dead and left in the ditch. Ravens and magpies helped themselves to the carcass.

Todd frowned at the wolf. "I heard they're trying to kill them all," he mumbled.

"I heard the same," Freda said, and they exchanged glum expressions.

"So," Todd said, lightening his tone. "You still haven't told me anything about yourself."

They stepped into the forest and walked past the tree Freda had slept beneath. She wrung her hands together as she followed him. How much should she tell him? He would be leaving town soon and probably wouldn't return. And it wasn't like the university or family would be hunting her down. She was free to share her story—or part of it, anyways. She told him about growing up in Twin Rivers and attending the archeology program.

"I didn't think women were allowed to pursue upper education." He sounded curious, not accusatory like the men who had said the same thing before.

"There are exceptions." Like her perfect grades and her father's prestige. "Rare, but there. It doesn't matter, anyways. I found the university system—*undesirable*."

Todd nodded. "I get that. But surely a professorship is more desirable than life out here." He gestured to the trees around them.

"Not in the slightest."

Todd looked over his shoulder and, seeing her serious face, laughed. "You remind me of my grandma."

"How so?"

"Well, you're stubborn. Any idiot can see that. And you're—strange. But not in a bad way," he added quickly.

She agreed with his assessment. They relaxed into a comfortable silence, and Freda decided she liked this Todd person.

The forest felt subdued around them. With winter breathing down the peaks, snow began to cover more of the ground as they gained elevation. The foothills crested and rolled back down into Owl Creek Canyon. The forest of these mountains grew sparser than the trees back in Taléria. Pine dominated the land, while deciduous growth populated the banks of Owl Creek.

They crossed the river, slow flowing in the late fall, and followed it up the mountainside. Yarrow Peak rose to their right. As they hiked higher, she could see hints of the excavation site beneath the grasses and smattering of snow. Freda assumed one would need to know the excavation happened to notice its lingering presence.

Other than hunters, people rarely ventured back here. Peak climbing had grown as a form of recreation in Lacuserra, but Freda hadn't heard of anyone pursuing mountains in the Cantons yet. She felt the absence of humans in the quiet around her. Hooves had flattened the snow, and they followed the ungulates' path. They passed a waterfall.

"That's Hidden Passage," Todd said over the roar resounding off the cliffs. "Owl Creek flows under the mountain for half a mile and comes out here."

Freda had seen the waterfall on maps before, but never in person. "Amazing," she said.

They continued up to the saddle connecting Yarrow Peak with Juniper Mountain. They lunched on the plateau. The day aged past noon, with a sun hidden behind overcast skies. Todd pointed down the other side of the saddle. "We're almost there," he said. "Just a couple more miles. You holding up alright?"

Freda gave him a deadpan expression. Did he really think she wasn't capable of another two miles?

He laughed. "Just asking."

They walked down the mountain, and the river began flowing above ground again. A copse thickened around them, and they followed a bend in the river. A mile later, the cabin appeared between the aspen stalks.

Freda braced herself on a tree.

Todd stopped. "Oh, sorry. Was I walking too fast?"

"No," she breathed, shaking her head.

It was as if she had dreamed this place into existence. The cabin was small and made of pine. It had a covered porch and intricate carvings on its door. Between the cabin and the creek was a garden, its size comparable to the garden back at the Haven. A fence, its iron wrought into vines and flowers, surrounded the garden. Beyond the garden and cabin stood a greenhouse and a shed. A tall wooden fence enclosed a chicken coop. She blinked back tears.

"Oh no," Todd said. "I feared this. I tried to warn you. Please, don't cry. You can have the brick house."

"Sorry, sorry," she said, still shaking her head. "I just—can't believe it sometimes, you know? How life. It just *gives*."

He looked utterly confused. Freda realized she probably wasn't making any sense to him.

She cleared her throat and wiped her face dry. "I mean, it's perfect, Todd. Truly perfect."

The animal pen's fence needed reinforcement.

"For the bears, you know," he said.

Freda figured as much. She helped him carry freshly cut cedar planks over to the fence. Todd proved to be a skilled woodworker. The shed beyond the greenhouse held many of his creations. He showed her inside after they finished the fence.

"Mostly bows," he said, opening the door. "My father and I hunted quite a bit." The bows hung on the wall. They appeared to be both delicate and strong, with graceful arcs and taut strings. "Do you know how to hunt?"

Damari had been the hunter back at the Haven. She had always wanted to learn—but, Damari. She touched the smooth wood of the bow closest to her. "I never learned."

Todd placed his hands on his hips. "You plan to live out here, and you don't know how to hunt?"

She shrugged at the disbelief on his face. "I've learned things before."

He chewed on his lower lip, studying Freda in that way of his. "I'll teach you. If you want. But really, want's got nothing to do with it."

"You'd do that?" She felt herself beaming.

"Let's see—you're a few inches above five feet, aren't you?" Todd scanned the wall. "A buck twenty, I'd guess. Plenty of muscle with more to come." He stopped in front of a smaller bow. "About the same size as her," he whispered.

Freda almost asked whom he spoke about, but she could tell he was talking to himself. He took a recurve bow down from the wall and handed it to her. Snakeskin covered one side of the limbs. As if woven by a master weaver, the red, black, and white scales formed a geometric pattern. She turned the bow over in her hand and ran her fingers along the bare wooden side.

"It's yew wood," he said. "And the skin belonged to a red-spotted garter snake. I harvested the wood from a dying yew tree. The snake was dead when I found her. The string is made of elk sinew, and the grip is from the hide of a mule deer." He took a quiver down. "The elk sinew is relatively new. I harvested him a few years ago. I replaced the grip when I replaced the sinew."

A cut of the snakeskin wrapped around the quiver's opening. Freda admired his attention to detail. He slipped an arrow out of the quiver and rolled it between his forefinger and thumb. "The shafts are made of dogwood. The feathers are from a turkey."

"You mean to say you make your own arrows too?"

"I'll teach you how," he said. "And I'll also teach you how to make strings from sinew, because those will wear through."

She turned the bow over and over, bewildered by this man's talent and his generosity. It was almost too much. "But don't you have to, I don't know, prepare for war?"

He grew visibly stiff. She wished she hadn't brought it up.

"We have the month off. To be with loved ones before…"

Silence passed between them. He hadn't pushed for her to share more than she wanted. Freda would gladly do the same for him.

She gave him a small smile. "I'd be honored, Todd. If your hunting skills are half as honed as your woodworking ones, I'll be learning at the hands of a master."

"Well okay then." His blushing face looked odd on his giant man of a body.

She laughed. "I hope you know what you're signing up for."

"Let's see. Now." He led her outside to a sack of grasses already riddled with holes.

He showed her how to shoot the bow, and she practiced for an hour before returning to chores. She cleaned cobwebs out of the cabin and greenhouse while he cut wood for the cabin's stove. They had the place in order before sunset. Todd insisted Freda sleep on the cabin's futon while he slept on the ground.

They left for Middle Fork at dawn and arrived before dinnertime. Freda stopped Todd at the edge of downtown and pulled the lockbox from her pack. "How much?" she asked.

"I've been trying to figure that out the whole way here," he said, crossing his arms. He looked as uncomfortable as she felt.

"How 'bout five thousand?"

"But that's more than I'm paying for a home here in town," he said. "You're honestly doing me a favor, taking the place off my hands. Three grand is more than enough."

She opened the box and counted four thousand dollars. "Let's call this a truce," she said, handing him the cash.

He frowned. "It's too much."

"Consider the thousand payment for your lessons—and insurance. I mean, no promises I won't accidentally shoot you."

He laughed. It was a boom of a laugh, from the gut, and she laughed as well.

"I want you to practice for the next two weeks," he said, growing serious again. "I need to head up to the base in New Headway for a few days. When I get back, we'll see if you're ready for a kill. It should be good timing, with winter almost here. The deer will be settling into the canyon."

Freda straightened her shoulders. "Will do."

"See you soon then," he said, sticking out a hand.

She stepped past his hand and gave him a hug. "Thank you," she said, releasing him.

Though he had felt stiff in her arms, he smiled down at her. "Every day," he said, turning and walking away. "At least one hour of shooting every day."

She saluted his back and walked the opposite direction, to the general store. She knew it would be her first shopping trip of many over the next few weeks. Winters were cold and long in Prominence. With no bounty canned, no herbs dried or meat yet salted, she had a lot of food to carry back home before the snows settled in for real.

☾

Freda could sense the snowstorm approaching, the air warm and calm, as they hiked in darkness to where the herd would be sleeping. She fiddled with the straps of her backpack. Todd had helped her pack it with meat bags, a bone saw, a good knife, a few extra layers, and a satchel of dried fruits and jerky. The quiver and bow were strapped to the outside of the pack.

The wind grew as they moved up and over Golden Falls Saddle. Gales swept in from the north, pulling a curtain of clouds. They descended into Echo Canyon, hiked south, and reached the chosen kill spot. They kneeled in the muddy snow. Close to the ground, she noticed the wolf prints. They were nearly as big as her hand, with four teardrops crowned by the puncture of nails. There were at least ten in the pack now.

She breathed slowly, deeply, with as little noise as humanly possible, just as Todd had taught her. The wind pressed coldness against her exposed face. She took off her pack and prepared her bow.

Perfect wind, Todd mouthed.

She tried to force her heartbeats to an even rhythm. The shot needed to be without error. He had told her stories of tracking wounded animals in blizzards.

*It was as if I was chasing my own death,* he had said.

The does appeared first. The white of their tails remained lowered, their steps delicate but relaxed. Dreadlocks and tangles hung along their backs. The wind brought their musty smell. She remained stock-still, knowing any movement could ruin the weeks of preparation.

The bucks followed behind their female companions. Without their antlers, they looked similar to the does. Freda silently slid the arrow's notch onto the sinew. The first buck plodded into the clearing and back into the growth. Two more bucks did the same, followed by the one they had chosen. He was old but not too old, strong but not genetically necessary.

She checked her breath and heart rate. They were erratic. The buck took another step, moving through the brief opening. The light prodding of Todd's elbow almost caused her to jump.

Now, he mouthed.

Twang of sinew punctured the silence. The buck groaned and staggered off, leaving a thin track of blood. The other bucks let out deep grunts as they charged through the juniper and willow. A flurry of snapping twigs. Silence followed the rush of loud.

"Great shot," Todd whispered at last, placing a hand on her back. "Well done. We'll stay here for a little while and let him slow."

They waited. Distant music of the Echo River floated to them through the quiet. Though cold pressed down from the storm-heavy sky, Freda felt sweat slide down her cheeks. What if she had hit the stomach? What if the deer died a slow, miserable death, and they never found him? Her breath and heart had been out of control. Surely the arrow flew untrue.

Todd handed her a handkerchief. "Try to relax."

She patted the sweat from her face.

"Let's see where he ended up," he said, standing.

They followed a faint blood trail along the river for at least a mile. As the blood grew thicker, she could hear labored breathing over the water's song. It was a terrible, rattling sound. She touched her ears beneath her hat, half expecting to feel blood on her fingers.

Red blossomed away from the creature onto the snow. They approached from his broadside. The shot had pierced his lower lungs. Fear flashed in his eyes when he saw his killer—the one he would sustain.

Todd nodded to the deer. "Quick like," he said.

Freda straightened her shoulders and drew back another arrow, resting her knuckle behind her ear. She held her inhale in for a second, maybe two, hesitating in the fullness of her own life. She released her finger with her exhale.

"Thank you," Todd whispered to the deer.

Stepping forward, she saw the radiance of storm in his glazed eyes cast skyward. She dropped to her knees and closed his eyelids. Todd knelt beside her and handed her the handkerchief again. Flakes began to float down, weaving through the red branches of willow and gnarly cottonwood limbs.

"No two kills are the same," he said. "But this feeling—it doesn't change. Try to stay grounded in gratitude."

Freda retrieved the knife and rope from her pack. Todd showed her how to press her fingers to the breastbone and knife from the belly to the throat, unzipping skin, guiding the blade with a V of fingers. He cut away the deer's penis and testicles as Freda watched in a surreal pairing of horror and wonder. He cut a circle around the anus, explaining how she needed to avoid the rectum.

"Pinch the bladder when you cut it away." He threw the bladder into the forest, and ravens swooped from branches in that direction.

Following his instructions, she tied a rope between the deer's esophagus and stomach cavity. Todd squatted beside the deer and pushed into his side. The guts spilled onto the snow.

"Use quick nips of the knife," he said, snipping away the membrane clinging to a steaming pile of organs. He gathered the remaining guts with his gloved hands and pulled them out. Freda gagged at the stench of fermenting things.

The forest felt pregnant with quiet. She whipped her head left to right, scanning the shadowed trees. She figured the wolves could smell it by now. Todd handed her back the knife.

"Stay present," he said, not unkindly, and he guided her through cutting the diaphragm away from the body.

He tied the rope around the deer's two front legs and walked toward a robust cottonwood, trailing rope from the spool behind him. He threw the spool over a branch, and she helped him heave the animal into the air. The deer swayed with head high, blood draining to the ground.

"Now we just need to wait for the meat to cool," he said.

She sat next to Todd and stared at the artless blood designs on the snow. Every creaking branch and flap of a wing tingled against her body. She could feel the Ghost Pack in the near distance.

"Wolves won't attack," Todd said. "And bears are already sleeping."

Still. They sat for what felt like hours. He stood at last and said they just needed to skin the deer and then they could head home. He showed her how to knife the hide away from the fascia. They cut the ropes, and he instructed her through sawing the carcass into quarters. They placed the quarters in the leather bags, two for each pack.

Todd placed the head in another bag and packed it. "Brains make for great tanning," he explained.

They tromped back through the new snow, stopping to drink from the stream flowing from Mirror Lake to the Echo. With elevation gain, she could see the Ghost Pack helping themselves to the guts. Ravens darted between the snapping of jaws. Yearlings tugged at the bones as the older wolves licked clean the legs and ribcage.

Snow continued to fall. They ate a late lunch at the Golden Falls. Icicles formed along the wispy streams of falling water, and snow gathered on the mossy rocks. The trees stood stark with limbs outlined in white. Freda removed her pack and sat on a lone granite boulder near the water's edge. The pool beneath the falls swirled, and a mist swayed upon its surface. The smell of death surrounded them. She thought of his rattling breath, the red blossom. She began to weep.

Todd sat beside her and wrapped his arm around her shoulders. "We must kill to live," he said. "My grandmother had called this the Holy Paradox."

☾

A smoked flank remained alongside a few jars of canned burger. She would need to hunt again, soon. A more important hunt, though, took precedence.

The snows had thawed, and Freda spent dawn to dusk preparing the garden. Her starters were thriving in the greenhouse and looked ready for life outside the safety of glass. With the summer solstice arriving in two days, she figured the threat of frost wouldn't return until the fall. She replanted the kale and lettuce first, alongside cabbage and chard.

She craved greens after a winter of potatoes, rice, meat, eggs, and carrots. The food she had packed in had sufficed for those months she had spent cooped up in the cabin. Blizzards had kept her inside, save for feeding the chickens and milking the goats. She had passed the time sewing pants from the deer hide. She had also read, again and again, the scroll and the books she had brought with her from the Haven.

With the hardier starters replanted, she returned inside to prepare a dinner of yet more meat and rice. She sautéed some fiddleheads she had found along Owl Creek that morning. They tasted as fresh as the mountains felt these days. She chewed them slowly, relishing the flavor of early summer.

After preparing a cup of tea, she settled onto the futon with the scroll. A few questions had been nagging at her throughout the winter. Most of all, she wondered who had been present when Flo died, and whether or not this person understood the meaning of her last words. It was possible. It was possible someone, or some people, had witnessed the last Anima's Death Revelation and knew where to look. These people, though, would need to know where the first Anima was buried to make sense of Flo's final words.

She rolled the scroll and placed it back in the box. Laurel was certain Freda would be the one to find the mushroom. Freda's faith in the woman hadn't failed her yet. Doubt wouldn't serve her, now or ever. She leaned back into the pillow and willed herself to sleep.

In the morning, after feeding the chickens and goats and checking on the starters, she packed for an overnight trip and headed toward Hidden Passage. The sun shined in an azure sky. New leaves fluttered in the aspen grove, and snowmelt gave the river a deep baritone. The afternoon felt ripe and whole.

She walked up and over the saddle, almost skipping the whole way. Arrowleaf balsamroot, lupine, and wild roses spread across the ground beneath Yarrow Peak. Freda walked through the flowers, picking a few as she went. When she came to the cave, she held a bouquet of yellow, purple, and pink. She imagined handing the bouquet to Tillie.

The cave smelled dank, with a hint of rusted iron among the redolence of moss and tannic waters. She spread out Javiera's blanket on a flat spot near the entrance and ate a jar of canned meat. She put the bouquet in the empty jar with some water in it. Leaning against the cave's wall, she pulled the satchel out from beneath her shirt. She opened it and placed a pinch of the apricot flowers in her palm.

They were crushed, brown and dry. She tried to smell the blood of her lover, but all she could smell was the iron of the cave. Her body yearned to evoke the petals. Freda knew Tillie would come if she did. She could come and help her look.

*No one,* Laurel had said. *No one.*

Freda touched the petals, feeling their brittleness. She placed them back in the satchel and closed her eyes against the tears. She would find the mushroom. She would return to her. She would be the Anima and all would be forgiven.

Freda woke sitting up. The solstice had come with rain and lightning. Water pit-pattered outside the cave's opening. Her neck felt stiff, her legs numb. She ate a breakfast of jerky and placed the blanket back into her pack. Thunder rolled through the canyon. She stepped into the rain and walked to the deciduous trees growing near the river. When she neared, she dropped to her knees and began crawling, seeking. The rain fell in slanting sheets. She felt as wet and heavy as the river itself. Lightning illuminated her surroundings.

Flash and boom. Flash and boom. The next lightning bolt revealed red mushrooms growing beneath the aspens in front of her. Thunder resounded with her cry of joy.

# III

## ORIGINS OF THE IMPERIUM

*Plants feed the caribou. Caribou feed the wolves. Wolves feed the plants. Men can kill all, but then men will be dead.*

\- Nukopan Proverb

# BAZI

## 1,366 YBP

### Jabira, Jafard

Milk streamed into the clay vessel. Bazi liked how the teat felt between her thumb and finger, how it listened to her touch. She liked how the heifer tangibly relaxed, how relief from the milk's pressure spread between them. She liked how she worked in the warm light of early morning, how the Alidima Mountains leaned into the dawn as if to hold the sun in place.

Yes, Bazi liked a few things about her life as a cow herder's wife, most of all her six-year-old son sleeping in the shade of the nearby fir tree. Though she did not choose to come here, she figured this was as good of a life as she could have hoped for. There were fates far worse for a Nyachian woman than being married off to a Kahalian, albeit a poor one.

The vessel filled, and she stood, brushing grasses from her haik. Careful of snake holes and rocks, she treaded barefoot back down the knoll with Yedder by her side. Unlike the mountainous skyline behind her, the southern horizon ran unrestrained. Summer heat blurred sky and land, and the horizon moved like smoke, dancing with no discernible rhythm.

She squinted, seeing if she could make out the sprawl of Raymina in that blur of blue and tan. She thought of the markets she had visited there as a child with her father and brother. In sharp contrast to the sage and garrigue scents kicked up by her feet here, the labyrinth of shops had smelled of cinnamon and honey, body odor, animal blood, fresh and rotten fruit. They would set up shop next to the other shepherds selling wool and dried lamb haunches. Bazi's father would always give her brother and her each a cowrie shell before day's end, and they would run through the maze of tents, seeking out a sweet or a toy or whatever the shell could afford them.

One quadrant of the Raymina market was easily four times as big as the village she walked to now. The huts below the knoll gathered between giant blocks of granite. She could count the homes on her fingers and toes and name the owner of each one. And while she walked home with a wanting stomach, knowing there would be food enough for her and her son, she kept her gaze south on the shimmering heat until a large boulder eclipsed the vista.

Children played a game with pebbles in the corridor leading to her husband's house. Bazi stepped over the game, ruffling hairs with her free hand as she passed. The weaver's daughter pretended to trip her, and Bazi feigned a stumble. Laughter ricocheted off the rock walls as she continued home.

Her morning's calm evaporated as soon as she stepped into the hut. Dassin's two-year-old daughter whimpered as Dassin pulled burs from the girl's gnarled hair. A three-month-old girl sat snug against Dassin's chest in a sling. The fire beneath a pot of boiling eggs filled the room with a thick heat. Bazi's clothes matted to her skin within minutes of arriving. Thiya plucked feathers from a chicken with her five-year-old and three-year-old daughters. She grunted at Bazi as if to say hello. The newest wife, Simma, threaded beads onto a headpiece. She alone looked serene sitting next to an open window, her face shiny with sweat and the glow of an expecting mother. If their husband's bad luck continued, another girl grew within Simma's womb.

Bazi placed the vessel on the table and set her sleeping child on a mat away from the fire. She helped herself to a glass of the fresh milk and a slice of honeycomb. Her fellow wives dwelled in their individual tasks, mouths stretched tight with concentration. Bazi scolded herself for remembering how her mothers had always laughed and joked together. Her twentieth year would arrive with the fall harvest. She had been in the husbandry of Amastan for seven years now. It was past time she put these futile comparisons to rest and release the nostalgia of her childhood.

She dipped the honeycomb into the glass and sucked the milk from the cells. Her slurping noises exaggerated the absence of conversation, and she quietly chewed down the remaining bites. She poured glasses of milk for the other wives and their children.

Amastan burst into the hut. "Great Almighty, women, it's hotter than an orgy of snakes in here." He laughed at his joke as he threw a dead oryx on the table.

The other wives and Bazi lined up to receive a kiss. She willed away the fact they stood like a palate of deepening browns, with her skin of sable in the back. It was coincidence and nothing more. Reading into such things had never served her before. He received each wife with bravado, sweeping her into his arms, telling her how he had missed her.

Bazi patted down her hair to no effect. When he brought her into an embrace, she breathed in the smell of his travels, the wood smoke and sweat and the sap of trees she imagined only grew where oryx ran wild. He released her, and she moved to the dead oryx on the table. She had never seen one alive, she realized, admiring the curve of horn atop his lifeless head. She ran a finger along the line where brown and white fur met, and she pressed a hand against the thigh muscle stiff with rigor mortis. What power it must take to run up the steep mountain slopes. What power.

A small *tsk* brought Bazi's hand back to her side. She looked to Thiya, thinking she had been watching her touch the dead oryx. But the woman was looking to the bedroom. Bazi noticed Simma missing, and she also noticed Dassin and Thiya exchange annoyed looks. It was no secret Simma was Amastan's favorite, being the most beautiful of the harem. Her swollen belly seemed to make her even more irresistible to him. The other wives returned to their work with movements made loud by anger. Bazi didn't share in their desire to be lying beneath Amastan's weight. The birth of Yedder had nearly killed her, and her root had yet to heal.

She doubted she would ever have another baby. Finding a seat beside her sleeping child, she wondered if Amastan knew this, too. She wondered if he could tell she fought back tears the entire time he was inside of her, and if this was why he no longer brought her with him to bed. Smoothing down Yedder's fuzzy hairs, she reminded herself that he was the first—and only—son in this family. A Nyachian may have birthed him, but he was a he. If she could, indeed, no longer birth children, she at least had that pebble in her corner.

☾

Simma screamed and screamed. Her bellowing voice shook dust loose from the hut's thatched roof, and it drifted down onto the women. Thiya cooled Simma's forehead with a cut of loincloth soaked in creek water. Her hands covered in blood, Dassin held the baby's cresting head and told Simma to push harder.

Bazi would bring Amastan updates as he paced the rock corridor. The vulva had opened. They could see the baby's head. Simma did well. She was strong and young. Amastan would nod at the ground and continue pacing. After a full day, almost exactly sunrise to sundown, the baby slid into the world.

Dassin lifted up the crying infant. "A boy," she said, bringing the newborn to Simma's chest.

Simma sobbed as she held her baby. He shrieked, and his slimy, red body writhed as if in protest to being pulled out into this world. Bazi didn't remember crying when she gave birth to Yedder.

Thiya snapped her fingers in Bazi's face. "You have one job," Thiya said.

Bazi ran out the door. The contrast of fresh air felt like a plunge into cold water. "It's a boy," she exclaimed. "It's a boy!"

Amastan rushed into the hut. Bazi watched him go and felt her excitement cave into an unexpected hollowness. Amastan had been hunting when she had birthed Yedder. But this wasn't about her, she reminded herself. She thought of how her mother had celebrated the birth of Bazi's siblings in equal measure. It hadn't mattered if the son or daughter had emerged from her body or that of a fellow wife.

Dassin and Thiya walked out, and Bazi forced a smile. They didn't smile back, doing nothing to hide their own jealousy and resentment. The three women walked silently through the dark corridors of stone. Their children were in various stages of disarray. The pair of twelve-year-old girls handed them over with obvious relief. Bazi received her hysterical son and hugged him into silence. The absence of his crying only amplified the snivels and screams of his sisters.

Bazi thanked the girls for watching Yedder. She knew they didn't have a choice in the matter, and they brushed the thanks away with flicks of their small hands. Girls of their age, a year, maybe two, before their moon-blood, took care of children when mothers needed to help other mothers. They stood before Bazi, only a little shorter than her, with chests still as flat as those of their boy peers. Soon their breasts would swell, their slender hips would unfurl like wings, and they would find themselves holding babies of their own.

☾

Milk and eggs sustained them all throughout the winter, but little else. Frost crept down the mountains by late fall, killing the deadnettle and purslane that had filled their bowls with green. The snow followed soon after, and with it a cold that made breath visible. Bazi's days began in a chilled darkness until dawn slit a crack in the sky and sunlight poured through like blood escaping a cut.

The oryx had migrated down to where the Eaznali River slowed its flow on the plains, a territory belonging to the hunters of Raymina, leaving the Jabira men to make tough choices about what to kill. The women dealt with the fallout of these choices. A moon after the solstice, Amastan slaughtered one of the heifers for meat. The decision turned him sour for the remaining course of winter. The cow had been a dowry from Bazi's father. It had been an expensive dowry compared to those of Thiya and Dassin, but that was the cost of being a Nyachian.

When she watched Amastan slash the cow's throat, she swore her own throat felt the knife. She helped process the meat, skinning and butchering the carcass with blurry vision. She did her best to hide her tears, but she knew the others saw her cry, though no one said anything. She remembered her father helping the calf emerge into the world. The death of this heifer felt as though the last thread between her and her family had been severed.

Yet when she fed Yedder little cuts of liver that night, gratitude flushed away the grief. The death of her childhood for the sake of her child became an ache soothed by necessity. Nature demanded it, and she succumbed to this order.

Bazi and the other wives sewed clothes from the cowhide. They adorned the pants and dress with beads Amastan had traded cheese for on his last trip to Raymina. He planned to sell the clothes to begin saving for another cow. Bazi threaded eggshell beads, creating a pattern that reminded her of the way light and shadow danced across the snow. A thought came more than once, each time causing her fingers to still: what Amastan really needed was another dowry.

Amastan threw the hut door open and slammed it closed, sending a shiver through the room. Simma's baby startled awake and began to sob. Simma gave him a nasty look as she set her beadwork down to settle him. Yedder stood leaning against Bazi's leg, watching his father unload chopped wood next to the fire.

Having stacked all the wood, Amastan slunk into a chair. "How much longer until the clothes are ready?" His question came out as a sigh.

"A week, at most," Dassin replied. Her oldest daughter sat next to her, handing her beads.

Amastan nodded and returned outside to fetch more wood. That night, he took no wife to bed. It was the same the night before and the nights to follow. His appetite for sex had seemed to dwindle with the food supply, and though Bazi was relieved, the other women began to whisper about it as they finished beading the clothes.

"His manhood shriveled with the cold," Simma said.

Thiya nodded with a smirk. "Good thing we all have able fingers."

They shared a laugh, and though it was at her husband's expense, Bazi relished the camaraderie emerging from these hard times. Maybe she would feel at home here after all. Maybe they would live like her mothers had—as a web of women supporting women.

☾

They were left with one heifer, and the milk proved insufficient for the ten of them. Bazi gave her share to Yedder. Her flesh began to evaporate. She could feel her bones pushing against the skin as if they wanted out of confinement. The other wives weren't any better off. Thiya's face looked like she sucked her cheeks in, and Dassin, an exceptionally robust woman, dwindled into a slender thing for the first time in her life. The young continued to grow as the mothers shoved as much of their portions into their children's bowls as they dared.

No one complained. There wasn't much to talk about, and so they spent the dark days of late winter in a numbing quiet. Amastan wore his shame like a beard. It elongated his face and aged him ten years. He told the women to stay in the hut lest someone see their withered bodies. Bazi alone was allowed to leave. She milked each morning with a deliberate slowness, soaking up the fresh air and the expanse of open sky and land. While she savored this luxury he afforded her, she sometimes thought Amastan treated her with particular coolness, and that her duty as milkmaid was one he reserved for her alone for reasons opposite to privilege.

Bazi focused on Yedder. At seven now, he reminded Bazi of her father with his dark brown eyes and large, flat nose. When they went out milking, she taught him words of her native tongue. She insisted he not say the words at home, and he obeyed. She wondered if he also understood.

The women finished the beadwork on the dress and pants. They were exquisite pieces of clothes, fit for a wedding. Amastan left for Raymina and returned two days before the new moon, bringing home a rooster. He also seemed to have brought the spring with him, for the snows melted and green shoots emerged from mud.

The clothes they made should have been enough to buy a cow. The decision to introduce a rooster to the coop made sense, as now they could breed the hens for meat chickens in the future. Yet they were still left with one cow. Milk was immediate and consistent, while meat chickens took time to rear. Bazi wondered where all that money had gone—all their time and work. As usual, no one said anything.

The largest profit from their beadwork was Amastan's lifted spirits. He took Simma to bed that night. It was the first time Simma had been back in there since giving birth to her son. Bazi could hear them moaning as she lay curled into Yedder on their mat near the door. She wondered if Amastan would bring her back there in the days to come. It had been over a year now since he took her. An uneasy feeling settled into the space created by this awareness, and though her scarred vagina ached with the thought of sex, she spent the night switching from hip to hip, unable to find comfort on either side.

☾

In the morning, in the pasture, with Yedder sleeping under the tree, the pulling of teats lulled Bazi into a daze. Green grasses of early summer stood out with individual radiance as dew on the blades caught sunlight. She worked half asleep. When a figure materialized on the knoll, she blinked and blinked, untrusting her tired eyes.

Yet there was truly someone approaching. The person neared, and Bazi recognized the narrow shoulders and long legs of her husband. He wore his indigo scarf around his head, and his face, freshly shaven, looked at her with shadowed eyes. She rose to her feet and walked to meet him.

"Amastan." She paused. "What a lovely surprise."

His mouth twitched. It was a thing he did when he had something important to say, and Bazi waited. She clasped her hands behind her back and rubbed her thumbs against one another.

"I, I do not bring anything lovely." He avoided Bazi's eyes, looking instead at the mountains as if he were planning a hunting route. "It was a hard winter, and I've been forced into an even harder place. We're in need of another cow."

His eyes found the cow behind Bazi. She turned to look as well. With a punch to the stomach she saw the clay vessel tipped over, the milk it had contained now soaking into the mud. Bazi braced herself for Amastan's wrath. He had never hit her, but he had once slapped Thiya for forgetting about a roasting leg of oryx. The meat had been ruined, and Thiya had been forced to spend the night outside.

Amastan, though, didn't seem to notice the spilled milk. His mouth continued to contort in its strange ways. "The thing is, Bazi, you're, well, you've been exhausted. Your worth, that is, to me, as a wife." The words dropped from his mouth one at a time, each blow separate and complete in its blunt force.

"I agreed to marry a Nyachian, because, well, you're beautiful. That is, for one of your kind. And the cow, it was a big asset to the family. But you've"—he continued to look anywhere but at her—"well, you're dried up, as they say, and while your cow served us well, her purpose ran its course. We'll be needing another. A dowry, that is, which will bring another mouth to feed. And more, the Almighty willing that my next wife is more fertile than the one I must now release."

Bazi rubbed at her temple. A cold sweat turned her white haik transparent. "Release?" The question gagged her.

He nodded, his eyes finally meeting her own. "Release. Yes. You must leave, Bazi. Today. Now. While no one can see. Go home. Return to your kind and never come back."

Everything slowed. "Your son—your firstborn son…"

"My firstborn son was birthed by Simma." His tone was stern.

"But to go home would be shameful. I would bring shame to my family."

"As I have brought shame to mine by marrying a Nyachian. Please, Bazi, do not make me grow violent. I offer an exit. If you refuse it, well." He patted the dagger strung to his robe that she hadn't noticed. "If you refuse, there is no one around."

Her inhale made a sharp sound. Yedder yawned and sat up. How had she not seen this coming? She had allowed his disregard toward her to become a refuge rather than a threat.

"What will I eat? How will your son and I survive the trek back?"

"This, thank the Almighty, is no longer my problem." He walked away, disappearing behind the knoll.

Bazi fell to her knees. The mud cushioned her collapse. She sobbed and sobbed, her cries an ugly noise, like the yelps of a dying rabbit. Yedder cried with her. They sang out as mother and child, disturbing the morning with their terrible harmony.

When Bazi rose, her haik hung heavy with mud. She tore it off and walked in her wool trousers and shift. Yedder continued to cry from hunger as they moved west. She prayed someone in Jabira would hear him and come running to save them. She prayed to both the god of the Kahalians and the gods of her people. If anyone heard Yedder's weeping, no one came to the rescue.

Her prayers crescendoed to curses. Her curses dissolved into more sobbing.

She followed a rough path where the foothills dipped before rising into the Alidima peaks. In other circumstances, the sun would feel like a smile upon her bare skin. It beamed down in a sky blue as a merganser tail feather. Poppies by the thousands splashed the green grasses with violent red. Meerkats darted between tamarisk trees, scurrying about on two legs like children playing hide and seek. A stag bounded across the path a stone's throw ahead.

Being in this wooded alley, between foothill and mountain, reminded Bazi of being a little girl. Her parents would tell her to stay out of the forest. They would describe clawed creatures with hungry bellies and pointed teeth. The forest, they had stressed, was no place for a child. Bazi felt like a child. She was in trouble and would return home to receive her parents' wrath. She wondered which was more dangerous: staying here in the forest with the predators, or bringing shame to her father and mothers in Mtoasili.

A singular hope kept her moving west. Her family would offer sympathy. They would take her and Yedder back into their fold, and she would live out her days helping her father and mothers as they aged. Her brothers had wedded and began families of their own in Mtoasili, and though she assumed they continued to help their father with the sheep, Bazi figured they were busy feeding their own children. She could help. She would help. This was the hope bringing one foot in front of the other.

Noon slipped by overhead, its passing obscured by the long limbs of cedar trees. She walked beneath a community of macaques. They chattered away, seemingly discussing her presence. Bazi made eye contact with one of the larger females. Her bright green eyes, set within circles of pink flesh, stared back at her without apology. The flat stretch of her nose and mouth twitched.

The shadows pooled deeper around them. Yedder began to cry again. Bazi pleaded with him to quiet. The predators could hear his screams. The predators would come. But she knew she couldn't reason with his hunger. He needed food. She took his hand and asked him to help her look. Yedder lifted up a cedar seed with excitement. She said no, not edible. His downtrodden face was a splinter to her resolve.

He brought his little hand up again. She unfurled his fingers and gasped with delight. A white and brown mushroom lay in his palm. Her birthmother had called them spicy penises because of their peppery flavor and phallic shape. Bazi figured that if there hadn't been this joke about them she may not have remembered them now, and she thanked her mother for her crude sense of humor, though as a girl it had always embarrassed her.

Yedder pointed to where he had found it. A dozen more grew in a cluster. They sat and plucked the mushrooms, wiping off the cedar needles and soil. Bazi brought one to her mouth and took a bite. Yedder watched, hesitating to do the same. She told him it was okay. It was time to eat.

Twilight quieted the forest around them, hushing bird song and muting the light. Bazi considered climbing up a tree with Yedder upon her back, but she figured most predators knew how to climb. She came to terms with their situation: if a tiger or lion were to attack, she would deal with it then. Was this delirium from exhaustion speaking, or good sense? She decided it didn't matter. What would be would be.

She and Yedder nestled into a nook within cedar roots. Sleep was a timid visitor throughout the night, coming and going like a mouse, and she met the dawn with part relief, part despair. Her child had slept, and they had survived. For this she was thankful. The true predator manifested as hunger, and it circled back in on them. Yedder whined.

Bazi hushed him and told him to help her find some more food. The growing light aided their search. Yedder yanked free his hand and ran to a tree. He plunked down, his back turned to Bazi. She heard the unmistakable snap of a mushroom stem. She ran to him, yelling for him to wait. But he already had the cap pressed to his lips. Bazi careened over to him, skidding to a halt on her knees. She ripped the cap from his hands and scolded him for attempting to eat something without her approval.

White dots spread across the red cap. Their pattern reminded Bazi of a snowflake. Remarkably clean of debris, the mushroom radiated in her upturned palm. The red of the cap rivaled the red of the poppy flowers. She sniffed at it, her hunger and curiosity merging into a formidable desire.

Dozens more grew around the trees. Most had sprouted up at random. Yedder had picked this one, though, from a perfect ring. Its absence in the circle appeared like a question written on the earth. She looked at Yedder watching her, expectant. He opened and balled his hands in front of him. One little nibble would tell her if it was safe. If it proved edible, there were enough mushrooms here to keep them full for another day. One little nibble. That was all it would take to know.

When the world spun, and the cedar branches grew together and apart, together and apart, shattering and swallowing the light in turn, she knew even the tiniest of bites had been too much. Of all the pain, all the heartache she had endured in her life thus far, this moment was the most wretched of all: watching her child watch her crumble to the ground, knowing she had failed him.

☾

The macaques shrieked and whooped, their voices vibrating through the lair. Bazi leaned against the coolness of a boulder. She watched as a cheetah tore into the hind of an impala and gave a bloody chunk of meat to Yedder. Her son ate with the largest smile she had ever seen on his face. It seemed plastered there, that smile, since she woke nearly a half moon ago. She didn't know his mouth had been capable of such a stretch.

His joy radiated around him, palatable almost, and if it weren't for her inability to move and thorough loss of control, everything would be perfect. Her son was fed, safe, and happy. He was eating raw meat, a traditional food of their people: he grew taller, stronger, more robust every day. That was all she had wanted all along. But despite the fact he was thriving, she sat with a rigid unease, as if her legs dangled over a precipice.

The cheetah feeding Yedder called herself Hamia. She had yet to fully explain to Bazi what was happening. Bazi knew she could hear voices she couldn't before. She knew her body, like that of her son's, transformed before her very eyes. And she knew there was a reason for these transformations, a reason named the Task, as Hamia had said. That was the extent of her knowledge—its incompleteness left her feeling deranged.

*I see you are as anxious today as you were yesterday,* Hamia said, tearing off another chunk of meat for Yedder.

*I am as ignorant of my situation as I was yesterday,* Bazi said.

Cedar needles rained down as a young macaque swung from one tree to the next, taunting another juvenile. They seemed unfazed by the cheetah below. Satiated, Yedder bounded over to Bazi and sat in her lap, resting his head against her chest. His hands and face were a bloody mess, and his breath smelled metallic.

*Your stress only prolongs your transformation,* Hamia said. She sat on a rock facing them, poised like a queen. Dark markings emphasized the gold of her eyes, and the intricacies of her lustrous coat, spotted with perfectly shaped black circles, spoke of a divine creativity.

*You've said that before,* Bazi replied. *And yet you do little to relieve it.*

*Little? Am I not feeding you and your child? Am I not ensuring your safety?*

Bazi looked away, ashamed. *It's not my fault,* she said. *I didn't ask to be banished. I didn't know the mushroom would leave me debilitated.*

*I'm not trying to chastise you.* The softness in Hamia's voice contrasted her usual gruffness. *You are only debilitated for the time being. Your transformation nears completion. Can you not feel the changes already?*

*Yes,* Bazi said. *I can. But why me? Why am I this Anima you speak of?*

*For reasons unknown you found the mushroom first, or it found you,* Hamia said. *Either way, you asking* why *this happened is like asking why the viper is born the viper, or why the sheep is born the sheep. There are mysteries the Salvagers don't even understand. These mysteries keep all creatures equal in their unknowing.*

*Salvagers are the people who can see into the past?* Bazi asked.

*Correct.*

Bazi stroked Yedder's curly hair as she considered Hamia's words. She had never asked why she had been born human, or why she had been born a woman for that matter. Why was being reborn as something else a reality in need of explanation? Why did she resist the mystery?

*You will walk again in two days,* Hamia said. *It is time for you to understand the circumstances in which you are born so you can prepare for what awaits.*

The cheetah before Bazi transformed. Her limbs grew ever longer, and fur gave way to skin not unlike Bazi's own. The cheetah's head had been smooth, her neck a triangle of white. The woman on the rock had dozens of long, black braids and a square jaw. Her eyes remained the same gold color.

Yedder yelped and Bazi gasped. Without a doubt, she was the most gorgeous human Bazi had ever seen. "Mother!" Yedder cried. "Who is that?"

"I am a Shapeshifter," Hamia said. The voice spoken aloud sounded just as it had in Bazi's head. "A Keeper, alongside Salvagers. Shapeshifters are your blood-bonded allies and will always answer to your call. There is one for every species—thousands in Baninchi alone. We will help you restore the Order to this land."

"The Order?" Bazi asked.

"The Sacred Balance preserving all Life. The Anima before you, an Alidiman named Avni, was born in northeast Baninchi. She freed her people from the Yiúsians. This warring kingdom hailing from southern Lacuserra do not abide by the Order. They spread Disorder in their quest for power over their fellow humans."

Hamia's full lips pulled back to reveal clenched teeth. Bazi didn't understand the grimace on her face. She didn't understand much of anything. She wondered if she had been hallucinating this entire time. Or maybe, it could be, she had died after all.

"The last Anima's efforts deterred the Yiúsians for over a millennium," Hamia continued. "But they have now returned in double the force. They have conquered Msivuli and plan to continue south, to Mamahali."

Yedder whimpered, and Bazi hugged him closer. "Have they reached Mtoasili?" she asked. "I mean, my family—are they okay?"

"I do not know your human kin," Hamia replied. "I do know there is a real and immediate danger to all Life. It spreads across the savanna. This Disorder leaves towering piles of tuskless elephant carcasses in its wake. It burns the homes of humans and lions alike. It takes without regard for the Sacred Balance and the honoring of otherness that sustains all Life.

"For the sake of your child—for the sake of all children—you must use your powers to end the spread of Disorder. We must kill the Yiúsians once and for all. Then, we will turn our attention north, to the Flüschen. Once we have unified all of Lacuserra under the banner of Order, we will look west, to the Lyziver and Guâdí Empires. This, of course, may not all happen in your life; there will be more Animas to continue the Task. But you, Bazi, must set forth the larger vision before it's too late."

Yedder began to cry. Bazi glared at Hamia for scaring her child. Powers? She sat here, unable to move, and this strange woman spoke as if she could overturn entire kingdoms. If invaders had come to Baninchi, she and Yedder should flee from the fire, not run into the flames.

Hamia studied Bazi's face. She seemed to have read her thoughts when she said, "The Disorder will spread. You can either meet it head-on, with the help of the Shapeshifters, or you can cower from your powers, and thus responsibilities, as the Anima reborn."

She morphed back into a cheetah. *The roller Shapeshifter will find you on the Bahyasi Grasslands. He will summon the Shapeshifters to your Task when you are ready to face it.*

Hamia stroked Yedder's head before slinking off into the tall grasses, leaving Bazi to gather the ashes of what she thought she knew about her place in this world.

☾

Hamia didn't return. Macaques brought them fresh fruit and water for the remaining two days. Yedder played with the macaque juveniles. Bazi thanked the monkeys for keeping her son entertained, but they insisted it was their pleasure. It wasn't often their parents allowed them to interact with their human peers.

Dawn dappled through the branches. It was like the fourteen mornings before it, filled with the distant drone of water falling, the sunlight filtered green by cedar needles, Yedder's head upon her lap. Yet now she could feel the force pumping through her legs and arms. She could feel her body's yearning to move, to run.

She gently shook Yedder awake, and they ate the rest of the dates and argan nut flesh the macaques had brought the night before. When she stood, Yedder gawked at her. She wiggled her toes and fingers and did a little jig.

Yedder laughed. "Mother, you are alive!"

They laughed together at this, at the absurdity of her transformation. They laughed with the joyful promise of their life together now that she stood again. She crouched to the ground, motioning for Yedder to climb onto her back. When she stood, his weight felt half as heavy as it had a moon earlier. If anything, he had grown with the ample nourishment Hamia and the macaques had provided. She stretched her arms to the side, marveling at the lines defining biceps, triceps, and forearm muscles. They reminded her of something, something her fingers felt.

The oryx. Her muscles reminded her of the oryx Amastan had brought home. She remembered the feel of the animal's muscles when she had pressed her fingers to his thigh. Though a day dead, she had felt their potential. She had envied their power. Now look, she thought, making a fist with her hand and releasing it. Now look. Now feel.

She took off running. Yedder whooped and hollered with delight. "Faster," he cried. "Faster!"

And she did. She ran so fast it felt reckless. It was reckless, and yet she didn't stop herself. Some part of her long leashed came unfettered. The way she ran felt as wildly intuitive as childbirth. Her body knew what to do. Yedder tucked his head into her shoulder to avoid the branches grabbing at them. He fell asleep. How he fell asleep she couldn't understand.

She was the opposite of sleeping. She was awakening.

☾

The journey home took half the time it had when she had left as a young bride. As she neared Mtoasili, she sped by places she and Amastan had passed on their way to Jabira. There were the watering holes her dowry had drank from, and then there was the flat spot beneath a cluster of juniper trees where Amastan had thrust into her virgin body with a violent urgency. She remembered feeling scared. Injured, scared, and alone. She remembered feeling betrayed by her father.

How had she forgotten that moment in all this time? Her memory, it seemed, had an agenda of its own, ensuring her survival with the erasure of distress. When Amastan had asked her to leave—where was that memory then? Why hadn't it told her to run, to take his demand to depart as an invitation to reclaim her sanctity?

As they neared Mtoasili, a breeze carried the undercurrents of smoke. It smelled like the time a bonfire had gone rogue and consumed the neighbor's house. Elephant grass burned hot and fast and fierce, smelling of hair on fire. The breeze carried this stench and heat now.

The first grievance of her homecoming would prove to be the fact she couldn't see the forests flatten into the savanna. She yearned to hold before her the forever stretch of grasses. More so, she yearned for Yedder to see it. He would better understand himself, she thought, if he could see where his mother came from. He would better understand why the boulders of Jabira and the walls of their hut there had been a sorry trade for the boundlessness of the savanna. Yet there was no savanna to behold, only smoke thick in the burning. This was the first grievance.

The second grievance would prove to be the absence of her parents, brothers, and neighbors. She and Yedder approached the town along its eastern periphery, trusting the smoke kept them hidden. In little time, the truth of this reality revealed itself: there was no one to hide from and no one to find. There were only the smoldering remains of houses, the black grasses breathing their wretched stench.

The third grievance would prove to be the absence of bones. In the same way she and Yedder had combed over the forest floor, seeking food and finding mushrooms, they perused the skeleton of Mtoasili, seeking remnants of her people, evidence of their demise. They found none. No graves. No bones. Bazi bent to the ground and wrung a fistful of the black grasses in her hand, smearing charcoal on her palms. She felt the agony yawn open in her stomach, drawing the blood from her heart to her womb.

But overcoming that anguish, in the way lions overcome an antelope, slowly at first, growing more fierce and deliberate with each snap of jaw, was hope. A hot, angry hope brought forth by the third grievance. An absence of bones, buried or not, meant they had survived. They could have survived. Her people could have survived this nonsensical demolition of their dwellings.

Yedder pulled on her shift, and she came back to him, to this moment, bringing with her the resolution to find their family, alive or no. He pointed up. A purple strip of fabric, centered by a yellow boar head, fluttered above it all. Perched atop the flagpole was a lilac-breasted roller. He had bright, iridescent feathers, pink down the neck and teal in the tail. The Shapeshifter, Bazi assumed, tilted his head once in mutual acknowledgement and took off south, into the smoke.

She and Yedder walked over to where the flag had been staked in the ground. Flattened grasses stretched in the direction the bird had flown. These Yiúsians did nothing to obscure their path. Bazi figured they had no need to do so. By the look of their wake, they traveled by the hundreds, if not the thousands. The smoke said it all in its silent and hovering presence.

These invaders feared no one. They had come to claim this land as theirs, and they would burn any who stood in their way.

Bazi and Yedder alternated between walking together and him riding upon her back. She snuck sideway looks as they strode hip to head, and she saw the serious determination on her child's face. At seven years old, he looked like a little man. She figured if she put a sword in his hand and told him to march, he could pass as a very short soldier. Just when she thought she would break down weeping for the death of her son's childhood, he would sprint ahead, chasing a rabbit, or he would squat low to the ground and pick up an object of fascination.

"Look, mother, obsidian!"

"Look here, a bird skull!"

"A giant dung beetle!"

Bazi thanked the world for reminding her son to dwell in his wonder, to continue believing he could catch a rabbit with his own two hands. These moments, though, became less frequent the more villages they passed. Every village was the same: deserted, smoldering, and free of bones or graves. The invader's wake continued onward, a stamp across the grasses announcing their mammoth presence. They chased the apparition of a giant through a cloud made of smoke and ash. It felt like they would never walk in clear air again. The only sign of time was the red orb overhead, though even the sun seemed to have been conquered by these invaders.

Why had they come? This single question was as relentless as the smoke. As much as she desired to find her family, she desired to find the answer to this question.

*Disorder,* Hamia had said.

They spread Disorder—but *why?*

The day drawled on, one step at a time. Other than the rabbit hours ago, the land showed no signs of life. In the macaque lair, Bazi had heard the forest community talk. It had sounded no different than the narrow alleyways of Jabira, where children had screamed with play and mothers had chattered idly. Bazi remembered the savanna being a vibrant place. Flamingos had exploded into flight, and giraffes had run with a peculiar grace.

She had wondered, on the way here, what the voices of her home would tell her. She had hoped that even if her people had been inflicted, the other animals of this land would remain in the routines of their lives. Though she couldn't see ten steps behind or beyond her, one thing was clear: no animal lived immune to human conflict. Only the roller, appearing at random as a brilliant bolt of color, accompanied them.

The absence of other life posed a greater complication than not being able to eavesdrop on their conversations. Bazi had only brought from the cedar forests pockets filled with dates. They stopped to eat. Yedder chewed his meager portion with slow, thoughtful bites. Black smears marked his face like battle paint. Bazi observed her son, noting the stark difference in even his eating mannerisms between now and yesterday.

"Do you want another date?" she asked.

He shook his head. "I'm not hungry."

"That's a lie."

He shrugged. "We'll need them for tomorrow."

She tucked a stray curl behind his ear. "You're right. We will."

Bazi slept little, the night being a terrifying presence. Yedder lay curled into her. Though the world around them felt monstrous, she abated her fears by cherishing her son's reversion back to his child self. He was seven years old in these dark and scary hours. In the morning, he would age twenty years. In the morning, she needed to tell him the worst of it.

The smoke shifted with the sunrise, and her son woke and stood. "We should continue," he said.

Bazi patted the ground beside her. "Yes, in a minute. I first need to tell you something."

He sat and stared at her expectantly.

"I…" She fiddled with one of his curls.

He caught her hand in his and brought it into his lap. "Mother?"

"I, well, we are walking to find my family," she began. "Our family."

Yedder nodded. "Ya, I know."

Couldn't they just sleep until the smoke cleared? Couldn't he stay safe in her arms, the two of them a snail in a shell? Yedder continued to hold her hand as she cried.

She hacked up gray phlegm and continued. "They may not be alive."

He nodded again. “Ya, I know.”

“I will—I have been called to fight. As the Anima, I have been called to fight this invasion.”

Yedder squeezed her hand. “Ya, I know.”

His little pink tongue licked at cracked lips. He looked beyond her, and she wished to be in his mind. She wished she could hear her son’s thoughts a hundred times more than she wished to hear the voices of savanna creatures. What else did he know? How many years had he aged in the last moon alone? All this time she had been consumed by her own transformation and so had missed that of her son.

“I know you are the Anima,” he said. “I didn’t know that was the name for it, but I see you, Mother. I see you, and I see the burned homes, and I see that we are not heading back to my father’s home. I know—I know that you are strong and fast now and that you could fight whatever made all this”—he waved an arm overhead, swaying the smoke—“happen. I know that you should fight it. And me, too. We should fight it.”

Bazi blinked, pushing a couple more tears from her eyes. “I didn’t know”—she coughed—“that you knew all that.”

“You didn’t know, or you didn’t want to know?”

She felt like Yedder had hit her over the head with a rock. She wasn’t even aware she was still crying until Yedder smeared the tears into her cheeks with his dirty fingers.

“It’s okay,” he kept saying. “It’s okay. I understand.”

“I know you understand,” she managed to say at last. “That’s the problem.”

He stood and offered her a hand. “It’s better this way,” he said, helping her to a stand.

They brushed the grasses from their clothes before brushing them from each other’s back.

“Let’s find water,” he said.

They resumed walking in quiet, and sure enough, an hour or two into the morning, they came upon a river. Nothing had ever tasted so sweet. They drank and drank. The water seemed to even lift the smoke a bit. It cleared Bazi’s mind, and she felt more able to think about what her son had said that morning.

"Wait a second there, young man," she said, her tone startling him. "You will *not* be fighting."

He crouched above the river like a tiger cub, a feral disobedience narrowing his eyes. "Yes. I. Will."

"No, you will not."

They glowered at one another. The veins of his lanky legs and arms revealed his intensity. He would grow to be strong. He could grow to be strong, that was, if he remained alive.

Bazi forced herself to relax, sitting down to soak her feet in the river. They left the argument untidy and continued resting in silence. The breeze gathered force. It commanded the smoke, pulling it across the grasslands, pushing it away from the earth. The sky broke through patches in the thinning haze. The strokes of blue felt as wonderful as the water had tasted. The wind cleared the smoke entirely, and they lifted their faces to the sun, welcoming its midsummer potency. Bazi shaded her brow with a hand and looked to where the path would lead them. Grasses flattened by the invaders continued to follow the water west.

She realized they sat along the Panpole River. Rising above the grasses, barely recognizable even to her Anima eyes, stood the multistory mud buildings of Mamahali. She saw no smoke columns drifting up from Nyachi's largest city. Either the invaders had not arrived to the city yet, or they had arrived and had yet to burn it down. Bazi retrieved the rest of the dates from her pocket and held them out for Yedder. He shook a hand, refusing. She thrust one at him.

"I can go longer without eating," he said.

"We'll be in Mamahali by day's end. Eat now. We'll need our energy once we're there."

He inhaled the date.

Let him be ravenous, Bazi thought. Let him believe he ate to fight.

They reached the city's outskirts by sundown. Huts built in the traditional Nyachian fashion spread out before the taller buildings. The grass homes looked shabby and tiny compared to the towering cityscape standing black against the red horizon. They approached low to the ground, using the riparian growth as cover.

The Panpole River flowed through the city center. She remembered swimming in it with her brother when their father had allowed them a break from helping at the market stand. Dozens of other people were always in the water as well: children like them playing while their mothers washed clothes nearby; old men with sagging skin and long, gray beards cleaning their armpits and feet. She remembered how the mud buildings, etched with patterns made of triangles and squares, seemed to grow out from the river like the baobab trees she and Yedder threaded through now.

They slowed to a crawl when the grass huts became denser. The outskirts had bustled with people when she had visited as a child. Now the shantytown dwelled in complete silence. The void of voices filled Bazi with a cold fear. She motioned for Yedder to quit moving. The river's song nearly drowned the noise out, but Bazi could just barely make out a couple of voices speaking somewhere in the near distance.

She whispered to Yedder to wait and climbed up a tree. The roller Shapeshifter landed silently on a branch near to her. Dusk had come and gone, and she could see firelight flickering up from the city center. Bazi climbed back down, moving quickly despite the dark. She thought nothing of it until she returned to Yedder.

"Your eyes," he said, "they flash in the dark. You look like a tiger."

She laughed, thinking that was absurd.

But Yedder grabbed her arm and squeezed it tight. "No, mother, listen. You are like a tiger." The seriousness of his voice quelled her laughter.

"I didn't mean to scare you."

He squeezed her arm again. "It's not me who should be scared. It's them." He pointed downriver, toward the firelight.

Her own son believed in her power—when would she as well? They continued to follow the river, passing a group of whispering warthogs on their way. The roller flitted from branch to branch overhead. The structures grew bigger around them, as did the light and noise downstream. Bazi could pick apart the human voices coming from the city center. One spoke in Nyachian, the other in a language she had never heard.

The river, though, remained too loud to make out what they were saying. She looked at Yedder pushing away the bushwillow as he walked, his face a portrait of bravery and determination. She wanted to tell him to stop, that it was time to retreat back to his childhood. But she knew there was something beyond mother-and-son bonding them together now. Their destinies were intertwined into a single river, and they could not move upstream.

They tiptoed onto a street. No one, not even a rat, moved across the dirt road. They scampered along the sides of buildings, moving closer and closer to the noise and firelight. The roller flew between window shutters and eaves. His feathers flashed in the twilight. Bazi smelled the fire. She also smelled hundreds of humans. She could taste the salt of sweat on her tongue. Coughs and moans punctuated the spaces between the resonating voices.

They came upon a ladder, and she began ascending without hesitation. She could feel Yedder's breath on her heels. When they reached the building's top, Bazi peeked over the edge. No one was there, and they pulled themselves onto the flat roof. Crawling on their bellies once again, they moved toward the fire. A man spoke in a booming tone, filling the night with his foreign language. Once at the roof's edge, Bazi gestured for Yedder to stop and to remain flat on his belly. She lifted her head just enough to see beyond the eave.

She hadn't smelled hundreds of humans, but thousands. A giant bonfire burned in the city center, its cavorting flames flashing across the sea of black faces. Light glistened off metal cuffs wrapped around wrists; it glimmered upon the silver heads of spears men held as they stood on platforms above the captives. Her people filled the square and the adjacent streets.

On a platform above the bonfire, nearly half as high as the building behind it, two men stood, each holding a bullhorn. The same purple flag she saw waving above the remains of Mtoasili stood limp on the side of the platform. The foreigner quit speaking, bringing the horn down from his mouth, and the other man brought his to his mouth.

Bazi recognized him before he even began speaking again. She had seen his face painted on tapestries and carved into wooden blocks at the Mamahali markets. There, in person, made larger than life by his giant shadow cast on the mud walls behind him, stood King Nabahu of Nyachi.

"Opposition demands death," he roared. "I relinquish my throne to the one and true king. The kingdom of Nyachi is henceforth under the rule of the Yiúsians."

The foreigners banged their spears on the platforms. Even over the thundering weapons, she could hear children whimper. Her family—they were in that mass. The thought forced the wind from her chest.

The whimpering she heard was Yedder. His eyes, glassy and round and huge, stared unblinking at the horror below. She yanked him away from the eave and into her arms. Holding him tight to her chest, their hearts rampaged against one another. His whole body shook. He grew cold with the shock.

They lay like this as the firelight dwindled. The people below continued to moan and cough. Now that the show was over, she imagined them sitting down, their wrists raw from the cuffs. She imagined them seeking comfort, heads finding thighs and hands finding hands.

A couple times throughout the night, screams of revolt erupted, followed by sobs and general commotion. She didn't dare look over the roof again. Her gaze remained skyward, to the stars traversing the sky with careless ease. Her people believed the deceased rose beyond the clouds to dwell forever as a star. If the belief was true, her ancestors watched this tragedy transpire. How helpless one became in death. Bazi hoped the stars were uncaring, for if they remained partial to earthly drama, it would seem the afterlife was a purgatory of empathy without the ability to act upon it.

She, though, was alive. She was alive and more capable than ever to do something.

The roller ruffled his feathers nearby. He studied the horror with black eyes ringed in orange. Squeezing Yedder closer to her, Bazi inhaled the oily earth of his hair. She felt the bones of his elbows, the pulse in his wrists. She held her son with the tearing emotions of him being hers to care for, and yet hundreds like him depending on her as well.

*For the sake of all children,* Hamia had said. *For the sake of all children you must use your powers to stop the Disorder's spread.*

Sunlight crept its way onto the rooftop. Yedder woke within her arms and brought a hand to his hair, feeling wetness.

"Did it rain last night?" he whispered. He looked at her bloodshot eyes and didn't ask more questions.

The smell of feces became as thick as the smoke had been. They listened to bodies by the thousands shifting to find elusive relief. The feeling in her stomach reminded her of those moons she had starved in Amastan's care. Was that just this past winter, not even six moons earlier? It felt like a lifetime ago.

Yedder sat up and brought his knees to his chest. Bazi figured he knew what needed to happen next. The knowledge grew between them as a palpable force. She would fight, and she may not survive. She probably wouldn't survive. The hunch of Yedder's shoulders, the solemn contemplation of his face told her he understood this, though she wondered if he still thought he would fight alongside her.

Let him believe, she thought again. His faith kept him strong, and he would need all of his strength when it came time to run.

The sun ascended into midday. She peeked over the eave. The men with spears still stood on the platforms, pacing back and forth, watching the mass of captives. With the daylight, she could see the cream color of the soldiers' skin. They wore metal shirts over yellow shifts. Helmets topped with yellow and purple feathers hid their faces. She counted at least a hundred of them spread out across a few dozen platforms.

Bazi turned to the roller. *We attack tonight,* she said, *after the sunset.*

The bird nodded once and took off, flying north. The teal of his feathers were luminescent against the white sky. She studied more closely the layout of the city center and the length and width of the streets leading to it. An alleyway ran behind one of the platforms. That seemed as good of a place as any to launch her attack. She squinted, trying to read the body language of the soldier pacing that platform. He was tall, strong, and proud.

Was it fear or rage causing her heart to rampage? The people below, her people, continued to sit and stand, urinate and defecate, moan and cry. The thought of killing that man, so aloof in the sway of his walk, so smug in the way he banged his spear, ground her teeth together. Her fingers clutched the roof, and bits of mud rained down on the man pacing the platform below. She slipped beyond sight just before the soldier looked up.

Yedder whispered, "Do you think they will leave before nightfall?"

"Let's pray not."

He started to pray. She could hear the susurration of his voice, like a breeze rustling grasses, begging for night to come swift and black.

The day dawdled by, hot and sticky. Dark descended with the casual ease of summer nights. It smelled as if the human waste had fermented in the heat. Why did these barbarians keep the captives in the streets? Why not at least spread the people out on the savanna, allowing the earth to soak up their urine and feces? It would have still smelled unnaturally foul, but at least the air opened up on the grasslands. The buildings kept any moving air from reaching the swamp of humans below.

As if in answer to these questions, the bonfire was relit, and the old king and new king of Nyachi returned to the platform. The show wasn't over. Bazi and Yedder rested their noses on the eave to watch.

The foreigner wore the same purple robe with golden threads as he had the night before. It looked as if he had wrapped his people's flag around him. With sunset still seeping light into the world, Bazi could better see his features. His pale brown hair grew in sleek waves, and a thin beard framed his face. The feminine shine of his locks contradicted his sonorous voice. He walked back and forth as he spoke, gesturing with long arms. From his tone, Bazi guessed he was trying to pacify the prisoners. His language sounded flat and long compared to the galloping cadence of Nyachian.

Nabahu's translation revealed she was right. "People of Nyachi," he cried out, "we are blessed to come under the rule of the Yiúsians." Bazi realized that Nabahu, her people's beloved king, might have been planning the invasion with these foreigners for some time.

"The Yiúsians will soon rule over the western world," Nabahu continued. "They intend to continue south to the dark forests and east to the monsoon seas. We, the Nyachians, are now under their protection and guidance. King Savas will serve as our father. He will nurture us with food and water. He will train us in advanced arts of war. He wants you all to be happy and healthy. He wants your sons to grow to be strong, your daughters to grow to be beautiful and fertile.

"But only," Nabahu raised his voice, "*only* if you obey. Opposition demands death."

Signaled by these three words, a dozen soldiers marched down the street, ushering before them around thirty naked Nyachian men. A strange wooden structure connected the Nyachians together by their heads, and they walked with forced uniformity. Rage radiated off of them. Behind the men, chained together, staggered nearly twenty children and women.

Bazi swallowed back vomit. She pulled on Yedder's shirt and motioned for him to look away. He jutted his chin out. No, he mouthed. They fought soundlessly over whether or not he could watch the atrocity unfolding below as the soldiers shoved the prisoners onto the stage.

"These slaves disobeyed," Nabahu called out. "Opposition demands death." And before Bazi could pull Yedder away from the roof side, the soldiers slashed their spears across the stomachs of the men, women, and children. The sea of her people exploded into a torrent of protests. Complete chaos ensued.

Bazi grabbed Yedder's arm, and they ran to the ladder. They flew down the rungs. Shapeshifters or not, now was her time. She sprinted through the empty streets. Screams, sobbing, chains rattling, metal clanking, moans and cries ricocheted off the buildings around them. Bazi found the narrow alleyway leading to the square and turned down it, leading Yedder with his wrist in her hand.

Soldiers hit the rioting prisoners over the head with the butts of their spears. Bazi stopped at a side door to a shop. She had grieved this moment a hundred times over in the past twenty four hours, and now that it had arrived, she realized she wanted her son to live more than anything. The painful thought of her potential death diminished with the hope that he could live. He could live free if she fought.

She thought she would cry. She had sobbed when she had anticipated this goodbye. But instead she held his shoulders tight, peered into his wet eyes, and said, "I fight for you. I fight for the love I have for you."

He sniffed and nodded. "Ya, I know."

"And you know you cannot fight, not yet?"

He nodded again. "Ya, I know."

She brought him to her chest and frantically kissed his dark curls. His little hands wrung the back of her shirt. He didn't sob, though. His bottom lip quivered, but he fought against the tears. It was the one fight he could own for himself in this moment.

Bazi kissed his forehead and opened the side door. "Stay in here," she said. "Stay in here and I will come back for you."

She shut the door and closed her eyes. Blood pumped against her finger pads. Her mind settled into its center, and the world purified into a matrix of smells, a map of sounds. When she opened her eyes, the night beckoned her to attack.

*You are like a tiger,* she heard him saying. *You are like a tiger.*

She sprinted down the alleyway, unhearing to the screams rushing out of her throat. Her primordial screeching spread over the open square as a terror. She leaped onto a platform and crouched, pausing but a breath to look for a target for her rage. A flood of strange creatures came pouring through the streets beyond the crowd. In both human and animal forms, the Shapeshifters roared into the center.

Prisoners grabbed one another by the arm and pointed up at Bazi. She saw a soldier beat the side of a man's face with his fist. She launched from the platform and dragged the Yiúsian down with her fingernails clawed into his eyeballs. He barely had time to cry out before she broke his neck. The veins in her hands pulsated as she looked around for the next invader.

One had his back turned to her. She slithered low to the ground as she approached. Her people created a path and quiet followed in her wake—everyone stunned into silence by the woman moving eerily similar to a snake. She took the soldier down by grabbing his legs and yanking them back. His face smashed against the ground, and his spear clattered to the side. She thrust it into his heart.

She spun in circles, seeking out the next soldier. No more stood within reach. The absence of noise in this corner of the city center was stark in comparison to the surrounding storm. All eyes nearby had found her.

"Look anywhere but here," she said. "Keep making noise!"

Whoops and hollers unrolled away from her. She found the key in a pouch hanging from a soldier's belt. Blood had already soaked through the yellow fabric, and it dripped from the key's cuts. She grabbed the wrist of a nearby child. The little girl looked up at Bazi with wide eyes.

There was no keyhole in the child's cuff, only chains threading through the binding. She moved to the next handcuff. No keyhole there. No keyhole in the next cuff or the next. Screaming grew louder a few heads away.

"Hold this," she whispered, thrusting the key into a girl's hands. The Yiúsian came charging through the crowd, stabbing a woman in the neck, seemingly by accident, as he ran with his spear. He thrust it at Bazi, and she ducked. Strands of cut hair fell from her head. He swung again, this time glancing her arm. The sting reignited her rage. She jumped away from the swoosh of metal and pounced back. Shrieking, she grabbed the man's arm and ripped it clean from the socket.

For a moment she stared at the arm in her hand. Had she, did she, how did she manage to do that? Now it was the man shrieking. She tossed the arm to the side and finished him quickly by breaking his neck. Finding another key in the same place she had found the last, she returned to the girl who held the other. She cowered away from Bazi, holding the key in an upturned palm.

"It's okay," Bazi whispered. "I'm with you." All the people who had witnessed her last kill looked at her with horror.

"Over here," someone yelled. "The lock is over here."

She ran to the man who had spoken and unlocked his cuffs. The connected cuffs fell free in a chain reaction. Thrusting one of the keys in the man's hand, she told him to find another lock. Rubbing their wrists, the freed people seemed frozen in place.

"Don't just stand there!" she yelled. "Run!"

They jumped as if whipped and took off in a stampede. Bazi found another lock and managed to undo it before a dozen soldiers emerged from the chaos. A pair of Shapeshifters ran after the soldiers marching toward Bazi. They managed to kill a couple Yiúsians before they were killed. Bazi yelped as the Shapeshifters crumpled to the ground.

She ran to meet the three Yiúsians approaching. Their spears slashed the air as she jumped up and right of them, landing on all fours atop the platform. One clambered up the stairs, and she charged, rolling below the spear's arc. She pushed off her hands and feet before the spear had a chance to swing back at her. The soldier crashed to the floor beneath her body, and she tore his head off.

Holding the decapitated head of the man, she noticed a small figure watching from a doorway. That was—that was her son. The recognition felt distant at first, as if her eyes had to adjust out of the dark and into light.

He seemed far away, even though she could toss the head at him, and he would be able to catch it. She knew that face. But he didn't recognize her. That was clear.

"Run," she roared, tossing the head to the side and dipping low before a spear could find her chest.

He stood still, stupefied with horror. To his left, a woman speared a Yiúsian through the chest. Her braids swung as she ripped the spear free.

"Hamia," Bazi yelled. "Hamia, protect Yedder!"

Hamia grabbed Yedder's wrist, and they took off running. He looked over his shoulder as a spear skimmed Bazi's cheek. Hundreds of Nyachians running down the city streets absorbed him into their flow. Some of the Yiúsians chased after the freed people, while a dozen soldiers ran toward the platform Bazi danced upon. The majority of the Yiúsians fought the remaining Shapeshifters in the city center.

Bazi glanced at the mayhem of soldiers and Shapeshifters exchanging blows before tumbling away from a spear and twirling away from another. She jumped up onto a windowsill as the platform filled with soldiers. A few more Shapeshifters tried to run to her aid but died with spears to hearts and throats.

Freed prisoners continued to run beyond the platform. For every Nyachian caught and killed, ten more escaped. It was beautiful, watching them stream down the city streets. Bazi thought of the waterfalls back in the macaque lair. She closed her eyes and listened, half expecting to hear the water's rumble that had been the music of her transformation.

The soldiers parted, making way for King Savas as he stomped toward the platform. The scowl on his face, the scorn in his eyes: they did not scare her. She met his fierce anger with a cool smile. She would not play his childish games. She was the Anima, and he was but a boy who hadn't gotten his way.

He barked something at his soldiers, and the majority of them scattered off the platform, chasing the people who continued to run free. More Shapeshifters tried to run to the platform, but the Yiúsians had formed a barricade. Looking up at her, King Savas continued to bark.

Nabahu walked onto the platform with tentative steps. His weakness smelled like rotten onions. Her dismissive attitude darkened in his presence: he was the reason the Yiúsians had come this far in their invasion. She no longer smiled. Nabahu noticed, and his eyes ran away from her. But he knew he couldn't run. Bazi knew this as well.

King Savas yelled and screamed at him in his droning language. He slapped Nabahu across the face and pointed up at Bazi.

Continuing to look at the floor, Nabahu said to her, "King Savas demands you to come down here and face him like a man."

Bazi laughed. She laughed and laughed. The soldiers exchanged terrified looks. Her laughter shook her crown of black hair. It set her eyes afire. She crouched in the windowsill, a black shadow save for the blaze of her eyes, and laughed until she was crying.

"Like a man?" she said, speaking directly to Nabahu in their shared language. "Does that mean like you? A coward who sold his people for his own skin? Or does that mean like him, an animal turned rabid with greed?" She laughed again, shaking her head. "I cannot do what he asks. I cannot face him like a man, because I will never be a man. I am the Anima."

She launched herself onto Nabahu and clawed at his face. She managed to break his neck before the first sword found her shoulder. The second sword found her leg. The third, her hip.

A tiger roared, and a gorilla screamed. Someone held her head up by her hair. She sat back on her heels in a pool of her and Nabahu's blood. King Savas looked down at her with an odd expression. Was it reverence or disgust? He said something in his strange tongue, and the fourth sword found her neck.

Her talking decapitated head would haunt all the men present for the rest of their days. She lived on in their nightmares. She lived on in her words. She lived on in the promise of the Anima's rebirth.

# OILI

## 844 YBP

### Grahimland Seaterra

Torches guttered as Oili swept past. The glass beads of her dress thumped against her chest. She ripped off the fasteners and threw them against the wall. The beads shattered into innumerable pieces; they glinted like stars on the floor behind her. Her silk dress fell from her body, and she kicked it free. Wearing but her underdress, she slipped out the cellar's window.

The moon, almost new, hung low in the west, its thin rays further dimmed by the Great Wall. Oili strutted through the icy streets lined by wood and stone buildings. She would pay for her insolence, but she marched forward nonetheless. He needed to know. The town's gossip would have reached him before sunrise, and she needed to be the one to tell him. She would take her father's wrath to do him this much. He had, after all, risked his life to be with her. She could risk a whipping.

Finn stood in his watchtower with his back to her. The broad angles of his shadowed body brought Oili's heart into her throat. Today was inevitable: they both had held this knowledge while holding each other. Of all the nights they had spent together, secreting away on horses to the steaming waters, this knowledge had been with them as much as the rowan trees and the wolves' howls. When Oili had visited the Crow for soapwort and juniper tea last year, she had swallowed the seed-killing tonic, though she had wanted nothing more than to allow his child to grow within her.

They both had known they could not live forever in their love, but when he turned to the whispered call of his name, the reality of losing that face, that smile, uprooted this knowledge. If her fate as the Princess of Grahimland were to marry the Prince of Nunlu, why would she have fallen in love with Finn Holt, her lord father's guard of the northeast tower? The gods surely had another plan.

Finn heaved her up to him on the turret's lift. He opened the door, and she embraced his armored body. "We must leave," she breathed into his ear. "We must leave. Now."

They unhitched the fastest horses and slipped out the door of his unmanned tower. The melted snows had left the ground soggy. They trotted too slowly for their haste. The wind tugged her hair free of their braids, and it flowed behind her like a bronze veil. Green lights danced across the infinite black above. Oili took the aurora as a good sign from the gods.

She reached out to Finn and squeezed his hand. "They won't know I'm gone until the morning. I told my guards to leave me be until dawn."

"But they will see I am gone within the hour, and they will check your bed."

"Do the other guards know? About us?"

"They have their suspicions."

Oili released his hand and willed her horse to trot faster. The muddy ground sucked at the stallion's feet, and he struggled to obey. She looked over her shoulder at the Great Wall fading behind them. Her father would be deep in mead's sleep. Her new stepmother, a year younger than Oili, would be curled into his massive body, waking throughout the night to feed their newborn.

They threaded into the dark forest. The horses slowed even further, timid in the lingering scent of wolves.

Finn stopped his horse. "When we are found, I will be killed."

"We will not be found." Oili's voice was louder, stronger, than his.

"And where will we go where the Princess of Grahimland will not be noticed?"

Oili halted her horse and turned to face him. Even in the shadowed night, she could see the resolve on his face, and her stomach dropped.

"We cannot do this," Finn said. "I cannot." He slipped off his horse, and Oili did the same. "Love," he whispered, reaching to bring her into his arms.

She stood defiant, her arms crossed before her. Why did he have to make this harder than it already was?

"What you ask of me I cannot do. Your betrothal, we knew…" His red, bushy eyebrows pulled together. "To abandon my position as a guard to spend a night with you is one thing. But to sabotage the Gelid Alliance is too much. It's treason, Oili. Treason against our lands, our people."

She knew it. She knew he wouldn't follow her into forever. He was too stubborn, too righteous. She wanted to claw at him, to tie him up and throw him over her horse. Wasn't their love untouchable? Bigger than the royal court? Stronger than the kingdom?

Finn pulled her into him. Though she was as tall and strong as most men, his strength always surprised her. She softened against the metal of his plated chest. The tears she had refused since receiving the news over dinner felt hot on her face.

"The mainland Flüschen will attack, and when they do, we will need the warriors of Nunlu. Do not think for a moment this is what I would otherwise choose to do." His voice cracked, and he cleared his throat. "Am I not here now? I would—I would do near anything. But not this. I cannot sabotage Grahimland's chance for independence."

Oili pulled away. She grabbed his hand and placed it with hers atop her stomach. "Then I must go to the Crow again. Tonight."

Comprehension slackened his face. Had two moons already passed since they had made love at the spring? The mist rising from the hot waters had danced around them as they devoured each other, their hunger overpowering any fear or virtue. It had just been them and the stars, the trickling waters, the pulse of union. Tonight the whole kingdom of Grahimland spanned between them. The merging of the Gelid Seaterras was dependent on her marriage to the Prince of Nunlu—an alliance demanding her womb to be vacant, free for the filling.

Finn's hand quivered beneath hers as if he was tickling their unborn child. She saw in his face the possibility of their life together: wrinkles growing from their eyes with the years of laughter; three, four, six children running around a small plot of land somewhere on the mainland; a life spent working the land, harvesting a garden, lambing, milking the sheep and goats. A simple life. A life beyond the realm of courts, swords, and Solerian silk.

His face hardened, though, and his hand quieted. He withdrew it from hers and held her with the firmness of knowing it would be his last time doing so. Oili breathed in the cold metal. She wanted nothing more than to smell his smell beneath the armor, the one of salt and wild onion.

"In the Afterworld," he whispered, the words wet on her ear, "we will be together. But for now our lives are not for us." He released her and jumped back onto his horse. "I assume you know the way and feel safe alone."

Oili nodded once.

"Then I will return to my post with the hope my absence has not yet been noted. Please do hurry, Princess. The sun will rise and with it our people's hope."

She cringed at the word *princess*. He had not called her that since the first time they met, two years earlier when he had escorted her to Helöf for the Whaling Festival. How could he switch back just like that? As if his love were a fire he could put out with a single bucket of water. She felt she would need an entire spring's worth of runoff to smother the wildfire within her.

Oili stiffened against the threat of yet more tears. She *was* a princess. Daughter of King Gunnar Ingesson the Huge. Finn may be a coward when it came to love, but his loyalty to her father, his willingness to sacrifice his own desires for the kingdom, was one of the reasons she had fallen for him in the first place.

"I will do my best." She took courage in the steadiness of her voice. She could survive this. She would survive this.

As he swiveled on his horse to head back north, Oili saw the glimmer on his cheek, and she knew he was right. They were meant to be together—but not in this life.

Oili tied up her horse to a rowan branch. She normally wouldn't need to hitch her horse, but he was acting spooked outside the Crow's home. Oili couldn't fault him for it. The cobblestone cottage leaned into the darkness, its roof appearing as if it would cave in at any moment. A dim glow leaked out from gaps in the shutters. When she raised her fist to bang on the door, it opened.

The Crow looked up at her with a passive face. Her eyes, an opaque blue, appeared unsurprised, as if Oili's visit had been planned all winter. She wore a long, tethered dress and cloak, both black as her namesake. Bright white hair stuck out at odd angles from beneath her fur-trimmed hood. Around her neck hung a vial of dried plants and flowers.

"I'm sorry to intrude," Oili said after a long pause had passed between them.

"No problem at all, Princess." The Crow stepped aside to allow Oili in. "Please, come warm by the fire."

The Crow had the short and stout stature and light brown coloring of her fellow Tuttuáns. The first time Oili had come, it had been treason. The Tuttuán were sworn enemies of her people since the Flüschen conquered Grahimland, confining the Tuttuán to the smaller of the two Gelid Seaterras, Nunlu. Six decades later, Oili's father initiated the campaign for Grahimland's independence from the mainland kingdom. The proposed alliance between the Grahimland Flüschen and the Tuttuáns of Nunlu would render Oili's visits to the Crow as gossip, but not as treason.

Oili had to stoop to enter the cottage. The Crow's home lacked the taller doorframe and higher ceilings typical of Oili's people. A hare hung from the wall, ready to be skinned for dinner. Shelves filled with dried herbs and canned animal parts obscured the cobblestone walls. A jar of eyeballs watched Oili as she moved to the fireplace.

"Were you awake?" Oili asked, though she knew the answer.

"Oh, I'm not much of a sleeper." The Crow poked at the fire with a spade. Sparks licked at a pot of water warming over the flames. "You come for more tea."

Oili studied the Crow's wrinkle-riddled face. Was that a question or a statement? "Yes. I have." Oili unfastened a leather satchel from her underdress's belt and plunked it atop the hearth.

The Crow dumped the coins into her hand and counted them with her gnarled fingers. She placed them back in the satchel and gave Oili a curious look. "I need one other thing in exchange this time," the Crow whispered, her words rushed.

Oili sensed a shift in the room, a presence arriving, and she looked around. Chills scattered across her ribs. Who would be listening? And why? She moved her fingers to the short sword hanging from her belt. "Who's here?"

The Crow's face remained passive. "You, me, your horse, and the creatures that be."

"Creatures?"

"Nothing out of the ordinary. There are no threats to your secrecy, Princess. Please, relax."

Oili kept her fingers around the handle of her sword.

"What I need of you is a promise," the Crow said.

Oili narrowed her eyes. This woman was bold. She knew Oili needed her. But did she know the whole kingdom depended on this one cup of tea?

"I need you to promise that you will make peace with the Tuttuán, and that you will destroy the Flüschen invaders seeking to conquer these lands."

Oili stared at the Crow, bewildered, before laughing a good laugh. The Crow knew more than Oili would have guessed. Of course she did. She was the Crow, after all.

"I'm here for tea, am I not? And I will marry for duty, not love. My marriage will make peace," Oili shook her head. "But how am I to promise I will destroy the Flüschen? I am but a sow sold for the alliance. My role will be served once I birth a son to the Prince of Nunlu."

A breeze swept through the cottage, and the fire's smoke swayed between Oili and the Crow. What was that countenance on the witch's face? Disdain? Impatience? It frightened Oili, whatever it was, and the humor of the situation blew out the shutters' cracks with the smoke. The haze now gone, Oili wondered if the Crow's face had even changed at all. Her usual impassive expression had settled back into her plump cheeks and narrow eyes.

"Yes, of course, of course," the Crow said, standing to prepare the tea. "I'm happy to hear it. A little bird told me about the Flüschen's plan to attack, and I became terribly frightened. Thank you for putting my unease to rest. You will make a lovely wife and mother, no doubt."

The Crow fetched contents from a shelf. She ground the pestle in the mortar, filling the cottage with the scent of freshly cut mint and something strange to Oili, dank like upturned soil. The Crow poured the ground herbs into a mug and mixed them with hot water. Handing the tea to Oili, the Crow grinned. A smile? Had the witch ever smiled in her life? The expression looked unnatural on her chubby face. Oili took the mug, thanking her.

"Wait," the Crow said. She hobbled away and returned with a goblet of wine. "To a new era," she said, raising her goblet.

Confused, Oili clinked her mug against the goblet. The Crow was even crazier than Oili remembered her being. Oili downed the mug's contents. The room whirled. Between blinding flashes of light, she could see the Crow preparing a bed beneath the shuttered window.

☾

Oili had woken on the day of her wedding. She grimaced now, thinking of how she had almost married a man she had never met. How had she almost killed the child now turning in her belly?

Finn had been the one to kick a bucket to her when she had woken with the need to vomit. She had retched and retched until bile dribbled from her lips. He had said when Oili's bed had been found empty the morning after they made the decision to part ways, he had spirited away from the Great Wall, back into the woods.

The Crow had said he nearly choked her to death, thinking Oili dead on the bed when he came storming into the cottage. But a Salvager was not so easily killed, and she had somehow stunned him while he tried to strangle her. Finn had told Oili he saw the vile around the witch's neck glow vivid green before he passed out.

The Crow had been forced to restrain him for the half-moon Oili had spent neither here nor dead. Like a pet, the Crow had fed him and gave him water and cleaned up his messes. He still glowered at the Crow for these days, for the humiliation he had endured. Oili asked him again and again to forgive the Crow—but only after Oili had found forgiveness herself.

After all, the Crow had poisoned her, killing the woman who had come to this cottage in the first place. She hadn't asked Oili if she cared to become the Anima. Playing the goddess, she had slipped her the mushroom and forever changed her body, her being, her fate. Oili had hated her for this, and for the first few nights after waking, she and Finn had whispered plots to escape confinement and kill this witch who called herself a Keeper.

One morning, a week after Oili woke, the Crow had returned from outside with a snowy owl gripping her shoulder. The bird had flown to Oili and perched on the corner of her bed. She called herself Neva and said she was a Shapeshifter. She had explained to Oili how she now shared an ancient language with the animal kingdom.

*You are the Anima reborn,* Neva had said.

She was no sow to be sold, no womb to be sowed against her will. She was the Anima: a power in her own body, her own right.

In her remembered years, no one would have ever called Oili, daughter of Gunnar the Huge, a delicate thing. But now her body, thewy as a caribou, made the old Oili seem meek as the hare. She feared, at times, Finn would one day discover he could not love the new Oili. She feared Oili the Anima would prove to be too much for him to hold.

She was the same towering height as before. She had the same golden brown hair, same slant of a smile, same burst of a laugh. But at night, when they had rediscovered one another's body, neither could understand the new lines of her arms and legs where muscle ran tight and enlarged. She wondered if either of them would ever become comfortable with her eyes' fire of emerald and amber.

Both Neva and the Crow promised Oili that she would not be alone in this new life of hers. With the help of her allies, the Keepers, she and Finn would keep their child now five moons growing. They would be together. But in exchange for her freedom, the Crow said she must first fulfill her Task.

☾

Oili's womb had swelled with the summer. When the elderberry harvest arrived with the season's end, she rested her basket on her belly as she filled it with the deep purple fruit. The Crow plucked berries beside her, working wordlessly. She had grown more quiet than usual in the last moon.

Oili stopped and turned to face the Salvager. "Crow," she said. "Is there something wrong?"

The Crow sighed. She set her basket down and motioned for Oili to join her at the wooden table beneath an oak tree. Oili sat across from her, and the Crow placed a hand on her arm.

"I can see the love between you and Finn is true and deep," she began.

Oili smiled. "I agree."

The Crow didn't smile. "Your Task, though, extends beyond the simple pleasures of a life as a wife and mother. This is both your blessing and burden."

Oili frowned at the Crow's hand. She was glad Finn was out hunting. He still loathed the Salvager and mistrusted the circumstances of their freedom. She withdrew her arm from the Crow's touch and placed her hands on her belly.

"But you said once I fulfill the Task, my family and I can live free."

"Indeed. But in fulfilling your Task, you will find yourself torn between the wants of someone you could have been, and answering the demands of the woman you are meant to become."

Oili felt the baby kick her hand. She thumped her hand against her womb in return. "You still haven't explained the Task."

"We're still waiting on Neva," the Crow said, looking to the north. "Once she returns, you can begin your life's true work." The Crow stood and resumed picking berries.

What did she mean when describing this tear between wants and demands? Oili remembered dashing across the soggy ground of early spring with Finn, desperate to escape her fate as a princess. She had wanted nothing more than to retreat into their love in a land far south from the Great Wall. If it weren't for Finn's initial refusal, she would not be the Anima now. They would not have this chance to live free together.

Once she fulfilled this Task, they could find a plot of land and raise a family. Of course Finn had his doubts; they festered like the rope rash that had encircled his wrists and ankles from when the Crow had tied him up. Oili couldn't blame him for his misgivings. And though she would miss some things about the Salvager's cottage—its music of creaking floors and chattering mice, the smells of fresh herbs and old wood—she looked forward to putting space between Finn and the Crow.

Oili looked around, hoping to see Neva gliding through the birch branches. Where had she gone? It had been two moons now since she flew north. Oili wanted to finish this Task and begin living on her terms for once. Had the Crow said her *life's* work? Perhaps Finn's mistrust wasn't as misplaced as Oili had hoped.

She brought her basket inside and dumped the berries into a large alder box. Looking out the circular window above the washing basin, she watched the Crow harvest with efficiency honed over millennia of experience. *Millennia.* She had forced herself to believe everything the Crow and Neva had told her. What other options did she have—return to her father and risk the lives of her lover and baby?

Even if they still tried to escape south, they would live a meek life, always in fear of being caught. If they trusted the Crow and Neva, there was a chance they could live their lives out in the open. Free at last.

The berries had stained her fingers scarlet. She did her best to wash them clean, but they remained red for days after.

☾

Neva returned the morning of the first frost and announced they would set out for the stoat's cave in the north, that day. Finn filled the horse saddle with oat bread, salted hare and pheasant meats, dried berries and acorn flesh. He moved briskly, as if the first winter storm would arrive by afternoon. Oili rolled their sleeping mats of stuffed burlap and brought them to the horses.

He secured the mats to the saddles. "There we are," he said, patting the bulky saddle. "We will not go hungry for at least a half moon." He kissed Oili on the nose. "Are you absolutely sure we should go north? Two nights' ride from here we could be on a boat to the mainland." His eyes found her belly as he spoke.

The soggy ground had hardened, and so had Oili's resolve. She breathed out a long, low whistle, and Neva floated down. Her wing brushed Oili's cheek as she came to rest upon her shoulder. Running the back of her hand on the owl's feathers, she said to Finn, "I'm as sure as I'll ever be."

Their goodbyes to the Crow were brief: an embrace between her and

Oili, curt nods between her and Finn. The Crow promised their paths would merge again in the future, a promise Oili wished away.

Gold fringed the birch leaves. The clouds hung low so the pine trees looked to grow into the sky. They trotted as fast as they dared over roots and rocks. Neva would fly away, silent and white as if she were a strand of the clouds gone rogue. She came back often to perch upon Oili's shoulder and confirm the forest was free of other humans.

"If the baby's a girl, I like the name Syvel," Finn said, looking at an apple core before chucking it into the forest.

"Syvel," Oili said. "I like its sound. What does it mean?"

"It was my grandmother's name. It's the flower of the apple tree. To me, it means home. It means apple pie and spiced cider."

Oili said nothing. She couldn't get the Crow's voice out of her head: *the demands of the woman you were meant to become.*

Finn reached out to squeeze her arm. "No worries, love. We don't have to name the baby that. It was just a thought."

She shook her head. "It's pretty. I like it. It's just—it's just I wonder *when* we'll have that home we crave." The cracks in her voice brought heat to her face. This baby made her feel more vulnerable to her emotions than ever.

Finn halted his horse and asked Oili to do the same. He swung down and helped Oili to the ground. Grasping her wrists, he found her eyes and held the gaze.

"I'm sorry I didn't come with you the night before, before you transformed," he said. "I'm sorry I left you to kill my seed, alone. I was weak—"

"You were loyal."

"I was weak," he said with conviction. "You, *you* are my home." He released a wrist and placed his hand atop her belly. "You and our child. But it's not too late to turn back south."

Oili shook her head. "You don't know my father like I do. He can be—ruthless. This Task is our best option. Though I fear that it will involve fighting. War seems inevitable."

"There will always be fighting," Finn replied. "There will always be war. What does that have to do with us starting a new life together?"

Thunder rumbled in the east. The sky above the treetops, though, remained a cold cobalt blue.

"I have a feeling we'll find out sooner than later," she said, hauling her body, seven moons pregnant, back onto the horse. "We need to go. *Now.*"

Finn leaped back onto his stallion, and they wove through the thick growth of evergreens. They paused at the trees' end, where the road between Drauhöir and Taliut ran along the edges of Eldis Forest and the Svetór Lava Fields. Neva swooped back, finding Oili's shoulder. She informed Oili of an army a league east of them. For as long as the owl could see, a line of soldiers on foot and horseback were moving north.

Oili relayed the news to Finn, and they exchanged sober looks.

"The fallout of the Gelid Treaty has begun," Oili said, giving voice to the obvious. "We must hasten our speed before war tears the seaterras apart on the eve of the Flüschen invasion. Neva says the western stretch of road remains clear of the army and its scouts."

Finn took a long drink from the water flask and handed it to Oili for her to do the same. They kicked their heels into their horses and took off faster than prudent on the rocky land. A thin path cut through the moss-covered boulders. Smoke from the army camps' fires faded behind them, and stars poured across a sky gone black. They camped beneath a lone tree within the seemingly endless lava field. The horses drank from a small stream running nearby. Someone had stayed here not long before, leaving behind charcoaled wood and an imprint in the moss. They unfurled their sleeping mats and decided against a fire.

Oili empathized with the baby's complaints. He or she had rolled about on the hard drive, movements that seemed to echo in the emptiness of her stomach. They ate the pheasant meat and dried berries for dinner, Finn insisting Oili take two mouthfuls for every one of his. She didn't argue.

They slept hard, waking only when sunlight split the horizon open. A quick breakfast of bread and butter later, they were driving again, spurring the horses forth with heels to hide. Neva rode on Oili's shoulder, having found their pace exhausting to maintain in flight. Moss glowed beneath the autumn sun. Foliage growing within the rocks interrupted the green with splashes of red and yellow.

Oili imagined the mosses trampled by horses and carcasses of both beast and men strewn across the field. She leaned her body into the horse's neck as far as her belly permitted and whispered her thanks to the creature for his strength and speed.

*The lives of thousands thank you,* she said, and the stallion ran faster.

Another sleep later and they were running again. The field rose into hills. The hills rose into white mountains. Oili and Finn slowed their pace. A plateau permitted a more inclusive view of the land. To the west of the mountains, where the risen earth eased into a peninsula, the Alba Sea lapped upon the shores. Ice blurred the line between land and water, creating intricate patterns out of rock and sea. Beyond the shore, dozens upon dozens of ships sailed across the Angust Strait.

"All their forces, I gather," Oili said, threading her arms through a coat of wolves' skin.

Finn squinted, straining to see Grahimland's most northern beaches, much less the ships dotting the waters beyond them. "And where will we find this stoat?" he asked.

"East of here, in a cave within a rock shaped like a turtle. Neva said we can't miss the rock, and the cave will be in the turtle's head, like an eye."

Oili took off, away from the ships, and Finn followed close behind. The horses trudged up the steep trails obscured with ice and snow; they faltered at times, knees buckling when a hoof slipped. Finn and Oili clung on, slipping back and forth on their saddles. They feared for their unborn baby.

As if sent to further challenge their determination, gales brought a blizzard down the mountains. The storm came like the spring, slow at first, but bursting once it had settled. They were forced to hunker in a small enclave until it passed. Ice fringed the tips of Finn's red beard, and his eyes looked gray rather than their usual bright blue. They didn't speak. What words could warm this moment? Any effort to dispel the dread would feel forced.

At last the storm calmed. They emerged from the cave and plodded over the new layer of snow. Each step sunk the horses in snow up to their knees. The sun hovered a finger's width above the hills behind them. Night would come, and with it a cold that may forever bind them to this land.

But then it appeared. Facing them was the turtle's head, and the black cave eyed them down. Neva pushed off Oili's shoulder and flew to the opening. Oili and Finn arrived at the cave in a sunset red as beet wine. The horses refused to move closer. They dismounted and pulled the horses, with effort, into the yawning. Without light they stumbled over slippery rocks. The dripping of icicles sounded between iron horseshoes clanking on stone. Neva, waiting atop a stalagmite, told Oili they neared the stoat's home.

A light from ahead grew stronger, smoothing out their steps. The cave narrowed and became drier and warmer. The passage was soon too small for horses. Finn and Oili reluctantly left them behind, Oili promising to return as soon as possible. They crawled on knees and hands toward the light, following Neva as she flitted from rock to rock.

A bend in the passage brought them to a large cavern. They stood with ample space above their heads. Oili felt she could breathe again. The light of two dozen candles revealed a kitchen, its wood shelves filled with jars of dried berries, burlap bags of oats, baskets of carrots and apples. Neva perched on a counter and ate from a plate of dead mice. A fire flickered within an oven. Oili marveled at the chimney rising from the oven into the rock. How far did the chimney travel to dispel the smoke outside this cave? Who made this place, and how?

Finn pointed to a man sitting cross-legged within a small loft. His face, narrowing at the mouth, was freckled and smooth. Oili frowned. Weren't all Keepers wizened with years, their powers earned through centuries of experience?

"You were expecting someone else," the man said, climbing down a ladder. Spry and wiry, he seemed to spring from rung to rung. "And all this time *I've* been expecting the Anima." He grinned. "You are every bit as impressive in person as I imagined. Though I doubt the feeling is mutual. I've never been one to demand awe." He laughed a high-pitched wheeze of a laugh.

Oili and Finn exchanged bewildered looks. They couldn't disagree with his point. Standing on his tippy-toes he might have come up to their nipples. He wore pants and a shirt made entirely from white ermine fur. He had bright red hair, much redder than Finn's auburn locks. Oili found him boyishly handsome with his cut jaw and shiny black eyes.

"I expected you to be more—mature looking," Oili said. "I assumed all Keepers to be, well, old."

The man gasped. "You mean to say," he said, turning to Neva, "that Neva has yet to show her human form?"

Oili gagged as a mouse tail slithered in Neva's beak. The owl shook her head.

"What did Esha teach you? The most important Keepers, and most beautiful, I may objectively add, are, of course, the Shapeshifters." He gave Oili a wink.

"Who's Esha?"

Again, the man turned to Neva. "Is she still going by Crow? That name is downright confusing for a Keeper. There was a crow Shapeshifter. A nice Alidiman lady named Rita."

"She goes by Crow precisely because of Rita." Neva's voice, barely loud enough to hear, startled Finn. Oili had heard her speak many times now, yet seeing her morph left both her and Finn blinking with mouths open. The snowy owl had transformed into a strikingly beautiful woman. With the palest skin Oili had ever seen, and white hair longer and more unruly than even Oili's own, Neva seemed to glow. Her eyelashes and eyebrows were bright white, too. Her lack of color exaggerated the gold and black of her owl eyes.

"Stian here," Neva continued in the whisper, "likes to hold the Shapeshifters above the other Keepers because we are blood-bonded to the Anima. Truth have it, he but envies their free will in matters of human conflict."

Stian's bemused expression melted downward. With his jovial persona deflated, he appeared much older. The two Shapeshifters looked at each other with an understanding beyond Oili's own.

"It's—true," Stian said at last, moving to the oven. He pulled out a bread loaf. "I don't always agree with the Task and what it asks of Shapeshifters. Nearly a third of the northern Shapeshifters have died for the Task. And Shapeshifters aren't like Salvagers, or even the Anima, for that matter. Once a Shapeshifter dies, that's it. They're *dead*-dead. There's no coming back for our kind."

Neva and Stian bowed their heads in honor of their losses.

"Let's slow down," Neva whispered. "There's no need to lay millennia of guilt upon our newest Anima. After all, she didn't ask to be our leader."

"Of course, of course," Stian said. He set the bread on a low table made of stone and motioned for them to sit.

Rocks, carved and smoothed into seats, were arranged around the table as if he often entertained guests. The room felt worlds away from the passage it took to find it. Warmed by the oven, with all the modern arrangements of a house back in Drauhöir, they would have thought themselves home if it weren't for the lack of windows and the stalactites reaching down from the giant arch of a ceiling.

"Thank you," Oili said, accepting a slice of steaming bread from Stian.

Finn offered his gratitude as well and all but inhaled a slice heavy with butter and jam. Stian set another piece in front of Finn before he could ask for it.

"Our horses—" Finn said.

"Have been fed and watered," Stian finished.

Finn raised an eyebrow.

"I have helpers," Stian said.

Oili shifted on her stone stool. Helpers? She spread butter on the bread and willed away her mistrust. Stian served bowls of stew, and Neva watched them eat. Oili could tell she had much to say.

"Now," Stian said, returning to the table after washing the dishes. "With all creatures fed and watered, let's discuss the Task."

"Keepers or no," Neva began, "the odds look good for the humans of Grahimland, should we succeed in forging an alliance against the Flüschen."

Oili wondered whom Neva meant by *we.* "Who exactly are the Keepers?" she asked. "The Shapeshifters and Salvagers?"

"And Mages working for Order," Stian said. "Humans trained in Florávo. That is, plant magic."

"Like the witch?" Finn asked.

Oili wondered if Stian and Neva could hear the disdain in his voice. She remembered Finn telling her about the vial around the Crow's neck—how it had saved the Crow's life when Finn had tried to kill her.

"The Crow is not your common witch, but an extraordinary Mage," Neva said. "But one does not need to have Keeper blood to practice Florávo, though it certainly makes for potent magic."

"Essentially, dear Anima, you have powerful allies ready to assist in your Task," Stian said. "You were to have the baby here, but circumstances have changed. The war between Nunlu and Grahimland has begun sooner than we had anticipated. Moons sooner. We cannot hide your pregnancy from the people—though this may be to our advantage, as recent knowledge reveals the Prince of Nunlu has his own lovechild in the womb of a mistress, and you two may find peace in your commonality."

Oili sat up straight—a lovechild? Like the one growing within her? What were the chances? Oh merciful gods! How perfect. She smiled at Finn. He remained stoic in the seat next to her. His ordeal with the Crow had evidently left him mistrusting of all Keepers. She turned back to Stian, bracing for whatever he had planned.

"So what next?" she and Finn asked at the same time.

"Well you, Anima, will stop this war," Stian said. "The Gelid Seaterras have yet to witness your powers, but when they do, you will be the bridge unifying the peoples. To do this, you will need to arrive to both armies in full expression."

"Full expression?"

"Rest tonight," Neva whispered. "Tomorrow, you will see what we mean."

The next morning they rode into the dawn, greeting the sun with bodies fully fed and rested. The horses forged through the snow with renewed energy. Stian rode on Oili's horse, clinging to her like a child. Her baby seemed to like his touch and kicked at his hands wrapped near her bellybutton. Neva rode behind Stian in her owl form. Finn laughed at the sight of it—Oili, Stian, and the owl, riding one behind the other. It was the first laugh he'd had since the forests; Oili relished its cascading sound.

They reached a knoll overlooking Grahimland's eastern shores. Oili wondered why they had traveled in the opposite direction of the Nunlu army.

"Stop here," Stian said.

They pulled the horses to a halt.

"There," he said, pointing to a thin peninsula below. "You will find a Keeper—an emblem, really, of your power. But you will have to go solo. We cannot be present, or he will not come. He is an ornery one, that Stor. Mistrusting even of his own kind. He answers to the Anima alone."

Oili quieted the voice questioning if this was but a ploy to have her killed, to have her lover, their baby, killed. How did she know these Shapeshifters didn't work for the mainland Flüschen? The Crow could have been in this all along, ushering her to some icy death. It seemed every step forward as the Anima would be an overcoming of doubt.

Finn helped her off the horse and asked for a private word. "Oili, please." The white puffs of his breath accentuated his whisper. "This is madness!"

"What is this war but madness? We have no other choice but to trust the Keepers."

Finn glowered, unconvinced, but consented. Oili began down the knoll, to the white finger of land pointing into an infinite horizon of water. The ground leveled, and she continued over icy rocks and snow. Walruses with tusks as long as her forearm balked at her appearance. She assured them of her neutrality: this wasn't a hunt for food. The land turned opulent, and she realized with a startle that she traversed frozen water. The ice thinned, revealing the sea moving back and forth below her feet. She stopped and waited.

The ice creaked and cracked. When she turned around, the great white bear stood behind her. On his hind legs he was easily double Oili's height. He roared. Oili dropped to her knees and pleaded with the polar bear for her life.

*Stand, Anima,* Stor said, returning to all fours. *You will never grovel again. Not in my presence, nor that of any other.*

Oili pushed herself back to her feet with effort. Had her child doubled in size overnight? She placed a hand on her womb and faced the bear. *I am told you will help me,* she said.

Stor approached Oili, each step a shiver down the ice. His black eyes, glinting with sunlight refracting off the ice, sized Oili up. *I will,* he said. *I am your natural born ally, as the blood-bond demands of all Shapeshifters.*

Neva floated down to them and perched on Oili's shoulder. Her presence brought Oili confidence.

*I will also be your legs,* Stor continued, *for I am much faster than you, and we do not have time to spare.* He lowered himself to the ground.

Oili grasped fistfuls of fur to climb onto the bear's back. They took off toward the knoll where the others waited. The horses whinnied and pranced. Oili and the bear kept their distance. She called out words of assurance to the horses, but the poor beasts fought against the sheer instinct to bolt. The sight of Oili and his unborn child, riding atop the formidable polar bear, drained the blood from Finn's face.

Oili wished to console her lover, but the impending war demanded haste. "To the Nunlu camp," she yelled.

Stor charged across the white expanse, his feet flying with knowledge of ice and snow no horse could ever possess. This was his land. His body was of this place. The horses and their riders quickly disappeared behind them as they sprinted for the western shores.

And this was how the Tuttuán first saw Oili, Princess of Grahimland, seventh Anima of the earth: seven moons pregnant, snow owl upon her shoulder, white wolf-skin coat fluttering in a wind created by the speed of a polar bear running at full capacity. It mattered not that they had been struck dumb by her surreal appearance; they had no time, wits or no, to gather weapons before she was past the camp borders, charging through guards, yurts, and men warming by fires.

She found the Kan and Prince in the camp's innermost and largest yurt. The bear managed to squeeze through the yurt's door with Oili still atop his back. The roasted duck leg in the Prince's hand fell to the floor. Camp whores screamed and ran away. The Kan nearly choked on a bite. He coughed and coughed. The servants stood gaping, too stupefied to pat their ruler's back. His face turned a violent shade of blue.

Stor lowered, and Oili slipped down to her feet. She stood next to the bear, drawing courage from her hand on his side. The Kan, having regained his breath but not his composure, gawked at the woman before him.

"I am Oili, daughter of your enemy," she began. "I have come to bring peace between your people and my own."

Over the course of three days, all the while her father's army waiting for war on the fields, Oili and the dynasty of Nunlu created a new treaty. Stian had served as mediator when he and Finn arrived shortly after. Oili apologized for shaming the Kan in her pregnancy, explaining that she had conceived before the marriage had been arranged. The fact the Prince also had a lovechild did prove to be advantageous, as Stian had presumed.

Oili emphasized the fact that her pregnancy had been part of a larger plan for her to become Anima. She also emphasized their common cause, and they agreed to a condition similar to those previously wrought around the arranged marriage: they would unite to fight against the Flüschen. Though in this treaty, Nunlu would remain autonomous from Grahimland, and they would reclaim all lands north of the Eldis Forest, namely the Svetór Lava Fields. They would each live as their own country, divided by culture and land, bound by their shared desire to defeat the Flüschen hailing from the mainland.

Her father had wished for unity. His vision had been two seaterras, one country. He had sold his daughter for this dream. But now his daughter was dead. He would have to face Oili the Anima and the terms she had created for the sake of her unborn child. Oili knew her father, and she knew his dream would not die as easily as her old self had.

Finn agreed to meet Oili in Drauhöir, for Oili still feared her father would kill him. They embraced, her belly, their child, a membrane between them. She mounted Stor, alongside Neva and Stian, and waved goodbye to her lover and the armies of Nunlu.

Smoke from dozens of fires announced the army camp's presence long before Oili could see any tents or people. It settled as a haze on the plains, obscuring the vision of horizon and sky. Stor moved slightly slower in this snowless country. Oili feared the bear would overheat. Snows would come to the entire seaterra within the moon, but for now the fields remained covered in moss.

The guards sounded the horns at the sight of Oili trotting across the plains toward them. A row of men with longbows formed along the camp's border. Another row of men dropped to their knees in front of them and arranged their circular shields into a barrier. Oili's father surfaced behind the protective force.

He rode atop a great black stallion, a horse Oili remembered being wild and fierce, unfitted to ride when she had last seen him in the stalls. Her father, the largest man in Grahimland by all accounts, appeared to be taller than even the tents. He wore his mink fur coat: the one Oili would sometimes take naps upon as a little girl. His long sword hung from his side, resting against the stallion's flank, and in his right hand he wielded his favored weapon, the axe.

Whereas she took the Nunlu army by surprise, her father's army watched her approach for a long stretch of field. Even with the smoke obscuring their view, the men soon recognized their princess. They visibly softened; arrows drooped downward, and gaps grew in the barrier of shields. Stor sauntered forward. Soon the entire army crowded along the camp's border. Dressed for war, weapons in hand, they stared at the bear, Oili with the owl, and the strange little man riding behind her.

Fires crackled and crows screeched, and women whispered in the tents. Oili only had eyes for her father. She wondered if it was horror, relief, or disbelief knitting his eyebrows together. She wondered if his shoulders rounded in a way only a daughter would notice because he felt betrayed or because his prayers had been answered.

"Father," she said, holding his gaze. She looked to the men. "My people. I come to you as the Anima reborn."

They didn't move. The whispers in tents quieted. She knew the word *Anima* was meaningless for now. How could she tell them all that she had experienced, all that she was? How could she convince her father that there was an even greater plan than the one he had created when he vowed to marry her off?

No words would do. She needed to show them. Was this her idea or one Neva whispered? Closing her eyes, Oili yelled for them to come. She cried out louder than her voice magnified ten times. No human could hear her yelling, but the ones she needed to hear heard, and the smoke shifted behind her as they answered her call.

Crows by the hundreds flew out of the smoke. They moved in concert, a black cloud overcoming the white haze. Oili's hair whooshed forward as they rushed past her. She asked them to fly over the camp, as low as they dared. Most of the men screamed and turned their heads away. A few lifted their faces to the murder flowing over them. The feathers tickled their foreheads and cheeks.

The crows danced in the smoke above the camp, following Oili's requests to dive down, float east, dart west. All stood mesmerized, her father included. She thanked the crows for their help, and they scattered, flying away in all directions. With the skies now quieted, Oili eased herself off the bear. She approached the barrier. A few gaps in the shields reformed, but more than one parting remained.

Oili watched her father's eyes find her belly. His face remained a grooved tablet, the language of his furrowed forehead indiscernible. When she reached his horse, he jumped off. The ground trembled, or had her legs gone weak? Neva's talons squeezed her shoulder, and Oili stood as tall as she could.

He tapped his axe's head on her belly. "And whose child is this?" The boom of his voice brought Oili to the halls of their home and the way she could hear him calling for her to come from the opposite corner of the Great House.

"Finn Holt, guard of your northeast tower."

He grunted, the singular nod of his head telling Oili he had already known as much.

Everyone watched on, a collective inhale held among the hundreds gathered.

"May I have a private word?" she asked.

He flipped the axe's handle in his hand again and again. He looked from her eyes to her belly to the sky, then back to her eyes. He slipped his axe into his belt and swiveled away from her.

"I'll need all the mead in this camp," he barked to a boy of maybe eleven. "Everyone remain in their stations." When the boy, gaping at Oili, didn't move, her father bellowed, "Now."

Oili moved to follow him but stopped short when a voice asked her to wait. She walked past the barrier again, returning to the bear.

*I will go back to my home now,* Stor said.

Oili felt compelled to wrap her arms around the bear's neck. *Thank you,* she said.

*Anything for the Anima,* Stor answered. *Give the command, and I will be there.* He turned from her and ran back north. All eyes followed him as his white mass faded into the smoke.

Outside the tent, Oili paused. She swiveled around to face Stian.

"I think it's best if you wait here," she said. "I'll call you if things—falter."

Neva still perched upon Oili's shoulder. Stian frowned up at the owl. "But Neva gets to go?"

Oili ran a hand down her feathers. "She's part of my presence as the Anima. You are a stranger to my father, and unless you want to morph—"

"No," Stian said, looking sideways at the men around them. Her father's soldiers pretended not to be eavesdropping. They busied themselves with sharpening blades and polishing scabbards. "Your kind has little love for the ermine," he whispered. "I will wait here."

Oili ducked into the tent. The boy was pouring mead into two drinking horns. King Gunnar sat on his war throne. It was lighter than his throne in the Great House, made of birch rather than oak. A wolf-skin draped over the back. He wore his leather armor with the bear trimming. His beard and long hair had faint gray streaks. Did he have those streaks the last time she saw him? She hadn't noticed them if he did.

He watched her approach with a flat expression. Dirt smeared with his black war paint, causing the steel blue of his eyes to pop against the dark skin. She sat in the chair opposing him and accepted the drinking horn from the boy.

"Leave us," Gunnar said. The boy bowed his head quickly and all but ran from the tent. Gunnar drank deep from his horn. He wiped the mead from his beard with the back of his huge hand. "You brought me shame." Though his voice still boomed, Oili thought she heard a quiver of sadness beneath the baritone.

She met his stare with a lifted chin. "I am sorry."

He grunted and took another drink of mead. She knew to let him speak. She had sat in on most of his courts as a child and learned her father preferred to drive the conversation. If one tried to take the reins from him, he would become less willing to hear.

"Now we go the wrong direction. The Flüschen could arrive tomorrow and take back our lands." He scowled at her womb. "Your insolence has ruined everything."

Oili allowed him to indulge in this belief for a moment. She had only seen him this mad once before—when the whaling crew returned with news of her mother's drowning. He refilled his horn with mead, the actions slow and calm. Were he not furious, he would be moving with the robust gestures of a man his size. His expressionless face also told her he was seething.

She took a sip of the mead and set the horn back in its stand. "What if I told you the alliance still stood?"

He guffawed. "And you are wearing a pumpkin around your waist?"

Her hand found her belly. "The Nunlu prince also has a lovechild."

"How could you possibly know this?"

"I am the Anima reborn, father. You saw the crows. The gods blessed me with powers. I went to the Kan and reformed the treaty."

Gunnar frowned as he considered these words. He set his horn down and placed his chin in a hand. She waited as he fingered his beard, thinking. Beyond the tent's walls, the soldiers talked and joked. A pair of men discussed the way the crows had washed over them.

"I saw the crows," he said at last. "Tell me more of the Anima."

Oili explained about the mushroom, the Crow and all she taught her, and the last few days in the north. The boy returned with plates of roasted goat and a dish of honeyed apples and onions. They ate in silence.

Gunnar used a sliver of bone to pick his teeth. "So the Nunlu will fight with us against the Flüschen, and these Keepers will as well, should we need them."

"Correct. But father." She paused, breathing out the fear. This was the moment she had dreaded most since arriving. "There will be no union. Nunlu will remain autonomous and will share the Svetór Lava Fields with our hunters. We will fight with a common cause, but remain divided by culture and land."

Gunnar threw the bone sliver across the tent. "What?" he roared.

Men near the tent quieted. Oili could hear Stian pacing outside the door. She stayed straight in her spine.

"The Eldis Forest will be ours, and Nunlu theirs, and the lava fields a shared territory. This is what is best for the Order."

Even with all the dirt and paint, she could tell her father's face turned red. His breathing grew short and loud. She took courage in his anger. He may come around after all.

"You—you sabotaged my life's work. Your—*whoring* has ruined it all."

Oili didn't flinch. He panted from the outburst.

"It was love, not lust," she said, her voice cool and steady. "I am my own woman, father. My body belongs to me. You sold me for your own agenda—did you ever consider that?" She could see him struggle against the words. They were foreign, even to the Oili she had been before becoming the Anima.

His beard swayed as he shook his head. "You are a princess, Oili. You belong to the Kingdom."

"I am the Anima, father." Neva fluttered her wings. "This treaty will bring peace to our people and freedom to the land. Is that not the essence of your life's work?"

Gunnar's knuckles were white from his grip on the horn. His face had turned nearly purple.

*Prepare to summon the Keepers,* Oili said to Neva.

The owl took off, her wings shining like sun on snow. Gunnar watched her fly from the tent. Oili observed him with a hand on her short sword. When Gunnar turned back to face her, Stian slipped into the tent. He crawled silently in the cover of his ermine form, his fur still dark with autumn. He held a knife between his teeth.

*Wait,* she told him.

He stopped behind Gunnar. Her father's face had turned back to a dirty white. He looked both angry and exhausted.

"You have shamed me," he said again. The sorrow was unmistakable this time.

She bowed her head and apologized again. "Tell them it was your idea," she said, lifting her face back up. "When the Nunlu arrive, greet them. Tell your soldiers the treaty was your idea. But either way, this is the only way forward. This is the way to peace."

"*Your* way to peace." He brought his chin back to his hand and ran his fingers around his lips.

The soldiers laughed, the bonfires crackled. Stian stood on his hind legs behind her father, his little black eyes glinting.

Gunnar spoke at last. "But gods damn it to Oblivion, it's either be slaves to the Flüschen forever or accept these new terms. I'd rather be defeated by my daughter than a mainlander." His eyes found her womb again, though the glare seemed less intense. "What of you? Of this lovechild?"

"After the war, we will leave the courts. You will be rid of the shame."

"This might not be necessary," he mumbled.

Stian slipped back out the tent, as quiet as he had come in.

☾

Oili bore a baby girl a moon before the war. Though still tender from the birth, she attacked alongside her father's men when the Flüschen breached their shores. Having no son of his own until last winter, her father had trained Oili in the long sword since she was old enough to walk. Her strength as the Anima gave a brutal force to this skill her body had already owned.

Neva remained on Oili's shoulder throughout the battle, ready to call upon the Shapeshifters should the Gelid Alliance faltered. Following three days of battle, with the ground churned into a mess of blood and muddy snow, the Gelid Alliance managed to defeat the Flüschen without the help of any Keepers. The Flüschen, wounded but not obliterated, rowed their warships back to northern Lacuserra with the memory of the Anima.

The Nunlu armies returned home, and the Gelid Seaterras settled into an unfamiliar peace. King Gunnar continued to rule Grahimland. He told Oili that she, Finn, and baby Syvel could stay in the Great House; Oili had cleaned him of shame with her prowess in war. Shame or no, Oili had plans of her own.

Stian and Neva had left Drauhöir shortly after the battle was won. They promised to be ready when the Anima needed her Shapeshifters again, an oath Oili considered unnecessary—she had fulfilled her Task at last. She and Finn took their daughter south, to the coastal village of Verkun. They bought a plot of land and a cobblestone cottage surrounded by evergreen and birch trees. Oili learned how to bake crisps with golden oats and how to make wine with plants ranging from nettle to elderflower. Goats, chickens, and pigs roamed in a pasture next to a large garden.

She was mashing apples for mead when a familiar figure came lumbering up the dirt path. As Oili watched the Crow approach out the window, dread twisted her stomach. She hadn't seen the Salvager since she and Finn had left for Stian's cave. The Crow's walking stick, its top carved into the form of her namesake, clunked against the stepping-stones.

Oili washed her hands and picked Syvel up from her crib, setting the one-year-old upon her hip. Her little feet rested against the swell of Oili's second child. When Oili opened the door, the Crow had made it to the front steps.

"Crow," Oili said. "Come in, come in."

She opened the door wide, and the Crow swept inside. Her black coat swished across the ground. It was a good thing Finn had gone hunting for the day. The Crow took a seat, resting her staff across her lap. Oili set Syvel back in her crib and prepared moss tea. She handed the Crow a cup.

"To a new era," Oili said, smiling.

The Crow clinked her cup. "Yes, the new era." She took a sip and leaned back in the chair. "The reason I have come."

Oili frowned. "I thought I was reason enough. We, I should say." Syvel stood in her cradle, grabbing the side. With puffs of red hair and dark blue eyes, she was the equal balance of Finn and Oili—Oili the human that was. Syvel had been born without any physical attributes of the Anima.

"I came as soon as I was able. Your decision to leave the court, it's not part of the Task."

Oili's frown grew deeper. "The Task has been completed. We have defeated the Flüschen."

Phlegm in the Crow's throat rattled as she laughed. "Far from it. You have only driven them away. The Task asks for all Disorder to be vanquished. You have abated, not vanquished, Disorder."

Syvel began to whine. Oili stood and lifted her out of her cradle. She sat back down with Syvel on her lap.

"You were supposed to stay on the court," the Crow continued. "Defending Grahimland was only the beginning of the Task. You were to bring all three kingdoms of Lacuserra under Order." The Crow set a gnarled hand on Oili's thigh. "The Keepers of Lacuserra are ready. Well-practiced Mages have gathered at a Haven in Nafáit, trained by the mother of Florávo herself. The Shapeshifters stand by, as always. The time is *now,* Oili." She squeezed Oili's thigh. "The plans are set for success."

Oili shifted Syvel away from the Crow. "These are your plans. Not mine."

The Crow coughed again. She looked older than Oili remembered, more wrinkled and frail. Oili glanced at the wall behind the Crow, where her battle shield hung. It had become a decoration, a commemoration. And it would stay this way.

"Unlike Shapeshifters, my life is my own. Is it really fair to command them to their deaths unwillingly? If they truly care for this Task, why do they need me to fight? Why do any of the Keepers? I have done my part, Crow. I cannot go marching back into war. I have a child and another coming, unless you haven't noticed."

"Do not mock me," the Crow said. The opaque of her eyes drew back. Oili startled at their unnaturally bright glare. "I may be dying, but I still can see."

"Dying?" Oili whispered.

"Salvagers are perennial, not immortal. Another will be born upon my death." The Crow closed her eyes and breathed loud and heavy. "Remember the elderberry harvest, when I told you—"

"I'd be torn," Oili said. "Very much so."

"But you seem to have forgotten the blessing and burden part."

Syvel pulled on Oili's dress, and Oili let her breastfeed. Oili winced as Syvel's new teeth grazed her nipple. "Trust me, I know blessing and burden," Oili said.

"Then it is as I feared. Seeing is one thing, but being with it is another." The Crow stood and brought her walking staff upright. "I warned Laurel of this when she told me to give the mushroom to you. She insisted your privileged position as princess would give the Task unprecedented leverage. I said privilege tends to blind and bind." She turned and lumbered to the door. "Should you change your mind, Neva will be there to hear you."

"Crow," Oili said. "There will be more Animas."

The Salvager nodded, her face a carving of disenchantment. Oili watched her lumber down the path and out of sight.

The Crow's face and words would haunt Oili for the rest of her days. It was always at night, in dreams and nightmares. Her days were filled with her four children running through the garden and pasture, laughing and crying. She and Finn rarely talked about the Keepers or the war. All around Oili could still hear the murmured words of her animal kin; their voices were like the white noise of the ocean just beyond the garden's southern border.

Sometimes Oili caught glimmers of Neva when she flew between branches. Once, a moon or two after the Crow had left, she had nearly called out to Neva, wishing only to feel the owl's talons again on her shoulder. Yet she knew better. Neva belonged to the Anima, to a lifetime ago. And so, like all white noise, Neva became part of the backdrop of Oili's life.

The kids had grown, wed, and moved away to begin families of their own. She and Finn's hair had turned white, and their house grew heavy with dust and mildew. They slept outside more often than not. It was such a night, beneath the stars, with her head resting upon Finn's chest rising and falling, rising and falling. She slipped deeper and deeper into dreams. When she murmured her last words, Neva, a white shadow above, heard what Oili said and knew life existed in a calm before the storm.

# ERIE

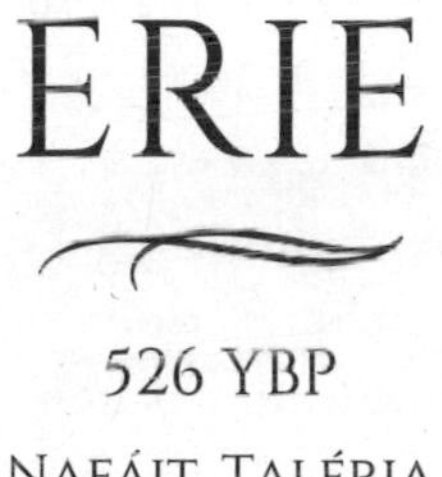

526 YBP

NAFÁIT, TALÉRIA

Erie's mother slipped one more eyebright into her braid. "You look divine," she said, squeezing Erie's shoulders. "He's the luckiest man in all of Taléria."

Erie blushed. Her mother was always telling her she was beautiful. But divine? It sounded blasphemous. Though when her mother held up a mirror, Erie saw what she had meant. Between the braid crown, the flowers, and her grandmother's satin wedding dress, she looked like a different person. Only the Divines could transform a pig farmer's daughter into a woman resembling a Desnordian princess.

Once the initial shock subsided, she recognized the young woman as her usual self. Her bright red hair still frizzed a bit out of the braid. The summer had left her cheeks pink, and the blue of her eyes popped against the splattering of freckles covering her face. She grinned at the reflection.

Her mother handed her the bouquet of angelica and heather. "It's time," she said, and she took her daughter by the elbow.

They walked out of the shed and into the honeyed light of early autumn. Vines crawling up the farm's cobblestoned fence had turned burnt orange in the last week. The entire world seemed to approve of this marriage, from the rainbow of foliage to the clear blue sky above. The dress trailed behind them as their feet crunched through the fallen leaves.

Erie could smell the ham cooking. Her father had butchered three pigs for the occasion: a small fortune for their family. Nonetheless, the dowry was a modest one, but Aodhan, son of a nobleman, said he didn't expect, nor want, a large gift from her father. His family was among the wealthiest in town, which was exactly why Erie had rejected him the first six times he had asked for her hand. When he would ask why not, she would point to the dirt on the hem of her skirt or the leaves stuck in the tangles of her hair.

He waited with his back to her beneath a yew tree. Erie's brothers, sister, and father stood in a circle and watched her approach. Aodhan's family had refused to attend. The priestess, standing in the middle of the circle, wore a dress the color of moss and an emerald circlet. Erie beamed at her family, dressed in their finest clothes. They smiled in return and laughed as Aodhan fidgeted with anticipation.

When they reached the circle, Erie's mother kissed her on both cheeks and went to stand next to Erie's father. Erie took Aodhan's hand, and he turned to see her. He appeared as stunned as she had felt looking in the mirror.

She was no longer the girl who had thrown mud balls at him when he would call her speckle face. Growing up in the village of Nafáit, they had known each other since they were toddlers. The seventh time he asked for her hand, he had sat her down and explained that he wanted to marry someone funny and kind and hardworking. Someone real, unlike the noblewomen his father wished him to wed. She had hesitated for another moon, but at last, at the vernal festival, she had told him yes.

He smiled now as he had then. Creases fanned out from his green eyes and the dimples of his cheeks and chin deepened. He wore a brown tunic and a simple wreath made of a rowan branch. A cluster of red berries nestled into his golden curls. The single telling of his nobility was his belt, ornate with gold symbols of the Divines. Erie figured that was the only thing of his family's riches he would keep following this marriage.

The priestess gestured for them to join her, and Erie and Aodhan walked into the center. She greeted them with kisses on each cheek. "Today we gather before the Four to wed the lives of Erie Dunn and Aodhan Crovan."

Erie felt Aodhan flinch at his surname. She squeezed his hand. The priestess looked up to the yew tree's branches, and all those gathered did the same.

"Water, Earth, Fire, Air, bless these souls in their union. May they never know thirst. May they always have food to share. May they be warm throughout each season. May they breathe easy in all their days. By the grace of the Four Divines, may their lives, now twined as root and soil, be blessed with abundance and health."

The priestess untied the strip of green linen from her waist. She wrapped the fabric around Eric and Aodhan's wrists, binding them together. "As the Four merge together to bring life to this good earth, so may your union. I now pronounce you, Aodhan and Erie, yoked together in this life, as with the last and the next."

Aodhan leaned in and kissed her like he had at the midsummer festival. His lips tasted of the mint growing wild along the river. She kissed him back, feeling as if she was watching from the branches above. This man, her childhood crush, the boy whom she had figured would always be looking down on her from his family estate upon Knockeye Hill, was now her husband. Her family burst out in cheers and laughter. They clapped and sang the yoking song as they hopped around the circle.

The priestess unthreaded the fabric and tied it around Erie's waist. They walked to the farm's front end, where the roasted pigs sat upon a table with apples in their mouths. Nearly the entire village waited at the tables set out across the yard. They greeted the bride and groom with hugs and congratulations. Erie drifted from one person to the next. She laughed and cried with her neighbors.

The blacksmith gave them a shovel, and the farmer next door set a jug of cider on the blessing table. Erie's best friend tied a homemade wool shawl around Erie's shoulders. Aodhan laughed with the peasant boys he had befriended despite his father's commands not to fraternize with the lower-downs. They clinked mugs of ale and sang bar songs about virgins.

Erie drank the ale and ate the pig and danced to the fiddles and flutes. She stained the train of her dress with the dirt turned up by their stomping feet. Aodhan spun her round and round and brought her close in his arms. They whirled like this late into the night, intoxicated by ale and love—and oblivious to the pair of men glowering beyond the light of the bonfire.

Aodhan secured the strap holding the burlap tarp over their trunks while Erie's father double-checked the mules' harnesses. The full moon alone allowed them to see. Erie and her mother stood off to the side, scanning the surrounding forest for the gleam of eyes. No one spoke. An unseen animal darted through the undergrowth. Goose pimples flushed down Erie's limbs, and she nearly screamed.

"It all looks good," Aodhan whispered. He looked as pale as a maggot.

Erie fought back the desire to wail and sob. She cried silently as she hugged her father goodbye. Her mother, blue eyes glistening, held Erie as close as Erie's swollen womb allowed.

"We will come visit," she said into Erie's ears. "I promise."

Aodhan couldn't watch. He stepped onto the cart's seat and stared straight ahead. Erie's father patted his thigh. He, too, was crying.

Aodhan managed to meet his eyes. "I'm sorry," he said.

Erie and her parents cowered at the loudness of his words. She whipped her head around but still saw no sign of onlookers. No one said anything in reply. They had told him over and over it wasn't his fault.

Her father helped her up onto the cart. She felt the baby push against her ribs as if she or he wanted to stay as well. "Well, goodbye then," Erie whispered.

Aodhan slapped the reins against the mules' haunches, and they took off with a stutter. Her parents waved, and Erie waved back until they and the farm shrank into the shadows. She and Aodhan rode in silence through midnight and into dawn. The western road led through forest. Erie kept the shovel in her lap in case anyone attacked. Though no weapon, the shovel at least felt heavy on her legs.

As sunlight grew, Erie saw the daffodils of spring lining the road. Dew sparkled on the flower's leaves. Moss grew across the forest floor and up the tree trunks. The world gleamed around them, and Erie found herself smiling despite it all. Aodhan still frowned at the road. Black circles and bloodshot eyes aged him ten years.

She ran a hand through his curls. "Please, love. We'll be okay."

His shoulders softened, but he continued to look ahead with a frown. "I should have known."

She had heard this a dozen times now and each time her reply was the same. "He was your own father. How could one even imagine?" She stopped herself. What good would it do to remind him of his father's violence? She touched where the knife had been pushed against her throat. They had been given less than a fortnight to leave town.

"It's a fresh start," she said, lifting the tone of her voice. "Look around, love. The Four are with us, blessing this beginning with their beauty."

He glanced at the forest. When he continued to brood in silence, Erie felt her temper flare. Her mother had called her kissed by Fire since she was a little girl. *Water be with you,* she'd say when Erie would throw a tantrum.

Erie gave Aodhan a stern expression. "Love, this is our situation now. We can either make the most of it or be miserable in each other's company."

At first his forehead furrowed deeper, and Erie feared she had said this too soon. But then he sighed. "You're right. It's just, your parents, I feel—"

"Stop," Erie groaned. "We will see them again. People marry and move to new towns all the time."

Aodhan raised his eyebrows. "What people?"

"People," she said, flinging a hand. "Láidun is supposed to be full of opportunities Nafáit doesn't have. Who knows? Maybe you'll become a nobleman with your own two hands. Heritage be damned."

This made Aodhan smile. She hadn't seen him smile since the night his father and brother had threatened their unborn child's life. She kissed his cheek.

"A fresh start," Aodhan echoed. He flicked the reins, and the mules trotted a little quicker.

☾

The summer came later in Nudom than it did in Taléria. The lands even further north were said to be covered in ice all year long. Erie didn't care to see if this was true or not. She pined for the vibrant ferns and mosses of Nafáit. Midsummer had come and gone, and yet the hills surrounding their new town rolled away in a pale green threaded with yellow. She felt as if she lived in either fall or spring, but never summer.

She helped Weylyn into his wool coat. He wriggled his little arms into the sleeve, insisting he could do it alone. Though he had his father's blond hair, he, too, had been kissed by Fire. He fumbled with the buttons. He was small for a three-year-old, and his little fingers made a task as simple as fastening a button troublesome.

The doctor ensured Erie he would grow to be an average-sized man, if not tall like his father. She had been malnourished during the last trimester and for that first year here in Láidun. Weylyn had sucked her dry and begged for more. Aodhan had found steady work with the town's logging company the winter after they arrived, and not a moment too soon.

Erie placed ten coppers from their coin box into her leather purse. When she secured the box back beneath the floorboard, she thanked the Divines for how heavy it felt in her hands. She put on her cloak and picked up the basket.

Weylyn reached up for the door handle. She helped him turn the knob, and they walked out holding hands. A pair of men trotted past on horses. They tilted their straw hats in greeting. Erie and Weylyn walked on the grass path running alongside the road, stepping around the horse and pig manure littering the way.

Most neighbors said good morning in Desnordian. Some, though, would see Erie's red hair and say their hellos in Talérian. As a child, Erie had hated the Desnordian lessons her mother had built into their homeschooling. *It's the language of the crown,* her mother would say. Now, living in a Desnordian protectorate, Erie felt only gratitude for her mother's persistence.

Weylyn stopped to pet a dog. Farmers walked by with bundles of wheat upon their backs. The second wheat harvest of the year had begun last week. Erie wondered what other new crops awaited at the market. She tugged on Weylyn's arm, and they followed the farmers into the town square.

A litter of piglets squealed as they ran across the road. Weylyn made to run after them but Erie said no. She remembered being a little girl, helping her father clean out the piglet pen. Once he had let her keep a piglet as a pet. She had named him Berry, and he had slept with her until he grew too big for both bed and house. When her father had butchered Berry the following winter, Erie had cried and cried.

*The only difference between that pig and the others,* her father had said, *was a name.*

Weylyn threatened to break down into one of his screaming fits. Erie guided him to the apple vendor. She bought a dozen and gave him one. He munched on the snack, content for the time being. She continued to a vegetable stand and further filled her basket with carrots, turnips, cabbage, and parsnips. A new vendor had set up shop between the woman selling wooden bowls and a man selling pheasants. Erie stopped to view the rows of mushrooms the stranger had set out on her stand.

The seller was neither Desnordian nor Talérian, but Tuttuán or Nukopan. Erie had a hard time telling between the two, just as it was hard to tell the difference between a Tal and a Des on looks alone. She had only spoken with a couple of the Taigas natives in the three years they had called Nudom home. Most of the surviving natives either lived in the Ollaoise Forest or the seaterras and islands north of the mainland.

The woman wore a brilliant blue dress. It cut low in the front and hugged tight around her midriff. The fashion was more typical in Taléria. Desnordian dresses, made with plain brown fabric that came up to the neck and fell loose in the bodice, were the standard in Nudom. Erie would only wear her Talérian dresses at home. This woman, though, seemed oblivious to the eyes lingering on her cleavage.

The women of Láidun glared at the mushroom vendor. Erie almost wanted to apologize to the stranger for her neighbors' behavior. They, too, had treated Erie and Aodhan with contempt until Erie had enough money to buy a Desnordian dress. Erie had also stopped wearing the pendant with the Divines' symbol, a circle quartered by two lines. Though there was no legal restriction against practicing the ancient religion of Desnord, the crown had converted to the Yiúsian worship of the Power over a century ago. It was only in northern Talérian villages like Nafáit where devotion to the Divines continued to thrive.

Yet this woman, with her light brown skin and white hair, wore a pendant not unlike the one Erie kept stashed in the coin box at home. Erie startled when she noticed it resting on her large breasts. A dozen silver rings lined each of her ears. Her hair had given Erie the impression she was very old, but now she could see the woman's face was as young looking as her own. Erie inched yet closer to the table, and the woman looked up. Her eyes, so bright and blue they were almost white, caused Erie to gasp.

The woman smiled. "Hello, dear," she said in Talérian, though her accent was distinctly Taigas native.

Erie noticed a silver reindeer clipped into the woman's hair and figured she must be Nukopan. "Er, hi," she said, pulling Weylyn away from the morel he was trying to grab.

He pouted, and the woman laughed. "He seems to love mushrooms as much as I." She picked up a swamp russula and handed it to him. "Just for playing. It only tastes good when cooked."

Weylyn took the mushroom and tossed it up and down. It looked like one of the Solerian porcelain plates Erie sometimes saw noblewomen buying. "I haven't seen mushrooms at the market yet," Erie said, examining the rows of fungi. She realized she hadn't eaten any since Taléria. She identified chanterelles and lion's mane, lobster mushrooms and puffballs. Most of the mushrooms, though, were foreign to her. "They're all edible?"

The woman nodded. "Yep. A copper a pound."

A reasonable price. Cheap, even. Erie withdrew a cloth bag and filled it with a variety. The woman weighed it, and Erie gave her two coppers.

"Thank you for your business," the woman said. Her smile was bright and full, as if Erie had just given her twenty coppers. "As a token of my appreciation, please accept this small pouch of dried delicacies. They are exceedingly rare and delicious."

Erie opened the pouch to see a few withered caps. Though the cap was a dull orange now, she recognized the white dots. They were the same dots atop the bright red mushrooms that had grown in circles within the forest surrounding her father's farm. "I thought these were poisonous."

The woman *tsked*. "An old wives' tale. Why don't you just try a nibble at home tonight? Take a little bite of the smallest cap. If you don't like the taste, it was at no cost to you. If you do, they're great in soups and stews."

Erie nodded okay. Thinking back, maybe her mother hadn't said they were poisonous after all. There had been enough morels and chanterelles in the forest to satisfy their mushroom needs. She thanked the woman and continued to the baker's stand at the opposite end of the square. After buying a couple loaves, she noticed the woman packing up her mushrooms. Strange, she thought, to leave the market so soon. But then again, Erie figured she would too if people were looking daggers at her as well.

Weylyn had turned his cap into a pulpy mess by the time they reached home. She helped him clean his hands before setting him down for his midday nap. She swept the house and mended a pair of Aodhan's socks as Weylyn slept on his bed in the corner. She washed vegetables in the basin, wishing she could grow her own, as her mother had done. For now they rented from a landowner until they could afford a wattle and daub house of their own.

Erie placed the vegetables in the pantry. She set the bag of mushrooms there as well and remembered the pouch the woman had given her. *A bite of the smallest,* she had said. Erie found the pouch alone in the basket. She had almost forgotten about it.

Weylyn continued to nap. He looked like a Water baby when he slept, all peaceful and serene. Light funneled through the window above the kitchen table next to his bed. She sat and lifted her face to the sun. It felt like summer in Nafáit, sitting here in the warmth. She could almost hear the lapwings of Lacuserra singing.

She placed all the caps on the table. Three seemed like an odd number. It wasn't enough, really, to affect the flavor of a pot of soup. Erie grimaced at her greedy thought. These caps had been a gift. The first, she realized, of their time here in Nudom, and from a stranger no less. If it tasted good, she would add them to a soup alongside a handful of puffballs.

The smallest had warped into a shape like a cup. She chewed a tiny bite. The mushroom tasted neither good nor bad, but plain, like water. Or maybe it tasted like dirt. She couldn't decide. Come to think of it, everything felt a little blurry. The sunlight on her face blinded her. She lay down alongside Weylyn and closed her eyes against the spinning room. She didn't open them even as her son stirred awake.

☾

"So you came home and she was just sitting there, playing with Weylyn?" Erie asked.

Aodhan nodded. He sat in a chair adjacent to the strange bed she had woken up in. "Then the guy, Kelvan, stepped into the room holding a handful of pansies. They were *glowing* as if he held a candle, not flowers. I wasn't sure whether to grab my axe or kneel to the Divines."

As Aodhan explained what had happened, complete strangers watched their son. Strangers, Aodhan insisted, Erie needed to trust. He was trying to help her understand. She found it difficult to focus as nausea and fatigue sunk her deeper and deeper into the mattress.

"They say you'll be able to walk again on the new moon," Aodhan said.

"But the moon was new the day I went to the market." Erie paused, trying to remember everything from that day. She had cleaned the cabbage and the carrots. Felt sunlight on her face. The mushroom—it had caused the world to spin away from her.

She tried to sit up, but Aodhan set his hand on her leg.

"You can't, or shouldn't." His voice was apologetic. "The transformation asks for you to be still."

"The transformation?" Erie looked at her husband as if he, like everything else around her, were alien. "Aodhan, what's really going on? Where *are* we?"

He stood and opened the curtains of the window on the wall in front of her. Green light streamed into the room. He could touch the oak leaves from where he stood. Vines wrapped around the trees' branches.

She knew that green. It brought tears to her face. "Are we—"

"Home," he said, smiling. "By the grace of the Divines, we are home again."

Erie wiped her face dry. "But Aodhan, we shouldn't be." Panic dispelled the initial wave of homesickness. "Where's our son right now? How do you know this isn't your father's doing?" She again tried to stand and immediately threw up all over the quilt spread across her body. Water spurted from her mouth and nose, followed by bile.

The woman from the market came running into the room. She wore a red dress now, but the hair and eyes were unmistakable.

Erie sank back into the pillow. She had never felt so exhausted in all her life. Though she yearned to stand and find her child, she could only lay back down. New tears sprung forth. They were hot with shame and confusion. She felt the Fire flicker in her stomach, but the fatigue even dampened her temper.

"I'm sorry," Aodhan mumbled to the woman as he helped her strip the soiled quilt off of Erie.

"It was bound to happen sooner or later," she said, giving Aodhan a pat on his shoulder. She smiled at Erie with the same bright, wide smile she had given her at the market. "My name's Uki," she said, taking Erie's hand in her own. "Please, dear, try to relax."

Aodhan sat on the bed next to Erie. He smoothed Erie's hair down. "Our son is safe. More than safe," he said. "We all are in this Haven."

Uki stirred something in a mug. She held the mug out for Erie.

"Why should I take anything from you?"

Aodhan grimaced at the snarl in Erie's voice. Before the woman could answer, Weylyn ran into the room and over to the bed. "Uki, Uki," he cried, tugging on the woman's dress. "Look! I finally did what Aife showed me!"

Erie reached a hand toward her son. "Weylyn—"

"Mother! Watch this." He cupped one hand over the other and closed his eyes. A small light began to form within his hands, turning them pink. At first Erie thought she was imagining the light, but when her son opened his hands back up, the glow within them was undeniable. Three bramble blooms cupped in his palms radiated a white light.

Uki beamed. "Exceptional," she said, squeezing Weylyn's shoulder.

"I haven't even come close to that," Aodhan added. He, too, beamed at Weylyn.

Erie gaped wordlessly at the shining flowers within her son's hand. The light began to dim. Weylyn grinned and ran from the room. "Aife," he called out. The pattering of his feet faded away.

"Children can elicit plant energy much quicker than adults," Uki said to Aodhan. She clinked the spoon on the mug's lip and looked at Erie. "I don't blame you for mistrusting me," she said. "But the era of the Anima had come again, and when I met you at the market, I knew you were our best candidate."

Erie saw a look of pride cross over Aodhan's face. It was the same look he had just given Weylyn. She felt her own face twist even more with confusion. The expression hurt after having worn it for an hour. "Anima?"

"Yes, the Anima. You are the Anima. We've been waiting for your rebirth now for over three hundred years."

Erie rubbed at her eyes. They wanted to close. She wanted to wake from this dream. Or was it a nightmare? The only comfort she found was the familiar smell of her husband.

"Please, before you sleep, drink." Uki held out the mug again.

Aodhan took it and placed it in Erie's hands. "Drink, my love." He kept his hands wrapped around hers. "You are safe. We are all safe."

The sureness of his hands told her refusing the drink would take more effort than she had to spare. He was her husband, after all, the father of her child. A child with flowers like stars in his palms. Or had that been a dream too? The warm liquid flowed down her throat. It, like the mushroom, tasted of both water and earth.

☾

The lapwings sang their fall songs. Their chicks had flown from the nests, and now they all talked solely of preparing for the flight south. They had sung the same songs in all of Erie's autumns. But for the last two falls, Erie could understand the words of their warbling voices.

She ran with the wolves again. They wove through the forest. The bird song streamed alongside the flow of their bodies. Nearing the outlying fields of Nafáit, the wolves ran to the east, away from the presence of humans. Erie continued south. She did this, though not often and always in secret. If the Keepers or her husband knew how close she came to her parents' farm, they would be angry.

Yet she liked to watch her mother kneeling in the garden, pulling up weeds. She liked to see her father throwing buckets of scraps into the pigs' pens. They both looked like they had aged more than the five years that spanned between now and the night she and Aodhan had secreted away. Silver streaks threaded her mother's black hair. Her older brother often helped her father. That would have been Aodhan had fate unfolded as expected.

She couldn't decide which life she would have liked better. She yearned to hug her parents. She wanted them to know Weylyn—to see how he had her father's pointed nose and her mother's quirky sense of humor. But they would never know him. They would never know her, now, as the Anima.

She watched them from a shadowed recess in the forest edging the northern fence. They probably still sent letters to the address in Nudom.

Erie wondered when, if not already, they would discover she and Aodhan no longer lived there. She wondered if they grieved her as dead, or if they cursed her name and the mystery her sudden silence created. Uki insisted, though, that her existence as the Anima must be kept secret until the time came.

The time for what, exactly, remained to be revealed. For now, Erie ran with the wolves while her son was busy with his afternoon lessons. Her body, swollen with strength and pulsating with energy, demanded she enjoy it. Enjoy it she did, more than most things.

Even had Uki not forbade her from revealing herself as the Anima, Erie doubted she would have anyway. Her parents wouldn't recognize her now, what with her severe jaw, astral eyes, and large muscles. The woman—the Anima—Erie saw in the mirror was completely foreign to the bride her mother had crowned with flowers a lifetime ago.

Her parents returned inside, and Erie took off back north. Fallen oak leaves hid the path. She flew over rocks and roots. Her body knew what to do. She could release into its power, allowing it to guide her through the trunks.

When she crossed over the Haven's invisibility border, the cottage appeared. Vines, red with early fall, crawled all over the cobblestone. The stream lazed beside it, and a small waterwheel spun in the waters. Ferns grew by the hundreds along the banks. Erie hopped across the rocks leading to the front door.

Aife and Kelvan were preparing dinner in the kitchen. Kelvan was a tall man with a blond bun. He stirred the soup while Aife peeled garlic.

"Smells divine," Erie said, taking off her boots.

Aife smiled. She wore her long, brown hair on top of her head in a pile resembling a bird's nest. "We had a perfect garlic crop this year," she said.

"Is my son in the greenhouse?"

"How'd you guess?"

Erie walked down the hall leading to the cottage's greenhouse. She opened the door and a warm air, fragrant with mud and blossoms, felt wet on her face. They kept the outside trees well clear of the glass enclosure, allowing sunlight to pour in through the ceiling. She found her son with Aodhan and Camden. Standing nearly seven feet tall, Camden towered over Aodhan. His hair, as red as Erie's own, reached well past his chest. He wore two small braids on either side of the part while the rest flowed freely in waves. Like Uki, many piercings lined both of his ears.

"My love," Aodhan said, kissing her temple. "You taste like you had a nice run."

Erie smiled. "I did. How are your lessons?"

"Weylyn's doing great. I, on the other hand…" He held up the bowl, and Erie breathed in the smell of freshly mashed mint.

"You're doing great as well," Camden said in his thick Jornorgudian accent. "It's just, Weylyn is doing extraordinarily well."

Her son held the bowl with his eyes closed. Rather than being torn and broken like Aodhan's leaves, his mint remained intact. The leaves began to glow.

"Yes, extraordinary," Aodhan said. He patted his son on the back. The two looked more alike than ever. It seemed to Erie the only things her son inherited from her were his blue eyes and the Fire.

Weylyn slumped, exhausted from the effort. "There," he said. "They're ready at last."

Camden placed the leaves into a mug and poured boiling water over them. "Uki will be thankful."

"Does she have a migraine again?" Erie asked.

"They're only getting worse."

The tone of Camden's reply crept down Erie's spine. She sensed the energy darkening in the Haven lately, yet it could be the fading light of fall. Camden ducked out of the room as Weylyn and Aodhan cleaned up.

"Make sure to thank Camden later," she said to Weylyn.

"I will." He dried the cleaned bowl and placed it back on the shelf. "I'm gonna wash up for supper." He skipped out the backdoor.

Erie watched him dunking his hands and feet into the stream. "Are you sure they don't mind teaching him?" she asked Aodhan.

"They insist. They say the world needs more Mages, and yet there aren't enough teachers spreading the art of Florávo."

He had said this before, yet the generosity of their time continued to bring Erie discomfort. Weylyn was thriving under their mentorship. While it brought Erie joy to see her son happy, she questioned if the time they invested in his education was entirely altruistic, or if they had other purposes in mind. "Why?" she wondered aloud. "What need is there of magic? We got along fine without it."

Aodhan shrugged. "I suppose we'll learn sooner or later."

"I'm not sure I trust it. The magic, that is. It feels like there are intentions we don't know about. You know, our life here—it wasn't by choice. I didn't ask to be the Anima."

"I thought we like it here."

"I do." She sighed. "We do."

Weylyn shook water from his hands and turned to come back inside.

"Something tells me that change approaches," Erie whispered.

"Change is always approaching," Aodhan said. "It's the way of the Divines."

Erie clenched her teeth. The Mages insisted they did not receive their gifts from the Divines. They didn't worship the Four, or any deities for that matter. Yet Aodhan still believed Erie had been transformed by the will of the Four; Uki had simply been the facilitator of the Divines' will. Erie knew this belief was why he had accepted their new life with relative ease.

Weylyn opened the door, and Erie withheld her response. She didn't want her son to know that she, unlike his father, felt their future wasn't as safe as they might hope.

When they walked into the kitchen, a stranger sat at the table with the Mages. Uki emerged from her room for the first time in three days and took a seat next to the stranger. She looked like she hadn't slept for months. Dark circles exaggerated the white of her eyes, and her hair was a tangled mess.

"Thank you, Weylyn, for the mint," she said, setting a hand on his.

Weylyn always sat between Uki and Erie. She was like a grandma to him, a relationship making Erie both happy and sad. Weylyn tilted his chin down once with a small smile. His humility made him seem much older than his five years. This, too, gave Erie conflicted feelings: she was proud of her son, but she wondered what he might be missing in this abnormal childhood of his.

"I'm happy you feel better," he said. He looked past Uki to the stranger sitting on the other side of her.

Erie found herself bristling at this man's presence, even though he looked remarkably similar to her youngest brother. Freckles spread across his nose and cheeks, and his dark red hair was cropped short. He fidgeted in his chair as his eyes darted between each person.

Opening an arm to the man, Uki said, "This is Stian. He is the stoat Shapeshifter."

Uki had mentioned Shapeshifters in those first few months following her transformation. She had said they were Erie's blood-bonded allies. When she had described them as capable of both human and animal form, Erie had imagined people more—impressive. This newcomer seemed too young, too jittery to be of any true help to Erie. Though really, what help did she need?

She tried to smile. "Hello, Stian."

"Anima," he peeped, bowing his head.

"Stian has lived in animal form since the last Anima's death nearly three centuries ago. It may take a few days for him to readjust to his life as a human. But rest assured," Uki continued, giving Stian a wink, "he was quite the eloquent diplomat in the last Anima's life."

Again, Erie tried to smile, but the resistance she felt kept her eyes narrow.

Uki cleared her throat and sobered her own expression. "As you all know, migraines have kept me bedridden for near a fortnight now. Stian comes as the envoy for the Shapeshifters of the north. I have seen this for myself, but he brings words to confirm the Flüschen are preparing for war."

Stian's fidgeting calmed. His face, tapering to the chin like the stoat's own, darkened. The Mages set their spoons and forks down and also looked at Uki with grim faces. Erie had no idea why the kingdom beyond Táléria's northern border was cause for such palpable tension.

Weylyn squirmed in his seat. "What?" he asked.

Erie wrapped an arm around her child. "This can wait for after dinner," she said.

"He needs to know, too," Camden said. "He will not be a child for as long as we wish."

Erie whipped her head to the man. "How *dare* you presume to know the fate of my child's life?" Her hands gripped the table. All the apprehension she had felt earlier roiled to the surface.

Aodhan frowned at Erie's white knuckles. "Love, please."

"It's okay, mother," Weylyn offered. He set his tiny hand over hers. "I saw blood in the mugwort leaves last week."

Though Erie's knowledge of Florávo remained nascent, she did know a red mugwort leaf meant impending bloodshed. Erie turned her anger to Aife, who had been his teacher last week. "Why didn't you think to tell me?"

Aife shook her hair behind her shoulders. "We have all decided to wait to tell you of your Task until the time came. Your son's natural propensity for Florávo wasn't part of this plan. I left it to him to decide whether to tell you what his gifts revealed."

"I'm sorry," Weylyn said, his eyes glassy. "I didn't want to scare you."

Erie shook her head. Here she was, trying to protect him from fear, and all the while he had been doing the same. They all had—but why? "I'm not weak," she said, looking at Uki. "Why all this stepping around me as if I were?"

The Mages exchanged apprehensive looks. Uki opened her mouth to speak, but Stian's words came first. "Of course you're not weak. You're the opposite. Which is why the Flüschen are looking for you."

"Me?" Erie asked. "Why me?"

Stian squinted at Uki. "Does she know nothing?" He flipped his hand to the side as he spoke, and the cadence of his words, paired with their high pitch, sounded strangely feminine to Erie.

"The Flüschen amassed faster than expected." Uki sounded defensive. "I wanted to give her time to adjust to her new body before setting the Task upon her shoulders."

"The Crow took the same approach with Oili, and we know how well *that* worked out," Stian said.

"Enough," Erie yelled, slapping her hands on the table. A couple of glasses tipped over. Wine and water pooled together. "If you continue to talk about my life as if I am irrelevant, I will take my family and leave tonight."

Aodhan moved to place a hand on her shoulder. Erie swatted it away.

"Take our son into the bedroom and close the door," she said. When both Weylyn and Aodhan began to object, Erie closed her eyes. "Please," she whispered to Aodhan. "*Please.*"

Aodhan studied her before consenting. Stian pushed the soup around in his bowl with a spoon, and the Mages looked between Uki and Erie. Weylyn continued to argue as Aodhan led him down the hallway. The bedroom door closed.

"Why are the Flüschen looking for me?" Erie asked.

"Because you are the Anima," Stian said, as if this was an obvious answer.

"The Anima before you—Oili, Princess of Grahimland—defeated the Flüschen in the Gelid Alliance's war for independence," Uki explained. "Three centuries later, the Flüschen still remember the Anima. They seek revenge."

"But how do they know of the Anima's rebirth?" Aife asked. "I thought the Haven would keep her secret, at least for a while longer."

"I was hoping you had the answer to this question," Stian said, looking at Uki.

Uki rubbed her temples. "I've tried. There's something blocking my Hindsight, I can feel it."

"A block?" Erie asked. As far as she knew, Salvagers could see anything that had happened, as long as they knew when and where to look.

Uki glanced sideways at Kelvan. "Last I saw, Jaco was talking with the Flüschen king. This was years before Erie's rebirth. He said he had discovered a way to prevent a Salvager from seeing."

Kelvan ran his hands through his hair. Erie had heard about Kelvan's son, Jaco, only once or twice before. He had been trained as a Mage until his mysterious departure from the Haven. From what Erie understood, Jaco hadn't spoken with his father in over a decade.

"So my suspicions were correct," Kelvan said. "He's warped at last."

"I believe so," Uki whispered. She reached across the table and squeezed Kelvan's hand.

He hung his head. "I don't deserve to fight."

"We need you," Stian said, his voice intense. "We need all of you."

"There are at least fifty Mages stationed in the Havens," Camden said.

"*Fifty?*" Stian looked like he had been punched in the gut. "There are ten *thousand* Flüschen gathered in Fretadt alone."

"I still don't understand why the Flüschen seek me," Erie said. "I'm not Oili. I had nothing to do with Grahimland's independence. I'm Talérian, for the Divines' sake. Besides, I heard the Flüschen reclaimed Grahimland a few years ago. What is there to revenge?"

Stian shook his head with disbelief. His flamboyance seemed to increase each breath he took in human form. Erie couldn't tell if his resemblance to her younger brother was comforting or unsettling. At least he offered the truth. As she was suspecting, the Mages and Uki had been hiding their intentions this entire time.

"What good is it to be a Salvager if you're not going to learn from past mistakes?" Stian asked Uki.

"What do you mean by that?" Erie asked.

With a pale complexion and hunched shoulders, Uki appeared unlike herself. "At least I haven't been hiding," she said to Stian. "At least I've been doing something for the Task."

"Stop fighting," Camden said. "The true enemy is Disorder, remember?"

Erie could tell Stian's cheeks flushed red only partly from shame. Stian had been sneaking glances at Camden since they all sat to eat. Uki also blushed. Erie had never seen her act in any way but buoyant; her ashamed behavior further alarmed Erie.

"What I mean, Erie," Stian said, moving a finger back and forth with each word, "is that the Salvager Uki replaced was the Crow. She only revealed parts of the Anima's Task that best served Oili. When it came time for Oili to fight Disorder in Lacuserra, she was already disconnected from her Anima self. She withdrew from the Task."

Uki had explained Disorder and Order to Erie, but apparently little else. "Withdrew?" Erie asked.

"She lived uncaring to the world beyond her own," Stian said.

"She raised her children," Uki said. "We can't blame her for wanting a life apart from the Task."

Erie scoffed. "You mean she lived a life like the one I had. You mean you can't blame her for wanting her life to be her own."

"Exactly," Uki whispered.

The rage, it throbbed. Erie wanted to turn the table upside down. She wanted to scream and thrash.

"There's something you need to understand." Hesitation made Uki's words slow. "Disorder would have reached Taléria sooner or later. It would have reached you in Nudom. The three kingdoms' peace was coming to an end. We saw this in the Flüschen's retaking of Grahimland. We see it in the Desnords' campaigns against the Lyziver Empire for rule over Taigas. And after millennia of disarray, the Yiúsians have also returned to power.

"The thing about Disorder, Erie, is that it will continue to grow wherever greed and fear are allowed to thrive. As long as Disorder rules the three kingdoms of Lacuserra, there will never be true and lasting peace. The Task asks the Anima and her Keepers to restore Order to the world. This requires stopping Disorder by any means necessary."

Erie folded her arms onto the table and leaned toward Uki. "I still don't understand why I am the Anima. Why me, Uki? *Why?*"

Uki's face, still pale, held a helpless expression. "I struggled with the decision. I really did." She reached out to touch Erie, but then stopped. "Laurel and I both decided to give the mushroom to someone who had something to fight for."

"Who's Laurel?"

"She's the Salvager of the Center," Stian said.

"And the mother of Florávo," Aife added.

"When Oili had freed her people," Uki continued, "she no longer had a reason to fight. She was afforded the privilege to withdraw. Your family, Erie, will never be safe as long as Disorder reigns in Lacuserra. But now, instead of living powerless, you are the Anima. You are your family's greatest hope."

Erie and Uki stared at each other. Uki's eyes, wet with tears, shined brighter than ever.

"And your family, Erie, extends beyond Weylyn and Aodhan," Stian said. "It includes the Shapeshifters. It includes all creatures."

Erie poured herself some wine and took a few deep drinks. "Why wait until now to fight?" she asked. "Why haven't the Keepers been fighting Disorder in Lacuserra between Animas?"

"Shapeshifters cannot survive in climates dramatically different than the native habitats of their animal forms," Stian said. "Half of the Shapeshifters of the north have died in previous demonstrations of the Anima's Task. Only five thousand remain able to fight in Lacuserra."

"Of which few would fight on free will alone," Uki said.

Stian shifted in his chair.

Uki gave him an apologetic expression and continued. "Previous wars have left many Shapeshifters—*disenchanted* with the Task."

"None of the Shapeshifters know where we come from," Stian said. His hands shook as he spoke. "None of us know who, or what, mandated this Task, and yet we all risk our lives for it, again and again. You, Erie, are the Anima, and yet you don't even believe in it. The Anima doesn't believe in her own damn Task." He caught his breath. "The Shapeshifters, regardless, will fight for you. We have to, as your blood-bonds. We don't have a choice."

Stian looked around the table. "And what of the Salvagers and Mages? They haven't been fighting, either. Fifty Mages, you said? Human complacency is as much to blame as Shapeshifters' *disenchantment.*"

Aife bristled. "We can't go out and train any old Commoner to become a Mage. Warping poses too great of a risk."

Kelvan brought his head to his hands, and Camden patted his back.

"You know as well as I do that Salvagers shouldn't fight," Uki said. "It's a waste of our purpose for the *enduring* Task." She sighed. "But you're right. You're right, Stian. The humans of Lacuserra have become complacent. Many don't know any better. Even if more people were trained in Florávo, few would be willing to use it for the Anima's Task. We're left with fifty Mages, five thousand Shapeshifters, and the Anima."

"Is Laurel even planning on coming?" Stian asked.

"She is to remain in the Machida Mountains," Uki answered, "where she's building the fourth Haven. It was too long of a trip to be here in time. And besides, we all know Laurel's purpose for the Task extends far beyond any singular battle."

"I thought there were three Salvagers," Erie said. "Where's the third in all this?"

Stian's smile was ironic. "My point exactly."

Uki agreed in the shrug of a shoulder. "The Salvager of the South has opted out of the Anima's Task. She doesn't believe it's possible. Frankly, we're just waiting for her to die. She's over three thousand years old, so it'll be any century now."

Tension grew thick in the pause. Erie could hear Aodhan trying to console a crying Weylyn. She felt strangely relieved to hear her son throwing a temper-tantrum. He was still a child—though maybe not for long, as Camden had said. She looked out the window, half expecting to see the Flüschen charging through the forest. Twilight cast the evergreens in shades of gray.

Uki broke the silence with a quiet voice. "It's common knowledge among my people who the fiercest creature is in all the world," she said. "It's the mother bear, Erie. She's feared by all." Uki reached for Erie's arm again, this time without hesitation. Her hand felt cool on Erie's hot skin.

"I chose you, Erie, because you are a mother bear. You are more powerful than any human or beast. The Flüschen would have eventually come to conquer Taléria whether or not you were the Anima. Now you have the option to fight. Now you have the ability to defend what you love most."

☾

The fire hissed as Erie doused it with water. Smoke swirled, filling the room with a haze. She walked outside. Early spring kept the evening cool. She trotted down the narrow path, moving like a fluid shadow in the dawn. The wolves waited at the foot of the hill. When she approached, they began running up the hill, Erie at their heels. They reached the top, and Erie could see the smoke billowing up from a large bonfire more than ten leagues to the northwest. Her stomach pulled tight.

*I see they've reached Hellörf,* she said.

Keno paced back and forth. His silver fur glistened in the rising sun. *They've killed two packs already,* he said. *At least twenty wolves dead. And the humans*—he paused, eyeing Erie—*more than a hundred.*

Erie said nothing. She thought she had smelled burning flesh. She fought back a scream. They were coming for Nafáit. They were coming for her family.

*We should get off this ridge,* she managed, turning to run back down the hill. The wolves and their Shapeshifter followed. They weaved through the trees, stopping at an opening in the grove.

*We attack tomorrow night,* Erie said. *We have fifty Mages and all the Shapeshifters of the north.*

*What's left of them,* Keno reminded her in a quiet voice.

The wolves exchanged glances.

*Would you prefer to wait for them to hunt us down?* Erie snapped. *Or would you rather take them unawares and fight for your life?*

The youngest wolf slunk before Erie. *But Anima,* she said. *There's no way we can win.*

Erie softened. The wolf was but a pup, not even a year old. It was Erie's idea to ask the wolves to fight alongside the Keepers. The Flüschen had been killing them indiscriminately for centuries. Erie knew she asked the impossible of the allies circumstances had left her. Yet she could smell the burning flesh. Her mother and father wouldn't smell any different in the fire the Flüschen spread.

She squatted down, meeting the pup's eyes with her own. *You, my friend, do not have to fight,* she said. *None of you do.* She looked around to the wolves standing in the trees. *But more will burn whether we continue to hide or not.*

Somewhere in the far distance, a tree crashed down.

*We are but vile creatures to them,* Keno said at last, looking to the wolves around him. *They will kill us all.* He morphed into his human shape, shedding his fur for tattooed skin. The linen tunic of his animal underskin hugged tight to his body, revealing the contours of his muscles. His hair, black streaked with silver, was smoothed back by the wind of his running.

"You're right," he said. "We either wait for our death, or fight for our lives. We will join you, Anima."

Erie knew Keno, as one of her blood-bonds, had no choice. Nonetheless, his spoken agreement brought Erie to her feet. "Gather the Shapeshifters and any animals willing to fight. We meet on the hill at midnight."

She sat at the hearth, staring at the coals. Sunrise filtered through the trees, filling the room with an orange and green light. She thought of a thin river running between here and Hellörf. They would cut northeast, across the river and into the lower hills of the Hoeden Mountains. From there they would continue north and attack the following evening.

Someone placed a hand on her shoulder. Erie jumped to a stand, reaching for the short sword hanging from her belt.

Aodhan looked at her with concern. "It's only me, love," he said. "You didn't come to bed last night." He moved to embrace her, but she stepped away, shaking her head.

"They've reached Hellörf." She squared her shoulders to his. "We leave, tonight. If we attack from the north, they won't expect us."

Aodhan's face grew gray. "And Weylyn?"

"You will stay with him." She slumped back onto the hearth bench, her whole body shaking. Aodhan pulled her close, and she began to sob. He cried silently with his head atop hers.

"He will need you," Erie said. She composed herself with a couple trembling inhales and walked into the kitchen to wash her face in the basin. When she turned back around, Weylyn entered the room.

Erie forced a smile. "Good morning," she said, smoothing down his golden curls.

Weylyn wrapped his arms around her hips and rested his head against her stomach, saying nothing in return. He had grown quiet throughout the winter. Erie had seen him watching her and the Mages practice weapons through the greenhouse's windows. He and Aodhan had continued their Florávo lessons while she had trained for war.

The three of them had all slept in the same bed since the day Stian had arrived, though Erie rarely slept anymore. She had spent the last six moons tossing and turning throughout the night, thinking of how she had Uki to blame for her family's entanglement in this bloody mess. When Erie would cry to Aodhan about her unfair transformation into the Anima, he would remind her that Disorder would exist with or without her as the Anima. *The Divines chose you,* he'd say. Though some days, Erie could tell even he didn't fully accept what he said.

Weylyn's sixth birthday was this summer. Erie started to cry as she held him close to her legs. She knew she most likely wouldn't be there to help him celebrate. She would miss this birthday and all the ones to follow. This knowledge—that he'd live a long life here in the Haven—brought her both relief and a terrible, terrible pain. She wouldn't see him grow into a man. She wouldn't stand in his circle, should he choose to wed. She wouldn't see her husband's hair turn white. She drew Aodhan into their hug, and the three of them cried together.

Stian and Camden emerged from Camden's room together, holding hands. Stian stopped giggling at whatever Camden was saying when he saw the three of them by the hearth. He and Camden slipped outside without a word. Weylyn released the hug first and looked up at Erie. He withdrew from his pocket a white wood anemone. It still glowed with the elicitation he had brought forth through its nectar. He placed it in her palm.

She knew this flower, as a charm, offered protection against evil or condolence for the death of a loved one. She ran a finger along a petal, feeling the warm light pulsate against her skin. Which purpose had he brought forth in it?

Weylyn closed her fingers around the flower. "You were born to do this," he whispered.

Erie hung her head. Her son—he wasn't normal, she knew this even though normal had been fragmented the day she ate the mushroom. His wisdom and magic had never found true comfort in her heart. She wanted him to be silly and blissfully ignorant like she had been as a child. But he would be who he would be. Now or never, she needed to embrace this. She tucked the flower into her pocket and kissed him on the forehead.

"Thank you," she said, and he smiled.

The others had readied breakfast, and the three of them sat at the table with the Nafáit Mages, Uki, and Stian. The cottage was too small to house the dozens of other Mages hailing from the three other Havens stationed around the world. Few spoke the same language. They had slept and ate outside since arriving over the last moon. With the canvas tents and weapons sprawled across the premises, the Haven felt like a real army camp.

"So you leave tonight," Uki said, handing Erie a plate of poached eggs atop steamed greens. She also handed her a cup of mulled wine.

The Mages gave Uki a confused look.

Erie took a deep drink of wine. Her food remained untouched. "The

Flüschen have reached Hellörf. The Wesgriech pack told me"—she gulped down more wine, emptying the cup—"they told me at least a hundred burned."

Kelvan slammed his fists on the table. Aodhan wrapped an arm around Weylyn.

"We'll meet the Shapeshifters at midnight," Erie said. "Come ready to fight to the death." Though she spoke to the Mages, she looked at Aodhan and Weylyn. They looked back with faces nearly identical in their jaws jutting forward. Weylyn lifted his chin up at her. She felt the warmth of the flower he had given her press against her hip.

The humans dressed in all black. Black tights and shifts, black gloves and boots. They ran through the forest as extensions of the night. Wind distorting the shadows. An overcast sky blessed their stealth.

The Shapeshifters running in animal form forged the river and traversed the rolling hills as a wave of fur. All ten surviving wolf packs of Taléria had rallied alongside other creatures threatened by the Flüschen's invasion. Breaks in the overcast revealed golden eagles soaring above the bird Shapeshifters. Neva flew in her snowy owl form between the great gray and tawny owl Shapeshifters. Foxes slunk out of tree hollows and hidden dens, joining one by one as the army ran through the hills. The boars spread out to thin the rumble of their hooves.

They paused a few leagues southeast of the Flüschen camp. Erie called Sabaa and asked her to scout the land. She reported a guard placed every league in a circle around the camp, each guard at least two leagues away from the camp's center. Erie thanked her and told the others they would cut further east now, up into the mountains.

Dawn flirted with the horizon. They ran toward the coming light and spent the day crowded into a recess in the cliffs. Erie knew it was risky—all of them here like fish in a barrel. But Sabaa and the other golden eagles took turns on watch.

The day passed slowly. Flies amassed around them as a roar of tiny wings. The boar threw back their heads, and the wolves snapped their jaws, but the flies continued to torment them. Smoke from the Flüschen fires settled into the recess. Erie pursed her lips against the taste of charred flesh.

She hopped atop the boulder and tried to count how many fighters had answered the Anima's call. Her stomach dropped. The army had felt much larger when they were running. A small stream trickled down a rock face, and the animals took turns lapping up the water. Erie knew they couldn't stay here all day. The sun had only just crossed the sky's apex. She swung her braid over her shoulder.

Sabaa flew down and morphed into her human form. Her hair fell to her bellybutton in waves the same red-black color of her feathers. A series of tattooed red dots mirrored the arches of her black eyebrows. "Anima," she said, loud enough for only Erie to hear, "another five thousand Flüschen arrived in Hellörf, bringing their total to fifteen thousand. We're now outnumbered three to one."

Erie hugged her knees and looked away. She felt the phantom of Weylyn's hands around her waist. She felt Aodhan's breath warming her neck. Sabaa eyed her with golden-orange irises. Erie could feel all the animals' eyes on her.

They should have fled. They all should have run west, to the lands beyond Nudom. But they would have met the Lyzlvers there. Disorder surrounded. She wanted to pull her hair out in fistfuls and curse Uki, the Divines—whomever was to blame for transforming her into the Anima. The spiral threatened to pull her under.

Sabaa wrapped an arm around Erie. "We are here," she whispered. "This is not all on you."

Erie leaned into the woman's curvy bust. The Mages had gathered around as well, echoing Sabaa without saying a thing. Stian morphed into human form and joined the circle. The linen of his animal underskin was soaked with sweat. Neva floated down and morphed as well. She preferred nudity to her underskin and joined them stark naked.

"We could have run," Erie whispered.

"They would continue to hunt us all to the shores and beyond," Stian said.

Erie closed her eyes and remembered running up this canyon, her feet barely touching the ground as she threaded between juniper and pine, the forest a blur around her. There was a gully that cut north leading to a low ridge. They could cross the mountains there. By the time they reached

Hellörf, darkness would shroud their attack.

"Prepare to depart," she said, standing. She turned to the animals corralled in the slot canyon.

*Finish drinking water and get in formation to run again,* she called out to them.

All the animals stopped moving. The only sound was the fly swarm droning. They erupted back into movement, slurping and shuffling.

When all was still again, Erie yelled, *Now*.

Neva and Sabaa morphed and soared back up to the sky. The humans and animals ran up the canyon, slow at first as they bottlenecked out of the recess. The gully appeared as she had remembered, and they continued toward the ridge as a river moving backward, upward, breath and paw, foot and muscle rippling like water freed from gravity.

Flames licked at the stars. They crouched behind trees and bushes, spread out in a line running nearly a league long. The heads of men stood among the trees on top of spikes. Erie avoided looking up at the severed necks.

Sabaa landed next to Erie. *We are ready,* she said, flexing her talons.

Erie tilted her chin once, and Sabaa took off, the force of her wings a welcomed breeze on Erie's face. "The eagles are in position," she whispered to the Mages.

Aife lowered her head toward the Deadly Charm in her hands. The mountain laurel and snakeroot flowers within the wicker ball began to glow. Camden evoked a large jar of Wolfsbane Decoction he held. When the liquid emitted a bright purple light, he unscrewed the lid and passed it around. Erie dipped her arrowheads into the jar. Around them, a dozen other jars began to radiate the same lavender light. They waited until all weapons had been coated with the poison.

Erie drew the bow from her back and rolled an arrow between her fingers. A wolf paced to her right, a boar to her left. *The time has come,* she whispered to them. *Spread word.*

They loped off in opposite directions, returning moments later. The wolf snarled. The boar kicked dirt behind him. Erie breathed into her stomach. She pictured herself holding Weylyn to her chest; she felt the soft press of Aodhan's lips on her forehead. Whispering goodbye, she stood.

With a lion's scream, she released the arrow. Roars and bellows whooshed across the earth. The Flüschen scrambled to find weapons as the animals flooded their camp. Their flags, black with a red bull, hung limp in the windless night. Aife and Camden threw Deadly Charms at tents, and the canvas caught on fire. Half-clothed men and women came out hollering.

Erie released arrow after arrow, her eyes training from one Flüschen to the next. Every wound the Flüschen incurred from arrow and blades proved lethal with the wolfsbane poison. Erie left the women alive: they were the surviving Hellörf townspeople with blood streaking down their inner thighs.

A man charged at her, and she slung her bow onto her back. He raised the sword in his hand, and she ducked, punching him in the gut. He stumbled, and she grabbed his arm, ripping it out of the socket. She took his head and twisted, breaking his neck. Someone, something primordial had taken over, and she moved with her eyes cold and mouth fixed.

The boars weren't faring well. They managed to stab a leg here and there, but their carcasses began to pile. Wolves took down men in small groups, but they, too, were killed faster than they could kill. The Shapeshifters, still strange to Erie, fought with skill gleaned over millennia. Yet they, too, began to fall, and Erie leaped over the bodies of foe and ally alike.

The titanic expanse of an eagle's wings flapped as his talons dug into a Flüschen's eye sockets. Erie released an arrow into the man's neck, and he collapsed. The eagle began to fly up, but an arrow pierced his wing, and he crumpled to the ground. Erie moved to help the eagle but an arrow found her arm as well. She yelled, ripping the arrow from her bicep and ducking to miss another. Keno ripped out the throat of a Flüschen. Beyond him, Aife threw a Deadly Charm. A man screamed as a hole burned through his face.

Erie managed to kill four more Flüschen before another arrow found her leg. She growled, pulling it free, but yet another pierced her shoulder. She turned and saw Camden's head fly off when a sword sliced through his neck. A cry caught in her throat. An eagle pummeled down from the sky, his body filled with arrows. The fur of foxes floated in the air. Stian ran to

Camden's body, crying. A sword slashed where his human head was a breath earlier, and he scurried through legs in his stoat form.

They were losing. Erie could only hear her blood pumping. She drew her short sword, and screaming her eerie lion scream, she rampaged. The arrows continued to find her body but she ran, jumped, thrusting her sword into stomachs, necks, faces. All she saw was red. All she heard was her own rage.

The Flüschen surrounded her. She saw Neva and Sabaa trying to fight their way to her. Blood was everywhere: smeared across faces, soaked into clothes, pooling on the ground in puddles dark and shimmering as obsidian. She could taste the iron. An arrow found Kelvan's heart. Had he managed to kill his son in this chaos? The tawny owl Shapeshifter lay dead by her feet. She never even knew his name.

"I command you to flee," she called to the remaining Shapeshifters. "Retreat! Retreat!"

Neva and Sabaa morphed and flew upward, dodging arrows with erratic flight. Erie heard Keno yelling for the wolves to run back into the forest. Aife and a couple of wolves stood beside Erie, surrounded by Flüschen. Despite her shaking hands, Aife slit the throat of one wolf and then the other. It happened so quick, so wildly intuitive, it seemed as if it was done in slow motion. The Flüschen yelled in their harsh language and rushed to stop her.

With an odd calm in her eyes, Aife raised the dagger to Erie's throat. "See you beyond the shores," she whispered.

Taken aback, Erie stood with arms open. A mercy kill, she realized as Aife crumpled to the ground after a dozen arrows hit her at once. Erie fell to her knees next to Aife's dead body. She reached to touch the Mage, but four arms wrapped around her and lifted her up.

They spit in her face. They punched her head left and right. Erie couldn't hear what they were saying. Her head rang and the words were like the roar of a waterfall. They threw her to the ground and kicked her, one boot after the other. Erie murmured the names of her husband and son. She rolled onto her back and looked above the men to see the stars. Even as urine rained down onto her face, into her eyes, she could see the stars giving space to the infinite darkness.

They yanked her off the ground and shoved her through a narrow parting in the standing and slain bodies. Erie stepped over Kelvan, and her feet brushed a wolf. She tripped over an eagle and landed on the body of a Flüschen. They jerked her back up by the hair.

A stake waited for her. They piled the carcasses of her friends, her allies. They strapped her to the stake and lifted her into the air, chanting something Erie couldn't understand, something about Oili. They used the pile to keep her upright.

The smell of fish overwhelmed the mutilated flesh as the Flüschen doused the bodies with oil. Here, with hopelessness surrounding, warmth spread from her hip to her heart, her heart to her head. Despite the abundance of death, she could only smell the wood anemone. It reminded her of the spring, of her first kiss with Aodhan at the vernal festival, of birthing Weylyn.

She managed to open a swollen eye enough to see the flower shine a brilliant white light in her pocket. The flames reached her, and though she shrieked, her body writhing in protest of its end, Erie could feel only love. She didn't hear herself scream her final words—words belonging to everyone and yet to no one at all.

# IV

## A GIRL NAMED ELLE

*"All people of the Imperium live united under a single Power."*

\- Declaration of the Three Kingdoms Union

# ART

## 95 YBP

TWIN RIVERS, PROMINENCE DISTRICT

When Elle came screaming into the world, a mess of black hair covered her head. Her father's hair, the nurses whispered, as if they still found it hard to believe an Imperial would marry a Montane Indigenous. Art only left the birthing room to fetch Elaine food, taking the whole week off work at the flight academy. It was an early birth, about six weeks premature, and Elle weighed an ounce shy of four pounds.

They returned home to their small, blue house on the Avenues, Elle wrapped up in a fleece blanket and Art's canvas jacket. It had snowed the day before. The world shined a dazzling white, and icicles decorated the porch railing. The first weeks they floated, sleep deprived but elated. They would lie for hours on the bed, fondling Elle's toes, kissing her blotchy skin. No one could say she was a cute baby, but she was the most beautiful thing they had ever seen.

Six weeks after the birth, postpartum depression seized Elaine, overnight almost. Darkness seeped out of her. Elaine had felt her entire life as if she was running from her dead father's fists. The ghost of him haunted her, demon-like in her visions, and she always felt but one step ahead of it. The postpartum left her exhausted, leaving her guard free to crumble. The demon sprinted in, victorious. In some ways it felt better to let it win. The fight was over. She waved her white flag and fell into the grace of defeat.

Art would come home from work to the baby squealing and Elaine crying silently in the nursery's rocker. He felt he was drowning in the darkness. Elaine would tell him about visions of herself bleeding out in the bathtub, and he would hold her and say she was strong and loved and this too would pass. He and Elle needed her to come back to the light, to the bliss. She did, months later, and Art thanked his people's gods. Elaine thanked Art, knowing his patient, fierce love had saved her from herself.

Though she also knew the darkness had changed her. It had claimed her, or some part of her she could never amputate. Art sensed this too, and they both decided it best if he underwent a vasectomy. They wouldn't talk about those months again; they both feared giving voice to the darkness would give it power. So they wished it away with silence, for Elle's sake.

Elle grew without haste, never plumping out. Strangers would eye Elaine and Art skeptically, wondering if the child was malnourished. One older woman even slipped them some money, for the babe, she said. Art tore the bill in half and handed it back to her without a word. That was Art. A quiet fighter. His war buddies called him the Silent Killer, a name that gave Elaine shivers. But even if he was a Silent Killer, he was also the Silent Healer, the Silent Lover, the Silent Rock the family stood upon.

☾

For Elle's third birthday, they loaded up the car and headed to visit Art's parents in the Openland District. They lived year-round on the prairies their ancestors had called home in the winters. When the Imperium had colonized Montane, the indigenous nations were given two choices: assimilate or live removed. Art's parents had chosen the latter, while he, after boarding school, chose life in the Imperium. He was the rarity for a Bilawáxan, not the norm, and his parents had never truly forgiven him for leaving the Openlands.

Their rustic house sat on a hill next to a creek and an aspen grove. They treated Elaine with respect but not acceptance. Elaine wondered if they somehow knew about the pre-Art years spent at bars and in beds. Art knew the truth for his parents' distance, and he couldn't blame them. Elaine, with her cream-colored skin and dirty blonde hair, was their painful history walking.

Elle was their common ground. Her grandma decorated the yard with clay models of all types of animals: bears, mountain goats, mice, hawk, goose, deer, and beaver. One of Elle's earliest memories was sitting on their lawn of wild grasses, playing with the figurines.

*She's a Bilawáxan*, her grandpa had said. *No doubt about it.*

Elle wouldn't know what that meant until years later, in school. She knew she was different from most of her peers. Their skin color spanned out as a selection of white paint, eggshell not too different from oatmeal, ivory but a touch darker than snow. But Elle, she was closer to the brown aisle of paints, a couple shades away from white. Half Imperial, half Indigenous, she knew her body belonged to two worlds long before her peers even knew multiple worlds existed.

It didn't matter as much in the first years of school. She had many friends, especially in the Avenues. They spent hours after school playing alongside a creek running in a park between Fourth and Sixth. Elle and her best friend, Sara, built a tree house in Elle's backyard with the help of Art. They would watch the squirrels, draw and read and talk about all kinds of things in that tree house. They would have tea with Elaine's shortbread cookies.

Elle would remember her mom in these days as beautiful and happy. Her hair combed, her body thin as always, but strong. She would remember coming home from walks with her dad to a roast cooking in the crockpot. She would remember the gentle way her dad held her mom, like she was a baby bird fallen from a nest. She would remember the clean bathroom, porcelain shiny enough to see her reflection in the toilet seat. She would remember the white whites of her mom's eyes.

Elle wouldn't remember the darkness that lingered, a shadow abated by her father's radiance. He laughed often, his laugh a contagious boom. She would later hold close a memory of the three of them on the living room rug, rolling in laughter. Yet she hadn't noticed the way her mom had stopped short, sober and cold. Her father had pulled her into his arms, kissing the nape of her neck at first, then blowing raspberries until a smile cracked the ice.

She would miss the laughter the most and the walks with her dad. Mostly they took their mutt, Jasper, down to the park. They threw rocks into the creek, and Jasper chased the splashes. They shared in his simple amusement. Some weekends all four of them hiked into the Crazy Mountains west of town. Art taught Elle the names of the animals. He also taught her the names of the wildflowers, pointing out bluebells and fireweed. He bent down to lift a glacier lily's head with a finger, telling Elle how bears ate these flowers.

"Everything has a purpose out here," he said. "Everything gives, and everything takes, and somehow, if left to do its magic, it all maintains a balance."

One Saturday, he, Elle, and Jasper went into the mountains without her mom. She stayed at home that day, sick with a cold. Elle suspected her mom didn't care much for hiking anyways, but did it for the sake of Art's love of the woods. Elle knew it was more than love for her dad, though. It was a belonging, each hike a homecoming.

They hiked up to Grayling Lake, right below Trapper Peak. Facing west, they sat and ate ham and cheese sandwiches. Art told Elle how his people, her people, came from the mountains.

"These mountains are part of a much larger chain of mountains," he explained. "It's called the Spine of the Earth."

Elle rolled her eyes. "Dad, I know. We learned that last year."

Art patted her head with his giant paw of a hand. "Such a good little scholar. Did you learn about the Bilawáxan?"

She shrugged. "A little."

"You know that's what I am, and half of what you are. But did you know our ancestors have lived in these mountains for *thousands* of years? It's hard to really wrap our heads around how long we've been here before the Imperials came. We would summer in the mountains, and winter in the valleys."

He pointed to where Trapper Peak cut the skyline. "You know how in town we can see the white peaks beyond these mountains? We call those Cenataan. Home of the Gods. We believe humans are the only animals without a god in their form. Every other animal has a god. There's a cougar god and a bear god, a raven god and even a mouse god. And all these gods taught humans how to live within the Sacred Balance."

Elle listened closely, absorbing the words. She would remember them all, nearly verbatim, and that afternoon would play over and over in her head for years. It was as if her eight-year-old self could see into the future, and she paid attention with mindfulness beget of foresight. The overcast sky, the mayonnaise on the corner of her dad's mouth, the language and beliefs of her ancestors: the details kept him alive. She inherited her father's long nose and face, hazel eyes, steady gait on long legs. But his endowment of their culture would end with this memory, a memory caught in an eddy—his words made all but myth with the wash of time.

☾

The following week Elle and her mom waited at the dinner table. The chicken was cold. Her mom stood and paced the kitchen, again. She had already called a dozen times, but she reached for the phone and redialed the Twin Rivers Flight Institute. Her dad had left a couple days earlier for training in New Headway, three hundred miles north. He had last called this morning, before taking out a young pilot. They were to fly until noon, and he'd be home by dinner. The sun had set, and the driveway remained empty.

Elle's mom told her to eat, and she did, nibbling the chicken, swallowing a couple bites of salad. A sick feeling gathered in her mouth and everything tasted like bile. It was an hour past her bedtime when her mom tucked her in. She read from the book her dad had been reading her. It was her dad's job to put her to bed, her mom's to wake her. Her mom wasn't giving the characters the right voices, and Elle didn't want her dad to miss out on the story, so she asked her to stop.

"It's okay, mom," she said, and Elaine began to cry.

They curled up together, on Elle's twin bed, and Elaine fell asleep. Elle was restless, and for the first time in her life she stayed up all night. She went to the back porch with their thickest blanket and watched the stars tiptoe across the black.

The phone ringing woke Elaine. She rushed from Elle's room and answered it. Elle stood behind the porch's screen door, watching her mom drop the receiver. Her face whitened, and a long, deep howl rushed from her gaping mouth. Elle watched her through the screen, in horror, like someone watching an animal dying at the zoo. She knew then her father wasn't going to come home. Her mom crumpled onto the ground and into a fetal position. Elle whispered for Jasper to come, and they ran to the park.

Elaine found her there, hours later. She was still white as a ghost, her eyes bloodshot and puffy. Elle hadn't cried yet. The tears would come, but for now she threw rocks into the river and watched joylessly as Jasper chased the splashes.

They both stayed home from work and school. Friends and neighbors came and went, dropping off casserole dishes and takeout. Elaine stayed in her pajamas for days in a row. Her friends, the ones she had made after becoming sober nearly twelve years ago, urged her to shower and put on different clothes. They helped Elle do the laundry and clean the kitchen. There always seemed to be people around that first month. Elle would walk into the living room to find them whispering. She'd try to listen in before they could see her there. They talked about keeping eyes open for bottles, getting Elle back to school, planning the funeral.

Her dad's best friend, Walter, flew in from Desnord a week after the death. He arrived at the house at midnight in a cab, and Elle woke to find him on the couch. She had only seen him twice before: first on a family vacation to visit him in Lacuserra, when she was still a baby, and again a couple years ago, when he had come to visit. Walter and her dad had gone hunting, though, so Elle had only spent an evening getting to know him.

But when Elle saw Walter in their living room, she ran and jumped onto his sleeping body. He woke to her sobbing into his armpit.

"There, there," he cooed. "Just let the tears come."

It wasn't just that Walter looked like her dad, also standing well over six feet with the mahogany coloring of the Montane Indigenous. He shared his woodsy smell, the musical cadence of his voice, the peculiar poetics of his talk. They could be brothers, people would say, twins even. Except Walter was missing an eye, and her father had left the war remarkably unscathed.

Walter let Elle soak his shirt before sitting up, setting her next to him. He pet her hair as she continued to cry. His touch made her self conscious of the grease and tangles. "When was the last time you took a bath?" he asked, not unkindly.

She looked sheepishly to the side, trying to remember. Her mom's friend had made her bathe a few days ago, but she had since gone swimming in the creek with Jasper a half dozen times. Walter drew a bath for her and cooked up some eggs and leftover pasta while she washed.

When Elaine came out of her bedroom a couple hours later, she found Walter cleaning dishes in the sink. "Where's Elle?" she asked.

Walter lifted sudsy hands up. "Elaine." He dried his hands and opened his arms wide. "Oh, Elaine." He began to cry.

She ignored his gesture to embrace. "Where's Elle?"

"I took her to school," he said, wiping the tears from his face.

Elaine narrowed her eyes. "She wasn't ready to go back."

"She told me this morning that she'd like to return. I think she needs to regain some sense of—normalcy."

"By what right do you have to come here and decide what my daughter needs?"

Elaine wore Art's army sweater and flannel pajama pants. They realized they were wearing the same sweater.

"I've come here to help, Elaine. Steve called. He said, well, he said y'all needed some reinforcements. There's no shame, Elaine. Not here. Not with me. I married the two of you, for crying out loud."

Elaine poured herself some coffee. "I know, Walt, I know." Her shoulders slouched toward the mug in her hands as if the hot beverage could make her feel warm again. "I'm not ready to go back. I won't ever be ready."

He held her from behind as her body shook with the sobs. His tears wet her hair. Elaine pulled away and set the coffee back down.

"I've gotta go back to bed," she breathed.

Walter nodded, and she faded back into the bedroom.

The funeral was held in their backyard. Elaine and Walter had debated about what to do with Art's remains. Only his charred bones were found in the plane's wreckage. Elaine ultimately agreed to hold a ceremony for him in Twin Rivers, but she decided they would scatter his ashes near where his parents were buried. Walter thought she should scatter them in the mountains, where their people's gods lived. Elle agreed with Walter, but she remained quiet.

Her mom was a ticking time bomb. Elle never knew what would trigger her to explode. Some days she would come home from school, and Elaine would hold Elle on the couch, stroking her hair and asking her about her day. Other days Elaine would be shut up in her room, only to come out when Walter would knock on the door to announce dinner. The wild look in her mom's eyes scared Elle.

One afternoon, Elle came home to Walter sweeping up broken glass beneath a giant hole in a window. He said something about a bird, but the glass was outside the house. Elle knew her mother had done it. Elaine cut up Art's old uniform with a pair of scissors the next day. Life felt like it would never be normal again, and Elle cried in her bed at night, holding Jasper close. Even Jasper didn't have the same buoyancy as usual. He followed Walter around as if waiting for Art to jump out of him.

Elle held hands with Walter at the funeral. She wore her dad's favorite dress of hers, one with red ruffles and a white collar. Her mom wore a black dress that revealed the thin contours of her hips. The low cut showed where her breasts converged as a line pointing down. People sipped on beers and glasses of wine, talking in hushed voices.

Elle had only been to two other funerals, her grandparents' in the Openlands. Even though the memory of each was foggy, she could feel that something was off here. No one laughed. There weren't any other kids. People looked tense, expectant. They looked like she felt when she came home from school.

Her mom floated from one group to the next, receiving their condolences with a vacant face. Walter followed in her wake with Elle. She watched him watch her mom, noting how he kept looking at the beer and wine table. Elle avoided people's eyes as Walter shuffled her from one group to the next. She leaned into their hugs, felt the warmth of their words wash over her.

Your father was my hero, they said.

She would thank them and move on. They were people who had come over for dinner, neighbors they'd run into and talk with on their walks. But Elle didn't know them, and she gripped Walter's hand, even as sweat gathered between their palms. It almost made her cry there, in front of all these people, the fact he didn't let go.

When they came to Sara's parents, Elle asked where her friend was.

"Oh, she wasn't feeling good."

Elle said she was sorry, but she saw the way Sara's mom's eyes darted to Elaine when she spoke. And for the first time since her father died, Elle didn't feel sorry for her mother.

"I want to go into my tree house," she told Walter.

He nodded, releasing her hand. They both wiped their palms on their clothes. She climbed up the rungs and watched the funeral from above. Eventually Elaine clinked a fork against her glass of water. Everyone inhaled into quiet.

"Thank you all for coming," she began. Her voice rang steady but distant. "Elle and I—where is Elle?"

She looked around, and Walter pointed up to the window framing Elle's head. Elle ducked down just as a few dozen eyes swiveled toward her. Heat pushed against the skin of her face. She remained hidden from view and listened to her mother continue.

"Well, Elle and I appreciate your support. Art, Art…"

A chipmunk trilled. Leaves shifted in a wind. Elle pulled her knees to her chest, waiting for what her mother would say. What could she say? What words could possibly make anyone understand what was lost? When her mother didn't continue, Elle exhaled. She heard the porch door slide open and shut, and she heard Walter thank the guests for coming. They streamed out the backyard gate as a murmur. A cold absence followed their departure.

Walter stood at the bottom of the tree. "You okay, kid?"

Elle didn't answer.

"Can this fort hold my weight?"

"Sometimes my dad came up here with me."

He told her to wait a second. When he returned, he crawled into the tree house with a backpack on. Elle couldn't help but giggle as his six-foot-five body strained to squeeze through the entrance. It was like watching a bear wedge into a fox den. He sat across from her, taking up two-thirds of the space, and pulled cheese, chips, chocolate, and cards from the backpack.

They played pairs and ate the snacks, mostly in silence. Again Elle wanted to cry with relief, this time because he didn't expect her to talk. It was like when she and her dad would go hours without saying a word: the quiet a sanctuary they would build together. An hour passed, maybe two. Walter shoved the cards back into their box.

He cleared his throat, and Elle's whole body went rigid.

"Elle," he said, bringing her into his arms. "Know you are loved. Know his love will always be with you."

The death of her father had made Elle a spectacle at school. The kids watched her with caution and curiosity, as if she had rabies. Sara escorted her from class to class, and for a week after his death they were permitted to eat lunch together in the teachers' lounge. Sara wore a blue dress, and her long, blonde hair fell down her back in perfect ringlets. Elle looked down at her grass-stained jeans and loose, gray t-shirt. How different they looked. How different they must feel.

"My dad packed me extra cookies today," Sara said, opening her lunch box. She winced. "Oh geez, Elle. That was stupid of me."

Elle took out the pasta leftover from the funeral Walter had packed for her. "Just 'cause my dad's dead doesn't mean you're not gonna have one. Your hair is pretty," she offered, desperate to change the subject.

Sara flipped her head to the side. "My sister did it for me. She's back from university."

Their history teacher, Ms. Fitz, walked over to the table. "Um, Elle," she said, "I lost my mom around your age. If you ever want to talk—"

Elle put a giant forkful of pasta into her mouth and nodded. Tears leaked from her eyes, despite her fight to will them away. The pasta forced its way down her throat, past the big lump.

Ms. Fitz placed a hand on her shoulder. "Anytime. You come find me anytime."

She preferred her peers' wariness, their awkward silence and deliberate avoidance, to her teachers' kindness. Whereas the kids looked at Elle as if she was feral, dangerous even, the adults looked at her as if she was fragile. The worst was the school counselor, Mr. Simmons. Elle would go in to see him twice a week, during gym class.

Mr. Simmons would study Elle with intensity. Silences extended between his questions and Elle's reluctant responses. Elle would watch him write on a pad of yellow paper, his tongue licking at teeth stained yellow with coffee. She didn't consider herself an angry person, but the way he stared down the crooked bridge of his nose at her stirred a feral thing inside. Elle thought of it as an animal, like a cornered wolverine. He would ask her how she was feeling, how things were at home, and Elle would imagine feeding the wolverine slices of meat.

"I hate my counselor," Elle told Walter as they took Jasper for a walk after school. "He smells like onions and looks at me like, like I'm a speck on the carpet. You know, like I'm dirty or something."

Walter chuckled. "Smells like onions, huh? So says the girl I have to bribe with candy to take a bath."

Elle glared at Walter. "He makes me feel small."

"I'm sorry," he said, wrapping an arm around Elle's shoulders. Her shoulder bones pressed hard against his hand. "Are you eating enough, Elle?"

Elle shook Walter's arm away and repeated his question with a nasal voice. "That's what Mr. Simmons asks."

Walter stopped walking and asked Elle to do the same. He crouched down so he could look into her eyes. He placed both hands on her shoulders. Elle watched her sneaker kick at a rock in the path.

"Elle, look at me."

She reluctantly met his eyes.

"I know this is hard. I honor your pain. But you can't let it turn you cold. You can't let it make you mean or angry. There's a light in you." He tapped a finger on her chest. "Right there. A beautiful, brilliant light. Art had it. Your mom has it. I have it. We all have it. And real bad stuff happens in life. Things you can't change. We don't know why, and we don't have control over most of it. But we do have control, or at least some control, anyways, over how it changes us."

Elle thought she had cried all the tears there were to cry, but there it came again, the sobbing. Walter pulled her into his chest, resting his head on hers, and they leaned into one another for a while. People stepped around them on the path, unable not to stare. When she calmed down they began to walk again. They stopped at the creek, and Elle threw rocks for Jasper.

Walter sat next to her. "Your father probably didn't tell you much about the war," he said, his words hushed. "But we both experienced terrible things—things we can never unsee. It put me in a bad place. A real bad place. Your dad, well, he wasn't immune to the agony, to the horror. But it's like the gods gave him extra light to share with us all or something. He helped me through the darkest times of my life. And I've always felt your mom and him, that, well, that he was sent to her or something like that. He saw in her what other people couldn't or wouldn't.

"It's hard. It's really hard to make sense or justify his death. But sometimes I feel that people like your dad, that they've got just too much light for the human body to handle, you know? Like, there's too much light for this little body to hold."

No one would call Art or Walter little, but Elle could see what he meant, even then. She watched Walter fiddle with his eye patch and wondered if the socket could shed tears or not. He cracked his neck and looked at Elle as if he had been talking to himself and he was embarrassed someone else had heard him.

"Sorry, Elle, that probably didn't make any sense to you."

"I think I get it." She threw another rock and watched Jasper charge after the splash, scattering the rock's ripples.

☾

Walter left a week later. Elle asked him to write. He promised he would. She received a letter from him a month later. He told her about the fall colors up in Desnord, the unbelievable yellows and oranges, like the forest was on fire. He also wrote that she was always welcome to come visit. She wanted the words to read *come stay*. She could always come stay.

Elaine resumed working at the library soon after Walter returned home. For a while, things seemed to be settling into a new normal. She made dinner every night. Her friends came over at least once a week, and they listened to jazz on the radio and chatted. Everyone expressed awe of her resilience.

But no one, not Elle, not her coworkers or friends, knew of what Elaine called her Silver Bullet. A little flask, the one she had carried everywhere before Art, found its secret pouch in her purse again. She took little sips. Not enough to tip the scales, she told herself. Just a little gin medicine to numb the pain. And it worked. For a while, it worked.

One night Elle came back from Sara's to Elaine packing boxes with her dad's things. She had written "keep" and "give away" with permanent marker on the cardboard. A glass stained red with wine sat on the floor next to her.

"We've got to get rid of what we can, Elle," she said. "It's gonna help. It's gotta help."

Elle stole little things from the boxes after her mother fell asleep. From the give-away box she took her dad's pocketknife, the one he used to cut cheeses with on their hikes, his Imperial Bombers canvas jacket, and a t-shirt. From the keep box she took a couple photographs of him. In one he was holding her as a baby, his face aglow with wonder. In the other, Elle and he stood smiling side by side on top of Yarrow Peak.

She slid the pictures into the book they had been reading together before the accident. The book remained unfinished. Elle would never find out what happened to the little boy who got lost in the woods. And with time, she stopped wondering how the story ended.

☾

Two years later they sold the house. The mortgage proved too expensive for Elaine's salary from working at the school library, and they were moving to a place called Mountain View. It sounded nice. Their moving truck was packed, the house hollow, cleaner than it had ever been. Elle hated the spotless floors. There should be mud there, big old footprints.

Elaine did detail work, erasing pencil marks of Elle's growth from a doorframe. Elle let Jasper into the backyard and followed him outside. She climbed into the tree house and walked around, having to duck a little. She drew circles with her finger around the screw heads, remembering her father pushing the drill into the wood.

When their moving truck pulled into Mountain View, Elle wondered where the houses were. The truck stopped next to a metal trailer refracting the summer sun, and she realized the doublewide was their new home. Her mother hadn't mentioned they were moving to a trailer park. She had just called it Mountain View as if it were like the Royal Heights or the Avenues in town. When Elle had told Sara she was moving, she promised to have her over to their new house for sleepovers. There was no way she would bring Sara here. Why would anyone ever want to sleep here?

"Where are we going to eat?" Elle asked as her mother showed her around inside. She felt like she had walked into a tin can. The ceiling hung so low she wondered if her dad would have even been able to stand tall in here.

"We'll eat at the bar." Elaine rapped her knuckles on the kitchen counter. She opened a door. "Here's your room, Elle. We'll share the bathroom."

Elle peeked her head into her new room. It was half the size of her old one. White paint gave the room a clean look, but the brown shag carpet came apart in some places. She doubted all her things would fit, though they had gotten rid of most of their stuff. Her mother had called it a liberation movement. She had packed boxes with a frantic energy, slurring her words and breaking a few of their nice dinner plates. Elle knew her mother wasn't herself some days, but she had yet to understand what caused her to change. She had yet to name the bitter smell chasing her words and lingering after her kisses.

When friends had come to help with the moving, her mother was more herself, though less pleasant. She had even snapped at a couple of their neighbors. Elle had watched a look pass between the two other women, and she had wanted to pinch Elaine. Elle almost preferred the frantic and sloppy version of her mother that seemed reserved for her alone during their private time at home.

She described their new house to Walter in a letter, trying not to sound mean or angry. She had kept her promise to him as best she could. *My room feels cozy,* she wrote, though the word she wanted to use was claustrophobic. *And I'm getting used to the train when it passes. It doesn't wake me up as much. The best part,* she continued, *is that we're right by the mountains.*

That last part she truly did feel. The Crazy Mountain foothills rose above the trailer park. Elle yearned to hike again, though Jasper had developed arthritis in his old age of fourteen and couldn't walk up steep trails. Not that it mattered. Her mom refused to go into the mountains. She spoke of ticks, cougars, and bears: things her father must have kept away when they had hiked together as a family. Elle took Jasper on walks down the dirt road, toward town. When she would look at the mountains on their way back home, she would think of her dad, of the last hike they had together.

It built resentment toward her mother, the way she forbade her from returning to the mountains. Even as her dad's ashes settled into the riverbeds and grassroots of the Openlands, she knew his spirit lived in those peaks rising above the foothills. She imagined his face in the mountaintops, the shadows on snow forming his nose, eyes, and mouth. She imagined him with grandma and grandpa, and she wondered if the gods decided they would be remade in a different form—if their spirits had found new bodies.

☾

Jasper died a year after the move. They walked a mile south of Mountain View to bury him in the forest. Elle carried the shovel, and Elaine carried Jasper. Elaine was a skinny creature, like her daughter, but she could carry weight, though not gracefully. Jasper's back legs dragged on the ground, and she cursed half the way there.

"This'll do," she said, placing Jasper on the dirt littered with orange pine needles.

The trees, dead with beetle-kill, stood as gray and red matchsticks, prone to catch fire. Elaine took the shovel from Elle and began digging. The ground was hard and rocky. More curses filled the afternoon. Elle stroked Jasper's fur, crying. She thought of how lucky he was to have died of old age. Maybe he had held on for her, like he knew she needed him as long as he could manage. But death came for everything. Elle knew this well, and she pet his rigid body without flinching.

"This'll have to do," Elaine said, using her shirt to wipe sweat dripping down her face. They both lowered him into the three-foot deep hole she had managed to dig. Elaine shoved the dirt back on top, and Elle watched as Jasper disappeared in fragments. Once finished, patting the soil down firm, Elaine reached for Elle's hand. In that moment, with only the dead standing witness to their funeral, Elle thought her mom had maybe come back. She squeezed her hand and looked up to her. But Elaine was gone, remembering when Art had brought Jasper home as a puppy. It was as if Elle held onto the hand of her mother's corpse. She released it, both their palms still dry and cold.

A week later Elle returned to the grave to say hello. Something had dug Jasper's body up, leaving half-eaten legs and clumps of fur spat out. Elle gaped at the mess. She sprinted home, tears streaming behind her. That day Elaine quit her job at the library. It didn't surprise Elle.

Elaine announced that she'd taken a bartending position at the Susie Blue. "I'll be making real money," she said.

Elle didn't tell her about Jasper's body. She dreamt that night of the brains remaining in his skull. The flies buzzed all around her, and she swatted, swatted. They kissed her with their bloody legs.

☾

At twelve years old, Elle knew the smell of alcohol like a rancher knows the smell of cow shit. She never told anyone about her mother's drinking, especially not Sara. She had been to Sara's house countless times over the last two years. Sara always asked why not her place for a change. Elle said she wanted to be in the Avenues, something about her dad and being close to their house. Which was true, making her reason only a half lie.

Sara's mom always asked how Elaine was doing. "I just never hear from her anymore," she said to Elle one afternoon. "I called and left messages, but she doesn't call back. Is everything alright? I heard she doesn't work at the library anymore."

Elle pushed the ice cream around in its bowl. They sat out on the back porch, enjoying some spring sunshine after a particularly harsh winter. Little chickadees flitted between budding branches. Elle missed the enclosed feel of the Avenues, the giant oak and poplar trees in nearly every backyard. Trees grew along the Birch River near Mountain View, and plenty of pines populated the foothills. But the trailer park itself felt barren.

"She got a new job, something to do with—banking," Elle lied. She felt slimy when she lied, but more often than not, she was finding little lies easier than the truth.

"Well, tell her I say hi. And goodbye," Sara's mom said.

"*Mom,*" Sara whined. "I haven't gotten around to telling Elle yet."

"What? Tell me what?"

Sara and her mom exchanged the Pity Look. It's what Elle called it now. She hated it more than anything. *More than anything.* The wolverine inside clawed with hunger.

"We're moving, Elle," Sara said.

They both knew what this meant. Ever since entering secondary school, Sara had remained Elle's friend, her only. Sara had many friends. She was popular and pretty, with glossy hair and clothes that always matched her shoes. Elle had her outfit: jeans, a t-shirt, and her dad's canvas jacket that came to her knees like a dress, the sleeves hanging half a foot past her hands. Her unruly hair, the color of wet leather, was often greasy because the shower at home grossed her out. And she was skinnier than ever. Bones, they called her at school, and the Elle Who Smells, or just Smells for short.

"When were you going to tell me?" Elle asked, keeping her eyes on the chickadees' erratic flittering.

"Soon, I promise," Sara said. "I just wanted to wait for Jasper's death to, you know, have some time."

In that moment Sara became like all the rest—all those people who treated Elle as something fragile, something to tread lightly around so as not to break. Elle wanted to scream at her. It made it worse that Sara was so nice, so loving. She looked at Elle with those big, blue eyes; the tears made them two pools of perfectly clean water. She was an angel, and Elle wanted to rip off her wings and eat them like a cat devouring a songbird.

But Elle finished her ice cream and pretended to be okay, to play off Sara's move as an exciting next chapter. Anything to make the Pity Look go away. They were moving to New Desnord. Her father's promotion was located there, and they'd be leaving in a month. Elle set the ice cream bowl down, saying that she needed to go home. As she biked back to Mountain View, she wondered why anyone even bothered loving anyone at all.

# LUNA

83 YBP

TWIN RIVERS, PROMINENCE DISTRICT

Girls started menstruating. Boys began asking the girls to the school dances and to go steady. Elle tried her best to avoid people's attention. Before Sara left, she had brought Elle to a table at lunch, introducing Elle to all her friends. But the day after Sara moved away, Elle had walked up to the table, lunch tray in hand, and the girls had pretended she wasn't there. Elle had slunk away, hearing them whisper *Smells* as she retreated.

Since then Elle had tried finding her people. All the kids had broken into tribes, and she wasn't sure where she fit in. It was as if a switch flicked when people turned twelve, initiating some biological instinct to form cliques. To thrive in the schoolyard wilds, one needed her pack. Elle attempted to fly below the radar, to not stand out. She felt like a mouse trying to scurry between holes without being seen.

Yet the claws of ridicule always found her hiding. Her skin was too dark, her body too thin, her clothes too worn for her to go unnoticed. She begged her mother to take her to the mall. She needed the pants, the shirt, with this or that nametag. When she looked into the mirror after biking to school, she saw her black hair knotted from the wind, her off-brand clothes faded and torn, and she hated herself. It was contempt so intense it felt like the wolverine gnawed on her ribcage.

Perhaps more than her body or clothing, though, Elle's home life cast her from normalcy. When her classmate's dad went to the Susie Blue one night, he told his son that Elaine had served him beers. Word spread like a bad cold, and before lunch every kid in school knew Elle's mother was a bartender. Elle soaked her t-shirt in sweat to the point she had to wear her coat all day to cover the dark stains. Did they also know her mother sometimes came home so drunk she slept next to the toilet?

Elle's mother the bartender remained a hot topic for all of two days. The kids moved onto the next gossip, leaving Elle back in her hole, safe in obscurity. No one had asked if her mother was a drunk. The teachers continued teaching, the parents continued parenting, and Elle prayed silent thanks to whatever god that had allowed the truth to remain hidden. Her mother's alcoholism would stay their secret. Elle knew, from an estranged vantage point, that the sacredness, the purity of her childhood was being sacrificed. But she couldn't bear losing another parent. She refused to seek help in fear the help would only bring more suffering.

☾

Shortly after Elle's thirteenth birthday, her mother brought home a man for the first time since her dad's death. Elle woke to his rumbling voice coming through the thin walls. The dream world and actuality blurred from just waking, and Elle fumbled with reality. Was her father? No, of course not. She shot up in bed, realizing that her mother had slept with another man.

And something more sacred than even her childhood writhed in its death.

Elle hadn't heard from Walter in nearly a year. Their letters had dwindled to one every other month, then one every few months, then silence from his end since last spring. But it didn't matter. He'd still take her in. He was the one person in this cruel world who wouldn't betray her.

She stuffed an extra pair of clothes into her backpack and found an envelope with his address neatly printed on it, someplace in the Lacuserran palatine of Desnord. People must be driving there all the time. Someone would pick her up and give her a ride out of here.

She closed the trailer door behind her without a sound and biked to the Twenty-fourth Avenue interstate exit. A light snow began when she reached the overpass. Cars whipped the snowflakes into flurries. She forced a smile and stuck out her thumb. Her torn jeans revealed skin pink with cold.

It wasn't long before a police car pulled over. The officer, a young, tall woman with curly hair, walked up to Elle and asked where she was going.

"Desnord." Elle avoided eye contact.

The officer knelt. "All the way up to Lacuserra, huh? Do your parents know you're going?"

Elle jutted her chin out. "Yep. They helped me pack."

"Well, how about you come to the station, and we'll get you warmed up before your travels. We have hot chocolate and donuts. Once the snow stops, you can try your luck hitchhiking again."

Elle knew she was lying, just as the officer knew Elle had lied to her. She was going to take Elle back home, and the wolverine growled. Or was that her stomach? Knowing there was no point in refusing, Elle followed the officer back to her car.

Elaine stomped into the station, eyes bloated with hangover. She had showered and smelled like soap. She had even curled her hair and wore a collared dress. Elle almost laughed out loud. She looked like a real mother. The officers assumed she had been crying.

"We found her at the Twenty-fourth Avenue exit. Someone called her in. Said there was a stray on the road, and that we should probably rescue her before the blizzard hits this afternoon."

Elaine thanked the officer and told Elle it was time to go home. Elle plopped into the car. Elaine sat in the driver's seat and lit a cigarette. She rolled down her window and blew the smoke out into the falling snow. Elle circled a hole in her jeans with her finger. Her mother's silence bore down with its heavy hand. Elle couldn't decide if she wanted to scream at her or sob into her shoulder. Her eyes welled. It was just the smoke, she told herself. The smoke stung her eyes.

Elaine flicked the cigarette butt out the window. "And where were you going to go?" She started the car and began driving home. They pulled into the driveway, the question still unanswered. "You need to know something, Elle."

Elle turned her shoulder, reaching for the door handle to escape.

"Walter died a few months ago. From cancer."

The words stabbed Elle in the back. Breath whooshed from her lungs. She fumbled with the door handle, but Elaine wrapped both her arms around her, restraining her. Elle bit at her mother's hands, at the stale stain of cigarette smoke. She screamed profanities she had only murmured before. Her mother's strength surprised her. She held on until Elle grew limp in her arms.

"I'm so sorry, Elle. I'm so sorry," she said over and over again.

"Why didn't you tell me?" Elle moaned.

Her mother hugged her tighter. "I didn't want to lose you. I didn't want the darkness to take you away."

They went into the house together. The blizzard hit an hour later, rocking the trailer as it wailed across the valley. Elaine heated canned soup on the oven as Elle sat on the couch, looking out the window at the whiteout. Elle couldn't remember the last time it had snowed so hard. How far would she be by now if someone had picked her up? She imagined herself out in this blizzard, still waiting for a ride, and pulled the blanket closer around her.

It was like no man had been here at all. His shoes were gone. Elle wondered if he'd be back. Elaine handed her a bowl of soup and sat beside her.

"I'm going to date again," she announced. "There will be more men. It's been five years now, Elle. I need to move on."

Elle slurped the soup down, feeling the wolverine pace back and forth, cornered. The stranger who had slept over last night didn't even matter now. Walter. Gone. How could she forgive her mother for not telling her about his death? She glowered at the dirty mirror reflecting them sitting next to each other. Elaine looked at her with pained worry. Elle hated her. And she hated this hate, because Elle also needed her. She needed her now more than ever.

"I need you, Elle." Elaine's voice cracked, and a few tears slid down her cheeks. It was as if she had heard Elle's thoughts. "Please. Don't leave me."

"How could you not tell me that Walter died?" But really—how had he not told her he was dying? Did everyone think secrecy protected her from the hurt?

Elaine tucked Elle's hair behind her ear, and Elle could see the Pity Look on her mother's face. "I was going to tell you. It's just with Jasper dying and then Sara leaving—I needed to know you could handle it."

"I can handle the truth." Soup sputtered from Elle's mouth. "I deserve the truth." She felt the anger caving like a piece of metal melting into its middle. But if the anger gave way, sorrow would overcome her. The pain would prove that she *was* too fragile, that she couldn't handle the truth, that she deserved the Pity Look. She resolved to stay strong. The anger was her strength. The wolverine would protect her.

Elle stood and said, "I won't leave. But I'll never trust you again."

☾

As two more years passed, Elle forgot about the wolverine. The anger became less of a creature separate from her and more of a second skin. The anger was she, and it felt good and right to let it blend seamlessly into her way of being. She knew she was breaking her promise to Walter. But if he didn't think she deserved to know he was dying, then why would he care if the anger won?

The anger felt good. It felt really, really good.

It also felt good to see the Pity Look turn into no look at all. The girls blossomed into young women, growing curves beneath their tight-fitting clothes. The boys remained boyish, though some sprouted chin hairs and lean muscles sooner than others. They entered tertiary school in a whirlwind of hormones, sex, drugs, and alcohol. People whispering Smells, like it was an inside joke they all shared, would follow Elle onto the new campus. Her quietness and sulking, dark body added Weirdo to her list of nicknames.

Elle grew subtle curves of her own, breasts filling a modest cup and hips expanding enough to demand a new pair of jeans. The nickname Bones still fit, and it also continued to follow her in the halls. She was a bit taller than average, though not enough to make her stand out. She let her hair grow to the small of her back, its black even blacker now that she didn't spend much time in the sun. Her front two teeth settled in large and straight, but the rest crowed toward the center in slightly crooked positions.

One day while walking to class, a girl behind Elle said, "I just wanna throw a cheeseburger at her."

Elle imagined pouncing on the girl and biting her arm, screaming, *You're a cheeseburger!* The thought made Elle laugh out loud, and the girl behind her sneered, "Weirdo."

Elle didn't feel like a weirdo. In truth, her routine was drearily normal: school, housework, and under-the-table jobs like washing windows and weeding gardens. It seemed most of her peers babysat or mowed lawns, though Elle figured they probably spent their earnings on going out with friends, rather than helping out with the mortgage like she had been doing since last year.

Even her grades were average—that was until science class her second year of tertiary school. Her teacher, Mr. Hansen, pulled her aside after class one day. A little shorter than Elle and at least four times her age, Mr. Hansen reminded Elle of a chipmunk. He wore old-fashioned wool pants and a tweed vest almost every day.

As he ushered the kids out of the classroom, Elle fiddled with the jaw of a plastic skeleton standing next to his desk. She hadn't done anything wrong. Why would he punish her? When it was just the two of them, he came over and asked Elle to take a seat.

"You know, Elle, if you applied yourself in school you could go anywhere you wanted." He examined her through his circular glasses. "It's never too early to think about university. You show real promise, Elle. You could go places."

His words stupefied her. Her? Promise? What did he know?

"Universities offer many scholarships for students who demonstrate academic commitment," he continued. "If you want, I could show you what they look for. You could be paid to go to university anywhere. But you'd need to start planning now."

She could go places. She could be paid to leave. Why hadn't anyone told her this before? Elle thanked Mr. Hansen and said she'd need to think about it.

That night, while her mother was at work, she wrote in her journal about the possibility of leaving Twin Rivers. Graduation was still three years away, but he had said she needed to start planning now. Her mother never mentioned anything about university; women in her generation typically hadn't attended. Occasionally she would ask to see Elle's grades, and when Elle would show she wasn't failing, that was good enough. Elle had never thought of herself as a serious student, but why not? What else did she have going for her? Elaine certainly didn't have the money to send Elle to university. And even if she did, she would want Elle to stay in Twin Rivers.

Elle unfolded a world map she had torn out from a magazine. Her experience of the planet included Twin Rivers and where her dad's parents had lived in the Openland. She ran her finger across the map, imagining the expanse of tundra in northern Taigas, the lush rainforests of Suqwas, the unyielding steppes of southern Lyziver. For the first time in years, Elle felt hope. Mr. Hansen had shown Elle a portal door, and through it waited the world.

She wasn't destined to poverty, to this trailer home, or even Prominence. She could live on the white sand shores of Cactia. She could move to the ancient mountains of Shénchåo. She could even visit Walter's grave in Desnord if she ever found the will to forgive him. She scribbled over this last thought with her pen.

The next day at school, Elle asked Mr. Hansen if she could talk to him again after class. She could barely focus on his lecture, something about genetic mutation. When all the other kids had left, she told him she had thought about what he had told her, and she was going to pursue academic scholarships.

"I thought you'd say that," he said, giving her a wink. "So I printed off some information about what universities look for."

Elle thanked him and slipped the papers into her backpack. She offered a small smile. When he told her to see him if she ever needed help, she knew she wouldn't. He had shown her the door, but she would walk through it alone.

☾

The school year ended. When Elle showed her mother her report card after the last day, Elaine blinked at the row of straight As.

"Well aren't you a good little scholar," Elaine said.

The words rippled across a reservoir of grief. She felt her dad patting her head when they were on their last hike together. She saw the waters of Grayling Lake, black in the overcast light, gray scree of Trapper Peak, her father's mass of a body.

"Elle? Elle?" Elaine waved a hand in front of her face. "Hello?"

Elle shook her head. "Sorry. I'm just—a little lightheaded. I didn't have lunch," she fibbed.

Elaine lectured her about skipping the free meals at school. She left for work, and Elle went for a walk. When she reached where Jasper's grave would have been, she crouched down and touched a glacier lily. She missed their dog's sure and simple companionship. Come to think of it, he had been the only stable figure in her life after her father's death, unless she counted Walter, which she didn't anymore.

An idea swooped in then, one she couldn't believe she hadn't thought of before. She ran back home and jumped on her bike. The shelter was close, just down Mountain View Lane. When she walked in, the receptionist looked her over with kind eyes, though Elle could sense the apprehension.

"Hello," the woman said. "May I help you?"

Elle told her she wanted to adopt a dog. The woman explained that a parent or guardian would need to be the one to sign the papers. Elle said she was here to look, and that her mother would come back with her for the adoption. It could be true. It would be true, she decided. It was the least Elaine could do.

The woman opened the door to the back. "You can walk around. Please don't put your hands in the cages. Some of the dogs are well-behaved, but others are still being sensitized to humans."

Elle thanked her and began the tour. Volunteers cleaned the cement floors with hoses, while others walked dogs in an open field beyond the kennels. They kept cautious eyes on Elle as she strolled in front of the cages. The dogs yelped, whined, wagged tails, and growled. Some of the dogs seemed nice, while others snarled and snapped at Elle as she passed. She wanted to take all of them home, the mean ones and the sweet. As she walked down the aisle, watching a terrier sleep, a black mutt pace back and forth, a hound yowl, she felt her throat constrict.

Toward the back of the shelter she came to a kennel with a puppy sleeping in it. Elle stopped in front of the cage, and the puppy stirred. She stumbled over to Elle on paws much too large for her body. With brown, red, and white fur, Elle couldn't tell what breed the dog was. She asked someone nearby if she knew.

"We're not sure about that one," the young woman responded. She turned off the hose in her hand and came over to Elle. "She's for sure got some Taigas wolfhound in her, but I also see some shepherd. This guy brought in the whole litter. Said he came all the way from Wolfkill. She's the last one. Gonna be huge. Just look at those paws. Here, we'll let her out for a moment."

The lady opened the kennel door, and the puppy rushed into Elle's lap. Elle laughed as the puppy licked at her face. Joy—that's what she was experiencing. It was a strange feeling.

She *had* to have this puppy.

"She's so fluffy," Elle said, petting the puppy's soft coat. She bit playfully at Elle's hand.

"Oh yeah. The couple adopting her was worried about her shedding all over their new furniture, but they're going for it. Coming back tomorrow for her."

The joy popped, and Elle felt the usual emptiness flood back in. Of course she couldn't have the puppy. Of course some other people, people worthy of happiness, would take the fluffy puppy home. Elle felt her throat constrict again.

"Hey," the lady said. "There's lots of other dogs here who need homes."

Elle put the puppy back in the kennel and finished looking at all the dogs. Anyone of them would do. Beggars couldn't be choosers, after all, and any friend on four legs would be better than none.

Elaine had the next day off. Elle came home from washing windows to her drunk on the couch, listening to some game show on the radio. Perfect. She would be more approachable a few drinks in. Elle sat next to her and waited for a commercial break.

"I want to adopt a dog."

Elaine laughed her high-pitched drunk laugh. "Oh yeah? And I want a new car." She took a drink of her gin and tonic.

Elle had prepared for the debate. "I will feed and walk it. You won't have to do a thing. It will teach me about responsibility and protect me when you work late nights." Crossing her arms across her chest, Elle paused for dramatic effect. "I can take care of a dog. If you trust me with this, it will help me to trust you again."

She knew she was being manipulative, calling upon the Walter fight to leverage her argument. She figured her mother still felt terrible about keeping the news from her, and that she craved for Elle's forgiveness and for them to be close again. Elle assumed those days were over, but she planted the hope anyways. Who knew? Maybe the dog *would* help heal their relationship.

"Elle, this place is tiny. How's a dog gonna fit in here?"

"It'll sleep in my room. I'll take it for walks. When I'm at school, it can stay in my room."

Elaine groaned and took another drink.

"We can walk there," Elle said. "It's not even a mile away."

When they arrived at the shelter, Elle prayed the receptionist couldn't smell the alcohol on her mother's breath. But Elaine was no amateur, and she had brushed her teeth and sprayed on perfume before leaving. The greeter, a man this time, didn't seem to notice she was inebriated. They followed him into the kennels.

"Which one did you want?" Elaine asked.

Elle felt all the dogs' eyes on her, pleading her to pick them. The power made her nauseous. Yesterday she had felt she could choose any one of them, at random, and be happy to simply have a friend. Today, the fate of another life in her hands terrified her. She walked the aisle, seeing the same terrier, the same black mutt, the same puppy. The same puppy!

"I thought this puppy was supposed to be adopted today," Elle said.

The man shrugged. "Those people called this morning. Said they couldn't make it work."

Elle didn't know she could smile so big. It hurt her cheeks.

"Oh, no. No, Elle," Elaine said. "A dog is one thing. But a puppy? No way."

Elle closed her eyes and inhaled through her nose. This helped, she had recently discovered, when the anger flared. Her fists unclenched, and she managed to reply in an even tone. "Mom, I want this puppy more than anything. We met yesterday and we—we have something like a connection. I promise I'll take care of her. I can't work a real job until next summer, and school doesn't start up for, like, three months. I'll have plenty of time to raise her."

The man stood awkwardly to the side, watching them argue for a couple of minutes.

"We'll take her," Elle said, beaming.

Elaine was already sauntering back to the lobby, defeated. A vague sense of guilt stirred in Elle. She all but called her mother an alcoholic, here in public. She had asked her why she even cared, being at work more than home. *Even today,* Elle had said, *you brought work home with you.* They had spoken in code. The man next to them would have no idea Elle was using her mother's alcoholism to get what she wanted. For all he knew, Elaine was a lawyer, and work was a pile of files on the coffee table, not a bottle of gin.

Elaine signed the papers as Elle leashed the puppy. When Elaine turned around, Elle was kneeling on the floor, letting the puppy lick her face. Elle looked up at Elaine and beamed.

"Thank you," Elle said. She stood and gave her mother a hug—their first real embrace in years.

☾

Elle proved true to her promises. She cleaned up the puppy's messes, fed her, and took her on walks, every day. They played together and slept together. When Elle left to do some random job, she put the puppy in a crate in her room.

Luna, she ended up naming her. Jasmine was a close second, as it reminded Elle of Jasper, but Luna's face was white, like the full moon. Luna grew a foot in a month and already weighed at least fifty pounds. Elle figured she'd at least match her one hundred and ten pounds.

Late summer came in hot, turning lawns yellow and exposing riverbeds. Elle opened the trailer door, and the heat hit her as a dry wave.

She and Luna walked down to the Birch River for Luna to cool off in the water. They continued toward town as usual, over the railroad tracks and down the dirt road. They never went farther than the bend in Mountain View Lane.

Elle didn't want to make it to where the pavement began. More cars drove there, and Luna preferred to be unleashed. Some days they walked the dirt road twice. Luna ran back and forth, back and forth, through the tall grasses growing alongside the road. She looked wild; people in passing said she resembled a wolf. Elle loved the way her fur flowed back when she really got going. She preferred her unleashed, too.

They returned to the river, and Elle threw a rock into the water. Luna just gave her an expression that said, *And?* Elle laughed. Jasper had been a lovable dog, but he hadn't been the brightest. She could tell Luna thought differently about the world than Jasper had. Luna seemed to her more human than dog sometimes, though maybe that was just her imagination, willing Luna to be a human. That way it would be less pathetic that she was Elle's only friend.

A car drove up the dirt road and parked near the Mystic Peak trailhead. Elle watched a pair of men slip on large backpacks and walk off into the forest. She continued to look at the trailhead. It felt like ages since her mother had told her no, they would not go into the woods, and no, she wasn't allowed to go alone. Did Elaine even remember telling Elle not to hike?

Luna sniffed at a dead fish on the riverbank. Elle realized she wasn't alone, not anymore. Luna would only grow bigger and more capable of protecting her. Elle looked back at the trailhead. Were there really so many bears and mountain lions out there? How dangerous could the wild truly be? She didn't remember ever feeling scared or threatened when she went hiking with her dad.

Maybe it wasn't the predators her mother feared about the mountains. Maybe she feared finding the ghost of her husband.

Elle stood, brushing grasses from her bottom. "Come, Luna."

The dog bounded out of the river and ran back toward the house. Elle hesitated. They should just go back home. How would anyone find her if she did get attacked?

A woman emerged from the forest. Silver streaks in her black hair glinted like polished steel in the sunlight. Elle couldn't tell how old she was from this distance. She might be older than her mother, but the way she strutted, lithe and deliberate-like, made her look much younger. She was alone. She, like the men, carried a huge backpack.

If that older woman could hike by herself, with weight, Elle figured she could, too.

"Luna, this way. We're going this way." They walked toward the evergreens. Elle felt her heart race, the adrenaline pumping, pumping. She stepped out of the parking lot and into the wilds.

# FORAGE

77 YBP

TWIN RIVERS, PROMINENCE DISTRICT

Elle took the long way to work, pedaling down the dirt path running alongside the Brother River. Her long hair flowed out from the newsboy cap she liked to wear these days. The world around pulsed with green life, and flowers unfurled out of pots hung from lampposts. She glided by couples walking arm in arm, groups of teenagers exuberant with the onset of summer, mothers pushing infants in strollers. People paused as she flew by on her red bike.

The path dipped under a bridge, and Elle noticed swallow nests constructed in the beams overhead. She followed a side trail into a thicket of poplar trees. A flock of grackles darted about overhead, whistling and humming. Elle tried to imagine what they sung, what they saw. Joys of flying. Tree branches, thin and graceful and leafing, reaching toward their underbellies.

The path ended at the back of a grocery store parking lot. She biked across the pavement, passing a large dumpster brimming with expired food, and merged onto Main Street's bike lane. Cars passed by with haste. After locking up her bike outside the Pizza Parlor, she slunk into the kitchen through the back door.

It was the lull before the dinner rush. Elle hung up her cap and her father's canvas jacket. The coat frayed at the hems, and its sleeves, rolled twice, no longer hung past her hands. She got to work, walking bins of dishes from lunch back to the sink and running loads through the washer in between sweeps. One of the servers helped Elle clean off the tables.

"Was it your last day of school today?" she asked, stacking the dirty plates and silverware into a bin. She was nearly a head shorter than Elle, with a curly blonde bob and breasts begetting generous tips from the male customers.

"Yep." Elle added to the stack. "I'm a free bird. Well, more free now, anyways."

"I always forget you're only like, what, eighteen? You could say you're twenty-something, and no one would know better. What are you going to do now? University? Work? Travel?"

Elle wiped off the salt and pepper shakers and put them back on the table. "University, eventually. Work, of course. Hopefully travel. I got scholarships to schools in all seven Cantons, but I've deferred them so I could take a gap year. I need some time to figure out what I really wanna do, you know?"

"Well, you're a smart girl, now aren't you? I always wanted to go to university, but, well, here I am." She rubbed her washcloth over and over a smudge before realizing it was a stain. "Thanks for helping me clean my tables. And congrats on graduating. Welcome to the real world." She picked up the bin and walked across the restaurant.

"Thanks," Elle mumbled to no one.

She finished bussing the tables and headed back to the dishwasher. The bussers arrived at the beginning of dinner hour and brought loads upon loads of dishes to Elle. Jazz streamed out of the radio above the sink. She thought about Luna, whom she had left at home after their morning hike. Elaine let Luna out before leaving for the night shift at the Susie Blue, but Elle knew Luna sulked around all this time, waiting for Elle to free her from hours of solitary confinement.

The bussers dropped off the last load of dishes and clocked out. Elle finished scraping off the plates, amazed by how some people would pay for a pizza and leave a third of the slices uneaten. Sometimes she would eat the leftovers, glancing over her shoulders as she shoveled the unwanted food into her mouth. But tonight she threw away the waste, finished cleaning the plates and glasses, wiped down the sink, and mopped the kitchen. At midnight, the servers, pizza chefs, and Elle sat for staff dinner.

In some ways the restaurant felt more home to Elle than her house. She figured these people were only nice to her because they had to be. Still, it felt good to sit around a table and eat in company. She listened to her coworkers talk about the customers this evening: a grumpy, old couple on table five; the stuck-up wife and her intoxicated husband on table twenty-three; beautiful women at the high top, to the chefs' delight. Elle relished the warm food in her mouth. She rarely realized her hunger until a meal was before her, and hers to eat.

"How was the dish washing?"

Elle looked up from her dinner to see that Nox, one of the chefs, had asked the question. A few years older than Elle, Nox had lean muscle, green eyes, and a sideways grin. Tufts of black hair curled out above his ears, and a hint of pine always lingered on his body. He was at least partially Native; maybe he also descended from the Bilawáxan peoples. Tattoos of black evergreens grew up from his wrists and into mountains. A starry sky extended above the mountains, disappearing beneath his t-shirt sleeves. Elle wondered what other tattoos hid beneath his clothes.

She swallowed. "Same as usual, I guess. How was tossing?"

"Same as usual." He leaned across the table. "Hey, you wouldn't be interested in coming to a party once we're done here, would you?" He tilted his head toward another chef a few seats away. "Mike and I are having a little get together at our place."

Was this a joke? She made eye contact with Nox before seeing her own reflection in the glass window behind him. The circles beneath her eyes looked like bruises. "Sorry. But I have to let my dog out."

Nox sat back in his chair. "Another time. What kind of dog you got?"

"I'm not really sure. I adopted her as a puppy. She definitely has Taigas wolfhound in her, though. She comes up to my hip."

"She sounds intimidating."

Elle smiled. "I guess she is, until you get to know her." She finished her last bite and stood with her plate in hand. "Thanks anyways for the invite. Maybe another time. See you guys soon," she said to the rest of the table. A few people said bye as she brought her plate to a bin by the dishwasher.

She biked through the chill to her home. The town had buzzed with drunken people as the bars emptied out, but on the dirt road, Elle passed no one. No one save a raccoon crossing the street, paws scattering pebbles, and an owl on a telephone post, watching. Her bike and body jostled as she crossed the railroad tracks before the trailer park. She veered into the driveway and locked her bike up on the old basketball-hoop pole.

When Elle opened the door, Luna dashed out onto the lawn to relieve herself. Elle lay down in the wild grasses with her hands behind her head as Luna sniffed in the night. Twin Rivers cast an orange haze over the valley, and the stars hid behind a milky veil of clouds. Luna licked Elle on the face. She brought her hands to Luna's muzzle and shook the dog's head back and forth.

"What are we going to do with our new life, Lu? A hike? Does Luna wanna hike in the morning?"

Luna wagged her tail and whined loudly.

"Okay, okay. Hush now."

Elle got ready for bed as Luna devoured dinner. She slipped out of her overalls and into her dad's shirt she had pilfered from one of the give-away boxes ten years ago. She wore it on nights her mother worked. The Imperial Bombers logo had faded entirely from it, and her skin peeked out in a couple dozen holes. When she washed her face and brushed her teeth, she avoided eye contact with the sullen girl in the mirror, focusing instead on the yellow rings rippling out from the drain.

Elaine had returned home from work in the middle of the night. Elle noted the half-finished beer bottles on the kitchen table. She also saw the man's shoes by the front door and the clothes—his shirt and pants, her mother's bra and dress—strewn on the couch. At least she had been too tired to hear.

Elle spread butter on a piece of bread and walked out the door with Luna. Dawn bled through the distant horizon. She ate her breakfast as they strolled past the other doublewides alongside the railway. It was impossible to tell where one property ended and another began. Luna trotted across the scraggly grass, zigzagging through faded lawn furniture, broken cars, the decaying forgotten.

Elle thought of her mother sleeping beside a stranger. She had yet to tell Elaine about the scholarships and her plan to leave. The thought of doing so brought breakfast to Elle's throat. Elaine could barely afford her half of the mortgage. Would she end up homeless without Elle's paycheck helping out? Maybe one of her lovers could actually pay up rather than eating their food and using their utilities for free.

She kicked at pebbles fanned out from a bend in the Birch. Maybe it wouldn't even matter whether or not her mother could make the mortgage. Mountain View resided in a two hundred year floodplain, which was why, she reasoned, a trailer park existed between estates. Elle had learned about the floodplain after researching "homeland" for a project last year in her geography class. A flood, Elle assumed, would take the mortgage with the trailer.

Across the Birch River, the giant windows of a log house flushed with the blossoming sunlight. Mansions spread out on that side of river, safe from the floodplain. Elle remembered peeking into the rooms while she had washed bird guts off their windows in summers past. The couches alone looked more expensive than their doublewide. She had once toyed with the idea of snagging small things, like a necklace or a vase, when the owners had left her alone to work. But Elle had decided early on that she would not be a criminal. She would not end up like her mother's father—a corpse hanging from a cell's ceiling. She was poor, but she was free. Or at least she could be free, *would* be free, when the time came to leave Twin Rivers.

Luna emerged out of the surging river and shook violently. They passed a wooden sign marking the beginning of the Mystic Peak trail. Morning light dappled through the evergreen boughs. Elle breathed in the textured smells of a forest waking: dew-moist earth, pine, sweetness of sap and wildflowers. She liked to imagine she looked like her dad, moving with deliberate strides over roots and rocks. She watched and listened for other life and tried to recall the creatures' names he had taught her. The swoop of a swallow, the scampering of squirrels, the chick-a-dee-dee-dees of chickadees.

The trail gained elevation, switch-backing up the small mountain. They stopped at the top of a plateau on the foothill's rounded top, where the forest parted, allowing for a panoramic view of the world around. She found her usual seat upon a rock. The valley to her east spread wide and undulated. Twin Rivers' roads, houses, and buildings seeped from a vague city center toward the creases in land where earth surged skyward. The Prism Mountains bordered the valley's east edge, cutting north to south as the Crazies did. Elle had learned the names of all of the surrounding ranges and their individual peaks. They were like friends, these royal blue giants.

Elle turned on the rock, to the Crazies plunging deep into the west. The foothills descended into a thin canyon where Owl Creek ran northbound. Aspens grew alongside the creek, their budding leaves cupped together as if in prayer. Yarrow, Mystic, and Trapper Peaks stood austere against the morning sky. Crescent Saddle dipped along the horizon, connecting the pinnacles of Yarrow and Mystic Mountains with an elegant swoop of earth. This curve in the ridge revealed the towering, gray presence of Bighorn Cirque. Beyond the cirque were the peaks her dad had called Cenataan, the Home of the Gods. They stood over thirteen thousand feet tall and boasted formidable names like Ghost Peak, Mount Shadow, and Froze to Death Plateau.

The day ripened. She pivoted again to observe the town's daily ritual of waking. Cars grumbled on, and the beeps and moans of construction resounded. Twin Rivers had grown in the past ten years from a small town to a medium-sized city. Since gaining vantage points afforded by hiking, Elle had witnessed the city expand exponentially. Condominiums and neighborhoods, giant grocery and department stores, streets and parking lots mushroomed across the valley. Elle had watched the paving-over of wild grasses once widespread. She found herself grieving sometimes for the loss of something she tried in futile to name: wildness, maybe, or a way of life, or the potential way of life that became more and more distant as Twin Rivers spread without restraint.

Nearly all the snow had melted in last week's warmth. The twin rivers, called separately the Brother and Sister, ran parallel to one another and divided the city into thirds. This past week Elle had witnessed the mountains weeping in the spring sun, releasing snowmelt into tributaries pouring out of the mountain recesses. She liked to imagine this annual purging as a shedding of skins. She saw parts of herself melt away, flowing into the rivers, gaining force until the collective energy united with one giant, pulsating body.

She decided to traverse south, toward Hidden Passage Falls. They walked on the rolling foothills for a mile before cutting down into Owl Creek Canyon. The green of new leaves and grasses glowed neon. Luna ran back and forth between Elle and whatever lay ahead. Elle, though, felt sluggish. She thought she'd be happy once she had finished school. The gap year had seemed like a good idea when she had decided to take it a month ago. But had she really taken it to decide what she wanted to study, or had she taken it because she feared telling her mom that she would be gone?

She imagined the majority of her peers were enjoying the start of their summers, sun tanning by pools, setting out on family vacations and trips abroad. And here she was, traveling alongside a creek with her one friend. Not even a real friend, but a dog. Sure, she could maybe call her coworkers friends, but not in any meaningful way. Those relationships were forged from circumstance. They weren't relationships like she had had with Sara. There was no Sara, not anymore.

Or not yet, she reminded herself, shaking a fist. In a new life, one she would create for herself once she moved away from Twin Rivers, she would meet new people and forge true friendships. There was no Smells living in Vallius or Paddock. There would be no Bones in Peatland or Gardenia. Like Mr. Hansen had promised a few years back, she could go places—places where she could shed old skins entirely.

Within this moment, within herself, she felt an impending transformation and yearned more than ever to be somewhere different—to be *someone* different. Elle promised herself that in her next life, the one she would soon create, she would find people who understood her. She would find community.

Elaine would have to learn to fend for herself. It would be good for her, Elle told herself adamantly. It would be good for Elaine to grow up. Elle wondered if she would miss her mother. Though a drunk and irresponsible, Elaine had never abandoned her. All these years it had been just the two of them, working together to pull through. The men came and went, but they had stuck together. Together, they had survived.

But could they apart? Elle knew there was only one way to find out.

A woman and man approached. They both used hiking poles and wore khaki shirts and pants. Bear bells tinkled as they stepped down rocks on the trail. A pistol sat snug on the man's hip. Luna trotted up to greet them.

"Good morning," Elle offered.

"Why, aren't you out early?" the man replied, stopping to take off his hat and wipe his brow. He gave Elle a closer look and raised his eyebrows. "And by yourself."

"The bears are out," the woman said. "Do you have a gun? I saw a sow and her cubs up here a few weeks ago. They come out earlier and earlier it seems. You do have a gun, don't you?"

Elle resisted the urge to roll her eyes. "No, I don't have a gun."

"Well you should. It's not smart to be alone, and such a skinny thing, too," the woman said, eyeing her closer. "Are you from around here?"

"Yeah. I've only seen bears from a distance."

"So you've hiked here often then?" the man asked.

"Kind of." Elle inched forward.

"Well good luck," the woman said. "There's mountain lions too, you know," she added. "And they'll kill you without you even knowing they're there. Just snap"—she snapped her fingers—"your neck in half."

"Geez, Martha," the man groaned. "Why do you have to scare her? She's got her dog after all."

"I just don't think her parents should let her out here alone. They probably don't even know their daughter's hiking in bear country by herself."

The voices faded as Elle continued up the steepening path. The trail cut left across the creek, and Elle hopped over the waters on granite stones sticking out of the flow. Little waterfalls gave the stream a silvery staircase look. She felt annoyed by the interaction. The woman's fear reminded her of the reasons her mother had used when she had prohibited her from hiking.

The forest opened to a large meadow. Arrowleaf balsamroot grew everywhere, the yellow flowers and sage leaves vibrant. A family of deer bounced off, white tails flipped up as they disappeared into the evergreens. The sound of water falling deepened, echoing off of rock and filling the forest with a subtle roar. Luna ran ahead, and when the path descended, Elle saw her dog wading in the pool beneath the cascading waters.

Although she had been here at least a dozen times, the beauty of

Hidden Passage Falls never failed to fill Elle with a sense of relief. A lofty granite wall rose above the trees, and the waterfall poured out of a large opening in the cliff face. A cool spray misted her face. She felt the beauty of this place had been reserved for her alone, and she now relished her solitude. Within her, always, this contradiction: a delight and despair in being alone.

She remembered her mother's bra and dress upon the couch. Could Elle blame her for seeking comfort in sex? She thought of her coworkers, of the missed opportunities yesterday to connect with others, to maybe experience the feel of Nox's sinewy arms wrapped around her. The thought made her tingle in places she had only explored with her own fingers and the company of a shame she didn't totally understand.

With no one around, she peeled off her clothes and walked naked to the riverbank. She submerged into the pool without allowing herself time to reconsider. Underwater, the waterfall rumbled even louder. The coldness of snowmelt brought her to the surface with a gasp, and she swam back to land, stepping out of the river quivering.

Her clothes hung damp from her frame as she and Luna walked back home. Elle felt a renewed sense of direction. She would move away from Twin Rivers as soon as she could afford to. A thousand dollars were already rolled up and stored in a jar, secreted behind a panel of drywall above her desk. She would only need maybe two hundred more. She would relocate to wherever she decided to go to university. Meaning, in the next few weeks, she had a tough choice to make and an even tougher conversation to hold.

As her feet moved across the earth, her mind moved through the details of the next few months. She saw herself getting her driver's license and buying a car, probably a truck or a jeep. She saw herself hugging her mother goodbye, and though Elaine cried, she felt the surety of this cleaving's necessity for both of their growth. She saw her books and clothes in boxes, shoved into the back of her new truck with Luna squeezed in between them. And she saw Twin Rivers fading in the rearview mirror as she wound down the valley on the interstate.

*Goodbye, mother,* she heard herself say. *Goodbye, Bones.*

The man's boots were still strewn by the front door when Elle and Luna walked back into the trailer home. It was half past noon. Elle filled Luna's water dish and opened the pantry. She heard her mother giggle in her bedroom. Oh no. They were awake.

She warmed a can of tomato soup on the oven and plopped down on the couch with the pot and a spoon. Elaine opened her bedroom door and cigarette smoke seeped into the living room. She slipped out of a cranny she made for herself and closed the door behind her.

"Hi, Ellebell," she said, her voice scratchy. "How you doing?"

Elle slurped up a spoonful and looked at her mother, standing there with a red satin slip clinging to her collarbone, hair shaggy, eyelids heavy and smeared with leftover makeup. "Fine. How was your—night?"

Elaine sighed. "Oh, Elle. This one is the real deal. Really." She walked over and sat on the couch next to her daughter.

Elle felt her body tense. Her mother had been touching a strange man minutes earlier. Elaine moved to bring her arm around her, but Elle shrunk away, sloshing some soup onto the couch. Luna licked at the red spill.

"Geez, Elle. What's wrong?"

"Sorry," Elle mumbled. "Maybe shower first?"

"That's mean." Elaine frowned as she stood. "Can't you just be happy for me?"

Elle snorted. "I'm sorry. Sometimes I just feel a *little* uncomfortable when I have to eat my lunch between your bra and yet another man's underwear. You know, you're my mother. Not my roommate."

"Shhh," Elaine hissed. But the man was already moving behind the closed door. Elaine spun around and returned back into the room. "Everything's fine," Elle heard her mother say through the thin walls. "Elle's just being—moody."

*Just being moody*. Elle felt the rage throb. Here she was, sitting on a pile of scholarships, and yet she couldn't even tell the one person who was supposed to be happiest for her. She should be gone already. She should be unpacking in a new place, far from here, far from the grumbling baritone of whatever strange man stood on the other side of that door. Yet instead she had been too scared to leave her mother alone.

Fuck her. Fuck her for holding her back.

Luna sniffed at the bra, its hooks clinging to the couch's faded upholstery. Elle ripped it off and threw it at the closed bedroom door. She took one of the man's boots and threw that at the door, too.

"Come on, Luna." She slammed the trailer door shut behind her, sending a quiver through the tin siding.

The sun glared off the Birch River as the two of them moved upstream, following an old path alongside the riverbank. Elle decided they would walk back into the Crazies until Elaine left for the Susie Blue. Elle didn't have to work tonight. The rest of the day lay out before her as a blank expanse, and her mind ran wild across it.

She stopped and screamed. Ravens in a nearby cottonwood took flight. Luna ran back from where she had been sniffing at something. She sat and nuzzled her head into Elle's hand. Elle couldn't decide if the dog was confused or understood her anger. Luna had been investigating the leftovers of a mountain lion kill. Flies buzzed everywhere, and ravens cawed as they circled above the deer carcass. Elle remembered finding Jasper's remains.

Tears found the corner of her mouth before she realized she was crying. When was the last time she had cried? It felt like a long time. She sunk down and watched the river run, the waters weaving around boulders and smaller rocks. Sometimes Elle wondered if she sat and observed because she wasn't sure what else to do. She had nowhere to go, no one to talk this through with. Feeling the entirety of her exclusion from community, she propped her elbows on her knees and held her head as sobs shook her whole body.

The only thing to do now was to move. In movement there was less room for thought and feeling. She and Luna hiked up the foothills again. The sun dropped in the sky as they walked south. After a few hours of mindless wandering, Elle decided it was safe to return home. Elaine would be gone by the time they returned, and Elle could make dinner and get to bed early.

A rainstorm edged in from the southwest, unfurling across the valley as a purple wall. It reached Elle and Luna as they descended the foothills. Elle welcomed the storm. The rain weighed down her hair and pressed her clothes against her skin.

Elaine was gone, as were the man's clothes. Elle warmed up another can of soup and scooped dog food into Luna's dish. She bathed in lukewarm water drizzling from a calcified showerhead. She took out her journal and scribbled fiercely across the pages. The anger bled out through the pen until her hand cramped.

Elle finished a predawn breakfast of instant oatmeal and packed a butter sandwich into an old backpack. She also packed the book she wanted for today, a book she had found at a yard sale. *Wild Foraging: Gather edibles while enjoying nature.* Elle had flipped through the pages on the pedicured lawn of the book's previous owner. She figured she might as well find free food while she hiked and save a few extra dollars for the move. Last weekend she had stumbled upon a small grove of morels, but when she had tried cooking them at home, she had burned the mushrooms in the pan.

She and Luna made it to the plateau before sunrise. Yarrow, Mystic, and Trapper peaks gleamed white against the pink skies of dawn. They hiked down into Owl Creek Canyon. Elle replayed the fight with her mother over in her head. Elaine had not come home last night. Maybe her mother would move in with this new man, making Elle's plan to leave much easier. Had Elle been in the wrong yesterday? She knew her lash of anger had surprised them both, but a girl—or was she a woman now?—could only push things down for so long. She resolved to apologize to her mother the next time she saw her.

Babbles of the creek grew louder as they walked through the dim forest. The pine trees eased into hardwoods. A bridge over Owl Creek appeared through the lines of birch and aspen. Elle cut off-trail, dipping under the red branches of dogwood with Luna at her heels. She walked carefully over loose rocks and hidden roots. The quaking aspen thickened around her. She remembered her dad telling her they were one of the largest living organisms. Below her feet an intricate and wide root system intertwined—all the individual aspen lived connected as one.

Luna chased a squirrel. Elle's booted footsteps sent an unseen snake slithering away through the grasses. A red tail hawk glided overhead to the northeast. Elle watched through a parting in the canopy as he dipped and sailed, riding and slicing the wind in turn. She touched where a birch's bark peeled, thinking it looked like an ancient scroll. The trees parted to reveal the creek. She ran her hand along the velvet-smooth underbelly of a rock submerged in snowmelt and listened to the water sing.

Luna fell asleep in the shade as Elle foraged. She moved low to the ground, using her dad's pocketknife to snip watercress, glacier lilies, and wild spinach. Her cloth bag filled with bright green leaves and the yellow lily heads. Elle hoped to find morel mushrooms again. She wanted redemption.

Vivid red caught her eye. She knelt beside a ring of mushrooms below a large birch. She slipped the knife into her pocket and removed the foraging guide from her pack.

"The Fly Agaric," she whispered. She double-checked the top corner of the page describing this mushroom. *Edible,* it stated. Without reading on, she put the book back in her pack.

She plucked the smallest mushroom from the ring. The cap was a vermillion red, and the white dots spread across it in a geometric pattern. Playing at its gills with her finger, she decided to try a nibble before another cooking venture could spoil her find. The mushroom tasted damp and old. Its chewed pieces moved around her mouth like larvae. She swallowed with compulsion.

Trees throbbed. Sky shifted between blues and blacks and blinding white. Luna came to Elle's side, asking with worried eyes. Elle was still holding the mushroom as she collapsed to the ground. When her head hit a rock, she was already gone. And the river sang on and on.

# V

# THE MODERN ERA

*"Meaning and chaos are either the same cloud in different light, or forces as unlike, yet equally influential, as sun and rain."*

- Rua Munu, personal journal

# WINTER

321 YBP

RICHFIELD, PRINCETON CANTON

"And this, gentlemen, is our prize possession." The Madam pulled back the curtain. "Her name may be Winter, but she's anything but cold."

The Madam wore her finest corset, the pearly white one from Soleria that must have cost more than what Winter made in a year. The strings of her mantua were unlaced to reveal her tremendous cleavage. Her long, red hair, wavy from braids, shined from a hundred brushings. Unlike many of the whores, she was full-blood Desnordian, which was why, Winter figured, she was the Madam.

The Imperial soldiers exchanged glances. Winter lifted her chin up, swept her honeyed hair to the side, and gave them her signature coy smile. The Madam ran a hand along the back of Winter's head. Shivers danced down her spine.

"She's well versed in the language of pleasure." The Madam winked at the men as she slipped a hand under Winter's dress and tickled her crotch. Winter feigned a moan.

One of the shorter men stepped forward. "I'll take her."

"For how much?" the Madam asked, withdrawing her fingers. She licked them as she stared down the men.

"Fifty copper."

The soldier next to him scoffed. "I'll pay double. As long as I can do anything I want."

"Of course." The Madam bowed her head. "Though with Winter, we usually charge two hundred."

"Here's three hundred." A brawny soldier withdrew the copper coins from a side pouch and pressed them into the Madam's hand. "For anything."

The Madam smiled and tucked the money between her giant bosoms. Winter pretended nonchalance, though the price was double her highest bid yet. The soldier offered his hand to Winter, and they walked to a back room. Moans and ecstatic screaming filled the hallway. Winter's white, transparent dress trailed behind her. She could feel the other soldiers' eyes on her backside. The man's hand was calloused, and she imagined a gun in it as he marched into town, claiming this land as his own.

The Imperium had arrived. Again. Winter and the other whores had spent a day hiding in the brothel's basement with the rats. When the Imperium first invaded ten moons before Winter's birth, the Tatankoy, with the aid of the Jmu'neböna, had managed to defend their territory, though just barely.

Last week, the Imperium had devoured the Openlands whole. Only the foolish had fought. *War is good for business,* the Madam had said. *Victorious soldiers make for hungry men.* And she had been right. Winter's vulva had begun bleeding along the edges by the end of the week. She had resorted to using her mouth despite her hate for the taste of penis. The Madam had finally given her a rest yesterday. Today, though, the Imperial generals had reserved the brothel for their needs. The Madam had promised gratuities.

Winter closed the bedroom door behind her. The soldier stripped off his jacket and cotton pullover shirt, revealing whipping scars across his massive back. She ran her finger along a scar, startling him. He spun around and grasped at her hands. She yelped.

"Don't touch those," he growled, releasing his grip.

She composed herself. Gratuity. Gratuity. She may earn enough to finally escape. "My apologies, sir."

She pulled down his pants. He tore her dress over her head and pushed her on the bed, front side down. He took her rough and quick from behind.

When he lay relieved, he said to lie next to him. She did as told, resting her head on his chest. Men liked when she did this—more, it seemed, than the sex itself.

"You remind me of my wife." He toyed with her nipple. "She was Torerran. Tan skin, like you. And green eyes, too. You are Torerran as well, no?"

Winter traced the ridges of his abdominal muscles. "Maybe. My mother was 'böna. The man who got her pregnant was an Imperial soldier, like you."

She felt the ridges of his abs deepen. He pushed her away with enough force to knock the air out of her. She hit the ground next to the bed and struggled for breath. What had she said? Had she blown her gratuity?

A slap to her face knocked all questions from her mind. Blood filled her mouth.

"Muckbreed cunt!" He slapped her again. "You, your people…"

Winter noticed the shadow of grief cross over the face glowering down at her. His scars. His wife. He didn't need to continue.

"You look, you look Torerran," he muttered. "You look—like her."

He slapped Winter again and the blood splattered from her mouth across the rug and walls. The mess! Any extra pay would be used for cleaning. Winter swallowed the blood and struggled to stand. He hit her back down, this time with a punch to the jaw. Hot pangs echoed the loud crack. She crawled behind a chair. He lifted the chair and threw it across the room. He wasn't a man hungry for pleasure anymore. There was nothing victorious about this anger. The fist above her was primal, the next blow defeated.

Blood continued to gush from her mouth. She would be blamed for the mess. Forget gratuity. Forget her standard wage. She would owe money for this spoiled transaction. He raised his fist again, and she ducked just in time. His hand punched a hole into the wall.

That hole alone would cost all of her escape money. As he struggled to free his hand from the wall, Winter snatched her dress and sprinted down the hall to the whores' living quarters. She pulled a pouch from a recess cut into the bottom of her cot's mattress. The Madam's voice grew closer, quickening her motions. Despite the pain, the panic, blood in her mouth and black bubbles popping across her vision, she moved fast enough to scamper out of the window. She kicked away a hand grabbing at her ankle.

This was not the secret escape she had been planning for years. She had always imagined herself running away in the early dawn, while the whorehouse and town still slept. The Madam calling her name faded away. Bare naked, her dress clutched in one hand and the pouch in the other, she ran down the dark alleys of Richfield. The white fabric swayed behind her like a foxtail. Men smoking outside bars and other whorehouses catcalled as she sprinted by.

*You're a natural runner,* her mother had once said. Winter ran through the matrix of dirt roads, leaping over piles of horse dung. Shadows flickered over her. She ran beyond the city's edge, into the open land. *Look at you go,* Winter heard her saying. *Look at how you fly.* She kept running. Wind dried the blood around her mouth. She ran into the forest, the dark growth folding her back into her ancestors' home.

She woke within tree roots to the undulating notes of a flute. Sunshine shimmered down through a thick canopy. The music and green light appeared like a dream at first. Birds sang in harmony with the flute. The notes crescendoed and fell, and the birdsong responded, high then low. She curled up deeper into herself, holding her pouch close to her stomach, and fell back asleep.

When she woke again, there was no flute and little birdsong. The forest purred, subdued by midday. She sat up, leaning her back against the giant oak. Blood stained the collar of her dress and where the fabric had pressed between her legs. She touched the tender places. His blows would leave blue and black blossoms. Her jaw felt out of place, and her fingers ached where he had crunched them together.

She may be fractured, but she was alive. For this she could be thankful.

Depositing the pouch's contents in her lap, she counted the copper coins. There was no need, really, as she had counted them again and again in the witching hours of night, moving the coins between her fingers, feeling their angles, the promise of their solidness. Four hundred coppers. It would be enough to live on for at least three months, maybe four if she skipped meals. She had been waiting for five hundred to leave: the amount, she had figured, to get her to Greenwood on foot. She would still head south as planned, to her mother's birthplace. Though why, now, she had no reason. If the Imperials hadn't killed or imprisoned her relatives yet, they would soon.

She fastened the pouch around her neck and began walking. Light waned as she moved deeper and deeper into the trees. The forest smelled oddly familiar, like the feeling of getting into bed and remembering a dream from the night before. A low purr continued around her, interrupted only by the demands of her stomach. Her last meal had been breakfast yesterday. Or was that two days ago now?

She continued with hunger and without hope. The only compass directing her south was moss on the trees. *The moss will grow on the north side of trees, away from the sun,* her mother had once told her. As a child growing up in the city, such things her mother said had seemed silly. Winter figured they were but stories she shared to remind her of their 'böna roots. Now Winter felt chilled by their foresight, as if her mother had seen a day would come when she would need the knowledge.

Yet if her mother had known her daughter would almost die at the hands of a client, Winter figured they would have run into these woods together years ago. She hoped so, anyways. Why hadn't they escaped after that first whore was murdered? The brothel was no place to raise a girl into a woman. For the innumerable time, Winter wondered why her mother had ever left Greenwood and her 'böna relatives to work in a brothel in Tatankoy territory. It was a decision that had dug her mother's own grave with the busy shovel of syphilis.

Day leaned into night, and the cold of her mother's memory sunk deeper. She found another nook within roots and shivered back to sleep. Hunger dragged her out of dreams. There. She sat up. There was the flute music again.

She felt like a husk, a brittle shell without meat. The music grew louder. Someone must be playing it, someone who might have food. She stumbled to a stand and followed the notes. They bounced up and down, growing loud one moment, quiet the next.

The flute music stopped. Winter froze.

"Hello, Anima," a voice said.

Anima? A figure materialized within the trees. The flute hung around his neck. He stood half a head shorter than she was and wore a dark green tunic and pants. His hair, a soft brown, was pulled into a high bun. The deep tan of his skin brought her comfort; she figured he was either of 'böna or Tatankoy descent. His face was clean-shaven, and large black stones studded his lower earlobes.

His eyes reminded her of the Madam's bright blue eyes, though his were even lighter. White, almost. He unlatched a leather canteen from his belt and handed it to her.

"Water?" he asked in Imperial.

She snatched the canteen and drank its entire contents.

He took off a rucksack and retrieved a small loaf of bread. "For you," he said, tearing a large chunk from the loaf.

She took the bread from him, too hungry to ask questions. The chunk of bread held an unexpected center. She worked its curious texture around her mouth. It was bread, sure. But a mealy undertone spoke of something more than grains and yeast, salt and water. The taste reminded her of the forest itself; it reminded her of that familiar smell. When she swallowed the bite, the world spun around her. She felt the man easing her body back down to the earth.

☾

Winter chopped wood, placing the logs into a basket. She strapped the basket to her back and leaped across the river stones, returning to the grotto. Rua skinned rabbits while Stian hung herbs to dry. Winter placed the logs in the hearth, and Keno started a fire.

The stew bubbled over the flames. They sat on stumps, warming their hands and feet. Candles flickered from nooks and crannies in the rock walls. Water falling a dozen yards away filled the grotto with a drone. At first the constant white noise had agonized Winter. Everything had felt dire those first moons after her transformation.

Keno came to sit next to her, brushing her shoulder with his hand. Rua eyed them over his bowl of soup. Winter sensed that Rua knew of the kiss she and Keno had exchanged the previous night. Sometimes she wished she could block Rua's Hindsight. Privacy seemed out of the question when it came to Salvagers.

Neva swept into the cavern, her long, white wings backlit by the summer sun. She hovered to a perch next to Winter. When she morphed, the snowy feathers gave way to skin just as white. Her hair fell past her breasts in wind-tousled locks of ivory. With pale lips and eyebrows the same color as her hair, her yellow owl eyes looked unnatural on her human face.

"They've cut over five hundred trees in the half moon alone," Neva said to Rua. She spoke like she flew, the words an intense whisper.

"Hi, Neva. How are you?" Stian said. He smiled his impish grin, knowing the Shapeshifter cared not for extraneous formalities.

Neva rolled her eyes.

After spending seventeen years in a brothel, Winter could tell the sexual preference of a person within ten minutes. Between the feminine intonations of his voice and his flamboyant hand gestures, Winter knew Stian preferred men within ten seconds of meeting him. She wondered if he was gay in his stoat form as well.

"I was just about to get to that," Rua said. He tipped his bowl back, slurping up the rest of the contents.

Winter felt the reprieve from her past funneling to an end. Her breath grew short and quick. Keno placed a hand on her thigh and gave it a squeeze.

"My migraines have been getting worse," Rua said. "Unbearable, almost. They're preparing another attack on Greenwood."

"They now occupy forts along the forest edge from Richfield to Longmeadow," Neva said. "They're razing the forest for their houses and fences, and there are more cows and sheep being brought onto the land. I don't think the 'bōna will be able to defend their territory much longer."

Rua brought a branch between his legs and used a knife to carve the end into a point. The shavings gathered in a pile at his feet.

"So we will fight their guns with a wooden spear?" Stian asked, smirking.

"This is not a game, Stian," Rua said. "My hunting spear snapped today when I hit a rock and not a rabbit. My accuracy, it's been off lately. You know as well as I we will fight with magic."

Stian's smile withdrew. The grimace looked foreign on the Shapeshifter's narrow face. Winter had a hard time imagining their resident joker in battle. She had a hard time imagining any of them in battle—most of all, herself.

"The Mages will arrive within this moon," Rua continued. "All four Havens will be here. We'll have the Shapeshifters able to survive in this habitat, bringing our numbers close to ten thousand. Allied with the 'böna and Intlyvwi, our army will stand fifteen thousand strong."

Winter grew rigid. She remembered the rumble of the Imperials as they charged into town. The way the brothel's ceiling had rained dirt and dust onto her. The Tatankoy had been more powerful than the 'böna, more trained in battle and larger in numbers. The surviving Tatankoy had been shoved off to lands further west from here.

She rubbed at her jaw, its fracture healed by the cut of her morphed skull. She had been so naive then: her armor the curves of her body, her shelter the entrapment of bedroom pleasure. Her whoring had been both her prison and her protection. She remembered the soldier's fist on her jaw, the blood splattering.

"It's not enough," she murmured. "It's not enough."

Keno massaged her shoulder. "The Mages are well trained," he said. "Laurel's knowledge of Florávian martial arts has expanded significantly since the battle of Hellörf. I suppose we could ask the predators of this forest to join us, as they joined Erie."

"The humans and Keepers will be enough," Rua said. He ran his finger along the point of his spear, drawing blood. "There's no need to drag animals into battle again. We've been preparing for this war to end the Imperium once and for all since Erie's death. Hamia will join us with the Vipers, further improving our chances. They've been training tirelessly in the Kawaitu Forest south of here. Though I will admit, they remain bitter about Laurel's refusal to send aid when the Imperium conquered Baninchi."

"The Vipers?" Winter asked.

"They are descendants of people freed by an Anima named Bazi when the Yiúsians first invaded Nyachi over a millennium ago," he explained. "Hamia, the cheetah Shapeshifter, has been training them to fight Disorder ever since. Although they've managed significant successes against the Yiúsians over the last thousand years, the union of Lacuserra's three kingdoms proved too great of a force. All of the Baninchi seterra came under the Imperium's rule by the end of last century."

Winter stared at the senseless dancing of the flames. She figured the Imperium had turned its attention west, to Montane, after conquering Baninchi. Where would they stop their campaigns to dominate? How big was this world after all? Was it large enough to satiate the unknowable hunger spreading their guns and steel across the land?

She looked at Rua. "Why didn't Laurel help Hamia?"

"The Havens were only beginning to recover their populations after every single Mage died in the battle of Hellörf," Rua said.

"But what about the Shapeshifters?" Winter asked.

"We don't have to answer to Laurel or anyone apart from the Anima," Neva said. "Given the option, most Shapeshifters choose not to fight in human conflicts. Without the Anima's blood-bond, the Shapeshifters' participation in the Task relies on free will alone."

"And we all know the fickle nature of free will," Rua said, his voice dark.

Winter glanced at the Shapeshifters gathered here. Did they actually believe in the Task—or did their blood-bond alone bring them to this circle?

Keno, as usual, seemed to have read her mind. "We are here by choice," he said, rubbing her thigh.

Rua narrowed his eyes at Keno's hand. Keno returned the stare, staying his hand.

"I will admit, it wasn't until Erie that I fully believed in the Anima and learned to embrace my blood-bond to her," Stian said, smiling.

Despite the infectious nature of Stian's exuberance, Winter couldn't return his smile. "I'd hate to feel like I'm enslaving anyone," she said.

"The smart Shapeshifters know the fate of humans is intertwined with the fate of animals," Keno said. "If any of them feel enslaved, it's not because you're the one doing the enslaving. We're all subject to the spread of Disorder."

Neva regarded Winter with the glimmering orbs of her eyes, saying nothing. Winter wondered if she was thinking of Oili, the Anima who refused to fulfill her Task.

"You must grow stronger," Neva said, her voice barely audible over the fire's crackle. "We are going to *war,* Winter. The Shapeshifters need a leader whose whole heart is in the fight."

Rua agreed with a nod. "If all goes as planned, this will be *the* war to end the Imperium once and for all."

Winter opened and closed her mouth. Neva morphed into her snowy owl form and took off, leaving them in quiet. For once, Stian had no sarcastic remark about Neva's warmth. The fire and water alone sounded in the dusk.

Winter ran her hands over her arms. They felt strong. They were strong. But she knew exactly what Neva meant.

"Winter?" Keno whispered.

She took a seat next to him, smelling the musk of his bearskin bedding. The silver streaks in Keno's black hair glinted in the candlelight. She ran a hand through it, thinking of how his wolf fur was the same pairing of black and silver. Winter had slept with over a hundred men. Some tall and brawny like him, some with the same straight nose and teeth, the same dark stubble. But with his hoary eyes and a brow often furrowed with thought, he was, by far, the most alluring man she had ever met. She wanted him in a way she had never wanted another before.

They kissed until Winter drew back.

"What is it?" Keno asked.

She wished Rua from her mind, but his glare on Keno's hand continued to bother her. "It's—"

"Rua."

Winter nodded. She could hear Keno's frustration in his exhale. "He questions my intentions," Keno said. "Salvagers—well, they sometimes view Shapeshifters as prone to bestial tendencies, especially lust. Their mistrust is particularly bent toward Shapeshifters who prefer their animal form, as I did following Erie's death."

Keno grew somber, and Winter shuddered, remembering the story Rua had told her about the Flüschen burning the last Anima alive.

"There was this incident," he continued, "a long time ago, between a Shapeshifter and an Anima. But it's not important, not to us anyways."

"What happened?"

"The story is irrelevant to our own. Besides, who's to say that Shapeshifter didn't truly love the Anima?"

The wind rushed from her lungs. Love—her? Is that what she felt for him too? Since she woke as the Anima a year ago, they had spent nearly every afternoon together, laughing and talking and hunting. But she knew of only one love in her life thus far, and that was her mother. When she thought of her mother, she felt mild warmth in her body, like drinking a cup of tea. When she thought of Keno, she felt hot, especially in her root.

"Is *this* true?" she whispered.

"True?" he asked. "Do I truly love you? Yes. Of course I do."

Hesitating at first, she touched his knee. "I think I love you, too."

She resisted the urge to move her hand further up his leg. He knew she had been a whore. They all did. But he had never revealed what he thought of it. He said he loved her. But could he *make* love to her whored body?

Neva had said she needed to be stronger. She needed to gather courage. Here was a start. "Keno." She forced her eyes to stay locked with his. "Would you—could you have me? Knowing what I was—what's been done."

He looked confused. When he understood, he rushed a hand to her jaw. "I'm no one to judge."

It felt as if a chain broke. Freed, she kissed him, fully this time. He pulled her to him. After they made love, she lay on the bearskin, cradled by the sturdiness of his arm. Yes, she had been with hundreds of men. And yet for the first time after sex, she dwelled in her body rather than wishing she was someone else.

☾

Stian and Keno played a game of cards. Rua sat in the corner, meditating, while Neva paced the grotto. The waterfall had grown quiet in the last moon; autumn arrived with its thinner flow. Winter looked out on the forest, admiring the mosaic of red and yellow across the canopy. The trees spread into the horizon and beyond.

Rua stood. "They're crossing the log."

Keno put the cards away, and everyone stood. Booted steps grew louder. The Vipers emerged from the trees and navigated the rocky path leading to the grotto. They hurried up the slippery stones despite the muskets secured to their backs. Their black skin glistened with sweat.

Winter gasped when she realized what these strangers were wearing. Whereas she and the Keepers wore simple wool tunics over leggings, these men and women were in jackets and pants identical to the ones the soldier had worn. She remembered her blood splattering across his white pants. Though the golden emblem—an X with a boar's head on top and a bull's head on bottom—had been ripped off the jackets, it was unmistakable: the Vipers marched in Imperial uniforms.

Two-dozen strangers filed into the cavern. Their jaws dropped when they saw Winter. She felt like she often had when men would barter over her as a whore. And yet their expressions were of awe, not hunger. Once their shock wore off, their faces returned to stoic countenances. With straight postures and flexed muscles, they looked entirely different from the Nyachians Winter had seen attending to Imperials in Richfield.

"Where are the rest?" Neva asked.

A woman with full lips and long, black hair styled in hundreds of braids stepped forward. Her breasts gave a peculiar irony to the Imperial jacket. "Come, Neva," she said in a husky voice. The words were Imperial, but thick with an accent Winter had never heard. "That's rude, even for you."

Though Winter thought her incapable of being bashful, Neva blushed. The woman's smile was broad and bright. She pulled Neva into an embrace and went down the line, hugging Rua, Stian, and Keno. She stopped in front of Winter and leaned a shoulder back.

"It's been far too long since I've seen an Anima with my own eyes," she said, shaking her head. When the woman hugged her, Winter could feel her strength. She figured her capable of crushing a large man to death.

"Hamia?" Winter asked.

"Guilty as charged." Hamia winked and sauntered back to the men. "I'd like you all to meet my right hand." She nodded once at a tall man, and he stepped forward. He had the largest lips Winter had ever seen. His head was shaven, his cheekbones high and defined. He seemed maybe two or three years younger than Winter's twenty-two.

"Meet Yedder. He's a descendant of Bazi's son. The forty-second of his name."

The Shapeshifters offered a small bow, and Winter did the same. Yedder examined the Shapeshifters and said something to Hamia before stepping back into formation.

"We are Keepers, not Imperials," Rua said.

Hamia agreed. "He said they *look* like Imperials. But he brings up a good point about your choice in Anima. An Imperial? Really?"

Rua stiffened. "I may have carried the mushroom, but she came to it. Or it went to her. Besides, Winter is half Jmu'neböna, a people sharing ancestry with Yedder's own. We all share ancestry. We must look beyond the warp of time. This is what the Order asks of us. The same Order his ancestor, the mother of Vipers, died for."

Yedder stepped back forward. "Look beyond time and what—forget the last millennium my people endured?"

Though his accent was even thicker than Hamia's, Winter understood what he said. His anger, in any language, was impossible to mistake. Winter studied her hands as if seeing their tint of white for the first time.

"Of course not," Rua said, his voice softening. "I'm asking you only to look past the smoke that is skin. Her mother was raped by an Imperial. She has reason as much as you to fight."

Winter flinched at the word rape. Yedder noticed and looked at her anew. She willed herself to return his stare.

Hamia set a hand on Yedder's shoulder. "The Imperium has brought much suffering to the people of Nyachi. It's only natural we have our reservations about allying with those who resemble our enemy. But you're absolutely right, Rua. The Task is bigger than any one of us here. Besides, we don't fight against Imperials, necessarily, but the power structure oppressing people and nature alike."

Rua relaxed. "Couldn't have said it better myself."

Hamia placed a hand behind her ear and leaned forward. "Was that—was that *humility* I heard? Rua, you grow soft in your old age." She grinned.

A blushing Rua looked even stranger than a blushing Neva. Winter decided she liked Hamia.

"When do the others arrive?" Hamia asked.

"By the new moon," Rua said.

"We'll be back then with the others." Hamia tightened the musket's strap on her shoulder. "Anima, it's been an honor." She took Winter's hand in both of her own and looked at Winter with intense golden eyes.

Winter told her the honor was hers. The Shapeshifters said their goodbyes, and the Vipers strode in a line from the grotto.

Yedder paused on the way out, turning back to Winter. "You're the Anima above all else." His musket rested unmoving across his back as he walked away.

Winter wished more than anything she could believe what he said.

Neva raised her eyebrows at Winter. "Like mother, like daughter, huh?"

"Excuse me?"

Rua groaned. "Neva, no. Just, no." He slapped a hand to his forehead.

"You don't mean to tell me she doesn't know?" Neva sounded scandalized.

"Know what?" Winter looked between Neva and Rua glaring at each other. "Know *what?*"

Stian grimaced and retreated to his chamber. Keno kissed Winter's cheek before leaving them as well. Winter waited for Rua to speak with her arms crossed.

"Your mother," Rua began, giving Neva another glare, "she was forced to leave Greenwood."

"Forced?"

"Please, sit down," Rua said.

She remained standing and asked the same question.

Rua explained how her mother had been threatened when Winter came out half-Imperial. "All the women who had been raped were forced from the village. Most left years sooner than your mother. She endured the ridicule until a group of men came into their home one night and said they would kill you if she didn't leave by the morning."

Neva set a hand on Winter's shoulder. "It's best you know."

Rua obviously disagreed, but he said nothing. Winter processed his story. She had always wondered—and yet she had never dreamed it had been the 'böna that had sent them away. They were supposed to be her people.

"They're not all like that," Rua said. "Many of the 'böna disagreed with the Purge, as the faction called themselves. But war, it leaves wounds that can fester in strange ways."

Winter nodded, remembering the soldier's whipping scars. "Why didn't you tell me until now?" she said at last.

Neva gave Rua a deadpan expression.

"We need to help the 'böna, for the Task," Rua said. "I was afraid if you knew why your mother had fled to Richfield, you'd refuse."

Winter watched the water falling behind Rua. Sunlight glinted off the drops moving erratically off of the flow. The temptation to revenge her mother's memory was there. And yet the Order, the hope for preserving peace in Montane: it was bigger than any one of them, as Hamia had said. Her story, her history, was but a drop in a river.

She looked back to Neva and Rua. "Thank you for letting me know," she said. "But it changes nothing."

Neva offered a rare smile. "You took my words to heart."

"I'm trying."

"Well the time for trying is quickly ending," Rua said. "Execution is imperative. The Imperium is planning its advance on Greenwood as we speak. The future of Montane hinges on this war."

Neva morphed. Hovering in midair, she said to Winter, *I will gather the Shapeshifters at your word.*

☾

The elm and maple trees had shed their leaves seemingly overnight; the brown foliage filled the forest with decay's sweet fragrance. They had stocked the grotto with dried meat, berries, and tubers. Fur skins hung in the driest nook, ready for trade in Greenwood. Should they succeed, they would be ready to survive the winter. The preparations felt reassuring. Life as they knew it could be preserved.

Winter practiced her scythe as she had for nearly every waking hour since the Vipers left. She figured if she could get close enough to the Imperial soldiers, they wouldn't have time to reload their muskets before her blade found their necks. Her deadliest weapons, Rua insisted, were her speed and strength. He had described Erie's prowess in war. The eighth

Anima sounded like a natural warrior. In practice, Winter could slash her scythe with precision and power. But to actually kill another human? Erie seemed to have had an impetus Winter had yet to find, or cultivate, for herself.

She had one more day to practice. The Mages would arrive tomorrow with sunrise.

Animals fled east. They scampered past Grotto Falls, silenced by fear. Neva had told Winter of a whole league of trees cut down last week. Voices of the forest succumbed to the machines' din. And while this filled Winter with remorse and dread, the desire to fight back remained elusive.

She whipped her scythe above her head and slashed it into midair. Bouncing off a boulder, she slashed again. She ran through the trees, imagining branches were swords slicing at her. *The key,* Rua had said, *is to move sporadically, without reason. A musket is a machine of logic. You need to be a weapon of instinct.*

Distant, high-pitched screaming halted Winter. She strained to hear it again. Something was being killed. But it wasn't the release of life: it wasn't death in the Order. The screaming sounded unnatural. She sprinted toward it.

*No, no, no,* a woman's voice bellowed.

"What are you waiting for? Shoot the sow."

A loud crack resounded. Winter slowed down and approached without sound. She climbed up a tree, her feet and hands moving as quietly as a cougar stalking her kill. The mother black bear bled out on the ground, her voice fading into whimpers. Her cubs—her children—yelped as they tried to crawl to their dying mother.

One of the men lifted a club. In that moment, his fist raised in the air, triumphant, Winter all but heard the click. The Anima's impetus. She leaped from the branch and landed on top of him. With movements as sure as the will to eat, to make love, she took his head and snapped it as she would a branch. She withdrew her scythe from her back and turned to face the half dozen others.

"What the?" a man shouted.

Winter roared. They tried to scatter but her blade found each body. Their heads and limbs fell atop the layers of dead leaves. The slaughter happened in a matter of inhale, exhale, inhale, exhale. She returned to the cubs curled into the warm body of their mother and lay down beside them. After a while, she cleaned her face of the earth and tears and told the cubs they could come with her. They wished only for their mother.

*It will be hard to survive without her,* she said. *Impossible, almost.*

When she walked back into the grotto, she carried a cub in one arm and another shuffled alongside her leg.

"Winter!" Keno gasped, running to her. "Are you okay?"

Seeing his panic, she looked down and realized she was covered in the sow's blood and fur. "No," she whispered. "I mean, yes, I'm not hurt."

The cub in her arm began to mew. Smoothing down his fur, she looked at the Shapeshifters gathered before her and spoke through gritted teeth. "But I won't be okay—none of us will—until this senseless killing comes to an end."

☾

The Grand Alliance arrived by the hundreds before dawn. Standing between trees and sitting on boulders, they sharpened spears and cleaned muskets. Snow dusted the bare branches around them. Over five thousand people from all across the world had come. She had never seen such diversity in her life: from their color of skin and hair to their height and build. A few whispered to one another while most prepared in quiet.

Winter saw Yedder and Hamia where the Vipers had gathered. They looked up and waved at Winter. She smiled and waved back. Laurel came to stand next to Winter, and Hamia turned away, frowning.

"It's a beautiful sight, isn't it?" Laurel said. If Laurel had noticed Hamia's evident disfavor toward her, she didn't seem fazed by it.

"It's breathtaking."

Rua had told her about Laurel and Uki, the two other Salvagers. While he described Uki as enthusiastic and Laurel as brilliant, he hadn't told Winter about Laurel's lilac-colored hair or the intense way she looked at people. It felt more like she looked *into* them. Winter avoided eye contact with her.

"Come," Laurel said, taking Winter's hand. "I have something for you."

She brought Winter to where Rua and Uki prepared. A little taller than Rua, Uki reminded Winter of the Madam in the way her eyebrows arched in a bemused expression. Rua was applying a salve to Uki's back. It seemed like an odd time to moisturize.

"Nothing like a good rub down before battle," Uki said with a wink. Her voice was bright and nonchalant.

"Does it help with the nerves or something?" Winter asked. Her own body felt rigid with anticipation.

"I suppose it does."

Winter had assumed all Salvagers were going to be somber and restless like Rua, but between Uki's sunny presence and Laurel's calm demeanor, Winter figured the Salvagers were just humans after all, each with their own unique personality.

Rua finished Uki's back and handed the jar to Laurel. "It's Armadillo Salve," he explained. "An enfleurage Laurel concocted with witch hazel bark, pine needles, and geranium petals."

"With this on, no blade or bullet can pierce your skin," Laurel said. "I invented it a couple decades after Erie's death." She lifted the jar up to Winter. "We'll want to cover your entire body. "

Winter peeled off her layers. The salve tingled as Laurel spread it with cool hands across her back. Winter felt her body relax.

"I've started mixing in valerian root as well," Laurel said. "For the nerves."

Stian walked out of his chamber in a strange outfit. Made of neither metal nor animal, the clothing and helmet shaped perfectly to his body. It looked like he wore a bodysuit made of cream skin patterned with black lines. He did a little twirl. "Don't I look *good?*"

Winter couldn't help but laugh. "You look something."

"Don't be jealous," he said, throwing a limp hand in her direction. "You'll have your own."

Laurel screwed the lid on the jar and motioned for Winter to join her next to a barrel. Inside, birch bark soaked in a light brown liquid. Laurel retrieved a large piece of the bark and molded it to Winter's skin. It felt like putting on a shirt that was somehow both stiff and wet. When it dried, the material became flexible.

"Another invention just a century too late for the last Anima," Laurel said.

Astonished, Winter bent her arm and straightened it. "It's unbelievable."

"It's Florávo." Laurel smiled, revealing a large gap between her front teeth.

Wearing but his animal underskin, Keno walked into the grotto. Neva, dressed in birch, followed behind.

"Where's your armor?" Winter asked Keno.

"I will fight as I did at the battle of Hellörf," he said. "In wolf form."

Winter wanted to embrace him and tell him how much she loved him, but the time for war had come. She could sense it in the soles of her feet. It felt like a hectic pulse, the way the earth pounded as the Imperium marched south. "Are the Shapeshifters ready?" she asked Neva.

"Those who aren't here will meet us at Greenwood."

Winter walked into her chamber. The bear cubs slept curled up, hibernating. She gave each one a kiss and grabbed her scythe on the way out.

Standing on the edge of the grotto, she looked out over the sea of her allies. In the past moon she had thought often about what to say in this moment. Words like courage, bravery, and sacrifice seemed appropriate. She had practiced many speeches. They all were about *how* to win. Now, none of those speeches felt right.

"Why?" she began, yelling loud enough to be heard over the waterfall.

All whispers and movement stilled.

"Why are you here? Not you as in Shapeshifter. Not you as in Viper or Mage. *You*. Why are you here?" Closing her eyes, she remembered the way the sow had whimpered. The cubs crying. The club raised. Her jaw cracking as his fist landed. The smell of upturned earth atop her mother's grave.

She opened her eyes. "You are here for the Anima's Task, and I honor you for that. But what are we actually talking about when we say Order and Disorder, Takers and Keepers? When we charge into battle today, death is a certainty. You may die. And if, by the grace of your god, you don't die, you will lose a friend—so *why?*"

The warriors looked up at Winter with dignified faces.

"Though our experiences may be as vastly different as our appearances, our reasons share the same blood. We fight for the earth sustaining us all. We fight for the freedom to eat and drink the gifts of the land—gifts given by *no man*. We fight for our birthright to these gifts. We fight for our animal kin's right to these gifts. And if we die fighting, we die knowing the earth will take us back in. No man truly owns anyone. We belong only to the earth."

She raised her scythe into the air. The blade, sharpened yesterday, did not glint in the gray light. "For the Order," she cried.

Snow shook free from the branches as everyone screamed, "For the Order!"

Winter pounced from rock to rock and sprinted through the crowd, bumping spears and muskets with her scythe as she flew by. They followed behind her, running. Keno sprinted in wolf form by her side. The ground turned to mud, and the forest vibrated with the clamor of boots and shouts and snapping branches.

Smoke began to gather between the trees. Screams, muskets firing, and men yelling grew louder. Winter slowed and motioned for everyone to approach in a crouched position. Tree stumps became more common than trees until the forest, once ancient in its growth, became a graveyard of severed trunks. Though they could hear the battle, they still could not see it. The smoke swayed as a solid thing, made more of ash than air. She fought the need to cough.

When she could taste the iron of blood, Winter stopped. Keno's eyes flashed in the shifting gray. Stian withdrew his short sword, and Neva ran the curved edges of her daggers along each other. Winter glanced once behind her, to the dozens visible in the smoke. The Vipers squatted low to the ground with spears, bows, and muskets at the ready. Mages held Deadly Charms; the wicker balls glowed vermillion with evoked bloodroot and fire lilies. They all leaned forward as if tethers held them in place.

Winter thrust her scythe skyward, and the smoke swayed chaotically. The Grand Alliance screamed as it sprinted by the thousands into Greenwood. Black smoke billowed from roofs on fire. The corpses of 'böna and Imperials alike had already begun piling in the streets. Red sprayed as they charged through puddles of blood.

When they reached a field beyond the city, about five thousand Imperials surrounded a thousand 'böna and Intlyvwi. The Imperial soldiers turned their muskets at the stampede approaching. Their eyes grew wide when their bullets did nothing to stop the flood. The Montanes drove their spears with the adrenaline of hope renewed.

Winter vaulted into the lines of men. Blades extending from the Imperials' muskets slid off her armor like water gliding over feathers. Her scythe found gaps within their suits of steel. Each strike to their skin proved fatal with the Wolfsbane Decoction coating her blade. The Imperial soldiers faltered with awkward movements compared to the nimble fighters protected by birch. A wicker ball flew past Winter's head. It hit the Imperial running at her, blazing a radiant cerise light. The Imperial collapsed dead.

She jumped off the piles of corpses forming, attacking again and again. Keno ripped an Imperial's arm from his body, and she finished the man with a stab at the exposed wound. A Viper released arrow after arrow into the diminishing swarms of glinting steel. For a pause, Winter marveled at the man's accuracy. Each arrowhead found a weakness in the Imperial armor. When one man dropped dead with but an arrow to his knee, Winter knew Laurel must have created enough Florávian poison for all those fighting in the Grand Alliance. The man turned to face Winter, and she smiled at the ash-smeared face of Yedder.

Her scythe swung less and less. Blood soaked the Birch Skin up to her knees. She maneuvered around the dead, seeking enemies until there were none to be found. Keno trotted through an opening in the crowd. He morphed and walked to her with arms wide. Part of his left ear was missing.

"We did it," he said, embracing her. "We did it."

Hamia strutted over. She held a piece of fabric to a gash in her right arm. A giant smile radiated against the blood streaked across her face. "Well fought, Anima."

Winter tried to return Hamia's smile, but the victory felt more exhausting than the fighting. She withdrew from Keno's hug and looked around. The sun hovered low in the west as a crimson sphere in the smoke. Mages tended to the critically wounded. Montanes and Vipers called out names as they shifted through the dead. The Shapeshifters began gathering in the open land adjacent to the battlefield.

Beside Winter's feet lay an Imperial. She knelt and removed the man's helmet. His eyes, a light brown, stared beyond Winter. A hole burned into his armor told of where a Mage's Deadly Charm killed him. She wondered what he had called himself. And his mother, what was her name?

Hamia frowned at Winter. "He wouldn't be cradling your dead head." Her words were slow with venom.

"I was just—wondering." Winter closed his eyelids and sighed. "Did he even know why he was here?"

Keno helped Winter back up. He glanced at the field of Shapeshifters.

"Words celebrating our victory are in order," Hamia said. She pivoted and marched to where Yedder and the other Vipers stood waiting.

Winter noticed the people watching her. They looked expectant, eager, tired but joyous. She, though, couldn't shake the haunting. Something kept her on edge. They had won, but it seemed too easy. Wasn't the Imperium a formidable force? Hadn't it conquered two seterras? Their weaponry had been useless compared to the Florávian martial arts. She felt confused by this unexpected sadness for the dead men around her. Even the soldier that had beat her at the whorehouse—he was probably in one of these piles. In some ways he seemed just as much a victim to Disorder as any of the dead 'böna.

Keno set his hand on her shoulder. "Winter, your people need you."

She nodded once and walked toward the open field. The smoke still hung heavy around them. With all the survivors gathered, Winter could see they had lost a few thousand. They lifted their faces to her. When she opened her mouth to speak, another voice cried over her own.

"Winter! Winter! Prepare to fight!"

Winter turned to see Laurel running out of the forest with Uki and Rua at her heels. They slipped across the snow and mud. The Salvagers were supposed to be waiting at the grotto.

"It's done," Winter said.

With her hands on her knees, Laurel caught her breath. She shook her head. "It's only just begun."

Everyone exchanged confused looks. Murmurs spread through the crowd.

"We didn't see it," Rua said. "They've hidden it from our Hindsight all this time."

"What?" Keno asked. "See what?"

Laurel stood back up. The look she gave Winter quickened the dread Winter had felt since the battle ended. "They know about plant magic," Laurel said. "Thousands of mages on horseback will be here by nightfall."

Though Winter knew she should eat, the cornbread and chili in her bowl remained untouched. She sipped on water and watched her allies pass around food. They all remained in the field, whispering and stealing glances at where Winter sat with the representatives of each faction from the Grand Alliance. Keno gave her bowl a little nudge.

"Eat," he whispered.

She managed a bite of the bread.

"But we're still twelve thousand strong," Hamia was saying. "We still double their forces."

"Birch armor repels ordinary weapons— not Florávian ammunition," Laurel said. Her voice remained cool despite the exasperation apparent in her furrowed forehead. "I saw them hauling carriages full of the seven Deadly Charms. They have twice the ammunition we do."

"Three times," Rua said. "Half of which is Belladonna Bombs."

Hamia stood and started pacing. Yedder sat between Stian and Neva. Two men on behalf of the 'böna and Intlyvwi also had gathered in the circle. They watched the Shapeshifters and Salvagers with bewildered faces. Winter remembered how unreal the Keepers had seemed when she first woke in the grotto. She offered the 'böna man a small smile when his eyes met hers.

"So you mean to say we can't fight their mages, even with our blades coated in evoked wolfsbane?" Yedder asked.

Everyone looked at Laurel. She, Rua, and Uki all seemed to be in more pain than any of those wounded in battle. Winter wondered how they managed to remain present when their migraines must feel overpowering.

Laurel took a drink from a glass vial containing a green liquid. "We could," she said, returning each person's look in turn. "We could. But we will be like flies fighting falcons. I just—we had no idea."

"It was the same with Jaco," Uki said. "He somehow blocked my Hindsight and revealed Erie's birth as the Anima to the Flüschen king."

"I remember well," Laurel said, rubbing her temples with eyes closed. A dark nothingness in her voice gave everyone pause. "I have no doubt it was Jaco who also revealed the martial arts of Florávo to the union of Lacuserra's three kingdoms."

Laurel's face contorted, and Winter leaned away from the woman in horror. She looked ghastly, like the knot of an old tree, twisted and shadowed. Hamia quit pacing and gaped at Laurel as well. Even Rua seemed utterly confused by Laurel's crazed expression. When she screamed, crows exploded out of the trees. The entire field stilled and whipped their heads at the screeching Salvager. Winter covered her ears.

"A thousand years," Laurel hissed. "For a *thousand* years I traveled the world, gathering knowledge of plant magic. And in *half* the time they beat me in my own game with their army of *Thorns*." Laurel's face twisted deeper, and she began shaking.

People in the field began to whisper again and shift. The Keepers frowned at the ground. Winter watched a box elder bug navigate boot prints in the mud.

"They haven't forgotten, have they?" Uki said. "They haven't forgotten about the Anima."

Everyone looked at Winter. She wished she could be as small as the bug and find a leaf to crawl under.

"They were keeping their memory well hidden," Rua said. He took off his coat and placed it around Laurel's shoulders.

Hamia sat next to the Intlyvwi man. "Well this is our reality now," she said. "Is anyone fluent in either of these men's languages to help them understand?"

"I remember a little," Winter said. Both of the men spoke 'böna. She did her best to tell them about the Imperium's return with mages. The 'böna man asked what the Keepers thought they should do. Winter relayed the question.

Laurel struggled against vomiting. Rua and Uki exchanged hopeless looks. The sun grew a deeper red each moment.

"We have to try."

They startled at the whispered voice.

Winter repeated herself. "For the sake of this earth, we have to try."

After a pause, everyone jumped into motion. Hamia and Yedder marched to the Vipers, yelling in Nyachian. Laurel began retching in the bushes. Uki and Rua also grew pale and looked like they would soon follow suit. Neva set off to gather the Mages while Stian helped the Shapeshifters regroup.

Twilight began to pour out from the forest. Winter stood with Keno in the trees' lengthening shadows. The Salvagers had retreated back to the grotto; fighting wasn't an option when Disorder in action caused crippling migraines. She looked to where she last saw Rua. The look on his face had told Winter this battle would be futile—a gesture of resistance and little more.

Neighing and grunting sounded in the dark. Hooves thundered across the land. The Grand Alliance stood in lines behind Winter. The Mages knelt in front, holding wicker balls and pouches Winter didn't remember seeing in the first battle of this day. Men and women with readied arrows stood behind the Mages, and all ten thousand muskets and spears pointed forward behind the archers.

Torches appeared on the hills north of Greenwood. As the sea of floating flames cascaded toward them, Winter turned to her army. "Remember why you are here," she called out. "Whether you die or live, your reasons to fight are impenetrable."

She raised her scythe in unison with the twelve thousand warriors.

"For the Order!" they yelled.

Horses weaved through the corpses. The Imperial Thorns threw their torches into the piled dead as they stampeded across the field. Stench of burning flesh thickened the smoke around them.

"Release," Hamia screamed.

Arrows whooshed past Winter and rained upon the charging Imperials. With the exception of a few felled horses, the arrows didn't seem to affect the Thorns, even though the arrowheads had been dipped in wolfsbane. Laurel had said Florávian armor didn't deflect evoked plants. Hamia seemed to be thinking the exact same thoughts. For the first time since Winter met her, she looked scared.

"Release," Hamia cried again.

Arrows flew, again to little effect. The Imperial horses ran at them even faster. Foam sprayed out from their curled lips. The Thorns riding them wore no birch armor. White woolen cloaks fluttered in the wind of their speed.

Winter tightened her grip on the scythe. She yelled and ran at the horses. The twelve thousand behind her joined in the cry. A Thorn threw a pouch a dozen yards from where Winter stood. An explosion of fire caused flesh and blood to erupt from the line of archers. That must be a Belladonna Bomb. A dozen more bombs detonated around her. She tried to avoid the horses with her slashing scythe, but it was impossible. The animals cried out in death. They were victims here, slaves to Disorder.

She ducked as a Deadly Charm sailed by her head. A Viper behind her took the wicker ball to his chest and collapsed. With a soundless cry, Winter realized the Viper was Yedder. The Mages threw Belladonna Bombs back at the Thorns. While their Deadly Charms only bounced off the Thorn's cloaks, the explosions managed to kill. Winter realized this battle would be a matter of how many bombs each side could throw. She could hardly see through the gathering smoke. Strips of clothing and particles she refused to name drifted around her. A Thorn appeared in the haze with his arm raised, and she dove behind a pile of the dead.

The pile contained Shapeshifters, Mages, Vipers, and Montanes. No Thorns. She looked at another pile behind her, seeing it was the same. This wasn't a fight. It was slaughter. She had led her people to the butcher's block.

Stumbling back to her feet, she screamed, "Retreat."

A few Shapeshifters close by heard and began running back into the forest. She sprinted toward the battle, yelling for everyone to retreat.

Hamia ran toward Winter, ducking in time to avoid the flight of a charm. "I can't leave the Vipers to die."

"Get them out of here before they're all dead," Winter yelled.

Hamia's eyes blazed, and Winter thought she was going to argue. But Hamia nodded once and began yelling in Nyachian. Winter looked for Keno but couldn't see him. A Thorn threw another bomb in her direction, and she screamed as her leg's Birch Skin caught on fire. She ripped it off and ran toward the forest. When she reached the trees, she looked back once. High on their horses, men in white cloaks populated the carnage, their faces hidden within the drapes of their hoods.

Winter stood on the edge of the grotto with her scythe in hand, watching the Thorns tromp through the forest below. A few looked right at her. One pointed in her direction, and they began hiking up the rocks leading to their cavern. They stood an arm's length from the invisibility border, craning their heads back and forth. When they saw nothing, they walked back down the rocks. Winter released her exhale.

"The wool's been soaked in some sort of protective potion," Uki whispered, sniffing at the Thorn's cloak. "But I cannot name the plants. Possibly pine..."

Uki set the cloak down and walked to where Hamia and Winter stood on watch. The bull and boar heads of the Imperial emblem, stitched onto the cloak's back, glared up at Winter. The cloak's owner lay dead in the corner. They had managed to tackle and disrobe him after he walked past the border, but not before he could injure Stian by evoking the Juniper Vial around his neck. Laurel covered Stian's exposed clavicle bone with a powder while Rua bandaged Keno's ear. Neva nursed her own battle wounds in the corner, rubbing healing salve over a severe burn on her leg.

No one said anything for most of the night while the Salvagers meditated, searching for survivors with their Hindsight. The Thorns withdrew from the forest by dawn.

Rua opened his eyes and looked at Hamia. "A few dozen Vipers and half as many Montanes are on their way back to the Kawaitu headquarters."

Hamia nodded once. A black eye deepened the grave look she gave Winter and the Keepers. "I need to go to them," she said.

"Of course," Winter said. "Will you, will you tell them..."

What was there to say? They had salves. They had bandages. But no words could heal what was lost—what would be lost.

"I will," Hamia said, giving her a hug. Winter could smell the blood soaked into her jacket. Hamia pulled away and held Winter by the shoulders. "Come see us when you're ready."

Winter agreed, and Hamia took off. She watched the Shapeshifter disappear into the trees. Uki stirred out of her meditation and blew her nose into a handkerchief. She dried her face of the tears and said nothing.

Around midday, Laurel opened her eyes. Her voice cracked as she spoke. "At least a thousand Shapeshifters are dead. The Imperium continues south today, to the Intlyvwi capital of Ashland. I imagine all of eastern Montane will come under the bull and boar banner by winter's end."

Laurel looked as terrible as Winter felt. Deep lines carved her face into a mask of torment. The Salvager had arrived as a radiant woman, commanding in her presence. She now sat cross-legged in the grotto's shadows with hunched shoulders and a bowed head. Seeing Laurel's utter defeat felt as harrowing as any of the tragedies Winter had witnessed on the battlefield. She looked away.

"So we will meet them at Ashland?" Neva asked, limping closer to the Salvagers sitting on the ground.

Laurel shook her head. "No, Neva. Meeting the Thorns again in battle would be a senseless waste of Keeper lives."

The waterfall droned on and on. A northern cardinal flitted into the grotto. The flash of its red plumage startled Winter. He perched on a pile of fire logs before darting back into the open air. They all watched him fly away.

"We begin again," Laurel said at last. She looked around the circle. A hint of her dignity had returned in the lift of her chin. "We have no other option but to begin again."

"But—*how*?" Uki asked. "This was our greatest chance for success."

"Hindsight may gift us the lessons of the past, but the future remains unwritten," Laurel answered. "True, we tried our best and failed. This reality is now history. But was this war our greatest chance to end Disorder? We can't know for sure. Where there is uncertainty there can be hope. Time continues forward, and while the Imperium will expand, we can learn and try again. Either that, or give up entirely."

Winter felt herself mirroring Laurel's inflating posture. Everyone sat a little taller. The grotto seemed to expand around them.

"Giving up isn't an option," Laurel continued. She turned to Winter.

"We will fight again, but not in this Anima's lifetime. It will take much longer than your remaining years, Winter, to rebuild an army."

"But—what will be my purpose then?"

Laurel gave her a half smile. "For once, Anima, that's for you to decide."

☾

The cubs grew fast with the spring. By midsummer they stood as tall as Winter's hip. They foraged for serviceberries and rosehips together in the waxing sun of late summer. By the end of autumn, they were over a year old and ready for their own territories.

She watched them trot deeper and deeper into the forest. Though Winter knew their time to diverge had come, and she celebrated the fact they had learned how to survive on their own, she still walked back to the grotto with blurry vision. Keno waited, his arms open. They would never have children, and she cried into his shoulders for both his infertility as a Shapeshifter and hers from chlamydia a lifetime ago.

Winter well knew some wounds heal but forever change the body. She reached up and cupped the remaining half of Keno's ear. He placed his hand over hers, and they looked at each other, silent in their shared knowing. They sat near the fire and ate soup.

Keno stayed behind the next morning when Winter left to visit Harnia in the Kawaitu Forest. The following spring, Winter returned, and they decided to move to Keno's homeland in northern Lacuserra. Without the other Keepers, the grotto had grown formidable in its quiet. The lack of community made the Imperium's expansion to the west louder than ever. Every felled tree echoed through Winter's heart cavity.

She and Keno built a small cottage in the Värtop Mountains. Winter's hair turned gray while Keno's appearance remained the same. He told her she was as beautiful as ever, and she decided to believe him. They hunted together and gathered wild edibles.

One fall afternoon, Winter watched someone walk up the path to their house. The woman's white hair and pale skin glowed against the red rowan leaves.

Winter opened the door. "My dear friend."

Keno pulled out a chair at the kitchen table, and Neva took a seat. Winter prepared a pot of tea.

Neva looked around. "It reminds me of Oili's house," she said.

Winter flinched.

"I don't mean that as an insult," Neva said. "It's—different now. Oili had a choice. We're, well, figuring it out."

"Any news from the Salvagers?" Keno asked.

"They're hard at work repopulating the Havens," Neva said. "Finding orphans to train into Mages. Uki returned to the Northstar Haven to find her daughter, Ada, has gone missing."

Keno raised an eyebrow. Winter didn't know Uki had a child.

"Did she warp?" Keno asked.

Neva shrugged. "We hope not, but you know how it is with Duals."

"Duals?" Winter asked.

"Children of Salvagers," Keno explained. "With magic in their blood, they are terrific forces if they warp into agents for Disorder."

They sipped their tea. Winter rubbed at the throb in her hands. The arthritis flared on these colder days. She ran a finger along the wrinkles of her palm. Callouses from her scythe had long disappeared. "I can't just stay here," she whispered.

Keno and Neva looked at her.

"I don't want to wither here in meaninglessness," she said, louder. "Old and unable to move. To help in any way. There's got to be *something* I can do." Winter took Keno's hands and said, "I can't. I won't. I'm—sorry."

He nodded. "I understand."

Neva set her teacup down. "What, exactly, do you plan to do?"

Winter squeezed Keno's hands before releasing them. "The Imperium's axis works from three nexus, right? Milloposil, Spítheo, and Starktell. If I could just get into one of the—"

"It's impossible," Neva said. "We've tried."

Winter frowned at the table. If she couldn't attempt to kill the people in power, there had to be another way to affect change. She remembered holding the Imperial soldier's head on the battlefield, wondering why he had come to Montane. For all Winter knew, he was only following orders.

"I don't want to hurt anyone again. Not without knowing his heart's true intent."

"Then don't," Keno said. "The Anima's Task isn't only to fight Disorder, but to spread Order."

Winter and Keno smiled at each other.

Neva didn't share in their budding optimism. "It's your life," she said. "But be warned, Winter: the Sacred Balance asks humans to share. Those raised in the belief system of Disorder worship control above all else. Greed does not take kindly to sharing."

"What did Laurel say?" Winter asked. "Giving up isn't an option? I'd like to think that includes giving up on the potential everyone has to change."

Neva studied Winter with her yellow eyes narrowed. She sighed and shook her head. "Oh to be young again," she said to Keno.

Winter laughed. Young? Nearing her seventieth year, Winter appeared to be three times older than either Shapeshifter. "Oh to be impervious to the decay of age," she quipped in return.

"Decay happens to all, regardless of appearances," Neva said, her tone sober.

They rose from the table, and Neva gave them hugs goodbye before morphing. Winter watched the white blur of her wings disappear into the evergreens.

☾

"That's right," the woman said. "Two sons now." She sat in an oak chair by the hearth, rocking back and forth as she nursed her baby.

Keno and Winter glanced at each other. It had been the same story on the farm before this one, and the farm before that one. It had been the same story across all of Etalv, Stamden, and Jornorgud. Families living under Imperial rule were allowed to keep one son to help his father. The Imperial Army came for all following sons once they turned twelve.

The baby began to cry and the woman stood to change his diaper. Her husband, a grizzly of a man with a bushy beard and long, brown hair, examined Winter over his cup of mulled wine. She smiled at him.

"You're the Anima, aren't you?" he asked, not returning the smile.

"We've heard rumors of you, traveling with your—*son* here." He frowned at Keno. "Story has it you fought down in the new protectorate."

Again, Winter and Keno exchanged glances. She had expected that news of her mission spread out before her, as words traveled faster than walking feet. Yet in all her conversations thus far, she had never mentioned fighting in the battle for Montane.

"It's William, right?" she asked. "Can I call you Will?"

"Bill."

"Well, Bill, I'm not sure what rumors you've heard and haven't heard about me, but I will say my truth, clear and simple: I'm here to offer an alternative way of being than what is currently available in the Imperium."

The woman returned to the room, the baby asleep in her arms.

"Imagine if you didn't have to give a third son to fight and die for the Imperium's expansion."

Drawing the baby closer to her chest, the woman shot Winter a scathing look. "Treason," she hissed.

"I only asked you to imagine." Winter spoke with the quiet, patient tone she had mastered over the last three years of talking with families. They had all reacted to her words with resistance made harsh by fear. A few houses she left feeling heard and understood. Most houses, though, slammed the door shut behind her.

"It is what it is," Bill said. "We make an honest living here on the land of our ancestors. The Imperium protects us from our enemies in the west while we ensure there's food enough in the pantry come winter."

"And pray for daughters," Keno added. They had heard this common adage whispered across the countryside. Bill and his wife looked at each other, and Winter knew they, too, prayed for baby girls. Daughters meant more hands to help on the farm. They meant more food on the table—and less tears come the age of twelve.

"I'm not here to out you to the Imperium for wishing life was different," Winter said. "I'm simply here to tell you that it could be."

Bill finished his mulled wine and gestured for Winter and Keno to do the same. "We'll feed you breakfast before you leave," he said. "You can sleep in the bunkhouse out back."

Winter had learned some fights weren't worth the effort. She nodded once and drank the wine. It tasted of serviceberries, and she remembered the cubs. They were long dead by now. She hoped they had reached old age. "Delicious wine," she said. "Thank you."

The woman smiled, the first and only on their behalf. She led them to the bunkhouse. Keno and Winter curled up on the thin mattress made of hay. Though the bunkhouse stunk of mice and mold, Winter could also smell the body oil of a person.

"Do you smell that?" she whispered.

"Someone lives in here," Keno said.

An owl cooed somewhere in the near distance.

She turned to face him. "We've had more failures than successes."

He kissed her forehead. "Sometimes successes aren't evident right away. While it may seem they do not hear you, they do."

"I know," she sighed. "It's just—sad. So many of these families seem defeated."

"They're getting by. They have food, water, wood for the fire, roofs overhead."

Winter sat up. "I know. So why does the Imperium continue its violent campaigns in the south?"

Keno sat up as well. "Greed. Glory. Power. Some unnamable want."

"Really—abstract words? Is that all we have to explain the thousands dead at Greenwood?"

Seeing Keno's knitted brow, Winter softened. "Sorry," she whispered. "I'm tired."

"I know." He tucked her hair behind her ear. "I am, too."

In the morning they walked west. The birch trees were budding by the time they reached the Värtop cottage. Winter cleaned cobwebs from the ceiling rafters as Keno hunted down dinner. And so they began again.

☾

Years later, midsummer brought an unshakable cold to Winter's body. Her coughs grew louder and more frequent until blood began to color the phlegm red. She could feel death settling into her bones. Once bedridden, Keno spoon-fed her warmed broth.

Laurel came up from the Nafáit Haven with a tincture of elderberries and echinacea. She set the tincture on the nightstand and sat on the bed beside Winter. Holding Winter's hand, she said, "You've lived a glorious life, my friend."

Winter tried to swallow but her throat would not, or could not. "I've tried my best," she managed.

"Indeed," Laurel said, smiling.

"But—"

"No, Winter. You've done remarkable work. Be at peace."

Keno sat across from Laurel and clasped Winter's other hand. She felt suspended between the Keepers, held aloft by their love. She died in the night with Keno sleeping next to her. Still sitting on the bed, Laurel bore witness to Winter's last words and looked to the south.

# HANO

## 200 YBP

### The Manduka Forest, Sypay

Hano pressed the wooden barrel to her lips. Her exhale, a strong *whoosh*, sent the dart zooming through the palm leaves. It hit the boar below his neck. His scratchy screams resounded as he ran away, thrashing through the thickets. She and Tenaria waited a few moments before pursuing him. The frog's poison worked quickly, and they found the boar next to the Grand River around midday. They crouched down next to the boar's still body and held hands. The river, still engorged with flood season, raged beside them as they murmured thanks to the Spirits.

They would need help carrying his body back to the village. Being much faster than her older brother, Hano took off running. Broad leaves swiped at her face, and strangling fig roots obscured the ground. She moved as a blur nonetheless. The forest felt like an extension of her arms and legs, as familiar as the broad flat of her feet.

A few young men followed her back to the boar. She made sure to trot slow enough for them to see her. Tenaria waited with his back leaning against a mangrove tree. He looked like a jaguar lounging in the sun. One hand rested on the boar, another atop his short grass skirt. A thin headband made of hide kept his hair pinned close to his head.

He opened one eye. "You're getting slow in your old age," he said, smirking.

Hano gave him a flat expression. She had turned fourteen this past flood, and he had since taunted her about being a woman. She hadn't told him her moon-blood had yet to come. Everyone just assumed as much, including the young men, Tenaria's peers at fifteen, straggling behind her. Both had asked for her flower. Both had been turned away.

They set the stretcher down next to the boar and collectively pushed his stout body onto the hide. Four people made the trip home a nearly effortless thing. Hano kept her dart barrel on the front of her body, just in case. It was unlikely a cat would attack four of them, but she would never forget the sight of Bly's two eldest boys left with throats torn open.

A fire had been stoked in the village center. They set the boar near the flames, and Hano helped her mother skin him. Her mother's swollen belly turned pink as it pressed against the boar's naked muscles. Hano figured she would birth the child, her fifth sibling, within the next moon. She had been pregnant with Tenaria at Hano's age. While Hano worked her knife beneath the skin, she wondered if she would ever be pregnant or if she, like their Healer, Koenia, would live her life childless. Two women couldn't make a child. Maybe when she got her moon-blood, she'd end up wanting men instead of women after all.

They roasted the boar over the fire. Half a dozen children, Hano's younger sister among them, chased each other with sticks. A year ago she would have been running with them. Now she helped her mother turn the boar on its spit. Little beads of sweat trailed between her nascent breasts.

Commotion spread from the village's west end. The children quit chasing each other and found their mothers. Hano's sister wrapped an arm around their mother's leg. Hano tried to look beyond the few dozen people now gathered in the village center. Everyone quieted. A brief parting in the bodies revealed why.

Nehini had his hands on his stomach as he caught his breath. All the villagers had emerged from their circular huts and stood waiting. "Make way," they said. "She's coming."

Koenia strutted toward Nehini. Even in the heat of this night their Healer wore her fur cloak. Hano had never seen a giant otter alive; her father often said they were more rare than they used to be. The cloak covered Koenia's entire body. It shined in the dim light, black then silver.

"Nehini," she said in her booming voice. "Stay where you are."

Nehini lifted his face. He was thinner than Hano remembered him. Much thinner. He had always been gangly, but the way his cheeks caved in told Hano he had been running for at least a few days straight. He wore a strange cut of fabric over his chest and another cut over his legs. She had never seen material like it before. It was the color of orchids: red and purple, white and blue.

"The Emperor," he breathed. "He's dead."

Koenia stopped a few body lengths from Nehini. Flies buzzed around them, and thunder rolled somewhere in the distance. Nehini's mother moved forward to embrace her son.

"No," Koenia said, stopping the woman midstride. "Everyone back up."

The villagers did as told. Hano whispered an apology to the woman behind her when she accidentally stepped on her foot. Another gap appeared in the crowd, and Hano could see Nehini's shoulders slouch. He alone didn't look confused by Koenia's strange behavior. The Healer had always been an aloof and rude woman, but this reaction to their Messenger's long-awaited return seemed exceptionally unkind.

Nehini lifted his chin back up. The crowd shifted again, obstructing Hano's view.

"The Emperor's head rolled down the temple stairs," he said, loud enough for all to hear. "There's a new king. He said he comes from the north. They fought with weapons called guns. They're not like us, not at all. Their skin is the color of bone. Whiter than yours, even," he said to Koenia.

Whispers spread through the crowd. Skin even whiter than Koenia's? Tenaria had come to stand next to Hano. They lifted their eyebrows at one another. Hano stood on her tippy-toes, trying to see how their Healer reacted. Though Koenia was taller than even the men of the village, Hano could only see the blue and yellow macaw feathers of her headdress.

"They also brought a sickness," Nehini said, dropping his voice.

Hano heard Nehini's mother gasp. Another series of whispers spread.

"And you carry it now," Koenia said to Nehini. Her voice was flat and chilling.

Hano smelled burning meat. She ran back to the fire. The boar hung above the smoldering logs, a charcoal black. Hano removed the spit from its stand and cut into him. The meat had charred to the bones. Hano bowed her head and muttered apologies. She prayed the Spirits would understand and not exact revenge for the wasted life.

☾

They set fire to his hut, possessions, and withered corpse. Koenia had called it the Snow Fever. Hano didn't know what snow meant other than certain death. The Healer had prohibited anyone from coming in contact with Nehini. She insisted this was for the survival of the village. Hano believed her, but the reasoning didn't make his end any less cold in her body. He had been a childhood friend, a few years older and a few strides faster than she was. His fate as the Messenger had been bitter, as if his gift of speed only served to bring him quicker to death.

The village had remained in an uneasy quiet in the moon to follow. No news of life east across the Grand River or west past the Forever Night reached their ears. Hano hunted and ate and slept all in the dim, green light of this jungle. Koenia hadn't emerged from her hut since Nehini's death. The villagers gossiped about what the Healer was planning. Would the next Messenger be sent? Would the Snow Fever come to them? Would the guns?

Hano walked to the Grand River. She found a seat on the grassy bank and stuck her toes into the flow. Clouds obscured the sun. She cracked open a maracuja with her machete and sucked at the juicy flesh. A kingfisher splashed into the current upstream. He flapped back to the skies with a piranha wriggling within his beak. A pair of dolphins dived in and out of the muddy waters. They turned their pink and gray noses toward her, curious but unalarmed, before continuing downstream.

She could spend all day here, eating the spoils of the dry season, watching the river life beneath a break in the canopy. If it weren't for the meeting, she would. She finished her snack and ran back home. People stood in line to fill their bowls with catfish soup. Hano skipped into her family's hut, grabbed her bowl, and filed in behind her brother.

"Did you see anything interesting at the river?" Tenaria asked.

"Nothing out of the ordinary." She leaned in close. "Any word about this meeting? It feels strange." People seemed to be moving self-consciously around her, avoiding eye contact and scooping soup into their bowls with haste uncommon to the village.

Tenaria met her eyes. "I believe we will have a new Messenger by tonight."

Hano's stomach flipped. So the time had come. Everyone knew who the next Messenger would be. Stepping closer to the fire warming the soup, Hano could smell the burning grasses and wood, Nehini's flesh and bone. She left the line.

All bowls filled but one, they gathered in the village circle. Hano sat next to Tenaria with the other teenagers. Her mother offered a limp wave from where she was fussing over Hano's newborn brother. Hano resisted the urge to run over and throw her arms around her mother, to lean her head against the fullness of her milk-filled breasts. She waved in return, feigning nonchalance. Her moon-blood had arrived with the orchid bloom, days after Nehini's death. She was truly a full-grown woman now. To run to her mother would bring shame to the family.

She traced the rim of her empty bowl with a finger, thinking of how the Messenger had been a coveted role in the village. Boys and girls spent their free hours racing through the jungle, returning home with bruises and scrapes and panting for water. Hano's body—thick in the thighs, curvy in the torso, even as a child—seemed an endless source of energy. She could weave through the strangling fig groves, her hands using branches to swing over speed-sucking mud. The other children had admired and envied her agility.

Nehini's death had changed that. Her peers slurped up their soup in silence. They offered small smiles, little pats on her shoulder, but no words of comfort. No matter. Words felt useless anyways.

Koenia emerged from her hut, and the crowd dropped into silence. The slick fur of her otter cloak glistened in the twilight. She wore her long, black hair in multiple braids, and her face, longer and fuller than any Hano had known, looked down on everyone sitting. Though she had been in the village since her grandmother's time, she appeared to be younger than her mother. Hano sometimes found the agelessness of her face unsettling, even if it was proof of her connection to the Spirits.

Her presence expanded above the thatched roofs and into the twilight skies. All looked up to her. "For a full moon we have lived in the shadow of Nehini's passing. He is well in the Spirit World. I saw him last night, still running, his body newly carved."

Koenia paused, allowing the sobs of Nehini's mother to quiet before continuing. "I gather you all because his words haunt my dreams. We live in a peace that will not endure. The Tawanians have succumbed to these Snow Men, and I fear the fate of the Sypayos follows suit.

"Yet I cannot be sure. So it is time to resurrect the Messenger. Our eyes and ears need to reach beyond our home."

Koenia's gaze found Hano. The others turned to her as well. Hano wobbled to a stand.

"As our fleetest feet, our largest lungs, I bless you, Hano, as our Messenger. Tomorrow morning you will leave for Killasi. May your fate be kinder than that of Nehini's, and may you return with news that gives shape to the darkness of my dreams."

Hano listened to her father snore. Her baby brother and mother had finally fallen back to sleep. She tried not to rustle the dried palm leaves of her bed as she turned from one hip to the other. Watching her toddler sister kick her feet as she dreamed, Hano wished Tenaria still slept in their parents' hut as well. He had finished building his own earlier this moon.

Rain pattered upon the roof as a thunderstorm rolled in. Even the baby slept through its booms and crackles. Dying Nehini's slow death played over again and again in Hano's head. She wanted to talk with Tenaria, to make him promise that he would shoot her with a dart if she returned from the mountains with the Snow Fever.

Shadows stirred outside the open doorway. A bolt of lightning outlined a figure dipping into the hut. Hano sat up. Another bolt revealed the figure standing above her.

"Come," Koenia whispered.

Hano stood, her rushed movements causing the baby to stir awake. She slipped out of the hut behind Koenia just as the baby began to wail. The rain fell in slanting sheets, and water ran in rivulets alongside the path. The flood season was fast approaching. Koenia dipped into her hut. Hano paused outside the door. She had never been inside the Healer's home; no one she knew had been. Her hair grew wet as she hesitated.

Koenia peeked out the door. "Now."

Hano scrambled inside. In the center of the hut, a sphere emitted a blue light. Hano stepped toward it. The sphere, made of a clear material Hano had never seen before, held within it a few dozen mushrooms. Hano recognized the luminescent mushrooms. She reached a hand toward the light. Was the sphere solid or liquid?

"Don't touch that," Koenia growled.

"Sorry," Hano said, drawing her hand back as if it had been burned.

The sphere emitted enough light to reveal the Healer's entire home. Her bed, cushioned with palm leaves like usual, was lifted off the ground by a wood structure reminding Hano of a boar stretcher. A wooden water basin sat atop a kapok tree stump alongside containers made of the same clear material as the sphere. Dried leaves, flowers, and fungi filled the containers. The room smelled of the rain outside and something even sweeter, like açaí juice.

Koenia told Hano to sit beside the glowing sphere. She retrieved a bag from beneath her bed and sat across from Hano. The blue light turned Koenia's red face paint purple. Her eyes were even more black than usual. Hano didn't know of anyone else with eyes the same color as the pupils. During ayahuasca ceremonies, people's eyes would become nearly solid black like Koenia's eyes, but this effect was always temporary.

One time, Hano had asked her mother if Koenia was always using ayahuasca. Her mother had laughed and said if she were, she would be vomiting all the time as well. She had said her eyes were all black because the panther's Spirit dwelled in her. This was largely why Koenia lived as the village Healer. It was why they all trusted her word above any other.

Koenia loosened strings threaded through the bag's opening. Hano didn't recognize the bag's material: it looked even suppler than monkey hide. Koenia withdrew a long cut of fabric from the bag. The fabric reminded Hano of the clothing Nehini had worn when he came back to them. She leaned away from its bright red color.

"This is a skirt Tawanian women wear," Koenia said. She withdrew another cut of fabric. "And this is a shirt." Koenia held out the shirt to her.

Hano hesitated. What if it carried the Snow Fever? Koenia thrust the shirt onto her lap. Hano pinched the fabric and held it up.

"You wear it to cover your breasts," Koenia explained.

Hano frowned at the lines zigzagging over and above her bare breasts. "Do they not like tattoos?"

"I don't know. But if you walk around with your breasts hanging free, you'll be asking for a child you don't want."

But—why? Koenia took the shirt back and stuffed it into the bag. She explained how Hano was to change at the forest's end. Hano had a hard time imagining the Forever Night forests being not forever. Koenia further explained how she was to continue to Killasi. She taught Hano how to ask for directions in Tawanian.

"When you get into the city, find a corner and pretend to be homeless," Koenia said. "Beg for food."

"Beg for food? But why wouldn't I just go hunt some down?"

"There's much about the city you won't understand." Koenia did nothing to hide the irritation in her voice. Her long face darkened. "Just sit, beg, and watch. You won't speak the old or new tongue of Killasi, but the language of the body is universal. Observe what these Snow Men do and how they act. From this we might learn why they're here and where they plan to go next."

Hano nodded. Nerves beat against her ribcage. She slipped her arms through the bag's straps and moved to stand.

Koenia wrapped a hand around her wrist, causing her to still. "Above all else, Hano, you need to return if anything happens to you."

"Like, if I get sick?"

Koenia tightened her grip. Hano gritted her teeth.

"*Don't* return if you get sick. But if anything *else* happens, come back as soon you as you are able, and not a moment later. Do you understand?"

No, she didn't understand. What else could possibly happen?

Koenia wrung her fingers even tighter. "Do you?"

Hano gasped. "Yes," she lied.

"Leave now," Koenia said, releasing her hold.

Hano stumbled to her feet, nearly knocking the sphere over in her haste. The clear material proved to be hard. As Hano ran into the forest, she wondered if it was made of solid air or solid water.

☾

Broad leaves whipped at her forehead and arms. The dew mingled with her sweat. She moved through the forest, slower than an hour ago but still running. Last night she had slept in the branches of a wimba tree. When she had woken, a sloth had hung not an arm's length away. He had stared at her as if asking, *What brings you here?*

She didn't have an answer to that question. Was it her speed? The foreigners? An order as old as her people? She picked up the pace again despite the burn in her legs and lungs. Little welts on her feet seeped blood and pus. She allowed her mind to find the discomfort. This was what it felt like to be alive, to have sensations, a living body. If nothing else, she would dwell in her aliveness.

Nehini had shared stories of the empire from his first few trips to the Tawan capital, floods before the Snow Men invaded. He had told her about the homes and walls made of rock. Killasi sat within a cradle of earth giants; Tawanians called them mountains. Even if she met the same fate as Nehini, she would see the giants, and for this Hano ran a little faster.

Dusk slipped in through the canopy, and she stopped to eat the dried boar meat Koenia had packed in her bag. She ate freshly plucked maracuja for breakfast and continued running. Her legs felt heavy today, her feet a little clumsy. She slipped and launched into the ground face first. Pain like no other seared from her mouth into the pit of her stomach. She spit into her hand and startled at a tooth within the blood and dirt. Bringing her fingers to her mouth, she felt a gap where one of her front teeth should have been.

Blood continued to gush as she returned to a trot. And how much blood such a little thing like a tooth unleashed. The forest morphed from benign home to foreboding darkness. Knowing predators could smell the blood, she whipped her head to and fro, looking for the green slant of eyes, the blur of spotted fur. When she settled into another wimba for the evening, she collapsed into sleep. Fear felt more exhausting than running.

Her fourth day on the move and the canopy thinned. She slowed as the jungle quieted. Trees spaced further apart, and sunlight grew from a trickle to a stream, from a stream to a flooding river. Her eyes blinked against its fury. The trees gave way to smaller growth, and Hano tiptoed from bush to bush. This was it—the end of forever.

Grasses spread across the rolling earth. There was no human life on the vista, only green grasses as far as her eyes could see. The sunlight was relentless. She sat on the ground and closed her eyes. The yellow-red of her lids terrified her. Inescapable light. That was what had waited all this time beyond the forest. She looked back to the trees and the comfort of shadows.

She scolded her weakness and ate a few pieces of dried boar meat. When she resumed running, the rise and fall, rise and fall of the land threatened to tear her legs from her torso. But she pushed against the cry to stop, halting only when the crest of a hill revealed the earth giants Nehini had described.

They were blue. Blue as the Grand River on a clear day after the floods had run through. She rubbed her eyes, blinked and blinked, but no, they truly were blue. In all her life she had never dreamed that the land beneath her feet would ever be blue. But there it was, living proof the earth could be the same color as water and sky. Clouds wrapped around the pointed tops and between the folds of blue. The city etched into the hills and valley below the mountains. Nehini had downplayed the extent of the homes and streets.

Between her and the buildings were a half dozen more hills. A strange pattern differentiated these hills from the ones behind her. The markings reminded her of an anthill's terraces. Although they were but tiny dots, she could see people traversing the land, their movements indiscernible if not observed at length. She decided to cut north, along an extension of forest. When she entered the growth, Hano wondered at the trees. They were much different than the trees of the jungle. Many branches worked their way up the trunks, and the leaves grew small and by the hundreds.

She retrieved the change of clothes Koenia had given her. The full-length skirt felt itchy and hot compared to the short cut of boar hide she wore for the run. When she slipped into the shirt, her breasts questioned the fabric. Fully dressed, she followed the forest edge. The bright colors of her skirt seemed to beg for others to notice. But the women and men stooped over didn't look twice as she moved past them. They acknowledged her with a nod and continued to pull up plants from the dirt.

Hano entered the city limits. She felt she had one foot in terror, the other in thrill. More people than she had ever imagined moved within a wilderness of stone structures. The smell of urine and feces grew as she walked deeper into the growth. A person opened the door of a house, and Hano jumped away from the wood swinging into the street.

The person's skin looked leached of color. A real life Snow Man blinked back at her. He asked something, and she smiled and nodded her head, pretending to understand what he had said. He said something else, his face narrowing. His tone brought both her feet into terror. He called to another man across the street, and they both turned toward her.

Hano took off running. The skirt shortened her stride. The men ran after her, but she was faster despite the unnatural constraint of her clothes. They soon gave up the chase, but she didn't stop running. More white men and women passed by as well as people of her color. They all blurred together as one face of surprise. The city gave way to a steep incline of rocks and roots, and she willed her way up the foothills. Closing in on the mountains, the blue earth revealed itself to be, in fact, green and brown.

The clouds she had seen wrapping the mountains from afar surrounded her. Her lungs filled with heavy air, and she felt the panic quiet into curiosity. What *was* this place? It smelled of mud and sap. She sat on a mossy stump and ate the last of her dried meat. The sound of water trickling nearby led her to a stream. She drank from it, and a strange pang filled her head. She rubbed at the pain until it faded.

She had failed already. How had Nehini slipped in and out of town unnoticed? She decided to try again in the morning. She would enter the city from the northwest. Surely no one would recognize the imposter who had outrun a couple Snow Men the day before. Between now and then she needed more food and shelter for the night. The forest shifted around her, questioning what she thought she knew. Nothing. She knew nothing of this place.

Footsteps across the stream brought her body erect, ready to run again. A dark creature lumbered not a stone's throw away. The mists shifted and shaped around his body. He turned in Hano's direction, revealing a masked face. His fur's markings reminded Hano of the way she would paint her body in ceremony, with dark circles around her eyes. The animal looked like a sloth, with long fur and nails, though he moved more quickly across the ground on all four paws.

Seemingly unaware of Hano watching him, he clambered up the mountain. Hano decided to follow. She stalked the creature as she would a boar, and he remained oblivious to Hano's presence as he continued moving deeper and deeper into the clouds. The trees grew smaller, and the mist grew thicker. The world itself shrunk around her. Hano wondered if she was even in the mountains anymore. Earth and sky had blurred together.

The creature came to rest. Hano watched him uproot plants for a while before the mushrooms caught her eye. They dazzled, even in light muted by mist. Their color reminded her of red-blood orchid blooms. She moved closer to them and wondered at the perfect circle they had created beneath the trees.

She could hear the creature munching on a root, his gnawing and swallowing a blunt reminder of her own hunger. Running her fingertip in circles around the stem, she thought it shameful to pick something so beautiful, so rare. Red warned of injury or worse. To pick a red orchid was to ask for suffering. And yet this mushroom could be like the other mushrooms her people ate. It could sustain her.

The pluck sound it made brought her eyes to the creature. Surely he had heard the pop. But he munched on and on, looking blissful while he gorged. She yearned to feel satiated in the same way. As she moved the tiniest of nibbles around her mouth and swallowed, his masked face turned to her. The world shrunk even more around them. He stared right at her, unmoving and unconcerned, as if he had known she had been there this entire time.

☾

The clouds hugged the ground, obscuring Hano's vision to a foot at a time. That was what she loved most about her time in these mountains; she took one step at a time, one day at a time. In this way the days moved neither fast nor slow. How many moons had passed? There were no moons, only hints of night and day. The lack of full sun made her feel at home.

She hadn't been imagining it when she had eaten the mushroom: the masked bear had known she was there, and he had brought her to the cave that would hold her transforming body. Upon waking, the bear had explained little. She was reborn as the Anima, and she could now speak the ancient language of the earth.

The bear was a bear until he was a tall man with large shoulders. He had a bald head, black, arching eyebrows, and the same lucid brown eyes of his bear form. He was the most stunning human Hano had ever seen, that was until she saw the other Shapeshifters in their human forms. The guinea pig, alpaca, flicker, goose: all the Shapeshifters Hano met could transform into beautiful people. They lived boundless, wild in their refusal to be defined solely by animal or human form. They were ancient, ageless, and free in all ways but one.

To some extent, Hano could relate to a fluid identity. She had always been the second fastest in her village, beating all the boys but Nehini. Sometimes she thought she was, in truth, a boy. As the Anima, she was faster than she had ever been. If she could race Nehini now, she would leave him to follow her footprints in the mud. Her body remained curvy, though more muscles had formed within the flesh. She felt honored to live in the strengths of both fat and brawn.

Yet her favorite part of being the Anima, by far, was the voices. She could remember first entering the forest, when this place had enveloped her in its strangeness. Now she could hear the subtleties. The world around lived as a village of its own: there were hunters and foragers; there were families, rivalries, dangers, and comforts. She heard a wooly monkey screech at her infant to be careful. Their bickering reminded Hano of her mother scolding her toddler sister when she would refuse to go to bed.

Her family—they had crept into her conscience over the last few sleeps. It had been easy at first to push away thoughts of her village and her responsibilities as their Messenger. What room was there for the past when the present offered senses on fire? What space was there for the future when this sky-like earth filled her mind with an ancient language?

And yet she could not deny the shadows, even if the mist all but erased them. She sat on the mossy ground, leaning her back against a tree, and remembered the fires' towering flames, that smell of grass and flesh burning. Koenia placing the torch to Nehini's hut and telling them all the Snow Fever had taken him. Koenia, above all else, haunted Hano when the mist darkened.

*You need to return if anything happens to you,* she had said. The Healer must have known Hano would become the Anima. Why else would she have told her this? Yet the Shapeshifters had said to wait; they had an important message for her. She figured she owed them this much for bringing her back to life. When she had woken in the cave, she thought she had the Snow Fever. The masked bear had said she was dying so she could be reborn.

He had spoken the truth. She had been reborn, and she loved her new body, her new life here in the mountains. But on days like today, when the mist gathered around her, pressing the memory of her family, Koenia, and her mission as the Messenger against her, she knew the time to return drew near.

Hano stood and slung her pack back over her shoulder. She could hear a tapir bedding downhill. It was time to leave behind these thoughts and enter her body, her power. It was time to hunt.

☾

She was drinking from a stream when an osprey appeared without noise. A knowing chill quivered through Hano's body.

*Follow me,* the osprey said.

Hano hopped from rock to rock across the stream. Newly blossomed magic-plants grew along the waters. The osprey continued up the mountain, soaring from one branch to the next, leading Hano back to the place of her rebirth.

Light dimmed around them as they entered the cave. Hano remembered the terrible nausea when she first woke, but the beauty also flooded back to her. Water and sunlight poured in through a hole in the ceiling, revealing the cave's marbled walls. Deep and light blues, teal and white swirled together. A small pool of water glowed emerald green.

The Shapeshifters she had met during her transformation gathered near the waters, the masked bear among them. Their voices quieted as Hano approached. She took a seat on a rock. The osprey morphed into her human form. Brown and white feathers gave way to light brown skin reminding Hano of Koenia's coloring. She had full lips, long eyelashes, and a hairless head.

"My name is Dailan," she said in Hano's native tongue, though with a foreign accent. Hano hadn't heard any of the Shapeshifters speak in her human language. Words spoken aloud sounded displaced in the cave.

"Hano."

Dailan grinned. "I know. I hope you have felt well taken care of during your transformation."

"Very much so." She couldn't stop staring at Dailan's head. What had happened to her hair? Didn't she need it?

"It's that strange looking to you, huh?" Dailan ran a hand over the smooth curve of her skull. "I shaved my head for the fourth Anima's Task, and I found the ease and simplicity of baldness suits me. I've shaved my head ever since. Over three millennia now." She filled the cave with the jaunty cadence of her laugh.

Hano smiled.

"There now," Dailan said, coming to sit next to her. "A smile to light the world. May I hug you? It's been so long since I've seen an Anima."

Hano shrugged. "I guess."

Dailan embraced her. She smelled like an orchid. "It hasn't been that long, truth have it," Dailan said, pulling away. "Only a hundred years have passed since Winter died. She was the Anima before you. A very lovely woman."

Dailan set a hand on Hano's thigh. "You probably have so many questions. Why don't you ask first? Oh, and I apologize if I'm hard to understand. I learned both Tawanian and Sypayos in preparation for the Anima's rebirth, but I fear I'm fluent in neither. I figured, though, you may appreciate human-to-human contact as it's more ordinary."

Hano blinked and shook her head. This woman—who *was* she? "I understand you well enough. Where are you from?"

Dailan touched her chest. "Oh. Start with me? An appropriate place, I suppose, given the news I bring today. Not the best news, no, sorry to say. I come from a—is there a word for it in your language?—a seterra. The seterra I'm from is called Shénchåo."

"Seterra?"

"It's as I thought then." Dailan gave Hano a look of wonder. "Laurel once told me about the Sypayos and your exclusion from the larger world. Was your trip to Killasi the first?"

"I had never left the Forever Night before then."

Dailan whistled. "Amazing. Truly amazing. To live your life—well, anyways. If you're not familiar with seterras, you probably know nothing about..." She looked up in thought. "No, there aren't any words for them in your language, either, are there? The Republic and the Imperium."

Hano shook her head at the foreign syllables. "Re..."

"Re-*pub*-lick. Im-*pure*-e-um. They are the two World Forces."

"Are you talking about the Snow Men?"

Dailan looked confused for a moment. "Oh, the white men in Killasi. You call them Snow Men. Clever."

"Our Healer calls them that."

"Well, the Snow Men are the Imperial Army. Or I should say they work in service of a power structure called the Imperium seeking to dominate your land. The land. All land." Dailan's voice grew dark as she spoke.

Though Hano had just met her, she could tell the glowering demeanor wasn't her natural self. "Dominate," Hano repeated slowly. "As in—?"

"As in conquer the land by enslaving its inhabitants and extracting whatever resources the place may offer. Things like metal for their weapons and coal for their trains."

Train. Coal. These words rung hollow to Hano with their lack of definition. "I don't understand."

"Of course not." Dailan's smile was sad. "You lived oblivious to the spread of Disorder across the world. You didn't ask for the invaders to come and take away your autonomy. But the Imperium takes what the Imperium thinks it needs. The Republic does the same. In fact, the Republic's armies reached Tawan's shores last month. The Imperium and Republic are warring this very moment in the forest south of here, near the city of Tinaku."

"Wait—there are new invaders?"

"That's exactly what I'm saying."

Hano jumped up. "I must warn my village. I must leave. Now."

The Shapeshifters stirred in the cave's shadow. Hano had forgotten they were there.

"That's not wise, Hano," Dailan said, soft but firm. "Your village is but one tiny leaf in this forest we now navigate. We need to get you to safety and regroup with the Salvagers before making any rash decisions. Once the Imperium discovers your birth as the Anima, you will be hunted. Relentlessly. Ruthlessly. They will not stop until they find you."

"But why? What have I done?"

"It's not what you've *done,* but what you can *do*. With the right strategy in place, the Anima may be able to stop the World Forces, once and for all. She may be able to bring together all peoples in service of Order and fulfill the Task. I say *may* because we've tried, Hano. We've tried for over nine millennia now. We thought we would be victorious with Winter. We had an army." Dailan pounded a fist into her palm.

Hano wondered if she was even talking to her anymore.

"We had an army," she repeated. "But the Imperium discovered our secret and used it for its own twisted ends. Many of us escaped, Winter included. But many Keepers died that day."

Hano shifted as Dailan grew quiet. While she knew this story had everything to do with her life now as the Anima, it meant nothing to her.

"I made a promise to my people," Hano said. "They need to be warned of these invaders, if what you say is true and they intend to conquer all of the land."

Dailan snapped her head back up. She pushed out a breath and examined Hano with a kind face. "Okay. We'll make a quick detour to your village. But first I want you to see what we're dealing with. I want you to see the war at play and why it is vital we begin your Task as soon as possible."

"We?"

Dailan raised her eyebrows. "If you think I'm going to risk an Anima dying under my care again, you're crazy. I'm coming with you."

The Shapeshifters made grunting noises in their animal forms. Dailan lifted her hands. "We all know what has happened when Keepers have tried to bend Animas to our will without heeding their own wants and needs," she said.

Hano looked between the animals and Dailan. "What's that?"

"Oh, Hano. There's just so much to tell you. But it can wait. Laurel's not going to be happy about this detour. But then again, she probably already knows and hopefully understands."

"Laurel?"

"You'll meet her. Sooner than later, if we're smart about this."

They traveled due south. Up and down the foothills, past people working the land. Dailan flew above, sunlight making the intricate pattern of her white and tan feathers iridescent. Hano ran until her legs utterly refused. She killed and ate a rabbit, drank the mountains' runoff, slept in a tree next to Dailan, and continued before sunset. A waxing moon lit her path as she charged through the night.

Smoke reddened the dawn. Birds' morning song grew quiet. Hano slowed to the sight of smoldering trees, their blackened carcasses breathing smoke. The inner body of their trunks burned alive as a red pulse. Dailan waited atop the next foothill. Hano crested the hill and dropped to her knees.

The valley was a black pit spotted with fires. Where once a town, a city of stone and dirt and trees lived, a giant pile of rubble littered the land. Strips of fabric, black with glints of gold, waved above the chaos. She recognized a boar's head on the fabric. Smoke drifted to a hazy sky from the burning carcasses. She curled into a ball on the ground, coating her body with charcoal. Nehini. All she smelled was Nehini's body burning.

Dailan morphed into human form and pulled Hano's head into her lap. She stroked her hair and whispered, "I know. I know."

Beyond the smoke, the sun moved past its apex. Hano forced herself to stand. Who had won this war? It didn't matter. Not to her. Not to the Tawanians of Tinaku. Whether it was the Republic or Imperium made little difference to the people born here, to this land. The victorious conquerors shuffled below her as black spots within a black expanse.

"Let's go," Dailan said. She morphed and flapped her way into the smoke.

Hano ran faster than ever before. She coughed up gray phlegm as she went. The land returned to the green of living things, and she breathed easily again. The sun set, the moon rose. The moon set, the sun rose. Grasses swelled into bushes, bushes thickened into intertwining branches.

She wove through the jungle in her animal body, smelling, hearing, and feeling things she hadn't ever noticed before. The forest had always seemed quiet, the jaguar's scream or monkey call a small slice of noise in the hush. But now, leaping over mud pits and weaving through strangling fig groves, she heard the textures of movement, the layers of voices. Birds whispered of her coming, and a group of sleeping tamarins stirred as she passed. She paused to drink from a spring, remembering when she had found this fresh water as a child after losing her way in a race.

Dailan flew between wimba branches, always close by. Hano slowed her pace to a trot for the last stretch home. An uneasy feeling crept into her stomach. What had she to fear? Her family waited in the village and would rejoice at her safe return. Koenia would be eager to hear of the war.

Yet she wasn't the Hano they had sent to Killasi. She felt the slant of her jaw, the muscle of her arms. Her boar hide skirt barely fit now around her thighs. She wished she could see her face. The Shapeshifters had said she looked different, as expected; but they hadn't offered any details.

She passed a growth of red orchids, their crimson faces smiling up at her. This time a flood ago she had begun her moon-blood. She realized she had been gone for nearly a year. She followed a path leading to the village center. The journey back had taken a quarter of the time as the journey away, even with the detour to Tinaku. She straightened her shoulders, gathering confidence from this knowledge. A flash of Dailan's wings against the leaves further strengthened her resolve.

Her people were crowded in the village center. The smell of roasting boar wrung her stomach; she hadn't eaten since the rabbit. A young boy pointed at her as she stepped out of the forest. Hano remembered teaching him how to skin a capybara. His mother looked up and gasped. The surprise rippled away from the mother and her son, spreading across all those gathered. She watched as the familiar faces of her mother and father, her brothers and sister, friends and neighbors fell into bewildered expressions.

She stepped closer to the fire but stopped when everyone shifted back from her. Unease flared within her again. She struggled against it, questioning an impulse to run away. She had just returned. Here was home. So why did her body demand her to leave already?

Everyone stared at her, eyes blinking. Someone swallowing sounded loud in the absence of noise. Even her mother looked at her as if she was an alien creature.

Hano willed herself to continue. "I know I look different, and I am. I was reborn as the Anima. I've brought urgent news of a war."

Movement unsettled the quiet as people parted to make way for Koenia. She wore her cloak open today. Many necklaces of beads, bones, and teeth layered above her large breasts.

"Koenia," Hano said, stepping toward her. "I have—"

"A contagious disease. Do not come any closer," Koenia said. Her words rang as cold as the look on her face.

As if told to do so, the villagers moved further back. Hano caught an apology pass over Tenaria's face. He diverted his eyes away from her. Was he crying?

"You bring the Snow Fever," Koenia said, stopping a few body lengths away from Hano. She sniffed at the air between them and wrinkled her flat nose. "Or something fiercer. Look at yourself, child. You are sick and swollen. Your eyes are crazed. You threaten us all with your mere presence."

Her words hit Hano like machete slashes. Hano blinked back tears. "But, I—I bring news as the Messenger," she managed, her voice cracking. "And I am the Anima. I thought you knew, Koenia. I thought you, our Healer, had sent me to meet the Keepers." Hano saw comprehension slacken Koenia's face. The expression was quick but unmistakable.

Yet then Koenia twisted her face in bewilderment. "The Anima? Keepers? You speak nonsense!" She turned to the others behind her. "This was what Nehini sounded like in his last days. He spoke crazy talk."

Hano heard the osprey's high-pitched call resound. Leaves rustled in the forest and branches moaned. Something large paced behind her. Koenia's eyes darted to the movement. The look on her face reminded Hano of the rabbit she had killed yesterday.

"I don't carry disease. Please," Hano said, lowering her voice. "Please, I stayed but a minute in Killasi."

"But you were gone for eleven moons," Koenia yelled. "We figured you dead. And you all but are, dear child."

"Koenia, you must have known."

"You must be killed," Koenia spat. "Before you infect us all."

Hano heard her mother crying. Tenaria brought her sobbing body into his chest, his own face wet as well. He wore his dart barrel around his neck.

Hano flexed her body against the mounting panic. "How am I sick if I am strong? How am I crazed if I speak clear? You all need to know of the war between the Republic and Imperium. You need to know what the Keepers told me."

Koenia revealed her understanding in lifted eyebrows, but again she slackened her face in feigned confusion. "Nonsense. She speaks with a tongue twisted by fever."

Hano remembered what the masked bear had said about Keepers rallying to aid her in the Task. If Koenia was truly a Healer, wouldn't she know and embrace her as the Anima? Hano looked at Koenia as if seeing her for the first time. "Are you not a Healer?"

The village gasped. "Blasphemy!" a woman called out. Others in the crowd echoed her. Koenia stood tall. Hano thought for a moment that Koenia resembled the Snow Women she had seen while running through the streets of Killasi. Hano had always viewed Koenia as larger than life. But her presence was only as big as the belief Hano had held in her, and now Hano saw her for what she was—an imposter. This realization set afire the landscape of her childhood.

"I see she has not only lost a tooth on her journeys, but her mind. The Snow Fever has spread to her brain," Koenia said to their people. "You can see it in those sickly orange eyes."

"You are not a Healer," Hano whispered to herself, still fumbling with this new knowledge.

People exchanged blank faces of disbelief.

"You are not a Healer," she said louder. "And you stand between me and my people, refusing to listen to truth because of your fear. You are not protecting them. You are only protecting the lie that you are a Healer. Are you even—are you even *Sypayos?*"

There was no going back. She couldn't unsay the words. She wasn't just arguing with Koenia. She was arguing with the belief her people held in their Healer. "If you were a true Healer, you would know me. You would know the Anima." Though a part of Hano screamed to run for her life, she stood unmoving.

"She's crazy! Crazy," Koenia screamed. "Shoot her before she infects us all!"

Twigs and branches snapped nearby. "Don't," Hano roared. "Please! You must listen to—"

The dotted fur of a jaguar flashed in front of Hano, followed by the similar fur of an ocelot. Dailan ran behind them with a long spear in hand. A puma jumped out of a tree and landed between Hano and her people, snarling. Dozens upon dozens of people emerged from the forest with spears like Dailan's in their hands. They formed a line in front of Hano with the blades pointing forward.

Hano recognized the people as Shapeshifters. Her villagers screamed. Most ran away. Tenaria and a few other men stayed put. They brought dart barrels to their mouth.

"No," Hano shouted. She tried to run through the line of people guarding her. "Tenaria, don't shoot. Please, no one needs to get hurt."

Dailan stepped toward Koenia. "*Ada?*" she asked.

Koenia whipped her head from Dailan to the villagers and back to Dailan. She withdrew a pouch from her hip. "Ada's dead," she snarled, lifting the pouch above her head.

"Run!" Dailan yelled. She jumped up, morphed into an osprey, and soared into the sky. A few of the Shapeshifters threw Hano to the ground and covered her with their bodies. The explosion boomed. Dirt rained down, and Hano's ears rang. The Shapeshifters on top of her grew heavy. She felt like she was going to suffocate. When she cried for help, she couldn't hear whether or not the scream made a sound.

Someone lifted a body, and Hano squirmed back into the light. The air smelled like it had at the battlefield, of charred flesh and turned earth. Dailan grabbed her shoulders and asked if she was okay. Hano still couldn't hear her but understood her moving lips and nodded yes. Dead Shapeshifters and Sypayos littered the ground. Hano screamed when she saw Tenaria's lifeless body next to those of his childhood friends. More than half of the Shapeshifters survived. Most, like Dailan, had morphed in time to scurry away. The three to protect Hano lay dead.

Hano brought Tenaria to her chest and sobbed.

Dailan placed a hand on her shoulder. "We need to go."

Hano heard her over the ringing in her ears.

"I'm sorry, but we have to leave right now," Dailan said.

"But my brother. My brother."

"I know." Dailan was crying as well. "But Ada has escaped and will tell the Imperial Army where you are. We need to get you to safety."

"Ada?"

"Koenia. She's a warped Dual, as we feared. But I'll explain everything at the Haven."

A Shapeshifter walked over with a cut of boar meat and a bowl of water. He carried the meat in the crook of his arm and the bowl in the same arm's hand. A wrap of bloody linen covered the stub of his other arm. Hano cried out with horror.

"I'll be fine," the Shapeshifter said. He appeared to be Sypayos and spoke without an accent.

Hano wondered if he lived in a nearby village or if he, like the masked bear, preferred his animal form and rarely morphed into a human. How many Shapeshifters lived in the Forever Night? How many lived in the world? She eased Tenaria to the ground and ate quickly. Her people began trickling back into the village, and she looked for her mother.

"Now," Dailan said. "We have to go *now*." She morphed.

Hano wiped her face and stood. She looked once more at her dead brother. Her people gaped at her, soundless. "I'm sorry," she breathed, and she sprinted back into the jungle.

She followed Dailan east of the battle, through the broadleaf evergreens of Tawan's southern forest. She ate fish Dailan caught from rivers and a pudú she hunted down. A few times the thought of Tenaria's death brought her sobbing to her knees. Dailan would fly down and wait until the grief passed back into its numbing presence. In a way, the grief worked in her favor: the numbing brought endurance to her running.

After two days of running through flatland, they reached the base of mountains. The peaks beyond Killasi had risen from the savanna, their presence on the landscape godlike in the contrast. These mountains, though, began in trees. Hano didn't realize they had reached the peaks until the earth tilted upward. The forest thinned, and fewer animals populated the land. Hano passed a pair of ungulates with forked antlers. Giant birds soared above Dailan.

The higher they went, the starker the landscape became, and the colder Hano felt. The trees faded behind them as they reached a plateau covered with bright green bushes and red flowers. Hano stuttered to a stop. Giant spears made of white-covered rocks thrust into the sky. A lake the teal color of a parrot's feathers spread out beneath the peaks. She found it hard to catch her breath.

Dailan swooped down and morphed. "We should stop for a while, let you adjust to the mountain air. It's much thinner up here."

Hano sat and ate some of the pudú she had smoked yesterday.

"The Haven is between the two tallest peaks," Dailan said, pointing across the water. "We'll be there before nightfall."

Dailan remained in human form the rest of the way. When they skirted the lake, Hano could see the water was clear up close. This change reminded her of how the mountains had looked blue from afar. Many things in this world seemed to be one way and proved to be another—including her life.

They navigated a field of boulders. "We're nearly there," Dailan said over her shoulder.

Hano looked around. Nearly where? Dailan stopped and reached toward Hano. Holding hands, they walked a few more steps. Hano gasped.

The Haven materialized within the mountain. Made of cobbled stone, it appeared to grow up out of the rock. Circular structures connected long walls. Hundreds of windows punctuated the cobblestone. Hano had no name for the building. It was larger and taller than any she had ever seen. It looked like a hundred Killasi homes conglomerated into one.

"Laurel went all out with this Haven," Dailan said. "It's a proper castle."

"Castle?"

"That's what an Imperial would call it. It's meant to house many people. An army, in our case."

Hano noticed the faces looking out through the windows. Hundreds of people were watching her. A few waved. Hano waved back with a hesitant hand. A couple people started cheering. Everyone began clapping, and the cheering spread. The applause and whooping echoed off the rock walls. Hano smiled despite herself.

Dailan placed an arm around her. "Our Anima," she said, giving her a squeeze. "Our hope."

The tall wooden gate opened, and a woman walked out. She wore a long, white fur coat and leather boots. Purple hair fell in loose waves to her shoulders. When she neared, Hano could see many tattoos adorned her neck. Her eyes rivaled the sunlit snow in their bright blue radiance.

"And this is Laurel," Dailan said.

Laurel stopped in front of Hano. Her smile revealed a gap between her two front teeth. "Hano, our Anima," she said in Sypayos. "It's an honor to meet you. Thank you for traveling all this way. I know you have many questions. Come. Let's get you fed and in clothes better suited for the climate." Laurel turned back to the castle.

Dailan gave Hano another squeeze and followed Laurel. The faces had left the windows. Hano looked behind her, to the lake turning a deep blue in the twilight. Yet she knew the color of water was an illusion. Water, in truth, was colorless.

"Coming?" Dailan called.

Hano pivoted around and walked through the open gate.

Laurel passed Hano a basket containing food called bread. Many things on the table were novel to Hano. She could eat the bread all day but found the pickled vegetables disgusting. They sat at a wooden table in a circular room, a fire blazing beside them. Hano found the hearths in the castle most impressive of all. Dailan had told her the smoke went out through tunnels within the walls.

Hano wore a dress similar to the one Koenia had given her to wear in Killasi, though the fabric was a single shade of green. Laurel wore a shirt made of fur with a leather string lacing up the center. With the shirt's low cut, Hano could see the tattoos began on her collarbones and extended up her neck. She wondered if Laurel received any of them from a Sypayos artist: the lines and triangles resembled the ink etched into Hano's chest.

She could tell Laurel herself wasn't from the Forever Night; they had similar skin colors but little else in common.

Hano sat between Dailan and Laurel. The two other Salvagers, a woman named Uki and a man named Rua, also sat at the table. Their eyes were identical to Laurel's in their unearthly glow. Uki wore her hair in its natural white color, while Rua, like Laurel, dyed his, though he went with a neutral brown color. All three Salvagers wore a silver pin of a leafy plant over their right breast.

Between the bread, the Salvagers, and the seat lifting her high off the ground, she found the situation entirely strange. Dailan alone brought her comfort. She gave Hano a wink as she spread something yellow on a slice of bread.

"I know none of our Sypayos is perfect," Laurel began. "But we should talk in Hano's language so she understands. Dailan, you mentioned you know of Ada's location."

Uki made a small noise and stiffened. Rua set his fork down and looked unblinkingly at Dailan.

"I do." Dailan reached for Uki's arm across the table. "All this time she was living in the Manduka Forest—the Forever Night, as Hano's people call it. She goes by Koenia and works as a witch doctor in Hano's village. She"—Dailan swallowed—"Uki, she warped."

Uki's eyes grew wide and watery. Rua said something Hano didn't understand, though it sounded angry. Setting her chin on steepled hands, Laurel closed her eyes. A grave silence gathered. The fire crackled and swayed. Hano continued to eat bread.

"We figured as much," Laurel said, opening her eyes. "The real issue, my friends, is why we couldn't see her. I scanned the Manduka for her many times."

"As did I," Rua said.

Wiping tears from her face with a cut of cloth, Uki cleared her throat. "And I."

"So *how* are they blocking our Hindsight?"

"Hindsight?" Hano asked with her mouth full.

Dailan leaned over. "It's Salvagers' ability to see into the past."

"What did she wear?" Laurel asked Hano.

"Nothing out of the ordinary. A skirt, her cloak, some neck—"

"Cloak?" Laurel said, her eyes flashing white.

"It's made of giant otter fur," Hano said.

Laurel asked a dozen questions about the cloak, from what it smelled like to its texture and color. Hano answered as best as she could, trying hard to remember all the details. She had always found the garment strange; apparently Laurel did as well.

"Did she ever soak it in something?" Laurel asked.

"Not that I know of. I only went into her hut once, right before leaving. She had this circle with mushrooms in it. It was like a miniature full moon."

"A Mycena Orb," Dailan said, looking at Laurel. "And she used a Belladonna Bomb to escape."

Hano didn't understand half the words Dailan spoke. Her stomach grew stiff and bloated, and she sat back in her chair, uncomfortable and confused. Uki began crying again. She and Laurel exchanged words in a foreign tongue, and Uki calmed down. Hano massaged her distended stomach.

"We all do our best," Laurel said, looking around the table. "We've all done our best, and it hasn't been good enough. But we can't give up. We simply cannot. Life on this earth depends on us to maintain our dedication to the Task, even when all hope seems lost. Even when our own children betray us." She turned to Hano. "Are you okay?"

"I ate too much."

Dailan laughed, and Laurel smiled. Even Rua managed a grin. Uki, though, was pale and absent.

"I remember my first loaf of Talérian-style bread," Dailan said. "It's truly irresistible."

"And not part of your natural diet, I assume," Laurel said. "I assume none of this feels natural."

"It feels like a dream," Hano said, shaking her head.

"Maybe it is. But if we are sleeping, then I'd call our reality a nightmare." Laurel tossed her hair back and looked to the Keepers. "Friends, I've gathered us here, at the Machida Haven, to not only celebrate the Anima's rebirth, but to discuss an idea I have for the current Anima, should you be willing, Hano."

Hano sat taller. "Willing to do what?"

"As we've mentioned, we tried to defeat the Imperium during the last Anima's life. With the Grand Alliance we created between Mages, Shapeshifters, and the humans opposing the Imperium's spread of Disorder, we thought we had, at last, found a way to stop the Imperium. Yet they had learned Florávo from a warped Mage, and our ignorance to their mastery of Florávian marital arts sealed our defeat."

Seeing Hano's confused expression, Dailan said, "Florávo is plant magic. It's what Koenia used to escape."

"And Mages are people trained in Florávo," Laurel added. "I established four Havens in the world to train Mages. While we have a few thousand Mages at this point, we need an army a hundred thousand strong if we are to defeat the World Forces once and for all. As my fellow Salvagers know, I've established an additional training facility in the Prajatuya Palace. What better place, I figure, to raise an army than a place the Imperium deems worthless because it doesn't offer any valuable resources to their growth."

Dailan nodded. "Brilliant, Laurel. Naturally. Old Makalon is a perfect place."

Uki seemed to be slipping further away in thought. She slouched in her chair and frowned at the fire. Hano couldn't imagine the pain of losing a child. As Koenia had said, Ada was dead.

"That's the hope," Laurel said. "Yet we cannot rely on Mages and Keepers alone to defeat enemies of Order. We must ally with more Commoners. We must create more resistance like the Vipers."

Again, Dailan helped Hano understand by explaining what Commoners meant. "The Vipers," she continued, "are a band of rebels in a forest north of here. A Shapeshifter named Hamia trains them to fight. I heard she's been successful in recruiting yet more displaced Commoners," she said to Laurel.

"Indeed," Laurel said. "My idea for Hano here is to return to her home and create a resistance much like the Vipers. This means, Hano, that you would live out your days as the Anima in the Manduka Forest. Your demonstration of the Task would not only be to spread Order to all Sypayos, but to prepare your people to fight for the Sacred Balance when the time comes once again to try and stop Disorder."

Rua scoffed. Everyone looked at him. "When the time comes?" he asked. "You mean to let an Anima's life pass without at least trying to fight? We have three more Animas including Hano, and we're not going to use one of our last chances to end Disorder? We may not be able to quell Disorder in her life, but we can at least slow its progress with a strategic attack."

Laurel lifted a shoulder. "These are legitimate concerns, Rua. I said it was an idea. A long-game strategy. In my opinion, Hano's life as the Anima would be better spent developing resistance—building the Anima's Army—rather than running into a war we cannot win. Between the Imperium and the Republic, such a fight would be suicide for Anima and Keeper alike."

Dailan whistled. "Hold on now, Salvagers," she said. "Listen to yourselves. '*Use* one of our last chances.' Her life would be 'better *spent*.' Hano is here, in case you've forgotten. In person. She's a real-life human with her own wants and needs. Don't forget Oili."

The mention of Oili made all the Salvagers uneasy. Hano wondered who she was and why the Salvagers shouldn't forget her. Was Oili's life debated over much like her own at this table? She wanted to hug Dailan for saying her thoughts aloud.

"Thank you, Dailan," Laurel said, her voice quiet. "Our apologies, Hano. It's far too easy for Keepers to get wrapped up in their own hopes for the Task, as our lives extend beyond any single Anima's existence. We witness both the triumphs and failures of our beloved Animas, and we feel, in no small part, largely responsible for her successes—and her defeats. But Dailan is absolutely correct, as usual. We can educate you on your Task and mentor you with the knowledge we have earned from trial and error. Ultimately, though, your life is your own, and you may do what you choose."

Hano rested her head on a hand and stuck her tongue in and out of the gap of her missing tooth. She listened to the fire hiss and spark, thinking of how the Imperium had killed Nehini with its spread of the Snow Fever. She remembered the enslaved Tawanians at Killasi. Houses turned to rubble and trees to charcoal at Tinaku. And her brother— above all, her brother, lying dead without his legs. Disorder had killed him, too.

She sighed. "The Imperium will eventually come to the Forever Night, won't they?"

"It's likely," Laurel said. "But there are *thousands* of Shapeshifters in the Manduka Forest. It's the largest concentration of Keepers in the world. Which is why I believe it's a perfect place to gather an army of Commoners. You'll have protection from any intruders. Besides, Imperials hate the jungle. They fear its poison and predators."

While Dailan nodded in agreement, Rua continued to look angry. Uki might as well have been in a different room entirely.

"I know you don't agree, Rua," Laurel said, "and you don't have to. But we must support Hano in whichever decision she makes."

Rua stood and smoothed his pants as he paced, exhaling laboriously. He stopped pacing and looked at Hano. "What will it be, Anima? Fight or flight?"

"That's not a fair question, Rua," Dailan said. "She will still be fighting, but for the next Anima's success."

"Or possibly the last," Laurel said. "Like I said, we need to build an army of a hundred thousand, if not more. The golden spiral is tightening. The periods between Animas grow smaller as the cyclic timing of the mushroom's growth shortens. Time may be our true adversary."

"Two Animas without resistance? That's madness, Laurel." Rua was shouting now. He startled Uki out of her brooding.

"*Again*, I don't need you to agree." Laurel's voice remained quiet and steady. "But I *do* need you to support the Anima in her decision. We must remain allies or we will be our own conquerors."

She looked at him in a way that reminded Hano of how her mother would look at her as a child when she'd return home from a run with scratches and bruises. *You're going to kill yourself out there,* her mother would scold. Hano thought of how she had been right, in a way. The old Hano died because she was fast enough to be the Messenger.

The new Hano, though, Hano the Anima, didn't need to die. She wasn't sure what Laurel meant by golden spiral, but she did know when one person offered a meaningful life, while the other offered a rash death. She had seen the devastation wrought by these World Forces. Hano believed Laurel—they'd need a hundred thousand to win.

"I will do my part," Hano said at last. "I will prepare my people to fight for the Order."

Rua's face grew red. He nodded once and left.

Uki's voice cracked when she said, "And I will hunt the earth until my daughter is dead." Her chair screeched against the floor as she pushed away from the table, and she slammed the door behind her.

Dailan and Laurel exchanged somber looks. Laurel set her hand on Hano's shoulder. She wore four rings, each one embezzled with a different stone. "If you ever need help, summon a Shapeshifter. They will be there, ready to aid. You need but call into the forest."

"Like you, Dailan?" Hano asked. She imagined touching her impossibly long eyelashes. She imagined touching her hairless head, her breasts—all of her. She wondered if Dailan felt the same way.

Dailan shook her head with a small smile. "I must return to Shénchåo to do my part for the long game, as Laurel called it. But I will see you to your home."

"You're welcome to stay here as long as you'd like," Laurel said. "And Hano"—she gave her a pat—"I'm glad the mushroom found you. I don't think I could have picked a better Anima."

"Was that even a choice?" Hano asked.

"Most Animas were given the mushroom by Keepers. But some, like you, found it for reasons beyond our knowledge. There is chaos and reason, randomness and meaning in this world. While we've tried to control the Anima's fate for millennia, there are always things beyond our manipulation. I'm trying to befriend chaos, to reinstate trust in a larger design. Yet it's been hard, as Keepers, to maintain faith in a benevolent force shaping our lives. We don't have any sure reason for the deaths of Animas past. We don't have any sure reason for your rebirth. We only have the facts and what meaning we make of them. And more often than not, the meaning is revealed long after we've forgotten the facts."

Hano considered these words and how they felt true for her own life. She knew the facts, but couldn't yet discern the meaning. Why had she been the fastest runner? Why did she stumble upon *the* mushroom of all the mushrooms in a mountain? And why had the Imperium come? She voiced this last question aloud.

"*That's* the question, isn't it," Dailan said.

"Who are they?" Hano asked.

Laurel folded her hands and set them on the table. "These are complicated and yet simple questions. Greed brings the World Forces to this land. Greed and fear, which are the same pool of water in different light."

For maybe the first time this evening, Hano knew exactly what Laurel meant.

"But *why* does one succumb to greed and fear?" Laurel continued. "The Imperium is ruled by men who were raised in the belief structure of their natural-born right to dominate other Life, including the lives of humans they view as lesser. They call this belief, a kind of religion, the Power. There is nothing inherently wrong with any of the kings and emperors and principals of the Imperium and Republic. They were born humans capable of either good or harm—just like you and I. It is their *beliefs* shaping their actions.

"That is the essence of the Anima's Task: to counteract the belief structure of Disorder with knowledge of the Sacred Balance. For as long as Disorder continues to spread, Life will continue to diminish. Forests will be razed. Animals will perish. Humans will be enslaved. And the world will become a barren thing. After a certain point, the Order will be so out of balance, there will be no going back. There will be nothing left to take."

The fire sputtered out. Embers glinted in the hearth. Hano wiped the tears from her face. Dailan brought Hano into her arms, and Hano breathed in her orchid-like smell.

"We can do this," Dailan whispered. "We at least have to try."

☾

Vítor banged the butt of his spear on the earth. He stood tall before them, with dark skin and shiny muscles. A hide skirt hung to his mid-thighs. His black hair was wet with sweat.

"Jaguars, line up," he called.

The Sypayos warriors shuffled into formation. They stood on beaten dirt with erect postures.

"You have worked hard today," Vítor said loud enough for the three hundred standing to hear. "Be prepared to bring the same intensity tomorrow." He hit the ground once with his spear's butt, lifted it high into the air, and hit the ground again. "For the Order," he cried.

The ground quivered as everyone performed the same brisk movements and yelled in return, "For the Order."

The Jaguars relaxed and began talking casually. Vítor turned to Hano. She sat on the ground, her back leaning against a tree.

"You went easy on them today," she said with a grin. Her voice was hoarse and barely audible over the other Jaguars talking.

He shrugged his massive shoulders. "They were tired."

"The tamarins tell me yet more are on their way. Dozens, all the way from Iomgy."

Vítor raised an eyebrow. "Word of the resistance continues to spread. This is good."

"We'll need to cut more trees to make space in the training ring."

"We'll only cut what we have to. It's good practice to spar between trees."

Hano nodded once in agreement. Vítor bent down and lifted her onto his back. He smelled of salt and dirt. A spear had glanced his chest, leaving a smear of blood. She relaxed into his strength. Walking hurt these days, and she couldn't go far on her own two legs. Yet she still enjoyed watching the Jaguars practice, so she sacrificed pride for pleasure and allowed Vítor to carry her between the town and the training grounds.

Watching made her feel closer to the days when she was in the ring with them, sparring and somersaulting and flipping. She had easily dominated in her younger years. Though she now grieved the loss of an able body, she felt pride in the Jaguars she had trained when they were but teenagers, awkward with their spears. They had grown to be fully capable fighters. She knew they would be ready for war when a future Anima called upon her army.

They walked into Beroka. Fires burned with capybaras roasting above them. A group of children peeling plantains smiled and waved up at Hano as she and Vítor passed. Other than the village circle, where they cooked food and gathered as a community, Beroka remained hidden in the trees.

Laurel had advised Hano to use the canopy as cover, so they had built their homes in the branches.

Vítor set Hano down next to her grandniece. The young woman gave Hano a hug and fetched her a bowl of water. Hano sighed and closed her eyes. She hurt everywhere today.

"Are you okay, Hano?" Vítor asked. "You smell sick."

"I think I've caught a cold. A little medicine from one of the Mages and I'll be fine."

Vítor left for the hut where the Mages studied and practiced Florávo. Laurel had sent a half dozen of the Mages from the Haven with Hano when she had returned to the Forever Night. The walk home with Dailan and those Mages felt like a lifetime ago. She wondered how Dailan fared. What was she doing in Shénchåo? Did she think of Hano as often as Hano thought of her?

Vítor returned and told Hano a Mage would be over soon to see what she needed. He crouched down and gave her a hug. "I'll see you in the morning," he said. He morphed into his puma form and slid away into the trees.

Hano took the bowl from her grandniece and drank all the water. Her throat still ached for more, but she knew it wasn't water she craved. "Please, help me to my bed," she said to her grandniece. They hobbled together to her home. She had moved to the ground three floods ago, when she was no longer able to climb into the tree house. Her grandniece lowered her to the bed.

Hano didn't get up again. The Mages brought her medicine until she asked them to stop. She was ready.

She spent the next moon in and out of dreams. Dailan came to her in one of these, or possibly she was there in person. Laurel and Rua came as well, and all the Jaguars she had ever trained. She knew she was dreaming when Tenaria visited. She asked for his forgiveness. He kissed her cheek and told her there was nothing to forgive.

Hano passed surrounded by Jaguars and Vítor, her siblings' children and their children. As she whispered her final words, the entire Forever Night seemed to be holding its breath.

# FLO

## 131 YEARS BEFORE PRESENT

### ALIMENDIA SEATERRA

The aliens' skin reminded Flo of the fishermen who washed up to shore weeks after a storm. She had only seen them from afar, but she could tell they were not like her or her sister or parents. They were as white as the albino girl in the village over, and they stood nearly a head taller than even Ana's giant of a son.

When the aliens' colossal boat first appeared, everyone had screamed about a monster. For all Flo knew, that's what it was—a monster glinting in the sun, moaning as it beached. The aliens had tried to speak with the elders, but they couldn't understand her people, and her people couldn't understand them. They had left last moon with a gestured promise to return.

Today, all the elders of the twelve Wharwi villages would be gathering at dawn. Flo stirred awake to the sound of Papi limping out of his home next door. She began to crawl as quietly as possible past her sleeping parents. Jedda was awake as well, and the two of them slid out of the semicircle opening in their dome of woven grass leaves. They grinned at each other as they ran to the cover of trees growing thick along the white sands.

Ferns tickled her ankles as they continued running to the peninsula. The forest remained dark while sunrise skirted over the bay's teal waters. A pair of kangaroos bounded away at the sound of their coming. The palm trees thinned, and they continued close to the ground. A few other kids were already hiding behind a bush. They waved them over with fingers pressed to their lips.

Flo sat next to Tai. A couple years older than Flo's eleven, he was hardly a kid anymore. He had received his first carving on his birthday four moons ago. The whale, made of black triangular shapes, wrapped around the emerging muscle of his shoulder. She hadn't seen it close up yet, and she admired her mother's handiwork. As the most talented artist in the village, she had been the one to etch the whale into Tai's skin with an albatross bone.

Tai winked at her, and they both leaned closer to the voices murmuring a stone's throw from the bush.

"—their intent."

"True, but we do know they will return. With more, most likely." Flo recognized the scratchy intonations of Papi's voice.

"Do you think coexistence is possible?" a woman asked.

"No," a man said. Flo didn't recognize his accent. The word barely sounded Wharwi. The sureness of his tone sent a quiver across her ribs. Jedda lifted her eyebrows at Flo.

"No," the man repeated. "I urge you all to come inland as soon as possible. There, we can gather our forces."

"Gather our forces?" Papi sounded as confused as Flo felt. "You don't mean to say—"

"I do." Again, the stranger's cool voice gave Flo the shivers. "These people do not come in peace."

"But how could you possibly know this?" a man asked. "We have only just met them. Have they been in touch with the Mauni?"

"They haven't," the stranger replied.

"So your people haven't even met them, and you presume to know their intentions."

"Trust me. We need the Mauni and Wharwi to join—"

"Children!"

Flo and Tai bonked heads when they simultaneously jumped. They rubbed their skulls as three seething woman strutted through the ferns toward them. Jedda moved to run.

"Don't you *dare*."

Flo flinched at her mother's fury. As a stout woman with short, black hair, Monti reminded Flo of a tassie devil when angry. She yanked Flo to her feet and grabbed Jedda around the wrist. The other mothers found their children and likewise pulled them away from the elder council.

"Nearly a man grown and all!" Flo heard Tai's mother say.

Flo looked back at Tai, and his lips flickered up with the hint of a smirk. Monti lectured them about respecting elders and their request for privacy. Flo stuck her heels into the dirt, causing both Monti and Jedda to stutter. "But, mom," she whispered. "A Mauni man said—"

"Things you shouldn't have heard." Monti sighed. "Flo, Jedda"—she looked between her daughters—"the elders will know what to do. We need to trust them."

Flo frowned at the ground. A snake slithered through the ferns beyond her sister's legs. She and Jedda nodded, and they continued home in silence. Her father was waiting for her at the canoe. He was ankle-deep in the waters, arranging the nets.

"Go then," Monti said, shooing Flo to him.

"What about me?" Jedda whined.

Flo took off running, flicking up sand behind her. The morning felt calm with a light breeze. A couple moons still spanned between now and the wet season, and the sky promised good weather in its cerulean expanse. It was a perfect day for fishing.

Her father made sure to hide his grin from Monti. Flo helped him push the canoe away from the shore and sat with her back against the prow's fin. It, like the rest of the boat, was carved from a totara tree. Monti had spent over three moons cutting spirals into the fin. An abalone shell inlaid the center of the carvings.

"So," her father said, sticking his paddle into the waters. "What did the elders say?"

She launched into what she had heard, telling him about the Mauni man's warning. Her father's brow furrowed as Flo talked. He slowed his paddling and handed Flo a net.

"The elders will know what to do," he said at last.

"That's what mom said."

"And we know it's best not to argue with her." He smiled at Flo, but she could tell it wasn't a real smile. She felt the dread settle as a weight in her stomach. They cast their nets out and pulled in fish by the dozens.

☾

Flo sat with her family, watching the aliens maneuver their boats onto the shore. Even from this distance, with the whole bay between her and them, she could hear them calling out to each other in their clunky tongue. The first boat grounded near her old home. The aliens poured out of the boat's stomach and spread out across the white sands. Waves from the boat lapped up to where she would have cleaned fish. They inspected the ghosts of their houses: branches scattered at random, fire rings left half intact. She saw them marvel at her family's canoe. It had been too heavy to take with them.

She looked out to the waters beyond the bay, beyond the boats, and felt the rocking when whales passed. She saw their ancestors, the dolphins, threading the water's surface. The horizon promising infinity. She knew their new home would never truly seal the void. Another boat groaned ashore, this time landing where Tai's family had lived. She turned to her mother and asked if they could return home.

"Not for a long time, if ever," Monti replied.

"No, I mean our new home," Flo said. Jedda echoed the want to leave, and together the family walked away from the ocean.

☾

"The lineages of sea and lake people flow into and out of one another," Rua said, first in Mauni, then in Wharwi. "This is the way of water and its children." He stood on the stump of a kauri tree; the very tree Flo and her family had used to build their new house.

The village gathered around. Papi sat beside the stump, looking much like a stump himself. The pain in his knees had tripled since they had moved to the lake two moons ago now, and he rarely stood anymore. Though both he and Rua had white hair, Rua looked and acted much younger than him. Without tattoos on his chest or face, Flo wondered sometimes if Rua was even from Wildwood.

"We are all one," he continued. "We are all born of water, and we will all return to water. Let us enjoy meeting our new neighbors. Let us learn each other's language, share the bounty, and benefit from the security union affords." Rua placed both hands over his chest and bowed to the people.

Everyone clicked their tongues and thumped on their breastplates in thanks for his words. Flo noticed how some of her people sat still and quiet. Though they had followed Papi's decision to uproot for the inland, they still harbored mistrust for the Mauni elder. Flo had heard Ana whispering to Monti one time about Rua's unnatural eyes and the strange way his face hadn't aged with his hair. Flo couldn't disagree with Ana. All the eyes she had known in her life, apart from the albino girl, were the color of bark and kookaburra tail feathers. Rua's eyes shimmered like the sun on the ocean. White, then blue, then white again.

Only half of Flo's village had followed Papi's decision to uproot for the inland. The other half had trickled into the Mauni villages that had chosen to stay, despite Rua's warning. Flo wished her family had stayed near the sea, but at least Tai and his mother had come to the lake as well. She sat next to Tai now, sneaking glances at his face. His newest tattoos were of spirals coming off the corner of his lips and down his chin. They, along with the kangaroo bone piercing his nose, made him look fierce. He was fifteen now, a man grown, and Flo willed her body to catch up.

Tai thumped a hand against his broad chest. Flo could tell the motion was half-hearted. Rua stepped off the stump and helped Papi to his feet. The lake spanned behind the elders as they walked away from the crowd, its aquamarine waters reminding Flo of the ocean. Rua had told her they were that color because of the ever-melting ice in the mountains west of the village. The lake was almost large enough to look like a sea, but she could see the green hint of a shore opposing them.

Flo filled her basket with sorrel leaves and blackberries. Jedda did the same nearby. They smirked at each other as they snuck blackberries into their mouths.

"One for the basket, one for me," Jedda said.

Flo laughed. "More like one for the basket, three for you."

Their bare legs glistened, wet with dew. Morning sun trickled in through the thick canopy. A couple of koala bears idly munched on eucalyptus branches above, and a treecreeper pecked on a trunk. This place was no oceanfront, but over the last year, Flo had grown to accept, maybe even like, her new home.

Jedda wore a beaded headband, crafted in the Mauni fashion, over her long, black hair. She had grown half a head in the two years they had lived here. Flo had grown a full head. She now stood as tall as her father and nearly as tall as Tai. A bone spiral hung from her right ear. It caught the corner of Flo's eye as she stooped forward to pick from the lowest branches. The earring's pattern reminded her of the spiraling snails' shells littering the ground around her feet.

They walked home with brimming baskets, passing their neighbors' houses. The wet season up here had proven much colder than those on the shore. Freezing winds would sweep across the lake, rattling the wooden planks of their square, fully enclosed shelters. At first Flo hadn't liked the angles and door of their new home. She missed the dome of grasses opening to the bay, sand shaping to her body as she slept. For a while she hadn't been able to fall asleep. The ocean had lulled her to dreams for the first twelve years of her life.

Yet the forest lived with its own cadence, its own lull, and Flo's body had learned to listen for the wetas. When those winter gales would charge into the foothills, and snow crept down from the peaks, the four walls became a sanctuary rather than an entrapment. There were times, too, on the lake, when the shore faded away and the sky met water all around, and Flo would feel like a girl again with the dolphins. She could almost reach out and feel their skin, slick and firm against her fingertips.

Yet there was no salt in the lake. There were no dolphins, no whales, no sharks. Plenty of fish filled their nets, even in winter. They had yet to live in want. This was enough. It would have to be enough.

Flo and Jedda ducked into their home and set the baskets before their mother. Monti finished threading shark teeth onto a thin strip of sinew and tied the necklace closed. Flo knelt before her, and Monti placed the necklace over her head. Flo pulled her hair out from underneath it and admired how the teeth filled the crevice between her bare breasts. She remembered the shark's spotted skin and the way the shark slithered across the ocean floor like a snake.

"My eldest daughter, a woman," Monti said, unable to cover the crack in her voice.

Flo and Jedda glanced at each other, both caught off guard by their mother's sentimentality. Neither had ever seen her cry. Monti retrieved the skirt made of flax she had finished weaving that morning. Flo slipped out of her chamois hide skirt, careful not to further rip it, and tried on her ceremonial garment. She admired the skirt's intricate black and tan geometric patterns.

"A perfect fit," she said, helping her mother stand. They embraced, Monti resting her head on Flo's chest. Her mother felt small but sturdy in her arms. "Thank you," Flo said.

Monti turned away, hiding her face. Flo and Jedda returned outside to help the others finish preparing for the ceremony. Flo found Tai digging a pit for roasting the boars. She began to help him. Tai complimented her new necklace and skirt.

"You enter your womanhood in full blossom," he said, brushing a finger along her jaw.

The skin flushed where he touched her. The tingle she felt every time he came around moved up from her root and into her stomach. Etchings covered his muscled chest. The whale now flowed into a snake, and the snake wound around his other shoulder.

He let his touch linger longer than usual. "Tomorrow morning, we ask the elders for their blessing," he said.

She looked around, ensuring their privacy. With an unfamiliar boldness, she kissed him on his lips, feeling their fullness against her own for the first time. The tingling spread through her entire body.

He pulled away. "Tomorrow morning," he repeated, leaning back in to rest his lips against her ear. "May the Mother bless your emergence."

The entire village gathered along the lakeshore. Voices and laughter, children yelling in play, rolled across the water's surface. The sun set behind the mountains, and the evening radiated with flushed light. A dozen strides away from the rest, Flo and three other women-to-be sat in a circle with Rua.

His white-blue eyes looked even more unnatural in the dim light. He wore a loincloth made of hedgehog hide while the girls were naked. At sixteen, Flo was at least two years older and a head taller than the other girls. For a while she had wondered if she would ever get her moon-blood. When it had come last fall, she had cried in relief. She and Tai could finally be together in that way.

Rua led the girls in a chanting of the moon prayer. Flo resisted the impulse to itch at the ceremonial paint on her face, trying instead to focus all her energy on the invocation for fertility. She imagined what her and Tai's kids might look like. She hoped they would have his strength and her height.

They continued to chant as Rua stirred the mushrooms into the warmed goat's milk and honey. Each girl would drink one sacred mushroom to connect to the Mother and thus to all things—all gods, all life, all energy. This was a tradition shared by both Wharwi and Mauni. Flo remembered last year's moon-blood ceremony, when the girls had violently vomited after submerging into the lake. She fought back fear, returning to the image of her children with Tai, of his touch, the tingling in her root.

The village stilled. Flo opened her eyes to see them gathering around their circle. Her family's faces, though sober, gave Flo courage. Rua raised his chanting voice, and the entire village joined him in the prayer. He handed each girl a cup. When Rua gave Flo her cup, she felt his eyes linger on her with a curious twinkle.

The drink felt warm in her hands, and steam twirled up from the milk. People shifted to form a narrow passage leading to the lake, their chants continuing to rise and fall, filling the twilight with a pulsating force. A part of her wanted to dump the drink and run. But she knew the purge would connect her to the Mother, to her motherhood. Her body craved this connection, demanded it. Rua motioned for all to be still. Quiet collapsed into the chanting's absence.

The youngest girl drank first. The next youngest began drinking, and the next. Flo brought the cup to her mouth and chugged. The chunky milk didn't taste as bad as she had feared. It warmed her stomach. All four girls finished and stood. They held hands and walked to the lake, their steps irregular on the rocky beach. The village remained still and silent but for a baby crying.

Flo's head began to swirl. Or the stars were spinning faster. One foot, then another entered the chill waters. Was she supposed to feel this way? White flashes throbbed against the black sky. The waters embraced her knees, her thighs, her root. Her entire body careened into the lake, and the dark waters swallowed her alive and whole.

☾

When Flo woke, the world around her was calm. Sunlight poured into her family's home through the open door. No one was in the room, but she could hear voices not far off. Her head swam in muck. She was on her bed, in her home—but how did she get there? The memories of her last waking moments crawled forth from the murk. Her moon ceremony. The mushroom milk, walking into the lake, stars spinning.

She attempted to sit up but nausea overwhelmed her. Leaning over the side of the bed, she vomited up liquid and bile.

Monti rushed into the room. "Flo," she whispered. "Oh, daughter." She held Flo close to her, crying into her shoulder.

Flo stiffened. Her mother was weeping. Something terrible must have happened. "What is it? Is Papi okay? Jedda?" Flo's voice came out grating. Her throat ached for water. She wanted to leap up from the bed, but her body refused.

Her mother softened her grasp. "Yes, yes. It's you. We didn't know where you went and if you'd ever come back."

"What do you mean? Did I leave?" What in the name of the Mother had happened in that lake?

"You were here the whole time. You've been gone a half moon now. Rua said you'd be back—he's been here every day, giving you broth."

A half moon? Flo tried to respond, but her voice caught. "Water," she managed. "Water, please."

Monti gave her a bowl of water. The need to vomit returned, and she leaned to the side of the bed, retching up all the water she had just drank and more bile. Her father ran into the room. Fresh from the lake, he smelled of fish. He wet a patch of hide and cleaned the sweat from Flo's face. Monti stroked Flo's hair, her face strangely contorted.

"What? Tell me, mother. What else has happened?"

Monti stood and busied herself with the mess on the floor. Her father avoided her eyes.

"*What?*"

"It's the aliens," Monti said at last. "The hunters spotted a group of them near the old grove. More have come over the last few days. They're digging for something, and it's not roots."

Her father flinched at the words. He gave Monti a disapproving look.

"She should know," Monti said.

He set the cloth aside and rested a hand on Flo's thigh. "Focus for now on your healing. Rua says you'll be stronger than ever in no time."

Flo felt like she was swimming against a riptide. The shore held the answers, but she kept getting yanked back into the unknown. "The aliens? What's happening to me? Are the other girls bedridden?" Her throat burned with the threat of more vomit.

Her father looked again at Monti with a frown. "It was too soon," he said.

Rua came swishing into the room. He wore his hair loose, rather than in the usual bun. It flowed past his shoulder in white ringlets. His flax skirt swept the floor as he strode over to Flo. He set a bowl in Flo's hands and said, "Nettle and tahr bone broth." His eyes had the same glint Flo had noticed at the ceremony.

She held the bowl away from her. "Why should I trust you?" she asked in Wharwi. They had mostly spoken in Mauni in the last year. Her parents stilled at the sound of their native tongue. It almost sounded unnatural now, in this square home of theirs.

"I know I don't look it," Rua said, also speaking in her first language. "But I am very old. Much older, even, than your Papi."

"But how?"

"There's much you don't understand yet." He glanced at her parents. "Much. I've chosen you, Flo, to be the next Anima."

Flo felt the tides ripping her further and further away from shore. She wanted answers, and all anyone offered were words breeding yet more questions. Her parents seemed just as confused.

"Anima?"

"I couldn't see another Anima life put to waste," he said, looking beyond Flo. She wondered if he was even talking to her. "Not when the Imperium continues its ruthless expansion." His voice held an edgy tone.

Shivers crept across Flo's chest. She remembered listening to him from behind the bushes when the elders had met following the initial contact with the aliens.

"Laurel is irate with my decision," Rua continued. "She and the other Salvager are on their way here now."

Monti stomped forward and placed her body between Rua and Flo. "What nonsense do you speak?"

"You have every right to be angry," Rua said. "You all do. Being the Anima has its—*complications*. But I knew you were the one, Flo, when I met you."

Flo pushed her hands out in front of her. "Enough," she said. "You're only making me more confused. And my head..." She rubbed at the throbbing.

"Of course." Rua stood, unflinching despite the anger radiating off of Monti. "But please, Flo, hear this above all: you are transforming into a power the world desperately needs. These aliens—the Imperials—they do not come in peace. But you, Anima, can stop them from spreading Disorder across your home."

Silence followed the sound of his skirt swishing away.

Tai visited daily with a fresh flower in hand. He said they should wait to ask the elders for their blessings until Flo felt better. She agreed, though unwillingly. She wanted his seed, and the want grew with each bluebell, daisy, and everlasting he brought.

Jedda would braid Flo's hair and tell her of the village gossip. Monti helped her bathe. Flo felt her face might never cool down from blushing. She yearned to stand, to forage and fish again. What she would give to swim in the lake. At least the nausea had subsided, and she was able to eat small portions of galaxias soup. Though her retching had quelled, the rest of her felt unsettled. Her muscles ached, as if she had spent the day hulling in big catches. Something was happening to her.

The only one with answers had slipped from the village. No one had seen Rua in days. The things he said about the Anima, Imperials, and

Salvagers—none of it made any sense. Flo was happy for the distractions her sister and Tai offered. Her parents had their own distractions; Papi had fallen last week, and he was now as bedridden as Flo.

That was until the morning Flo stood. Monti reached to stop her, but Flo became upright without toppling. After a half moon on the bed, urinating and defecating into a bowl, Flo felt her legs firm beneath her torso. She stretched her arms out to the side, watching in awe as foreign muscles shifted with the movement.

Rua ran into the room. A boom echoed in the distance, then another and another, each boom growing louder. Screams began to fill the spaces between the booms.

Flo's parents shared a look of comprehension. "The aliens," they said in unison.

"They know of your rebirth," Rua said between breaths. "A spy—even in the Wildwoods!" He grabbed Flo by the shoulders. "You need to run. Run into the mountains, and I'll meet you there."

"Where's Jedda? Where is she?" Flo asked, running to the door. "Jedda! Jedda!"

"She's in the berries." Monti's voice was a whisper. Her face turned white.

Rua shook her. "You all need to run," he yelled. "Run!"

They followed Rua out the door and into the smoke. The screaming grew louder.

"Run," everyone was yelling. "Run for your lives!"

Flo and her parents sprinted south, away from the fire and toward the foothills. Their friends and neighbors, new and old, ran in front and behind them. Flo whipped her head around, but she couldn't see Jedda or Tai in the blur of smoke and bodies. Her father continued to hold her wrist. Flo felt as if she were jogging, though her parents were struggling to keep up. Her father halted, and Flo almost tripped over him.

"Go," he said.

Flo shook her head. Tears blurred her vision. What was happening? Houses burned behind them. The booms grew louder each breath.

"Go," Monti screamed. "Go now! Don't look back. Now, Flo! Now!"

Her parents pushed her forward, and they all began running again. She turned around once to see Rua falling to the ground with blood covering his shoulder. Her parents' screams to run faster faded. Everything faded as her feet pounded earth. She ran into the forest, branches cutting at her face. The screaming and smoke were gone, but she ran even harder.

*Whoosh.* The canopy sucked up her body. Netting pressed against her skin. Her leg poked out of the net at an awkward angle, and her arms folded into her body. It took a moment to realize what had happened. She hung suspended in the air, the net cocooning her. In her panic she had forgotten about the traps the Mauni had built to catch game.

Flo struggled to free herself, but the twine only twisted above. Her heart wouldn't calm down. It beat faster now than it had while running full speed—and what wild speed. Her breathing softened, and she could hear soft voices surrounding her. She tried to look around, but the net held her head against her shoulder. The voices spoke of fire. They moved away from her. She didn't recognize any of the speakers' intonations.

"Help!" she called out. "Help me!"

*Human,* a voice whispered. *There's a human over there.*

Flo closed her eyes, straining to hear more, but the voices disappeared. Human? Who had spoken if it wasn't a human as well?

Branches snapped and grasses parted from the direction she had come. New voices filled the quiet. Alien voices. Flo begged the twine to stop twisting and untwisting. She wordlessly prayed to the Mother to keep her safe. The aliens grew louder. She held her breath.

The branches moaned with her weight. Standing beneath her, a man looked up to see Flo, her body cupped in the net. She made eye contact with him, and for a moment he said nothing, and she wondered if there was grace in those eyes, if the Mother had heard her and swayed him to let her go. But any shadow of mercy passed, and he pointed up to her, calling to the other aliens. They shared a laugh, and a couple of them worked their way up the trees to cut her free.

She hit the ground with a thud and struggled to get the net off her. One reached to hold her still, and she kicked him in the groin with her free leg. She growled and thrashed, managing to free the other leg. A few of them laughed at the man moaning. Another moved to restrain her, and she clawed at his face. A feral will to live pumped through her, and she crouched, snarling, ready to spring.

The laughter died off as the man held his clawed face and bellowed. A couple aliens pointed long, silver and wooden barrels at her. A man with hair the color of dingo fur motioned for them to drop the barrels down. There were ten or so of them encircling her. Flo looked wildly from one to the next. The blond man pointed at her face and spoke in a soft tone. She couldn't understand what they were saying, but she could hear the wonder in his voice.

Flo stood, and collectively the circle took a step back. She scanned for the weakest one, a potential break in the ring. A boy shifted his weight nervously to her right. She launched. A boom sounded, and she dropped midair. Pain shot up from her kneecap. She scrambled to stand, but the wooden butt of a man's barrel met her head with a crack. Searing light flashed, and she crumpled to the earth.

The swaying woke her. She opened her eyes to a world upside down. Hurt filled her mind. She moaned and blinked, the light still blinding her. After some time she was able to see the trees passing, their leafy branches reaching into a brilliant blue sky. Her head throbbed, and her back ached from its position of a severe arch. The strange creature her body was slung over clomped its way forward. It smelled like feces.

Behind her were dozens, no, hundreds of men on these giant, four-legged animals. As they ascended a hill, her body thumped up and down. The hill crested, and she realized, though the view was inverted, that they were heading to the bay—to her old home. She remembered the last time she saw the sea, when they had watched the silver monsters ground ashore.

The beach below no longer resembled anything from that memory or any memories before it. Giant wooden structures stood where the forest once crept up to the sand, and smaller buildings spread out along the hills. How long had she been away? Flo tried to remember, though it didn't seem to matter. It might as well have been a thousand years. She closed her eyes and allowed the pain, the blood in her head, the rocking of her body to pull her back into the darkness.

When she woke again, her body lay horizontal. She tried to move, but her hands and feet were strapped down. Cold pressed against her naked backside. Lights flickered all around, and a fire crackled somewhere nearby. It smelled of smoke and something stale. Their homes burning, her people screaming: it was all here with her, in that smell of smoke.

Her knee had been wrapped in a fabric stained red with her blood. She could hear the aliens nearby. A door opened, and sunlight flooded into the room. Flo struggled to free her hands. A clasp dug into her wrists, ripping her flesh. A pale man with brown hair covering his jaw and chin came over to her. He wore some kind of white dress. The blond man that had captured her stood next to him, and they exchanged words.

On the man's white dress and the blond man's green jacket was a strange pattern. An X crossed over their chests. On the bottom of the X was a creature's head that had horns, like a buck, but was much wider than a deer's head. The symbol on top of the X was unmistakably a boar's head.

Tears streamed across her temples as she continued to struggle. Her back thudded against the table. She understood a single word of what they were saying: *Anima*. They said it a few times. It seemed unlikely this name Rua had called her was a different word in their language. She didn't know if she was crying because she was breaking her wrists in the cuffs, or because Rua had betrayed her.

The man in white ran his fingers along the lines of her calves, quadriceps, up the crevice halving her abdominal muscles. He grabbed her by the chin and turned her head one way, then another, murmuring as he went. He parted her eyelids with his fingers. Flo fought to close them, looking beyond him as he examined the pupils and irises.

He released her eyelids and showed the blond man out the door. When he returned, he brought a tray with him. Flo could see little knives lined up, their blades scintillating in the candlelight. He set the tray down and grabbed one. His fingers were delicate and slow.

Flo screamed a scream that didn't sound like hers. She cried for her mother, her father, Jedda, Tai. The man continued his work with graceful precision despite her thrashing body. Her blood flowed from her, and in time the pain neutralized itself in its entirety. She could feel her body softening, growing quiet, and she closed her eyes.

Her sweat and tears found her tongue and she licked at the salt, at the memory of seawater dripping from wet hair. Fish dancing in nets; sunlight a dazzle upon the sea; dolphins weaving the water into a tapestry of waves—memories from a lifetime ago. She felt herself returning to the Mother. When she spoke, the alien's knife slipped at last. The meaning of her words dissolved into the absence of a shared language.

# VI

# THE FINAL ANIMA IS BORN

*"The Task grew from failings of Animas and Keepers past.*
*Any successes did little to mitigate the spread of Disorder.*
*To restore the Sacred Balance seems an absurd undertaking now.*
*The human world is clearly bent on chaos. What, then, to make of us?*
*What to make of the mess we have created from Order?*
*There's a reason somewhere in all of this for why*
*the Anima is always a woman. I am sure of it.*
*Yet I cannot think of any reason for why there should be*
*a final Anima. Why in the world not continue the spiral*
*until the Task is complete? It seems the Task is less a test of a*
*single woman, and more an evaluation of an entire species."*

- Freda Johansson, *Task of the Anima*

# DISCOVERY

## 77 YDP

THE CRAZY MOUNTAINS, PROMINENCE DISTRICT

Freda moved toward the herd's bedding place after spending another solstice searching the woods beneath Yarrow Peak. The mushroom hunt had proved fruitless. Again. As it was with all twenty-four solstices before, a few rings of Fly Agarics had grown among the aspens, but none with the pattern she sought. So Freda trotted north alongside Owl Creek, pursuing the hunt she preferred.

A low growl halted her mid-stride. She dropped to her knees and stretched out her hand. The dog sniffed it and whined.

Behind the dog, a young woman lay still as stone, her face turned up to the starry sky. The dog's owner, Freda assumed. She had nearly stepped on her face. She took the woman's wrist and found the pulse. It was steady, though faint. A little blood soaked into the side of the woman's newsboy cap. Freda unfurled the woman's clenched hand and found a red mushroom within it. Her stomach lurched. She tentatively brought the mushroom closer to her eyes, though she already knew. A part of her had known for decades now and didn't need to look.

Nonetheless, the white dots atop the cap knocked the wind from her. "No," she breathed.

She looked closer at the still figure before her. Of course the woman was much younger than herself. She inspected the white dots a second, third, and fourth time, tracing the Flower of Life pattern with a finger. It felt as if she dreamed, as if she had, at last, woken to the nightmare of her life. Moving with unnatural slowness, Freda tucked the mushroom into her front coat pocket and felt its colossal weight against her heart.

For a long while, she stared at the stranger. Incredulity alone subdued hysteria. After all she had done, after all she had left behind, this—this straggly *nobody* had robbed her of *everything*. Though she didn't move, her legs falling asleep in their crouched position, it felt as if she thrashed in waters, gulping for air, trying not to drown as a flash flood swept away her life's purpose in this single moment.

The dog growled with impatience, startling Freda. She saw the backpack and placed it atop the woman's stomach before lifting her. The woman was alarmingly light. She could feel her bones poking against her clothes. Freda hiked over Crescent Saddle. Though there was no defined trail, she moved quickly with the starlight of a day old moon. The dog followed at her heels, panting as the trail gained elevation. Up, up, up and over the mountain saddle and down into the canyon below.

They passed a cougar in a tree, eyes luminous. They passed an owl as she cut the darkness with white wings. They passed a caddis hatch, fish rising. They passed a spider weaving her immaculate web.

Freda laid the woman down on the futon and wrapped the wound on her head. The dog curled up along her person's side. She was a stunning creature, almost as long as Freda was tall, with a fluffy coat colored brown, red, white, and black. Freda pet her despite it all.

She remembered reading in Rua's book that the cognitive transformation would take a half moon spent unconscious. She found his book on a shelf and reviewed the recipes he recommended to help aid the metamorphosis. The dog watched her prepare a broth. She jumped off the futon and licked the air around Freda's legs.

Freda threw a few meat scraps into a bowl for her and sat at the kitchen table as the bones and herbs boiled on the stove. The sun rose over Crescent Saddle in the window above the stranger on her futon. The cabin, her home for over two decades now, felt unreal. Everything—the fire burning in the stove, the slurps of the dog eating, the woman, the girl, really, sleeping on her futon—it all seemed like any moment it would disappear, and Freda would wake in her bed, alone yet again, but still with hope.

She pulled the pot off the stove and scooped some broth into a bowl. The stranger's face was ashen. Freda checked her pulse once more. Her wrist felt so small, so thin and fragile. Blood had dried in the crown of her black hair. She had a long face and nose. Freda could tell she had some Indigenous blood in her.

She poured the broth down the woman's throat. The Anima's throat, she reminded herself. She retrieved a tincture of chamomile, peppermint, and lavender and placed drops under the Anima's tongue. The dog's red-brown eyes followed every movement. "I don't have to be doing this," she told the dog. But that was a lie. It was all one big fucking lie. It had been the entire time.

She began her day as usual. Feed the animals. Gather eggs. Harvest vegetables for breakfast. Make breakfast. Only once outside again, with food in her belly and her knees on the ground, did she cry. She pulled thistle from the garden and sobbed. Loudly, without restraint: the kind of sobs she had craved since leaving the Haven. She wiped snot from her nose, leaving a trail of moistened soil across her cheek. The thistle piled as she screamed and gasped for air. At one point she was on her back between the rows of kale and onion, pounding the earth with her fists.

Days slipped by, as they had for all these years. Each day, each moon, each solstice: they all had flowed forward with her buoyed by the fact she was going to be the next Anima. Not fact, but *dream*. The dream she was going to be the next Anima. The purpose for being here. The reason she endured. Gone, now, and replaced with a stranger on her futon and a dog eating her meat. She wondered when the Keepers would show up. Had Laurel seen the rebirth? Was she as bewildered as Freda was with the twist of fate?

Of course not, Freda thought, pitching soiled grasses out of the goat pen. Laurel must have known all along. Freda recalled every detail of the moment that had shaped her life to this point: the Salvager in the cave, her white eyes aglow, telling Freda she would be the one to find the mushroom. How convenient not to mention it would be in another's hand.

She would kill her. Freda stabbed the grasses with the pitchfork. She would kill Laurel the moment she walked onto this homestead.

But no one showed up. A week passed, and the woman still slept, the dog still ate Freda's meat, the weeds still grew, and the chickens and goats still needed to be fed. In the absence of change, a terrible alternative surfaced. What if the Keepers had all been killed? What if Freda, alone, was responsible for the Anima's safety?

Freda paced the floor of her tree house, wringing her hands together. Even if Laurel had used her like a pawn, sending her out here to nurse the next Anima, the Salvager had done it for a reason. Rua had presumably died revealing the location of the last mushroom to her. What had he said again—something about the Keepers not orchestrating the last Anima's birth?

She stopped pacing and looked out the tree house window at the cabin below. Yes, it was possible this entire time they had known she wouldn't be the Anima. For this Freda would never forgive them. Yet they had sent her here with the knowledge necessary to bring the Anima into the world. Freda was no Keeper. She was but a half-trained Mage, secreted away in the mountains with all the knowledge and tools necessary to midwife the Anima into existence.

Bracing herself on the windowsill, she remembered Rua in that hole, all but dead. She had always wondered why he had been willing to kill himself so she, alone, would know where the last mushroom would grow. The Keepers must have known the Imperium would be hunting down the last Anima. They must have figured the best chance for the Anima's survival was in the safety of obscurity.

This realization did nothing to mend the wound where her dream had been ripped from her. It did nothing to shorten the years where a love with Tillie could have grown. It did nothing to fix the shattered reality around her. It did, though, offer a way forward. Freda decided she would leave for Twin Rivers tomorrow.

Elle B. Morgan's address was clearly printed on the library card Freda found in her wallet. Freda had passed through Elle's neighborhood many of her trips to town; it was likely she and Elle had even walked by one another in years past. She thought it unusual the only form of identification Elle had, or at least carried with her, was a library card. The other things in the ragged, leather wallet were about five dollars in cash and two photographs.

Gray lines quartered the pictures and a few pieces of tape held them together. An Indigenous man was in both; Freda assumed he was Elle's father. The backpack contained a water canteen, a can of ham, a book on wild edibles, and a canvas jacket. Freda wrinkled her nose at the Imperial Bombers logo stitched across the jacket's back. She placed the items back into the pack along with the knife she had found in Elle's pocket and the newsboy cap Freda had cleaned of Elle's blood.

She hiked to the Mystic Peak trailhead. When she neared the Mountain View trailer park, she hid in a growth of ponderosas and watched Elle's doublewide. A woman opened the door and locked it behind her. Even from the fifty-yard distance, Freda could tell she was Elle's mother. They had the same skinny body and defined cheekbones. The woman sat in her car and lit a cigarette before turning on the ignition. Freda waited until the dust clouds settled back into the dirt road before emerging from the forest.

She found a key beneath a plant-less pot, surprised to find it there, in such an obvious place to hide a key. The fern root she used to cheat locks remained in her pack as she clicked opened the door with the spare. Cigarette smoke and garbage assaulted her nose. A battered couch faced a mirror opaque with grime. A notebook, a few empty beer cans, and an ashtray overflowing with cigarette butts littered a coffee table. There was no dining table. A bar with pizza boxes and more empty beer cans separated the living room from the cooking space. Yellow tinted the refrigerator door, and dirty dishes filled the sink.

Freda opened a bedroom door and the stench of sex submerged her. She found herself swimming in the memory of Tillie. Her back, white and curvy and smooth as a river rock. The play of her tongue. The song of her laugh. Freda clenched her fists against the aching want in her fingers. The woman's bedroom was strangely bare, especially in contrast to the claustrophobic feel of the living room and kitchen. Beside the bed was a nightstand with only a glass containing cigarette butts and ash. Soiled clothes spilled out from the closet. Nothing adorned the walls.

The only thing out of order in Elle's room was the desk. The drawers had been left open and the contents within were disheveled. She noticed the top drawer had a locking mechanism. Crowbar marks told of someone prying it open. Freda grabbed a black notebook from the drawer and read Elle's words about another day at school spent moving through the motions. She also had written about her job, and a coworker named Nox whom she evidently found attractive, though she also wrote that she was too ugly and weird to *go there*.

What Freda found most intriguing were Elle's reflections about the mountains. Even the handwriting seemed to beautify as her language waxed poetic about the trees and rivers and birds. In these parts of the journal, Elle's voice shifted from self-loathing to something lighter. It was as if the further Elle went from writing about her own existence, the closer she came to discovering joy and revelation.

Freda considered taking the journal home, but she feared Elle's mother would note its absence and assume her daughter had come back for it. She closed the door to Elle's room and sat on the couch to think. Another one of Elle's journals lay opened on the coffee table. Freda saw that the entry had been written the day before the summer solstice. Watermarks blurred the penmanship, but she could still discern the words.

The entry began with excitement as Elle celebrated finishing school and receiving *ownership* of her life. But the happiness on the page quickly slipped into melancholy as Elle retold the events of that day. She had returned home from a hike to find her mother's newest lover was still in the house. She described her mother's behavior as selfish and childish. *Doesn't she realize how hard it is for me sometimes? And she tells me* this is the one *as if I hadn't heard that before.* The entry escalated into impassioned writing about Elle's resolve to leave home and her mother's *drunken self-sabotage* behind. She detailed the plans she had conceived while hiking that morning. *A clean start,* Freda read. *We'll both be better off for it.* She wrote that she already had a thousand dollars stashed above her desk.

Curious, Freda reentered Elle's room. Standing on her toes atop the desk, she fumbled with the ceiling pane. She discovered nothing. She walked back into her mother's room and searched the closet. There it was, on the corner of a back shelf. A large jar filled with dollars rolled into wads. Freda felt even more confused. Was Elle's mother looking for her or not? She slipped off her backpack, dropped to her belly, and wriggled under the bed.

A couple hours later she heard two people enter, a man and a woman. They talked with slurred voices, their words dripping together. The mattress pressed down on her. Freda stayed awake the entire night, periodically rearranging her body to abate the discomfort. It was ten or eleven in the morning by the time the couple stirred awake. They lit cigarettes and smoked as they lay in bed, talking.

"You know what I was thinking?" the man asked. "I love how we can spend time together without worrying about upsetting your daughter. I mean—I know it's been really hard for you that she left, but, well, I think it may be for the best. For everyone."

Quiet. A lighter clicked and fresh cigarette smoke filled the room. Freda stifled a cough.

"I think you might be right," Elle's mother said at last. "I just wish she wouldn't have left on such bad terms." Freda could hear the rue in her words. She continued, her voice darkening. "Did I tell you about the journal of hers I found yesterday? She wrote that *I* was childish and selfish."

"It reminds me of something my brother would have said when he was doped up," the man said, his voice cold.

The bed shifted, and Elle's mother's feet appeared again on the ground. "How 'bout I take you out to eat at that pancake joint by the Blue?"

"Sounds good to me." He stepped off the bed and pulled on his pants. "Ready?"

"Almost. Go on and start the car. I'll be right there."

His feet left the room, and Elle's mother walked to her closet. Freda listened to the unmistakable sound of a jar lid unscrewing. That sound was part of Freda's everyday existence. At home, it was the noise of opening a food container; it was the noise of nourishment. In this smoky room belonging to Elle's mother, it was the sound of abandonment sired by willful ignorance.

The front door closed, and the lock clicked. Freda waited before pulling herself out from under the bed. Didn't Elle's mother assume Elle would return for her money? As she hiked back to the cabin, she figured Elle's mother had betrayed her daughter three times over: first by reading her private thoughts; second by abandoning her; and third by stealing her money. Each betrayal begot the next. It wasn't Freda's mother. It wasn't her old home, her old life. But nonetheless she trudged up and over Hidden Passage Falls, her walking made slow with sadness for the person who had stolen her future.

All in all, though, Freda knew she had completed her mission to Twin Rivers with the best results possible. No one was looking for Elle. The final Anima was free to be born.

☾

Freda finished planting winter squash and placed a hoop house over the crop row before plucking wild peppermint for the next batch of Elle's medicine. She could smell a rainstorm approaching and moved quickly. Thunder echoed into the canyon from the south. A silver lining above Crescent Saddle announced the coming of moon-dawn.

She returned inside as rain and hail began to pour down. After hanging the peppermint to dry, she prepared the dog's dinner. When she placed the meal on the ground, she noticed Elle's eyes moving sporadically in their sockets behind closed lids. The Anima dreamed again. Any moment now she would wake.

A full moon crested the cirque. The lightning storm hugged the west side of the canyon, sending electric veins throughout its mass with crackles and shuddering booms. The storm passed as quickly as it had come. Freda ambled toward the goat shelter and pet the bleating creatures longer than usual. She took her time with her evening chores, not wanting to be the first thing the Anima saw upon waking.

Elle opened her eyes. The smell of sage after rain washed over her. She could see a moonlit forest through a window. Her brain throbbed. She touched her head and realized it was bandaged. Quilts layered atop her, and Luna slept beside her. Someone had lit candles atop the kitchen table and counters. Their flames bounced and swayed with the breeze moving between open windows.

Plants grew where they sat tucked away in nooks and crannies and across windowsills. Ivy tendrils weaved up the walls and wrapped around ceiling rafters. Alongside the wall in front of her stood a tall, oak bookshelf filled with leather-bound books and random items like a large magnifying glass and old clay vessels. Beyond the sage, she smelled wood smoke, lavender, and cedar.

Elle tried to lean forward and immediately needed to vomit. She found a bucket next to the bed. Each dry heave brought tears to her eyes. It felt as if burning hands wrung her lungs.

Luna stirred and came face to face with Elle.

Someone asked, *Are you alright?*

Elle moved her eyes around, trying to keep her head still while searching for who had spoken.

*Are you alright?* the soft voice asked again.

Luna wasn't looking at whoever was talking. She stared at Elle and licked her face.

The voice said, *I missed you. I was worried.*

Elle forced herself to sit up and look behind her. The effort brought stars to her eyes, and she nearly passed out. There was only a wall with a tapestry hanging from it. She lay back down and again the voice spoke.

*Did you miss me? I've been here the whole time.* Luna peered into her eyes, and comprehension crept into Elle's mind. Luna was talking to her. She was hallucinating that Luna was talking to her.

*Are you—are you* talking *to me?* Elle asked without opening her mouth. It was a thought she felt in the depths of her brain. Elle knew she had directed the words to a particular place. The question had emerged and then escaped, like a bubble roiling to water's surface and popping into the air.

*Yes!* Luna replied. *And you can hear me! I've been here the entire time you were away. The strange woman and I.*

*Strange woman?*

*She found you next to the creek.*

Elle thought back, her mind moving through a muddy pool. She remembered leaving the house the day after graduating school. Hiking up the trail, cutting down to Owl Creek, sitting beside it. She remembered plucking glacier lilies, wild spinach. The mushroom. The mushroom!

*The mush—*, Elle said, or thought, to Luna, stopping mid-sentence. She was talking to her dog, in a strange place, unable to move. Panic descended, acute in its entirety.

When Freda walked through the door, Luna slunk outside. She met eyes with Elle, and they exchanged silence.

Freda spoke first. "I know you're scared and confused but please, don't move."

"If only I could. Who are you?"

"My name is Freda. It's nice to meet you, Elle."

Elle didn't say anything. Freda sat in a chair next to the kitchen table, leaving the door open behind her.

"Why am I here?" Elle asked, crossing her arms.

"Because most people would have no idea what to do with you, aside from the minor damage to your head when you fell. Nor do you know what to do with yourself, I can only assume. Have you and your dog exchanged a conversation yet?"

Surprise flickered across Elle's face.

"And you think you're now crazy, right? You took a bite of a mushroom, hit your head, knocked something loose up there, and for the rest of your life will hallucinate conversations with your dog."

Elle remained silent, her eyes staring out from shadowed holes.

She reminded Freda of a weasel she once cornered in her chicken coop, fierce in her fear. "You're skeptical. Not that I blame you. You've had quite a journey. And you have only begun your life's purpose." *My life's purpose,* she should say. She forced her voice even. "I'm here, though, to help you. Your guide, if you will."

Elle looked at the door and back to Freda. "How long have I been here? Where am I? Who are you, and why do you think you know me?" She tried to sit up but nausea and vertigo forced her to remain still. Her heart felt as if it would leap up her throat and out of her mouth at any moment.

"*Please,*" Freda said, getting up to stand but then deciding to remain seated. "Please. Don't move. Your transformation requires another half lunation of stillness."

"A half *what?* Are you crazy? This is crazy. You're probably a hallucination as well. I'm the crazy one." Elle kept looking at the open door and back at Freda. She pushed the blanket away.

"You need to calm down," Freda said slowly. "I can explain everything.

No one is crazy. I mean no one in this room is crazy. You are not hallucinating. Breathe and settle. I can explain everything. Well, some things. For one, you will be able to move freely again on the next new moon, which is in approximately two weeks."

"Two weeks?" Elle's voice soared. The strange woman flinched. Her eyes were a bright green, observing Elle observe her. Elle could see she had been crying. "Why are you upset?" Elle asked.

Why was she upset? Freda almost laughed. "I'm—I'm not as upset as before, but this is hard for me—you being what you are now..." She stared at the floor. "I thought for nearly thirty years your life's purpose would be my own. This belief is—I mean, *was*—what I lived for." Tears ran down Freda's nose. A cavernous hush filled the room.

Elle wondered what purpose this woman thought her life held. Beyond the open door, Luna chased a squirrel. Elle realized she could hear the squirrel yelling in fear as it sprinted across the ground. He scampered up a tree trunk. The indiscernible scream of terror turned to a clear and high-pitched voice yelling, *Predator! Predator! Everyone off the ground and into trees!*

Elle listened to Luna and the squirrel bicker at one another before yelling, "Come!" *You're scaring him,* she added.

Luna sauntered back in through the open door and jumped onto the bed next to Elle. *Fear is a part of death for any animal,* she said to Elle. *And I'm hungry.*

"Could you understand the squirrel?" Freda asked.

Frowning, Elle shook her head. "I don't know."

Freda brushed out the wrinkles in her pants as if she could smooth away her sorrow. "I'll start at the beginning of my story, which will help you understand your own. But first, some tea."

Elle watched Freda prepare the tea. She wore a beige t-shirt under faded and torn canvas overalls. Silver streaked her black hair, and the elements had carved her face, but she seemed youthful. Elle thought she must be thirty-something. Veins ran down her defined biceps and forearms. She moved with a deliberate grace, like water, gliding across the wooden floors as she retrieved jars of dried herbs.

Moonlight funneled into the cabin. Cobwebs in corners gathered insects and dust, their milky threads glistening. Water flowed somewhere close by. Elle could also hear many quiet voices outside, like conversational din at the Pizza Parlor. Next to the door was a woodpile stacked a dozen rows high. Another oak bookshelf, its shelves lined with jars of preserved food and herbs, stood next to the woodpile. A small wooden table and two chairs resided under a circular window. Wooden cabinets, a cast iron cook stove, and a countertop where a giant jug of water and a washing basin sat made up the kitchen. Elle noted the lack of a refrigerator. She remembered how proud her mother had been when they had bought one.

Her mother. A flare of anxiety moved through her. Freda walked back into the cabin.

"My mother," Elle said. "She has no idea where I am. She probably thinks I'm dead."

Freda poured tea into two ceramic mugs and brought one to Elle, saying, "For your nausea."

"Did you hear me?" Elle asked, taking the mug. "My mother must be sick with worry by now. How long did you say I would be here? A half moon cycle? How long have I been here already?"

"Yes, you need another half moon cycle. And you've been here for equal that time." Freda's voice remained calm but veiled.

Elle could tell she was holding something back. "Don't you think they are looking for me? Like, the police? Have you seen or heard anyone out there asking for me? Where am I, anyways?" Anger made her voice loud.

Freda sat back down at the kitchen table and took a sip of tea. "Yum. I love licorice root. A sugarless sweetener, you know. Take a sip of the tea, Elle. It will calm your stomach and mind."

"Why are you ignoring my questions? I don't care about your fucking tea." Elle dumped the tea on the floor. "I want to know why I'm here and why you're hiding me."

Freda studied the steaming puddle on the floor and took another sip of tea. The girl had fire. This was good. "Elle, I'm not trying to hide you. No one has been searching for you. And you are here for reasons largely unknown to us. You are this era's Anima. You are the one and only human alive with the ability to communicate with animals."

Elle understood one thing alone. "What do you mean, no one has been searching for me?"

"I mean—I did my homework while you were undergoing transformation. Your mother, she thinks you have moved on with your life."

"How could you possibly know this?" Elle was almost yelling.

"More tea?" Freda offered, lifting the teapot up. She filled her own mug.

Elle glared at her. "Answer me."

Freda calculated her wording in silence. "I went into your house while your mother was away at work. I believe she has accepted your departure."

"You're stalking my mother." Luna growled in blind agreement to Elle's rage. "How long have you been stalking her?" Elle paused. "Wait—how long have you been stalking *me?* What are you, you going to do with me?"

Freda grimaced. She wasn't prepared for this—for her.

Elle felt a twinge of guilt as Freda cleaned the tea off the ground.

"I understand your mistrust," Freda managed at last. "It's wise, even. But I was only *stalking* your mother to make sure no one was searching for you. Do you know how bad it could have been if someone had found you here, mid-transformation? Had you been taken from my care and placed in a hospital…" She remembered the way Rua's eyes had bulged as he revealed the last Anima's agonizing death. "It would have been—catastrophic. Please, Elle. Relax. You're safe and in good care."

Elle began to protest.

"Enough," Freda said, thrusting her hands to the sides. "Be quiet now."

Elle opened and closed her mouth. Freda added more wood to the cook stove's fire and walked out to the garden. She gathered a basketful of asparagus. The moon cast watery light across the forest. Trees murmured in the breeze, and an owl sounded nearby.

Back inside, Freda cut the asparagus and a handful of garlic cloves. Her movements felt clumsy. Elle looked out the window, crying. Freda pulled the pan of vegetables out of the oven and scooped them onto two plates. She cut the meat into bite-sized pieces for Elle.

"Please eat slowly," Freda said, handing Elle a plate. "This will be your first solid meal in two weeks. It's deer steak and asparagus with garlic and goat butter."

Elle wiped snot from her nose. "Goat butter?"

"Yep, from Dorthy."

Elle sniffed at a spear of asparagus. It was succulent, and she began devouring the food. With each forkful, a deep hunger calmed.

"You need to slow down," Freda said. "If you eat too fast on an empty stomach, your nausea will return with double the intensity."

While Freda cleaned up the kitchen, Elle finished her meal. Apart from staff dinners at the restaurant, she couldn't remember the last time someone had cooked her a meal. When Freda took her empty plate, Elle could feel herself blushing. "Thanks," she mumbled.

*What did I eat before this place?* Luna asked Elle. *Whatever that woman feeds me is delicious.*

*You're eating deer tonight,* Elle answered, glancing sideways at her dog.

*I had no idea food could be so—real.*

Elle watched her dog eat. Real? None of this felt real.

Freda continued to flit around the cabin as another pot of tea cooled. She watered the herbs growing on the windowsills and harvested some of their leaves to dry. Pouring tea into mugs, Freda said, "Please don't dump yours on the floor this time."

Elle accepted the mug with tentative hands.

"I added skullcap and valerian this time for your anxiety."

"I don't have anxiety. I think any sane person would be terrified if they woke up in a stranger's home. I mean, seriously, where *am* I?"

Freda handed Elle a picture frame from the bookshelf. The black and white photograph was of a man and a younger Freda standing in front of a cabin. The man, tall and broad, reminded Elle of her father. Freda held a bow in her hands. The forest swelled beyond the cabin, rising into a snowcapped, rocky cirque.

Elle pointed at the cirque. "Is that the Bighorn?"

"Yep. We're in Badger Creek Canyon, west of Mystic Peak. There's no trail leading here, at least no trail found on a map."

Elle's face went slack. "You mean to tell me that no one could find me if they were looking?"

Freda took the picture frame from her and rubbed grime off the glass. Had all the Animas been this difficult? "The *right* people can find you.

You'll soon discover you'd rather most people didn't."

"Or would you rather they didn't?" Elle whispered.

"I don't know what I'd prefer, truthfully." Freda rubbed at her jaw. "You just don't understand. You don't understand at all. But how could you? What you are now, you have no idea whatsoever." She gazed beyond Elle, to the box on the bottom shelf of the bookcase. The scroll was locked away in her tree house. She hadn't unfurled it since finding Elle. It had been the beginning of this mess. It was the net Laurel had cast out into the world, catching Freda with cruel disregard for her own wants and needs.

Freda shook her head and stood. It was what it was now. She brought the blankets scrunched around Elle's feet up across her legs and stomach.

Elle squirmed. "I need to pee."

"That's what the bucket's for. I'll have to support your head, and we'll need to move slowly."

It took ten minutes to sit up, inch forward to the bedside, unbutton her jeans, and slip her pants and underwear to her ankles. Elle struggled against both vulnerability and vomit. Freda looked away while keeping a steady hold of Elle's head. The pee resounded as it hit the metal, a long and full stream. When Elle reached toward her ankles to pull up her jeans, vomit gathered at the top of her stomach.

"Easy there," Freda said.

But Elle was already reaching for the bucket. Freda stood powerless as she watched Elle heave up dinner. Freda held Elle's hair back, fighting back her own need to vomit. When the dry heaving subsided, Elle leaned against the pillow, shuddering. Freda wet a towel and wiped the vomit from her face and hair. She emptied and rinsed the bucket in the creek. When she returned, Elle had fallen asleep with her pants still around her ankles.

Freda tucked her in and went to the tree house. Large windows on the south and north walls allowed the moon to light up the old mattress, blankets, and pillow nestled into the corner. A kerosene lamp sat atop the nightstand and a rifle leaned against the wall. She lit the lamp and lifted the scroll out of the nightstand drawer. She traced the words. Usually the feel of the engraved letters comforted her, as the touch of a familiar blanket comforts a baby. Tonight, though, she only felt her callouses falter across the engravings.

The scroll, she realized with a start. It wasn't the scroll she had found. It was and it wasn't. It looked the same, and yet it felt old and worn. It felt the way it looked.

Laurel's magic had run its course, and now Freda cradled a decayed strip of calf hide. She wanted to tear it to pieces. She wanted to light it on fire and leave it to burn down the entire homestead. Hyperventilating, she shoved the scroll back into the drawer and pulled a pillow over her head.

Her breathing slowed. The sheets, damp with tears and sweat, stuck to her face. She thought of Tillie, of course. She tasted the salt of Tillie's skin, felt the tickle of her fingers across her back. She remembered the strange pairing of her dark humor and sweet shyness. The thought of her mother, dying alone, brought another wave of staggered breathing. She pulled the pillow tighter around her head, pressing her face against the mattress.

The Anima was reborn. A new era had begun. And Freda of the Cantons couldn't imagine being more miserable.

# TASK

Elle's stomach growls woke her. She remembered last night with a wave of nausea. Freda had seen her private parts, but Elle hadn't had any other choice. Which was more alarming: the animal voices she heard in her head, or the complete vulnerability of her situation? The latter, she decided.

Everyone talked to animals. She remembered the birdwatchers on the Mystic Peak trail with binoculars in hand. They had whispered to the birds as they followed their flight through glass. She remembered the people walking their dogs around town, saying to come and sit. She remembered all the times she had told Luna her grievances.

But this—this new way of talking, of *hearing,* was entirely different. She couldn't rationalize it away, and terror washed through her anew.

*I need to go out,* Luna whined.

*I can't help you,* Elle said. *As you may have noticed, I can't move.*

The door opened, and Luna rushed past Freda as she stepped into the cabin.

"Good morning," Freda said. "How are you feeling?" The room smelled of piss, vomit, and wet dog. She left the door open.

"Better than last night."

Freda filled two glasses with water and brought one over to Elle. "I have to do a few things before I make breakfast." Freda filled a small wooden bowl with dried berries and handed it to Elle. "While you wait, eat some of these gooseberries. Slowly, of course."

"Thanks," Elle said, taking the bowl. "What are you going to do?"

"Make sure we survive the winter." Freda popped some berries into her mouth. She began making a fire in the oven's stove.

Elle furrowed her brow. "*We?* I'm leaving as soon as I can."

Freda sat on her heels, structuring the kindling into a small tent. *Good,* she almost said. She'd never be the Freda she had dreamed of being. She'd never be the Anima. She set a lit match to the kindling, and it caught fire.

Seeing Freda's face contort, Elle shifted. She had obviously upset her. "What I mean is, I'd just be a burden. Another mouth to feed. I'll—I'll just return to my life and you can return to yours. It'll be best for both of us."

Freda's laugh was harsh. "When you return to your life?" She swiveled to face Elle. How little this woman, this *girl* knew. Her ignorance, it was understandable, but tortuous nonetheless.

Elle nodded. "It'll be best for us both," she repeated.

Freda knew arguing with her was senseless. "Well, if that is what you must do then so be it," she said. "But according to past accounts of women who ate of the *Anima metamorpha,* you now need to learn how to cultivate your new powers with a knowledgeable mentor." She stood taller. "And you must use your powers for the betterment of the earth."

"Oh, is that all?" Elle said with exaggerated cheerfulness. "I don't understand what you say half the time. What is the *Anima metamorpha*?"

"It's the mushroom you took a bite of." Freda grabbed a jar housing the remains of the last *Anima metamorpha* the world would ever know. She handed it to her. "The exceedingly rare, magical, and life-altering *Anima metamorpha*."

Elle brought the mushroom to her face and rotated the jar. The red had faded to brown, and mold bloomed on the top as a blue and white flower. She remembered its funky taste, its slimy texture. Her bite in the cap was but a nibble, hardly noticeable. She untwisted the jar lid and smelled the decay. "Why don't you eat it?" she asked, twisting the lid back on. "I mean, if talking to animals was *your* life's purpose and all."

"It doesn't work like that. There can only be one Anima per era." Freda sighed. "I was supposed to find it. Or at least that's what I thought, since I was presumably the only one to hear the last Anima's Death Revelation."

Death Revelation? Elle looked up at Freda standing tall with her hands on hips. Amber rays of morning streamed through the windows, illuminating the dust drifting around her. "Will I—will I die because I'm this Anima thingy?"

Freda slapped her forehead. "You'll die because you're mortal, like the rest of us. But you're not going to die solely because you're the Anima, if that's what you're tearing up over. I mentioned the Death Revelation because Animas have revealed the location of the next mushroom when they die."

Why there even were Death Revelations, though, Freda no longer knew. Or cared to know. Rua had died for nothing. It had all been for nothing. "I need to begin my tasks for the day," she said abruptly, shrugging away the despair. "Eat those berries. They may grow on trees, but not often."

The berries had spilled across Elle's lap. "Sorry," she mumbled, placing them back into the bowl.

Freda fed the goats and cleaned their shelter. They chomped on their breakfast, eyeing the dog lying under a pine tree past the pen. Luna watched Freda as she moved toward the chicken coop. Freda decided the dog must be half wolf, half Taigas shepherd.

She could hear the chickens chattering inside their large house. With a lift of the vertically sliding front door, eighteen chicks, six hens, and one rooster strutted outside. A mix of heirloom varieties, the birds' plumage ranged from snow white to ebony. One hen boasted golden and turquoise feathers woven within darker plumes. She fed the chickens before collecting their eggs, a neat dozen today. Freda admired the eggs' beauty in the wool-lined wire basket. Tans and blues and whites and browns, all gathered together as an ova bouquet.

She thinned the carrots and beets, weeded out the thistle and dandelions, and harvested spinach growing within a raised bed beneath a hoop-house. Sweat seeped into her wool shirt and trickled alongside her hairline. She peeled off her sweater and noticed a large hole in its back; it was yet another item in need of mending.

She stood with a basket full of spinach and turnip greens and took a quick inventory of the food growing before her. A couple months earlier she had planned the garden to feed herself alone for the year. Would Elle really leave? If not, they'd need to work twice as hard gathering and hunting to feed them both throughout the winter. That was, if they were supposed to stay here. Perhaps the Keepers would come for them after all.

Come for *her*, Freda corrected herself. They would come for the Anima. She would be rendered obsolete once they came to take the Anima under their care. She was a pawn, a stepping-stone. Fucking tears. She wiped them from her face with shaking hands.

She could only plan as if. As if this was meant to be. As if the Anima should stay with her here. As if she was meant to nurture and mentor the one the mushroom chose. Freda scrutinized the meticulously planted rows running east to west. There could be enough for two there, she figured, given they froze and fermented the majority. But they would need more jars.

Backpacking glass jars from town to the cabin was the bane of her removed existence. The weight of the glass, of course, was challenging. Newspaper wrapped around the jars added heft. They'd need fifty more jars, she speculated, lifting the basket higher on her hip. The hike to Twin Rivers and back totaled sixteen miles, with a six-thousand-foot elevation gain. Freda knew they could do the trip physically. Elle was the Anima, after all, and by fall she could carry all fifty jars alone if need be.

Elle accepted a plate of eggs scrambled with greens. "These eggs are so yellow."

"Orange yolks, most of them," Freda replied. "The chickens eat a diet of ancient corn, seeds, and whatever bugs they can find."

"Huh. Do you make the chickens' food or backpack it in?"

"I grow the corn and gather the seeds. But you'll be learning all about survival on this homestead soon enough, given you choose to stay. If you don't, well, I don't see any point explaining how I keep this place up and running." Freda studied Elle for a moment, deliberating. "I'd like to know," she said slowly, "I mean, if you're willing—I'd like to know more about you."

"Don't you already know everything?" Elle quipped. "Breaking and entering my house. Stalking my mom. Stalking me, for all I know."

"I had never seen you before I nearly stepped on your face when I was out hunting." She could have let her die out there. Freda breathed out the frustration, remembering the stale smoke of her mother's room, the sound of the jar opening. Elle's childhood made Freda's own seem like a fairytale. She wouldn't tell Elle more than she needed to know about that trip to her house. Doing so would only impede her transformation. "No, I don't know anything, really, about you. Please. Enlighten me."

Elle finished her meal with a satisfied groan. "What would you like to know? I don't want to bore you."

She looked at Freda with sunken eyes. Her long hair fell greasy and disheveled around her gaunt face, and her shirt hung off one shoulder, revealing a protruding collarbone. "I'd like to hear about your life before you unknowingly became our era's Anima," Freda said.

"Key word *unknowingly*. But okay," Elle said with a little shrug. "My dad was a pilot and he taught others how to fly. One day he was out teaching, and his student flew the plane straight into a cliff. Other pilots at the flight school said the guy didn't know how to handle the strong winds blowing off the lake, and those winds blew them right into the cliff. They said—they said my dad should have known better." She felt her throat constrict. When was the last time she had talked about her dad? With Walter? Mr. Simmons? It felt good and terrible, all at once, and she demanded the feelings to go away.

"Anyways," she droned, rolling her eyes. "Soon after, we moved into the doublewide you visited when you were stalk—er, investigating me. My mother quit her job at the library and began pulling night shifts at the Susie Blue. Which brings us to now." Elle finished with little intonation in her voice.

The day outside hummed and warbled with the life of summer. Desire to be out there—to stand and walk and simply be in the forest again—crawled against Elle's skin. She tried to shake her legs against the futon mattress without moving her head.

"Thanks for sharing, Elle," Freda said, watching Elle twitch on the futon. "If you don't mind, I'd like to hear more about you. Knowing about your parents helps me better understand your—*election* as the Anima. Yet I still don't know much about your life before now."

Elle looked at the vines crawling up and under the beams from different pots hanging near the windows. The plants must have been decades old. She realized she and this stranger shared a commonality: voluntary solitude.

"I spent a lot of time alone," Elle said. "I think being as poor as my mother and I were after my dad died had something to do with my, um, decision to be a loner. Though I haven't been truly alone since adopting Luna a couple years ago." She paused. "And you?" she asked. "Why do you choose to be alone?"

Freda stopped scrubbing the cast iron. She could hear the way Tillie's accent softened her name when she had called Freda to her at night; she could feel the smooth curve of her lower back. Had she really chosen to be alone? It was Laurel, Freda thought, squeezing the dry sponge. She had forced her into solitude. "I didn't choose this life," she said at last. "It was thrust upon me."

She took the bucket outside, leaving Elle with the angry tone of her words. Perhaps they didn't share voluntary solitude after all.

Freda looked up to the sun from working a hide. It was past noon. She wondered how hungry Elle might be before returning to the task at hand. Sweat along her brow plastered hair to her forehead. The deer's hide spread out on the ground, and she used long, powerful strokes with a wire-bristle brush to soften it. Her body moved back and forth, back and forth across the buckskin. The smells of pickling salt and baking soda stirred as she worked.

She had traversed over twelve miles from the kill site back to her home. Her knees creaked as she shifted her weight to sit cross-legged on the ground, bringing the hide closer to her lap. She reminded herself to decoct another sage tincture on the new moon. Even with the Youth Elixir, though, Freda wondered how much longer she could hunt alone. The deer moved more frequently in recent years, and she had to hunt in the far reaches of these mountains.

She knew she could maintain all the chores on the homestead by herself well past her hundredth year, given the sage tincture and decoctions she took bi-moonly. But she still needed to hunt. The dollar didn't stretch as far as it had a couple decades ago, and the inheritance was nearly gone now. She needed the cash the stores in town paid for the goods she made with deer hide.

Luna growled. She growled again, louder and longer.

Something—or someone—had come to visit. Freda walked to her rifle leaning against the pen fence. The goats huddled up against the door to their shelter. She swung the rifle's strap around her shoulder and unlatched the pen gate. The chickens had retreated into their coop and sat within its wooden walls, eerily quiet. Luna's echoing barks filled the canyon with movement. Birds took flight.

Freda rounded the cabin corner. "Shhhh," she whispered, resting a hand on Luna's raised hackles.

A large black bear stood on his back paws ten yards away.

Freda observed the bear's body language. He was curious, sniffing the air, paws dangling. Cocking his head left to right, his neck moved as a giant mass. He was one of the big ones. She had only seen him twice before, though she had encountered his presence many times alongside her homestead borders in big mounds of scat.

But what was he doing out this early? The bear continued to shake his head. Freda stepped forward and brought the gun in front of her, angling it up toward the sky. "Git!" she yelled at the bear. "Go on! Git!"

The bear sat and yawned over his shoulder. Versed in ursine, Freda laughed out loud. His large belly rested on his legs, and his paws continued to dangle. He twitched his nose and clucked his tongue. Freda slipped the rifle's safety back on and slung the gun behind her back. The bear sauntered downstream, following the creek's meandering. Luna looked up at Freda with a cocked head. They walked back into the cabin together.

"Did Luna scare the bear away?" Elle asked, petting Luna's head. She had heard Luna's warning call about the bear from inside the cabin.

"Hardly. He was only curious and left after saying hello."

"I want to be out there," Elle burst. She winced at the whininess of her voice.

"In time." Freda realized how bored Elle must be. "Wait a quick minute," she said, spinning on her heels. When she returned to the cabin, she took pants, socks, and shirts out of a pack and piled them near Elle. She slipped off her sweater and placed it atop the pile.

Elle gave Freda a deadpan expression. "What, exactly, am I to do with these?" She picked up the wool sweater. It was a drab thing. Elle recalled a similar layer at home.

"Turn it around."

Elle did as told. "You want me to sew your clothes?"

"If you would," Freda said, almost shy. "I figured you might be bored. Do you know how to sew?"

Elle remembered learning in home education class. They sewed pillows, blankets. Simple things she still used. "Kinda," she said.

"Great." Freda smiled.

It was the first time Elle had seen the woman smile with her eyes. Crow's feet brushed across her temples, and crescents folded into her cheeks. Elle offered a small smile in return.

"Are you hungry?" Freda asked, handing Elle a spool of thread and a needle.

"I can wait."

Freda told her she needed another hour to finish up her chores. It took two, but Elle was busy weaving a needle back and forth, back and forth, mending the holes in Freda's worn layers.

Elle couldn't remember a time when she had sat and thought for as long as she had in the last week. Though she still couldn't stand up, she no longer vomited. Using the bucket had become easier. Freda could now wait outside as Elle used it. Elle had gained some weight, and her menses arrived. Freda gave her fabric pads and washed them for her. This altruism above all others shifted Elle's mistrust to confusion.

What, really, did this woman want from her?

After mending her clothes, Elle had conditioned Freda's wooden bowls and plates and sharpened her knives. She had then read a couple of books Freda had picked out from her collection on the shelves. The books had helped pass two whole days. Elle had lost herself in *Maps of the Crazy Mountains*. She learned the names of little streams and creeks she had no idea existed. It seemed the more she scrutinized the maps, the more vast and unknowable the land became.

On one ancient map within the book, presented as a mythological rendering of the landscape, she had found a small body of water called Moonstone Lake. The lake appeared to be in a cave deep within the Home of the Gods. Unlike the other maps in the book, this one didn't have a date or a cartographer's name. Elle had found it strange that none of the other maps included this lake, though they did include the cave: Headwaters of the Echo, the maps called it.

Elle didn't know why Freda had chosen *Singing Waters, Sacred Blood* from all the books on her shelves. Did she know her father had been full-blood Bilawáxan? Elle hadn't said anything about her heritage when Freda had handed her the book. She had found the Bilawáxan stories entertaining, like the myth about the beaver god bringing the rivers down from the mountaintops. The second to last story in the collection had called forth her dad's ghost. Humans finally emerged on the scene as creatures of salt and water, free of a deity in their form.

She had leaned into the memory of her dad atop Trapper Peak, the way his arm felt like a complete circle around her. She had read and reread that story, remembering how he had told her about the animal gods teaching humans how to live in Sacred Balance, whatever that meant. Freda had been outside all day, as usual, and Elle had cried as if he had just died yesterday. If only he had survived, she wouldn't be on this futon in the middle of nowhere. She'd still be in the Avenues, preparing to leave for university with his blessing.

The book's final pages told of the Bilawáxan creation myth. It was a story her dad hadn't told her. Maybe he would have someday. The Bilawáxan believed all life on earth came from stars, and this universe with its innumerable stars had emerged from oneness. Elle had read this and remembered learning a similar theory in science class. The only difference between creation myth and scientific theory seemed to be the language. She preferred the poetics of the myth. It somehow felt more real.

"I think my muscles are getting bigger," Elle said.

Freda turned to her from stirring soup inside a large pot. "Let me see."

Elle pushed up the sleeves on her shirt stained with food spills and sweat. Her skin, Freda noticed, had begun darkening from the pallid, gray tone into a richer shade. Elle flexed with a snarl. A small band of muscle wrapped around the otherwise boney stretch of arm.

"I've never had muscle there before." Elle pulled the sleeve back down. "I'm not even doing anything."

"And that's only the beginning of your body's development as the Anima. You haven't stood since eating the *Anima metamorpha*, and here you are growing muscle. Wait until you're active again. You can't imagine the gifts you will soon experience."

The hint of envy laced in Freda's voice wasn't lost on Elle, and though she wished to ask Freda to elaborate, she decided against it. She watched as Freda's arms flexed when she picked up the pot from the stovetop, her veiny muscles pushing against sunned skin. Elle flexed her biceps again. Maybe they hadn't grown so much after all.

Freda gave Elle a bowl of venison and vegetable soup. Elle ate it, thinking of her meals at home. Food from cans. Elle asked Freda if she thought her muscles not only came from being the Anima, but also from eating better.

"Maybe. You looked malnourished when I found you. I sometimes questioned if you would survive the transformation."

"Malnourished? How could you tell?" Elle braced herself for ridicule. *Bones,* she heard them say.

"Your skin," Freda answered. "You were nearly translucent the night I found you, and that was only a day after you fell. You continued to pale and thin throughout the transformation." Freda noticed the shame in Elle's eyes. "But you're the Anima now. You'll grow into abilities that surpass even the most extraordinary human capacities."

A mouse ran across the rug between Elle and Freda washing dishes.

*Hey!* Elle called out. *Hey!*

The mouse tumbled over himself. He stared at Elle with tiny eyes.

*Yep,* she said. *I'm the one talking.* But what did she have to say? The mouse scurried back into a box on the bookshelf.

Freda pulled a chair next to the futon and set the kerosene lamp on an end table. Shadows danced across the room as the light wavered into stillness. She retrieved an armful of books from the shelves. *The Wolfwoman of Taléria. The Keeper's Way. Secret Sibling of the Fly Agaric. The Task of the Anima.*

"Where did you *find* these books?" Elle asked. Time had made the books' brown and red leathers rough along the edges. The pages aged into sepia, with some sheets no longer bound but sticking out at irregular angles.

Freda placed the stack in her lap. "I found them at the—at a place in Lacuserra. Let's start here," she said, taking *The Wolfwoman of Taléria* from the stack and setting the rest on the ground. "It tells the story, or a story, about Erie, the eighth Anima."

Elle received the book from Freda. She recognized the words as Flüschen, one of the ancient languages of the Imperium. "Do you know what it says?"

Freda nodded, taking back the book. She closed its cover. "What do you know about magic?"

Elle's skin prickled. "Excuse me?"

"For centuries, most people, if not all, knew of magic and its potential for both good and evil. It was only after the Imperium's campaign to kill all magic practitioners that the existence of magic withdrew from common life."

Elle's face had gone slack.

"I know what you're thinking," Freda said. "Magic isn't real. What does this *myth*"— Freda created quotes with her fingers—"have to do me? What does this have to do with anything?"

"Why, yes—"

"Everything," Freda interrupted. "Everything and very little, depending on what you decide to do as the Anima." She placed a hand on Elle's leg. "Please, don't be afraid. You have allies. *Powerful* allies. You will live a life more meaningful, more rich and dynamic than any human could ever wish for."

Freda's veiny hand reminded Elle of that ancient map of the Bighorns. Elle cleared her throat. "So, are you trying to say this communication I have now is a form of magic?"

"For lack of a better word—yes. The *Anima metamorpha* changed the actual composition of your brain so you may talk with all vertebrates. It will also change the structure of your body so you may live as a true human animal. I see hints of the changes even now. One more week and you will smell, hear, see—*be* like a wild creature. You will experience the supernatural simply as that: super natural."

The cabin seemed to pulse. Elle felt hot and itchy. She looked out the window as the half-moon emerged in the overcast, ringed in red. It slipped back under cover.

Freda lifted the book up. "This story says Erie fought alongside the animals. She was burned. Alive, that is. But she had little choice. To fight was her Task as the Anima."

"Task of the Anima," Elle repeated, the words a whisper. "And if I am this thing you call an Anima—*if*—do I have a task?"

"You will. In essence you'll be working to restore the ecological balance sustaining all Life—a balance simply known as the Order. Though I'm not entirely sure what the particulars will be."

"*Order?*" Elle scoffed. "This is anything but orderly. This whole situation is fucked up. I have a life back there." She jerked her arm toward the window. "It wasn't perfect, but it was mine."

"No, Elle. You *had* a life back there. The Elle you were three weeks ago died when she took a bite of the mushroom."

"Why did I have to eat that fucking mushroom?" Elle asked, pulling fistfuls of her greasy hair.

*What's wrong?* Luna asked.

*I'm what's wrong!* Elle said. *I can talk to you. Do you know how crazy this all is? What if I never get my life back?*

"What happened to Erie, I mean, before she died?" Elle asked, gripping the blanket. "Did she have a good life?"

"Easy," Freda said, placing a hand on Elle's white knuckles. "We're getting there. Erie's Task was to protect the people and animals being murdered when the Flüschen invaded Taléria. They were looking for Erie, especially after the Anima before Erie utterly demolished the Flüschen in battle centuries earlier. They killed animals—wolves in particular—by the hundreds as they scoured northern Lacuserra in their search for the Anima.

"Magic, and wolves for that matter, was seen as purely evil by the Flüschen, rather than morally ambiguous. The wolves weren't blameless, of course. They've always killed some domestic animals, undermining people's livelihoods."

"That's what I don't get," Elle interjected. "I eat meat. I don't think I'm going to stop now that I can supposedly talk with chickens and cows."

"Nor do you have to. Does the wolf stop eating deer because the deer and wolf work as a whole? No. There is a deeper knowledge here neither you nor I completely understand yet." Freda remembered her first hunt, the blood blossoming on snow. Todd holding her as she cried. *The Holy Paradox*, he had said. "You might, Elle. You might discover such knowledge throughout your life as the Anima—or maybe at your death."

"It seems like when we talk about my death, it's not far off." Elle looked back outside. "I always thought I'd be old when I died. I even thought I might have a big funeral. You know—I thought I had time to meet people I could love and that could love me…" She trailed off. Tears were falling, and she rubbed at them with impatient strokes.

"You have time, Elle. There's no one saying you'll die young. I talk of your death as the unavoidable event it is. And also to warn you—you need to be *extremely* careful when revealing your abilities to anyone." Was now the time to reveal the Imperium's determination to kill the Anima and all Keepers?

"Never," Elle said. She tried to sit up taller. "I would *never* tell people that I talk with animals. They would throw me into a mental institution. I'd rather die first."

"Careful what you say, Elle. But I agree. You should *not* reveal yourself. It's imperative that we keep your existence secret, at least until the time is right."

"When would the time *ever* be right?" Elle threw her hands up. "Do I have to stay out here, hidden in the woods, until someone or something tells me it's time to tell the world about being this—this *Anima* freak? This all seems like a giant, fucked up mistake. This wasn't my doing. It wasn't my plan. I was going to move away. I was going to make friends. But I'll always be an outcast if I talk to animals. I mean, *come* on! That's just insane. I'll be insane."

Freda felt her patience unravel. "You have a new plan, a better plan," she hissed. "Do you not see the extraordinary circumstances of your existence now? You are the *Anima*. You are the bridge between humans and animals. The world needs you. *I* need—"

"I can't live as an outcast forever." Elle's voice was cold and distant. "I didn't *want* this."

"There are many things we want in life that we don't get." Freda spoke through clenched teeth.

Elle had fully withdrawn. She stared out the window as the moon continued to weave in and out of clouds. Freda picked the lantern up and left the cabin, taking the light with her. The black forest shifted around her as she stomped to the tree house.

When Elle woke, gray cloaked the sky. Was it morning or afternoon? After urinating into the bucket, Elle decided today, she would empty it herself.

The room wobbled as she stood. She took a few steps before collapsing. Her shoulder hit the ground first. The bucket clanked on the floor and piss sloshed across the rug. She moaned from a crumpled position, rubbing at pain searing across her clavicle. It felt broken.

Luna and Freda heard the commotion from the garden. Luna rushed inside and halted at the sight of Elle curled on the floor, the pee emanating around her. She tiptoed around the bright yellow liquid. *Elle, your urine smells strange. Are you okay?*

Elle rolled onto her back, squaring her face to the furry mass of her dog's head. *No, I'm not. I'm a freak. A weak freak. I can't even take care of my own piss.* Beyond Luna's head, spider webs stretched between the rafters and slanting ceiling walls. Flies and mosquitos and innumerable tiny bugs were caught in the threads.

Freda leaned against the doorframe, taking in the smell and sight of the Anima crumpled on the floor, her urine soaking into the blue rug Todd's grandmother had woven. "You're dehydrated." She squatted down next to the futon and moved Elle's hair from her eyes and mouth.

Elle flinched at the touch. "I hate crying," she whined, covering her eyes with her hands. "Why am I crying so much? It's like my tears are out of my control."

"You're grieving, Elle. You're grieving for the loss of your own life."

Elle relaxed her hands back to her sides, revealing a red, puffy face. Even with the bloat from crying, Freda saw that her face had changed more overnight. Her eyes appeared larger and rounder. Freda smiled. "You're so close," she said. "You're almost done with the transformation. I promise you, when you are fully the Anima, you will look back at this moment and laugh at your own ignorance."

Freda wrapped her arms under Elle's armpits. "Let go of your old life," she exhaled as she lifted the Anima off the floor. Together they took the few steps back to the futon. "Let go of your old life," Freda repeated, helping Elle sit back down. "Let go of your old self. Easier said than done, trust me, I *know*. But at least begin the process. What are you holding onto so tightly? Why do you want to be the same person you were before you ate the mushroom?"

Elle lifted her legs onto the futon and leaned into the pillows. Massaging the middle of her forehead, she tried to understand Freda's question. She saw herself walking into an ivy-shrouded building on a university campus somewhere; she saw herself hiking with friends she had yet to meet; she saw herself on an airplane for the first time, the metallic slant of a wing cutting through clouds. "I wanted to make something out of my life. I wanted to go places."

Freda filled a glass with water. "I had asked why you want to be the same Elle you were before the mushroom, and you answered me with who you were going to be." She handed the glass to Elle. "But why do you want to be the same Elle you *were* before you ate the mushroom?"

Elle sipped the water. "I don't think I understand what you're asking."

"What I mean is, when I asked you why you want to be the same Elle before the mushroom, you told me you were going to go places, but not anything about you then—you three weeks ago. You told me instead about the hypothetical you. The things you wanted to do in the distant future."

Elle drank more water. It hurt to think this hard. "I'm upset because my future is no longer mine," she answered at last. "I'm now something called the Anima, which I have no idea what that could mean. It all feels out of my control. I think talking with animals could be—*interesting*. But I have to keep it secret. I'll have to be a crazy lady who lives in the woods and has conversations with animals."

Freda tried to say something, but Elle continued, "I didn't *love* my life, that's for sure. I didn't have any close friends, or, I mean, any that stuck around. I mean I had my mother, and I had Luna. But Elaine's an alc—

well, she has her issues, and Luna's my best friend, but she's a dog. I was gonna make friends—*real* friends—when I moved away from Twin Rivers. I was gonna start over."

"Yeah," Freda said, her voice soft. "I picked up on some of those things in your journal."

Elle's mouth dropped open. "Did you—did you read my journal?"

Freda ran her finger around the top of her bowl. It had been necessary research, she reminded herself, feeling Elle's glare burning into her. "There was a journal left open on the living room table in your house. Your mother must have been reading it. I, well, skimmed a couple pages."

Elle's mouth tightened into a sneer. Freda saw the Anima's fierceness, her growing power, and gaped at her.

"Why are you looking at me like that?" Elle growled.

"Sorry. But—" Freda paused. "Your power is growing within you. I can see it now." She knelt and rolled the rug up, moving as quickly as possible. Elle fumed in the corner, her anger pressing hot against Freda's turned shoulder.

Freda brought the rug outside and washed it in the creek. The sky began to lift, to lighten. Large, white clouds remained woven throughout the mountain peaks and crevices. Bird song filled the late morning with a celebratory feel.

An ouzel waded near the riverbank. Freda looked up in time to watch as he walked underwater. Though she couldn't see him now, she knew the songbird strutted and swam across the riverbed, eating stoneflies and trout eggs. A thin, gray film covered his eyes, allowing him to see underwater. He was an animal of two worlds, existing seamlessly in air and water.

Freda wrung out the rug and hung it to dry on the front porch railing before harvesting vegetables. When she stepped back inside, Elle was petting Luna while looking forlornly out the window. Freda rocked a knife back and forth across the garlic, filling the cabin with its tangy smell.

"You know what's almost hilarious?" Freda asked. "That you are so resistant to being the Anima when I had dreamed of being it for more than half my life. Both of our realities got turned upside down, and neither of us are happy about it, but we're forced to figure out what, exactly, we're supposed to do now that you are the Anima and I am your mentor."

"We never agreed to that," Elle said, whipping her head from the window. "We never agreed you were going to be my mentor."

*Is everything okay?* Luna asked.

*No. We're stuck here.*

*What's so bad about that?*

*I don't want to live with someone as crazy as she is.*

*Why do you think she's crazy?*

*Because she's forgotten what real life is like.*

*Is this not real life?*

*Never mind, Lu.*

Freda finished chopping garlic and moved on to the onions. She knew the Anima and dog were communicating. Jealousy pumped through her. She dropped the knife, and her hand lingered above the blade. Why was she making food for this brat? She stomped out of the cabin, slamming the door behind her.

She walked barefoot along the creek and stopped at an eddy. Slipping her feet into the whirling waters, she caught her breath. How could Elle be the Anima? How was someone like her supposed to fulfill the Task? Elle would fail. The last Anima would fail the world unless she embraced her powers.

There had to be a reason Elle was the Anima and not Freda. There *had* to be. Freda ran her hands through her hair as if the answer hid in her roots. If only she could make Elle see, to make her understand who she was now. She had to try again.

Freda swung the door open and walked to the futon. Elle's eyes darted between Freda's determined face and the knife on the cutting board.

"I found you next to the creek for a reason. But we'll never know what that reason is unless you let me help you. If you leave, you could be caught and, and..." Be murdered—or worse.

Elle bit her lower lip. "I can't stay here. I'm sorry, but I have to return to my life. It wasn't a perfect life, but it was my own."

Freda's face hardened. There had been no map to navigate this resistance. Was she supposed to tie Elle down? She resumed chopping garlic. Silence now, but for the rocking of the knife and the sliding of pans over the stovetop. Iron on iron.

Elle watched the clouds crowd upon the mountaintop. They gathered as one mass, an east wind pushing down on them. They looked like they were flowing over the saddle as a giant swoop of white water. The forest spread below as a mute army of pines, some green, some left gray and skeletal from beetle kill.

Freda handed a plate to Elle. They ate without a word. Freda returned outside to finish her tasks for the afternoon. Luna followed her out and rested in the cool windiness of the day, leaving Elle alone with an overwhelming desire to leave. The afternoon drawled by, this day slower than the entirety of the previous week. As dusk moved into the mountain valley, fuchsia light fading to lilac, Elle sketched out plans in her mind for when she was able to stand again.

She would hike back into town with Luna. They would go to her house and she would apologize to her mother. She would tell her she had to leave for a little while after their fight. Maybe they could even start over; they had been close once, before Walter died. Wasn't it possible to be close again? They would never know unless they tried.

Once she and her mother made up, and Elle moved back in, she would ask for her job back at the Pizza Parlor. She would say she had to leave town because of trouble at home, a half lie. She only needed a couple hundred more before she could take off. Two hundred more dollars and she would set off for college. Maybe she would study biology. Her ability to communicate with animals would make her a leader in the field.

No, Elle wasn't doomed for isolation. She didn't have to stay out here, removed from the real world. Her life was still her own. She would make sure of it.

Freda returned inside. The quiet grew awkward, causing both Freda and Elle to move self-consciously. Elle shifted on the futon while Freda prepared yet another meal. When the vegetable and venison stir fry finished simmering, Freda dished up the plates and handed one to Elle. Again, they ate in silence. And so began the last days of Elle's transformation.

Even Luna avoided conversation with Elle over the next five days. Elle felt the pangs of a certain rejection when Luna chose to leave with Freda every morning after their breakfast. One night Luna even opted to sleep on the porch.

*Why can't we stay here?* Luna asked. *I'm happy now.*

Of course Luna was happier here. Elle thought of how most dogs lived far removed from their natural desires to be with others, to hunt and eat and sleep with their pack mates. Here, Luna could remember her wildness: the layers of a forest, the taste of game, the cold waters and fresh air of the mountains. And what of humans, Elle wondered. In what ways had they forgotten their wild selves?

Elle resented such questions. She felt herself staggering far away from the safe zone of normalcy and knew she needed to re-emerge into real life as soon as possible. Returning to the city was the only way for her to maintain sanity. She clutched this resolution as if her life depended on it. Her life *did* depend on it.

All the while Freda continued to feed Elle and wash out her feces and urine from the bucket in silence. She moved through her daily tasks with a growing heaviness. On the last night of Elle's transformation, Freda harvested her first crop of beets for the year. As she sautéed them, she glanced at Elle. The Anima was no longer solely human. Her face narrowed at the mouth, carved not by starvation but unbelievable strength. The skin was pulled tight around the bone, and she could see how high her cheekbones had come to rest. Freda remembered the skulls of Animas past looking at her from black hollows, their skeletons seemingly half-human and half-cougar.

Elle returned Freda's stare. It seemed Freda had shrunk in the past few days, as if only now revealing her true age. Whereas there once was a buoyant energy, maybe even a fresh smell to her, staleness had crept in. Freda now exuded an old, tired air. Remorse tickled at Elle as she reasoned that it was her decision to leave, most likely, that had caused the woman to depress. Freda had treated her with a kindness and care Elle hadn't known since Walter left. Nonetheless, she couldn't stay here. She just couldn't.

Again, they ate in a rigid silence, and again, Luna decided to spend the night on the porch. Elle didn't sleep. She listened to the mice clamber around the cabin, their voices and feet loud in the quiet. She heard them speak of tasks and safety precautions. An owl had discovered their main exit hole, and a member of their clan had been swept away.

Freda slept a dreamless sleep. As Elle had expected, she felt her age more than ever this past week. Now that the life she had lived for no longer existed, energy escaped as water from a punctured canteen. She had run out of Youth Elixir and didn't see the point in making more. Even as she slept her body aged, every minute passing like a week.

Before dawn broke, Elle felt blood surging through her. She wiggled her fingers and toes. She lifted one leg up, then the other. Her stomach remained calm though hungry. She swung her legs over the side of the futon, laughing at the sheer ease of the movement. She continued to laugh as she stood and stretched her arms overhead. She marveled at the muscles woven across the bones.

Luna scratched at the door to be let in. When Elle opened the door, the dog looked up to see her person on two feet.

*You look intimidating,* Luna said.

*You look confused. We knew I'd look different now, but I'm still the same person.* Elle doubted her own words.

Luna dropped her tail down and folded her ears back. *So we are leaving?*

Elle squatted down and placed an arm around her. She knew Luna would come with her, even though she would do anything to stay out here. *We need to return. We have to. I can't live out here.*

Luna yowled. Elle had never heard her dog cry so deeply before, and it made her feel ill. She didn't eat the meat scraps Elle placed in her food dish. Elle helped herself to jerky and buffalo berries. She filled a cup with water and chugged it, placing the empty glass in the basin.

She tried to ignore the nagging remorse when she realized Freda had washed her jeans and sweater the day before. She found them drying on the clothesline outside. As she fumbled with the clothes, sensations of the forest bombarded her body. An overwhelming orchestra of noises, a myriad of smells demanding her attention: it all flooded into her.

She managed to clothe herself before collapsing to her knees. She closed her eyes and placed her hands over her ears. Blood banged, banged, banged against her temples. Birds sung poems of greetings to the day. Squirrels announced her presence to one another. She could hear, in the near distance, a herd of deer settling into their beds, their voices a murmur.

She opened her eyes to see trees shimmering in the breeze, the veins branching through each leaf. An ouzel flickered down to a granite stone in Owl Creek, and Elle gasped at her ability to perceive the intricacies of the bird's feathers. The bird dipped into the waters. "It's too much," she whispered. It was too much to take in, to bear.

Her legs trembled as she stood. She stumbled back to the cabin and slammed the door behind her. Luna hadn't moved from her place of mourning. Inside, the quiet rang. How was she supposed to live out there? She placed her hands on the kitchen island, bowing her head. She had to do this. She had no choice.

She found her pack next to the futon and ruffled through the contents. Her father's jacket and pocketknife were in it, as well as her newsboy cap and wallet containing the photographs of her father. With everything she valued accounted for, she took a few more strips of jerky. The remorse dug in deeper as she realized the jar was nearly empty. She shoved the meat into the front pocket of her backpack and filled her water bottle. From this perspective, standing and close up, she realized how organized and clean Freda kept the cabin. All the jars of food were titled and dated with neat, cursive handwriting. The countertops were free of mouse turds and dust.

What if she stayed? What if she accepted Freda's help?

Elle looked to the futon, the bucket, the books on the shelves. She would only continue to be a hinder to Freda. She didn't know how to survive out here. Freda would have to teach her everything. A life waited for her back home, one in which she knew how to survive. She had to leave, even if it meant facing the world beyond and its attack on her senses. She slipped on her backpack, adjusting the straps to fit the new muscles of her shoulders, and walked to the door.

*Time to go,* she said to Luna, not daring to look her in the eyes.

They walked toward Mystic Peak. Elle started running and commanded Luna to keep up. They moved across the forest floor, the Anima faster than she ever knew she could be, ever dreamed she could be. As if both creatures ran on four legs, they cut through the pine trees, branches swiping at their foreheads and limbs. Elle wiped cobwebs from her mouth and eyes. Even when the ground surged skyward, scree turning underfoot, Elle didn't slow down.

The wild world was trying to swallow her whole. She had to outrun the voices. She had to escape the wildness pouring into her body. It would destroy her. Or at least it would destroy all that she had ever known to be real.

# HOME

They stopped running at the plateau behind her house. Luna collapsed on the ground beside Elle, panting. They had run from Freda's homestead to Crescent Saddle, where they had spent the day hidden in Silver Stream's riparian growth. Elle didn't want to see or talk to anyone on the more popular trails below in Owl Creek Canyon. Once the sun had set, they had continued to run the last eight miles, pausing a couple of times for water.

Elle's lungs heaved. She took off her backpack and sat on the rock she always sat on. The town below extended out as a grid of orange and yellow lights in the night; headlights of cars navigated the matrix at sharp angles. It had only been a month since she last saw Twin Rivers, but the stark contrast between Freda's cabin and the city below rushed through her body as a shock wave. The radiance of the city reached up to the sky, filling the valley with an electric vibration.

She stood with hands on hips and shifted her weight side to side.

*What are you thinking?* Luna asked.

*We should get this over with.*

*This was your idea.*

*Let's go.*

They walked down the path they had hiked together hundreds of times. Yet tonight, Elle experienced the forest in ways making her uncomfortably aware of her heightened senses. She could smell raccoon scat on the trail and residual elk odor rubbed off on a pine trunk. She could see the gleam of eyes watching them from the higher branches of a lodgepole. Elle stiffened. The eyes belonged to a cougar.

*There's a cougar in the tree over there,* Elle said to Luna. The flashing green eyes disappeared with a loud *thunk*. Pine boughs moaned and creaked as the cougar ran away.

River song resounded around them as they reached Mountain View. Her mother's home was dark. Elle assumed she was at work. Nonetheless, her heartbeat quickened as they walked up the driveway. Her bike was gone from where she had left it locked up to the basketball pole.

She used her key to open the door and flicked on the light. Her mother, as she had suspected, didn't need a clean house. In recent years, Elle had a feeling that if she didn't clean once a week, her mother would be fine to let the home go. And let go she had. Empty beer cans and vodka bottles, pizza boxes and takeaway containers sprawled out in a semi-circle from the overflowing garbage can. An off-white rectangle discolored the wall where the mirror once hung. Elle pinched her nose as she walked to her bedroom. She recognized a boot on the floor as the same one she had thrown at her mother's door a month ago.

Luna stayed in the kitchen, licking at the leftover food containers. Elle turned on her bedroom light and gasped. On top of the desk, across the floor, over her bed spread things belonging to someone else, presumably the boot's owner. T-shirts and jeans, camouflage jackets and baseball caps piled up on her twin bed. Rifles and shotguns leaned against her bookshelf. A few backpacks and coats littered the floor, and the heads of a mule deer buck and an elk bull stared up with blank eyes from atop her desk. Everything of hers seemed to be where she had left it. He had simply come in and dumped his life on top of hers.

Elle kicked his shit out of her way. She picked the deer head off her desk and looked into his fake eyes. She saw herself and realized she had yet to look at her reflection in a mirror since becoming the Anima. The creature reflected back at her appeared like a stranger. She yelped and dropped the deer head.

She stepped up onto her desk and removed the panel of drywall. Fumbling her hand around, she found nothing. She felt as far back as she could, the motions frantic. But she knew. She had already expected as much when she had opened her bedroom door. Her mother or this stranger had taken the money. They had taken the money and probably spent it on booze already.

Still atop her desk, she crouched on her heels and pulled at her hair. The elk bull antlers nudged her back. Luna slunk into the room and looked up at Elle with trepidation.

*What? What happened?*

Elle sat cross-legged on the desk. *This happened,* she said, sweeping her arm across the room.

Luna sniffed at the deer head lying crooked on the floor. She moved across the room with her nose, prodding at the backpacks and clothes. *He's a hunter,* she observed. *But his things aren't why you're upset, are they?*

Elle stared at the bookshelf. He had placed shed and skulls of various animals on a couple of the shelves. The books that had been there stood in a pile on the ground. *No,* she said.

*What is it then?*

She tried to swallow the lump in her throat but it only grew bigger. *They took my money. They took our way out of here.*

*So we were going to leave town?*

*Yes.*

*And when were you planning on telling me this?* Luna cocked her head to the side.

*I hadn't worked out the details yet. I was going to buy a car with that money. I was planning these things before I could talk to you—back when I was still normal.*

*What if I didn't want to leave?*

Elle hung her head back. *None of it matters now. We won't be able to go anywhere for a while. It took me years to save that money.* The word *years* rang through her mind. She picked up the bull's head next to her. With inhuman strength, she tossed it at the bookshelf. An antler snapped in half, and the bookshelf careened to the ground. Books flew and skulls crushed.

Elle wanted to light the house on fire. She wanted to dump gasoline all over his fucking shit and torch it. All of it. This stupid fucking house that had been the beginning of the end. She wanted to watch this trailer home burn, see the metal walls glare red and fold in on one another.

But then what?

Luna sniffed at the skull shards scattered across the floor. Elle pushed herself off the desk. In the refrigerator were half a six-pack, a blue and green block of cheese, and a container with the fuzzy remnants of some food item. She found a single can of stew in the pantry. While she warmed it on the stove, she searched the lower cabinets for Luna's food. She found the bag of kibbles pushed back into a far corner.

Elle slurped up a spoonful of stew. Nausea pushed up from her stomach as she moved the mushy food around her mouth. She swallowed with force, fighting back the desire to vomit. Luna seemed equally disgusted by her meal, nibbling at the stale kibbles. Elle finished her bowl while Luna left her dish half full.

*I can't eat this food,* Luna said.

Elle said nothing. They both knew Freda's food was far superior. Her stomach gurgled and churned. Luna moved to the door and asked Elle to be let out. Elle followed her dog into the night.

Clouds billowed up from the horizon, blotting out stars. She remembered waking two weeks ago and seeing the full moon in the storm-swept canyon. She remembered the smell of sage, the dust and dried herbs of Freda's cabin, the peace she had felt upon waking. She remembered the sheer number of stars, too, even if she had only seen a fraction of the sky through the cabin window. But here, at the edge of the city, she realized with new eyes how the glare of human development overcame the presence of the universe above.

Unlike in the mountains, where the night had hummed with voices of nocturnal creatures near and far, Elle could only hear the electrical line buzzing and the rumble of an approaching train, its whistles growing louder. Each railroad car contained piles of coal, the black rock nearly invisible in the night. Elle plugged her ears. Trains had always been loud, but now the noise rattled her brain. She ran back inside, Luna at her heels, and slammed the door shut.

*Did that seem incredibly loud to you?*

*Those things are terrifying,* Luna replied. *Too loud.*

The clock read half past midnight. *Let's rest while we wait,* Elle said.

They lay on the couch together, and Luna fell asleep with ease. Elle tried to imagine her mother's side of things. Elle had been gone for a month. Maybe Elaine thought she wouldn't return. Maybe this guy really was *the one*. Elle wanted her mother to be happy, even if it still hurt to see her with unfamiliar men.

She took her wallet out of her pocket and unfolded the picture of her dad cradling her as a baby. The piece of tape holding the photograph together veiled her father's face in gossamer. Though young and alive in the picture, he looked like a ghost. Elle licked a finger and tried to clean off the tape. Just because she had never healed from his death didn't mean her mother couldn't, or shouldn't. Elle placed the photograph back in her wallet and watched the minutes pass on the clock.

At half past two, a car grumbled down the gravel road. It turned into the driveway, the headlights circling the living room through a crack in the window shades. She heard their voices, thick with liquor, as the car doors opened and banged shut. Luna stirred awake, the hairs on her hackle rising. Elle sat up taller and put a hand on her dog.

*Calm down,* she commanded.

*Something tells me not to,* Luna replied. She relaxed her hackles nonetheless.

The door grated open. Elaine gasped when she saw Elle on the couch. She wore the low-cut red dress she liked to call her power suit. The curls in her hair had frizzed out with the humidity. Elle thought she resembled a fish, the way her mouth moved as if she were saying something.

The man placed his foot into the house and leaned over Elaine's shoulder. He stood slightly taller than she did in cowboy boots. Besides thick eyebrows and a dark goatee, the man's head shined with the absence of hair. Elaine's lipstick had made a blood-red mess of his mouth. He wore a blue jean tank top tucked into the largest belt buckle Elle had ever seen.

Elle laughed at their stupefied expressions. She couldn't help herself. Their gawking faces made her feel more uncomfortable than she had ever thought she could feel. When she had imagined this moment, this reunion, over the past two weeks, she hadn't imagined a man with her mother. And of all the situations she had imagined, all the possible reactions, she had conjured a warm embrace in the more forgiving visions, yelling and crying in the more realistic ones.

But looks of horror? Elle quit laughing and cleared her throat. "Hi, mom."

Elaine licked her lips, her eyes still wide and blinking. The man stepped past her and stood in front of the couch.

"How dare you. Breaking your mother's heart and then returning like you own the place."

Luna growled at him, baring her teeth and raising her hackles. He leaned away from her.

*Don't even think about it,* Elle said.

Luna continued to flare her lips and growl. Elle stood, keeping her hand on Luna's haunches.

Elaine looked between the man and her daughter. "Elle," she breathed. Her eyes moistened with tears, and Elle felt her own throat restrict. "Elle," she repeated, louder. "What—what *happened* to you?"

"Looks like drugs to me," the man said. "Heroine, I'd guess. My brother had the same dilated eyes. Though maybe steroids, too," he added, running his eyes over the muscles of Elle's legs and arms, exposed in shorts and a t-shirt.

Elaine continued to gawk at her. The man stood between them, his face twitching. Elle could smell his scent, laden with alcohol.

"You're barely yourself," Elaine said. She raised her hand up, as if to touch Elle's face, but then dropped it back to her side. "Your eyes. They're *orange*. Or are they green? Your face is changed, too. And your body." She leaned back, taking in the Anima. "You're—you're *huge*. Where have you been?"

Elle ran a hand along her bicep, the swell of it still strange to her. How *did* she intend to explain her enlarged muscles?

The man shook his head. "Drugs."

Elle glared at him. "You don't know me. You have *no* idea what I've been through."

"You selfish child," he spat back, the alcohol on his breath hitting her like a shot of whiskey. "You have—"

"I'm dead serious." Elle's voice was quiet. "Shut. Up."

Luna growled louder.

The man frowned at Luna. "Put that wild mutt outside. She's dangerous."

"Let's all calm down," Elaine said, grabbing his arm.

He softened. "Remember what you said?" he whispered to Elaine. "About not letting her take advantage of you anymore?"

Elle scoffed. "*Me* take advantage of *her?* You've been here all of what, a month? You have no idea what you're talking about."

"You broke your mother's heart!" Spit flew from his mouth. He continued to look the Anima up and down, his face contorted with either disgust or confusion. "I mean, *fuck*. Look at her. Was she always this big? I'm serious, Elaine. People on drugs are unpredictable. Remember what I told you about my brother…"

Elaine swallowed loudly.

"Mom, please." Elle lowered her voice. "Tell him to leave."

Elaine continued to shake her head. "Where have you been?"

Elle felt the extent of her transformation in relation to the woman she had always mirrored, whose slim frame she had inherited. She hunched her shoulders in an attempt to appear less intimidating, to feel less of her bulk taking up space. Though she hadn't grown taller, she felt like she towered over them both. She closed her eyes, trying to remember what, exactly, she had planned to tell her mother. "I had to leave. I'm sorry I left like that. And I'm sorry about the fight. I'm better now, I promise."

"Typical drug addict talk," the man said. He squeezed Elaine's shoulder. "Sweetheart, this is dangerous. She needs to come back clean."

Elle clenched her fists shut, resisting the urge to hit him. She had resolved to accept her mother's new boyfriend, not punch him. Luna continued to growl.

*Lu, please. Your anger is not helping my own.*

*Get him out of here.*

*Trying.*

*I'll attack on command.*

*On command.*

"What are you *doing?*" the man asked.

"I went away," Elle said. "I went away but now I'm back. You *have* to believe me when I say I'm not doing drugs. Please, mom." She stepped closer to her.

Elaine reeled away. "Elle," she wheezed. "You smell terrible."

Elle hadn't thought of that, but she imagined she did smell terrible. It had been a month, after all, since she last bathed.

"Like garbage," the man said. He stepped between the women as he walked toward Elle's old room.

"Hey," Elle called to his back. "Where's my money?"

He turned around. "What money?"

"The money I saved in the jar above my desk. Where is it?"

Elaine averted her eyes.

"No idea what you're talking about," he said, walking into her bedroom.

Luna jumped off the couch and moved next to Elle's side.

"Mother," Elle groaned. She ignored Luna's barking. "Oh mom."

"I was just borrowing it," Elaine said, her voice shrill.

Elle dropped her hands away from her face. "That was *my* money."

"I had no idea where you went. I thought you left me." Elaine's face was tear streaked and twisted. Elle could see the alcohol pulling down her eyelids at the sides.

"Where did you go?" Elaine asked.

"It's—*complicated.* Where did my money go?"

The man emerged from Elle's old bedroom, carrying a rifle. "Get your dog outta here."

"Richard! You're drunk." Elaine stepped toward him. "Put your gun away."

Luna began barking.

"That dog is out of control," he said, gesturing the gun at Luna. "This is too dangerous, Elaine. I'm telling you. My brother. If I could have done something…" He cocked the gun. "I want you both gone," he said to Elle. "Now. And don't come back 'til you're clean."

"This isn't your home," Elle said.

*Luna*, stop *barking.*

*He means to kill us.*

*He won't.* But Elle didn't entirely believe herself. She didn't know this guy. She realized she didn't know her mother anymore, either. Hadn't in years.

"Honey, put the gun down," Elaine pleaded. "Elle, he's right. You've gotta clean up before we can talk."

"I'm not on drugs!"

"That's what they all say," the man cried.

Luna barked louder, and the man lowered the rifle, pointing it at her. "Now I won't tell you again. Take your rabid dog and get outta here."

Elle looked at her mother. "Mom, please."

But Elaine stared at the ground with an expression of mourning. "Go. Come back when you're my daughter again."

Elle placed a hand on her stomach. Luna snapped and snarled, her anger controlled only by the slipping grasp of Elle's will for her to not attack.

"I'm gonna count to ten," the man said slowly. "One. Two. Three—"

Luna lunged at him and snapped her massive jaw down on his wrist.

The gunshot echoed against the trailer walls.

Elaine sobbed without making a sound. The man screamed louder as Luna bit harder. Blood sprayed out from his wrist, and the gun fell to the floor. Luna snarled as she ravaged his forearm.

Elle felt strangely apart. Warmth spread down her chest. She realized the bullet had gone somewhere. She looked down to see blood branching across the white fabric of her shirt. It reminded her of a red tree growing. With shaking fingers, she pulled her shirt down over the shoulder. The bullet had skimmed the bulge of her trapezius muscle. It was a shallow wound. She figured a month ago the bullet would have missed her entirely.

*Come,* Elle said to Luna.

Luna let go of his wrist. Elle put on her backpack and looked back one last time at her mother. Over the man's screams, Elle whispered, "You left me ten years ago."

Elaine opened her mouth but said nothing. Elle turned away, Luna by her side. The door clanged shut behind them.

A cruel wind pulled clouds across the sky. Elle and Luna trotted down the road, crossing the railroad tracks. Her shoulder throbbed, but it had stopped bleeding. The wound had closed itself quicker than she reckoned was normal.

A train released its wail in the far distance. It was a penetrating sound of loneliness made lonelier in the cold, dark night. Elle shivered, though she wore her dad's jacket. She figured shock was rattling her body. That man had almost killed her. She hoped Luna had ruined his shooting hand.

*Are you okay?* Luna asked. She licked at the dry blood on Elle's hand.

*The wound will heal.* Or at least one of them would.

*Where are we going?*

Elle didn't have an answer. The city droned on with its sleepless lights, and a stream of headlights snaked across the valley on the interstate. An owl watched them pass from a telephone pole. Elle sensed his presence but made no effort to communicate.

She saw again and again the look on her mother's face as she stood in the doorway. There was no doubt about it: her expression had been one of horror. Complete horror. The tears came again. Was she a monster now?

She quickened her steps, and Luna scurried to keep up. Elle remembered biking this road home hundreds of times. The Brother River rumbled ahead, the waters still boisterous with snowmelt. Twin Rivers' suburbs began as roads branched off Mountain View Lane. House after house lined up, one not unlike the other, their lawns and cars lit by a neat row of streetlights. Elle imagined the families inside sleeping: the parents spooning in bed, the children hugging their favorite stuffed animals. She spit a wad of snot onto the white sidewalk and looked ahead to a bridge crossing over the Brother.

*Let's try to sleep under there,* Elle said. Luna bounded down a small path leading to the river. Elle stepped over beer cans and the decaying remains of a raccoon. She lay down with her head on Luna's haunches. Exhausted, she fell asleep to the melody of water, rock, and gravity.

Dawn's golden light streamed in through the cottonwood leaves. She looked up to see a village of swallow nests lining the concrete beams. Their homes conglomerated as bubbly masses of dirt with circular doors. The birds' faces, red and blue, peeked out from the openings. Elle heard them sing and chit chat, loud as a busy market square. Children asked to be fed. Adults exchanged details on where to find food. A few of the birds debated the threat Elle and Luna may pose and decided they, like most humans and their animal companions, didn't intend to hurt their colony.

Elle propped her elbows on bent knees and held her pounding head.

She could still hear animals. She was still the Anima.

Her gun wound throbbed, as did her legs. She massaged her quads and calves, contemplating their muscularity. Running back to town, she had moved with the thoughtlessness of adrenaline. But this morning she realized the absurdity of her new strength and endurance. She remembered galloping over Crescent Saddle, across Owl Creek Canyon, up and down the foothills.

*Elle, come look,* Luna said.

She joined Luna by the riverside. A muskrat flowed with the water, carrying a mouthful of reeds.

*Hey!* Elle called out. *Over here, on the riverbank.*

He suspended his body in the middle of the current, looking at her and then behind him, to his push-up of mud, reeds, and grasses.

*There have been rumors that the Anima has been reborn.* His voice was slow and husky. He spun around and charged upstream.

Elle squinted her eyes as the sun refracted off the water. Luna waded out into the river.

*Did you hear what the muskrat said?* Elle asked.

Luna shook the river from her coat, spraying Elle. *There have been rumors about you. I had expected as much.*

*You expected the muskrat would know about me?*

*Not only the muskrat, but all the animals. Can't you hear the swallows now?*

Elle listened more closely to the overarching hum. She realized the birds were talking about her. Energy swelled in the colony. The word *Anima* echoed around as dozens of little voices exclaimed the presence of Elle as the Anima born again.

A swallow swooped down and perched on a willow branch. All the birds quieted. Elle cleared her throat, although she didn't need to use it to speak. She could see a scar where the bird's right eye would be. Her, or his, plumage shined blue and silver. She couldn't intuit the bird's sex like she had with other animals.

*I am the Elder of swallows,* the bird said.

*Er, um, I'm Elle, the Anima, or whatever. I'm homeless, without a job, and reek like garbage.* Her grating laugh echoed off the bridge. *Sorry I couldn't be more impressive.*

*What's so funny to you?*

Elle shifted from side to side, wanting to run away. But where was she going? She fumbled with a thread trailing down from her cut-off jean shorts. Across the river a few magpies had gathered and stared at Elle with the same mute expression as the swallows looking down. She wanted to scream. She wanted to pull her hair out or dive into the river. But instead, she dropped to her knees and cried.

*It's not funny,* she said between the tears. *I didn't ask for this. I didn't want to be a crazy person, talking with animals.*

*All you humans are lost,* the swallow said. *Time is running out. If you cannot own who you are as the Anima, it is far worse than I even imagined.*

Elle sniffled. *Running out?*

*You will learn all about our collective struggle to survive with time,* the swallow said, puffing out a red neck. *But only if you choose to listen. Only if you choose to own your power as the Anima.*

Elle wanted to plug her ears, but she knew that wouldn't block out the words. *That's what Freda said,* she mumbled. She hadn't meant to think it out loud.

*Freda? Who is this?*

Elle flung a hand in the air as if to shoo away a fly. *No one.*

*That's not true,* Luna interjected, shooting Elle an apologetic side-glance. *She's the woman who found Elle after she ate the mushroom.*

Cars thundered past overhead. Normal people living normal lives, Elle thought bitterly. Hundreds of silent, shining eyes blinked down at her.

*Time is running out,* the swallow repeated. *You need to go back into the mountains—*

*Enough,* Elle said, pushing herself off the ground. She wiped the wild grasses off her clothes. *I'm not going back into the Crazies.*

The Elder sang a low, long note. The other swallows responded with a chorus of deep intonations, their voices joining into a dirge. Elle grew heavy with dread. The birds dropped into silence.

*A disappointment,* the swallow cooed. *A grave disappointment. Silly human, don't you see? Can't you feel the world around you?*

Elle walked back up the riverbank. "Come, Luna."

The swallows exploded into flight, darting and swooping above, screeching with dismay. Elle and Luna walked out of the bridge's shadow and onto the side of the road. Cars droned by. The summer's heat felt oppressive. Elle took off her jacket and cap and placed them in her backpack.

They needed food. They needed a home. They needed money. She sniffed her armpit. Before stepping into any building, much less the one where she wished to resume working, she needed to wash away her stink. She also needed a shirt free of blood. Luna sat next to her, silent and sulking. Elle knew she had let her down. She had apparently let the whole animal kingdom down.

A person stared at her as he drove past. The man's eyes and mouth were wide-open, reminding Elle of her mother's expression when she saw Elle had returned home. Elle and the man made eye contact. She thought the man would look away, embarrassed, but he continued to gawk at her. His car glided away as another one approached. Out of curiosity, Elle looked through the windshield to see if this person would stare at her as well. The woman driving and a boy in the passenger seat gaped at Elle with the same befuddled face.

Was it the bloody shirt? Her muscles? She traced her fingers along the line of her jaw. The bone felt strangely angled. She decided she needed to find a mirror. To her left and right were homes, entire subdivisions. Upstream, a car rotted in the riverbank; its side view mirror jutted out of the grasses.

*Let's go,* Elle said to Luna. *I want to look at something.*

Luna jogged out in front and plopped down into the river. Elle bushwhacked to the decaying car, struggling through a thorny thicket. Roots of a cottonwood reached underneath the car as if in an embrace. Its teal paint blurred with the reds and browns of rust. The mirror was opaque with age. She first tried to clean it with her palm, but when that only smeared the dirt, she took a quick look around and stripped off her shirt. She wet it in the river and managed to scrub the mirror into a reflective state.

Her mind fumbled with the image looking back at her. How was that—*her?* The jawline angled sharply upward, and her cheekbones had come to rest unnaturally high. Her eyes stared back as fiery orbs: an emerald green encircled the pupil, and a glaring orange encircled the green.

She stepped back and tripped over a tree root, falling to her butt. She crawled away as her eyes remained fixed on the reflection. Her shirtless body moved in a weird, spider-like creep. The creature resembled the old Elle, yes. But the person, the *thing*, Elle had become was no longer solely human.

Was she more animal or less human?

Her reflection disappeared from view, and Elle quit crawling. Her pulse hammered against her ears. She curled into the grasses and closed her eyes. No wonder her mother had disowned her. She was a beast.

Luna dipped her head in and out of the river, trying to catch a fish, as Elle slipped in and out of dreams. She saw her mother, Freda, her new face, taut and fierce. She washed dishes, walked the hallways of school, biked down a path, played in the backyard of her first home. She heard her dad's booming laugh, the raspy laughter of her mother behind the closed door.

All the while, wild grasses cradled her body. Shadows stretched across the river, the waters changing from clear to pewter. Luna gave up fishing and slept near Elle. The sun set. Elle woke as stars emerged in a cobalt sky. She stretched out and rolled to her side.

*Lu. I'm sorry for being so…* What had she been? Irrational?

Luna faced Elle. *Where are we going? What are we going to do? I'm hungry, and I wasn't able to catch anything today.*

Elle dropped into the emptiness of her own stomach. *Let's find some food.*

She remembered the dumpster behind a grocery store near the Pizza Parlor. Its lid had been propped open with expired food. She remembered thinking the packaged food looked fine, though she had always been whizzing by on her bike when she noticed the waste. *I have an idea,* she said. *But we'll need to wait a few hours so we're not seen.*

Luna agreed and fell back asleep. Elle sat by the river and listened as twilight unfolded around her. The occasional passing car perturbed the calm. Otherwise, the night noises were as subtle as the darkness. Even the river seemed to quiet at dusk. Elle heard a creature approach. It smelled of a skunk.

*Hello,* she ventured, waking Luna.

The creature stopped moving.

*We won't harm you,* Elle continued. What else were Animas supposed to say?

*I heard of your birth,* the skunk said. *I also heard you don't want anything to do with us animals.*

This was true, perhaps, not even twelve hours ago. But now Elle wasn't so sure. *It's an adjustment, though I wouldn't go that far.*

Grasses rustled as the skunk moseyed on to the river. Elle realized the sensitivity, the tenuousness of her connection to the larger animal kingdom, and disappointment stirred as she reflected on her earlier interactions. She wondered at the swift communication between the various species, apparent to her now through short conversations with a muskrat, swallow, and skunk.

*So you knew the wild creatures speak to one another?* she asked Luna.

Luna leaned her body against Elle. *I thought they might, but I wasn't sure. Dogs don't talk with the wildlife. We're shunned, I believe.*

*Shunned?* Elle placed her arm around her dog.

*We're part of the human world. We're more human, I think sometimes, than wildlife.*

*Did you know humans domesticated dogs from wolves?*

*I have yet to meet a wolf, so how can I believe that?*

*I haven't met an ape, and I still believe humans descended from primates.*

*If humans domesticated dogs from wolves, who domesticated humans from apes?*

Elle shrugged. *I don't think it's a who, but a what, or a how.* She sensed the passing of midnight. *Let's go. I believe we're safe now.*

They crossed the bridge and stepped off the road, weaving through the trees again. Although Elle had walked in the dark as the Anima last night, she hadn't noticed the new way she could see. She had been too preoccupied with being abandoned. Tonight, in the murk of a moonless night, leaves stood out in shades of purple and green. Despite the dim light, everything around her looked distinct. Tingles spread down her arms. She had night vision.

Two does with three fawns stood across the river, partially hidden in willow branches. They stilled as Luna and Elle approached.

*We don't intend to hurt you,* Elle said. They bounded away.

You *may not intend to hurt them,* Luna said. *But I would love a meal.*

Elle remembered the taste of deer burger sautéed with vegetables from Freda's garden. She wouldn't mind some venison now, either. They moved out of the thicket and into a field riddled with prairie dog holes. They walked along fences of backyards bordering the vacant lot. A gravel alleyway appeared between houses. Elle turned down the alley, but Luna didn't follow.

*Where are we going?* Luna looked back at the trees. *You don't mean to take us into the actual city, do you?*

Elle crouched down beside Luna. *That's where the food waits.*

The dog whined. *Something tells me this isn't a good idea.*

*I promise we'll be okay.* Elle pet Luna's head. *We'll eat and return to the river. I know where we can find food. Trust me.*

She walked down the alley with Luna close behind. They crossed First Avenue and slowed their pace. Elle heard rumbles in a dumpster close ahead and stopped, placing a hand on Luna. They both watched the dumpster shake back and forth, the lid rattling.

*What is that?* Luna asked. The commotion in the dumpster stopped.

Elle couldn't smell anything other than trash. *Who's in there?*

The dumpster lid propped open, and the masked face of a raccoon peered out. Red smeared with the black and white fur around his mouth.

*Are you hurt?* Elle asked.

His tongue licked at the redness. *You must be the Anima.* He gave Luna a distasteful look.

*You have the same idea we do,* Elle said. *It looks like you might have cut your mouth.*

He licked at his fur again. *It's not my blood. Your dog is about to drink poison,* he drawled. *Poison meant for me, with love from your people.*

*Luna,* she gasped, spinning around to find her dog's nose in a dish filled with a green liquid.

Luna looked at Elle sheepishly. *It smells like chicken.* She stepped away from the container.

*You could have died!* Elle turned to thank the raccoon, but he was gone, the can's lid left open with a circle of containers and torn garbage bags cast upon the ground. *Come,* she commanded Luna. *Stay by me. And don't go eating anything. We're close to dinner.*

She marched to an intersection of alleys and hesitated. The inclination to turn left pulled at her, urging her toward the Susie Blue—toward her mother and the hope of reconciliation. A closed sign hung on a shop's backdoor in front of her. Elle saw her wild face in the glass, the orange and green glow of eyes. She shuddered and stepped right.

The entrance to the Pizza Parlor's kitchen was ahead. Elle passed the rack where she used to lock up her bike. Had her mother sold the bike already? It would be useful at this moment. Though she figured she was faster now on her own two legs—*much* faster. Her legs itched to take off running, to gallop through the town, weaving between cars and jumping over fences.

Luna, though, was walking more slowly. *Only a little bit farther,* Elle said.

Luna didn't respond.

The alley ended at Main Street. They ran across the road and down the sidewalk until they reached the grocery store. The parking lot ended where a bend in the Brother River pushed riparian growth up to the edge of pavement. They walked toward the dumpster, following Elle's path to work in reverse. As they neared, Elle sensed they were not alone. Although this dumpster was much larger than the trash can in the alley, it rocked with a similar commotion.

*More raccoons,* Luna whispered.

*Shhhh,* Elle said, motioning Luna to follow her into the trees. She counted the raccoons. *At least twenty of them.*

*Will they share?* the dog asked.

*Only one way to find out.* Elle stepped out from the trees.

*Wait,* Luna said.

The raccoons noticed Elle and stopped rummaging. She hadn't realized how loud they were being until now, in the eerie silence of their stillness. Forty bright yellow eyes glared at her from dark faces. She continued forward regardless. She had vowed Luna a meal. She owed her that much at least.

*Hello everyone. My dog and I have come to eat here as well.*

A couple of the raccoons hissed as they jumped down from the dumpster. They reminded Elle of small dogs. More pounced onto the pavement. The gang of engorged raccoons loomed in front, some baring their pointed teeth, some standing on their hind legs, rubbing human-like hands together. The raccoon from earlier swaggered behind the group, his blood-smeared face twitching. A few stepped closer, puffing up their backs. Elle stood her ground.

*Well look what we have here,* a larger one in the front leered. *If it isn't the Anima and her mutt.* He spit on the pavement.

Elle almost laughed, the humanness of the raccoon's actions nearly too comical to believe. Yet these animals may be rabid with disease, or something fiercer.

*We heard you didn't want anything to do with us animals,* a raccoon near the back said.

*Yeah, that you didn't want to go craaaazy,* droned another.

The group as a whole inched closer and closer. Panic wrapped around Elle's chest. She looked over her shoulder for Luna. Where was she? The raccoons smelled Elle's fear, tasted it, and advanced quicker. Elle walked backward, preparing to run. But where was Luna?

The raccoon with red on his face sniggered. *Lost your little friend did you?* he asked. *Or did you leave her dead in the alley after she drank that rat poison?*

Elle shook her head. *You said she was about to drink it.* The panic gripped tighter. She tasted bile.

*That's what I said, but not what I saw.* He smirked. *Now what, Anima? All alone. No one to help you. And we raccoons are hungry.* Very *hungry. We have been for years.* He licked his lips. A smear of blood remained, making it look like a red scar reached up from the corner of his mouth.

*Yeah,* another raccoon piped in. *Hungry.*

*Hungry. Hungry. Hungry.* All the raccoons joined together, their voices screeching in Elle's head.

She placed her hands over her ears. The curb met her ankles, and she fell to her butt. The raccoons charged forward, their paws thundering on the pavement. Elle crawled backward. In her fear she forgot her strength. She forgot her power.

*Enough,* a voice rang out, penetrating. *Enough.*

The raccoons skidded to a stop at Elle's feet.

*Fools,* the voice hissed.

Elle looked around but couldn't see who was speaking. The raccoons slunk away from her, their bodies no longer as big as they had appeared seconds earlier. Two golden eyes emerged in the trees, followed by a swaying body. Elle mistook it for a coyote at first; the creature seemed too large and long to be a fox. But as the fox neared, she could see the red coat, the tail's white tip. Looking at Elle, an expression of disgust crossed the fox's face, brief but obvious. The raccoons retreated back to the shadow cast by the dumpster, watching the fox with palpable apprehension. Elle wondered why they feared this fellow nightwalker.

The fox stopped sauntering and eyed the raccoons. *Were you planning on killing the Anima?* Revulsion in the fox's voice thickened the air. *She may look pathetic now, but she will come around. And when she does, not even a hundred of your kind could kill her. She would rip your throats out, one by one. She could now, surely—if only she knew.*

*There are greater purposes for her,* the fox added, sniffing the air as if this knowledge could be smelled. *We would not be pleased if you killed our best chance for success.*

The raccoon with the red smear stepped forward. *But do the Elders know she wants nothing to do with animals?*

The fox lunged at the raccoon and snapped at him. The raccoon tumbled back.

*Of course we do,* the fox snarled. *Her refusal is temporary, we are sure of this. Much like your life if you continue to display such insolence. You have all spent too much time in this human world.* The fox's voice was still sharp with anger, but Elle also detected a hint of misery. *You forget about your obligations to the Order.*

Turning back to Elle, the fox said, *Your dog is very ill. She is at the river, drinking water as if she hasn't for days. Last I saw she had collapsed.*

Elle jumped up without a word and sprinted to the river. She spotted Luna in a crumpled pile near a boulder. When she saw Luna convulsing, she screamed. *No, no, no, no.* The river roared, but all she could hear was Luna's breath, rapid and rasping. Next to Luna was a pool of vomit with green and red swirled together. Her body twitched, and her eyes rolled back in their sockets. Elle tried to remember where the emergency vet was in town. But she couldn't face another human. They would take Luna from her—she looked like a monster now. Helplessness bore down.

The fox pounced atop the boulder behind Luna. Its eyes glimmered like smoldering coals, and the sky tinged orange and yellow silhouetted its body.

Elle wiped the tears from her face. *Where should I take her? What can I do?*

The fox slunk off the boulder. Elle felt its fur skim her body, the hairs stiff, not as soft as she had imagined.

It sniffed at Luna. *Smells like poison.*

Elle sobbed.

*Quit crying,* the fox snapped, giving her the same look of disgust as before. *You know exactly where to take her. The dog may live, but only if you act now.*

She took a wobbly breath. *Where? Who could possibly help? She drank poison.*

*Where you belong,* the fox said. *You know exactly where I mean. And by the smell of it, you need to leave now and run. Run and don't stop running until you get there. If you're fast enough, she may be able to cure her. I think the dog could live.*

*It's possible she* should *live,* the fox added in a voice hushed and reflective. *Run.* Silent as the moon, the fox disappeared back into the dark.

Elle knew the fox was right. There was nowhere else to go. Really, she had known this since waking beneath the bridge. Luna entered another fit of seizures. Elle squatted and reached her arms underneath her jerking body. Though Luna weighed at least as much as she did, Elle lifted her up with a grunt and placed her atop her shoulders. She stood, her legs unwavering, and marveled at her freak strength.

She took off running, following her old route home. The pavement passed underfoot as a gray river flowing away from her speed. Luna jostled atop her shoulders. Two cars passed, both slowing as they neared. Elle ran with the singular thought to run faster. When she neared the bend in Mountain View Lane, she smelled the fresh slaughter.

*My child. My child,* a female voice wailed nearby.

A fawn lay crushed in the middle of the road. He must have died moments before. The animal's blood shined like new tar. A raven already poked at the body. Despite his mangled corpse, Elle recognized the fawn as one of the three she and Luna had seen from across the river. The doe continued to scream. Her cries—known to Elle through the ancient language of the earth—soaked through Elle's skin. She didn't stop running as her own beloved emitted the formless smell of death. But she knew those words, *my child, my child,* would never leave her. They became a part of her.

She had seen many creatures left dead in ditches. Deer guts, rabbit legs, the ravens themselves smashed and strewn feathers: commonness numbed Elle to the road kill. She knew animals didn't live alone. Who was to say wildlife didn't remember the loss of their mates, their offspring? Who was to say any animal existed without knowing grief?

*Stay with me, Lu. Stay with me,* Elle whispered again and again, the cadence of her words one with the cadence of her feet. She crossed the railroad tracks and snuck through Mountain View. The doublewides glinted in the dim rays of a few porch lights left on. She wondered when she would see her mother again, if ever.

Elle's strides remained long and quick as the trail ascended the foothills. Dawn illuminated the Home of the Gods. She gained speed as the trail cut down the backside of the foothills. Luna's drool dribbled down her back. The trail forked, and she took a moment to consider the quickest route to Freda. Up and over Crescent Saddle, or south around Yarrow Peak, crossing the ridgeline near Hidden Passage Falls. She figured the latter of the two routes may be longer in distance, but had less elevation gain.

Luna no longer trembled. Elle felt the dead weight of her dog and screamed. She moved across the rocky, rooted path at a flat-out sprint. How did her body continue like this with only a vague sense of fatigue? She pounded upward, back and forth across the creek. If she passed any animals, she didn't notice. Not until they were beyond Hidden Passage Falls.

Their stink was almost tangible: fish, sweet clover, oil, and death. The grizzly sow and her two cubs tore at the elk. A gale swept over the ridge, taking Elle's scent with it, and they hadn't noticed her yet. Freda's homestead was only a couple more miles away. Elle's legs and shoulders ached as she hesitated, watching the bears eat. Luna slipped closer to death each passing moment. Elle crept forward, baffled by how the bears had yet to hear her heart pounding.

The mother sensed Elle with a startle and turned to face her, grunting. Her massive head and shoulders swayed. The cubs watched Elle approach.

*Please,* Elle said. *I don't want any trouble. My dog is about to die, and I need to get her to help.*

The sow quit grunting and sat. Her tawny coat caught the morning light, outlining her giant body in an aura of white. The cubs plopped down next to her. Their faces were light like their mother's, but their bodies had darker fur.

*Though you may not intend to hurt us,* she said, *you do as long as you resist who you are.*

Luna grew heavier. *I'm not sure what you mean,* Elle said. *I don't know how I can help. I do know that I may be able to save my dog, but only if I go now.*

The sow faced her cubs. *This is the Anima reborn. Go,* she said without looking back at Elle. *Save your dog, but don't forget about the rest of Life.*

Elle offered a thank you as she sped by. She promised herself that she would return to speak with the sow again. Freda's cabin appeared beyond a growth of aspens, and she sprinted through the trees.

Freda pulled up weeds. The sound of Elle's voice sent chills through her body. It was just another haunting. She continued to weed, the elk thistle poking her through a hole in her gloves.

"Freda! Freda!"

Freda looked up to pacify her imagination and saw Elle running out of the aspens with Luna slung across her shoulders. She slowly stood.

"Freda, please," Elle yelled. "Please, help. Luna's about to die. She's going to *die!*" She set Luna on the porch and swung the garden gate open. Collapsing to her knees in front of Freda, she cried, "Please. *Please.* She's dying. I had nowhere else to go. There was nowhere else. No one else."

# YARROW

Freda stared at Elle, at the Anima kneeling before her, begging for her help. Part of her wanted to tell Elle to leave, to cause Elle the same pain she had inflicted on her. When she had woken two mornings ago to the rumpled blankets on the futon, the empty cup in the dishwashing basin, she had felt the entirety of abandonment.

Abandoned by the dream she would be the Anima. Abandoned by the Anima herself.

But a larger part, the important part, knew Elle's return brought with it redemption. The Anima hadn't been murdered. Hope still lived. For all Freda knew, the entire Imperial Army would arrive any moment. But for now, Freda hadn't failed the Keepers, not to mention the world. For now she could help in the ways she knew how.

"What happened?" Freda asked, stepping around Elle.

Elle followed behind. "She drank poison."

"What kind?" Freda crouched down next to Luna and placed her hand by Luna's nose. Her breath felt irregular and weak.

"I think rat," Elle replied, sitting down on the other side of Luna. "It was a green liquid."

"How long ago did she ingest it?"

"A few hours."

"Few?"

"I don't know how long it took me to run here." Elle threw her hands up. "We were walking down an alley. It must have been about one or two in the morning. Then we came across a raccoon, and he told me my dog was *about* to drink poison. Luna didn't mention drinking any of it. We went to a dumpster behind a grocery store on Main, only five or ten minutes away, where we found more raccoons. They tried to attack me, but a fox stopped them. I found Luna by the Brother and ran here right away."

When she said the story aloud she knew how crazy it sounded. She also knew the only person in the world she could tell it to was the woman before her. Freda pulled back Luna's eyelids to see bloodshot, rolled-back eyes underneath.

"Oh, and I ran into a grizzly—"

"That's enough." Freda quieted Elle so she could think. "You say around two in the morning, huh?" She looked to the overcast sun suspended above the cirque. "It's nearly seven now, so we're past the point of inducing vomiting." What to do instead? She jumped up, remembering. "Get a blanket off the futon and make Luna comfortable on the porch."

Elle did as she was told, grabbing the blanket with an image of a cougar woven into it. The lavender and cedar smells of the cabin calmed her somewhat. While she walked back outside with the blanket in hand, Freda rummaged around the jars on the bottom tier of the food shelves, murmuring to herself. Elle set the blanket down and lifted Luna onto it. Freda stepped out of the cabin with a jar of water and a spoon in one hand, a jar of black powder in the other.

"What's that?" Elle asked, looking at the powder in the jar.

Freda knelt on the edge of the blanket. "Activated charcoal. You don't know how much she drank?"

Elle shook her head. "I don't think she had much. I had my back to her for a second."

"She couldn't have had more than a tablespoon or she would be dead. Rat poison is an effective, although blind, murder weapon." Freda dumped ten spoonfuls of charcoal into the jar of water, twisted on the lid, and shook the jar until it turned black.

The jar seemed to be glowing. Elle rubbed at her eyes. The run here had been more exhausting than she realized.

"I don't know if we should do this while Luna is unconscious," Freda said, her voice hushed and intense. "But we don't have any other options."

She quit shaking the jar. "Open your dog's mouth."

Elle pried Luna's jaw apart, and Freda poured the liquid down Luna's throat.

"This will hopefully absorb the rat poison before all of it can pass through the kidneys. There is little else we can do but wait for her to wake."

"How long might that be?"

"A few hours. Or never. It's hard to say. But Luna's a big dog. Even if she had a tablespoon she could still live, whereas most dogs would be dead or dying from kidney failure by now."

Elle felt numb. She lay down alongside Luna and wrapped an arm around her dog. Breathing in scents of the blanket, Luna's fur, and the forest surrounding them, she fell asleep.

Freda sat on the porch swing. For the past two days she had continued life on the homestead as usual: tending the garden and caring for the animals, practicing her bow, preparing for another hunt, cooking meals, cleaning the cabin. Yet even the simplest tasks had felt monumental. The hours had dribbled out into meaningless space. She had succumbed to hopelessness.

Hope, after all, had brought her to this homestead in the first place. Hope that she would be the Anima and spin the world in a new direction. Hope that the love she lost, the mother she betrayed, the hours spent in solitude would not be in vain. She had failed to find the mushroom before another; she had failed yet again when Elle had fled the homestead and its protection.

Who had seen Elle? Did the Imperium now know of her existence? Freda's foot twitched as she resisted the urge to kick Elle. Selfish girl! How little she knew about the precarious circumstances of her rebirth. But really, it was Freda who had failed. Of course Elle didn't understand, as Freda hadn't properly educated her. She had tried, Freda reminded herself. She had tried to teach Elle the history of her existence. The sullen girl had been as stubborn and volatile as a wolverine.

She must have gone home to find what Freda had in that doublewide—her mother had moved on without her. Freda knew what it felt like to lose a mother before she was dead. She also knew this was for the best. There was no place for a Commoner like Elle's mother in her story now, at least none Freda could imagine.

Midday approached. Elle remained cuddled against Luna as they slept. Crusted vomit ringed around Luna's mouth. Elle's hair covered Luna's face like a black shawl. Freda walked back into the garden and finished pulling up weeds. The sun blazed down, hotter than usual, even for summer's peak. In one pile, she placed the uprooted elk thistle, hound's tongue, and bindweed. She heaped yarrow into a separate pile.

Once finished, she brought the yarrow with her inside, tiptoeing past Elle and Luna still sleeping on the porch. As a pot of water heated to a boil, she cleaned, chopped, and evoked the yarrow. The white flowers glowed even as they tumbled in the waters, and their musty-sweet smell filled the cabin. A package of venison burger thawed in a bowl atop the kitchen island. A happy coincidence, Freda realized, having ready enough meat for two, maybe three.

Elle woke disoriented, forgetting where she was and what had happened. The details around seeped in. Luna continued to sleep, motionless but for the air coming in and out of her body. Elle could smell her sickness, and she struggled not to cry more.

The surrounding world appeared as an uncaring juxtaposition to her dog's condition. Summer flourished in these mountains, with wildflowers exploding across the forest floor. Paintbrushes, dipped in fuchsia, and purple lupine grew among the drooping stalks of bluebells. Arrowleaf balsamroot continued to bloom, the yellow flowers exclamations of cheer. The creek chanted, and the birds whistled with the water's song.

Elle felt the seedling of knowledge that she had returned to a home—a little seedling taking root, its nascent shoot given courage with the sunlit life encompassing her. But Luna wasn't here to enjoy their homecoming. Elle's chin quivered. Why hadn't she listened to Luna's intuition not to go into the city? Why had she forced Luna to follow her where they no longer belonged?

Through a crack in the door, Freda saw Elle upright. She ladled the vegetables and meat into bowls and filled a cup with the yarrow infusion. Today, Freda realized, would be the first time the two of them shared a meal at the table. She was glad she had kept a second chair after all. Leaning against the doorframe, she waited for Elle to acknowledge her.

Elle looked up, her green and orange eyes glassy with tears. Freda placed a hand on Elle's shoulder, and Elle wept openly.

"She can't die." Elle sniffled. "I can't bear knowing it was me who killed her." She remembered adopting her, that puppy smell. Their bond had blossomed into kinship overnight. She scratched Luna's favorite spot.

"It's not entirely your fault," Freda said, her voice soft. She checked Luna's breath again. It felt like it had gained regularity. "Lunch is ready. Please, come and eat with me."

Light poured through the open window above the table. The window framed Bighorn Cirque towering beyond a sea of green. Snow remained in the jagged shadows of its granite face.

"What is this?" Elle asked, bringing the cup of mossy liquid to her nose.

"An infusion of yarrow."

When Elle took a sip, she almost spat it back out. "Ugh. It's bitter." She stuck her tongue out, gagging.

Freda rolled her eyes. "You need to drink the entire cup. It'll help you recover."

"I'm not the sick one." Elle placed the cup down and picked up her fork.

"Luna will have her fill when she wakes. It will help her organs heal. For you, the plant will help with your indisposition. It's an ancient and versatile medicine, yarrow. We're blessed it grows in abundance here. I merely had to weed the garden to harvest it."

"What do you mean by *indisposition?*"

"You weren't poisoned, Elle. But you've endured a lot of stress and sorrow. I mean *indisposition* as the natural low following troubled times. Please, drink up."

Elle stomached the unpleasant taste. The tea spread warmth throughout her body. They ate and drank in their usual quiet, Elle helping herself to seconds. Once they were both done, Elle washed the dishes.

She leaned against the counter. "Now what?"

Freda handed her a refilled cup. "More yarrow." She pulled a chair next to the futon. "Come, sit," she said, taking a seat in the chair and patting the futon with her hand.

Elle moved to her place of transformation. She felt much better after lunch and the cup of tea. The yarrow infusion tasted less bitter the more she drank it. She sat on the futon, wondering how often in her young life she had moved through trauma without acknowledging indisposition.

"We need to—talk," Freda said. How to begin again?

"I agree."

They held eye contact, but neither spoke.

Freda cleared her throat. "What's important here, Elle, is that we reach an agreement. The manner in which you left was rude, but more importantly, it was *extremely* dangerous. You don't understand yet how vital it is that your existence stays secret. At least for now."

"What I don't understand is why you didn't tell me how big of a *freak* I am now. You, um, failed to mention my crazy face, my creepy eyes." She pushed the skin away from her eyes and bulged them. "You didn't mention my freakish appearance. Not once."

"That's because I don't see you that way. You're the Anima. I anticipated these changes"—*envied* them—"and that's why I asked you to stay. Because I know *who* you are, Elle."

Elle glided her hands over the contours of her arms. "I know," she said quietly. "I know, and I'm sorry for leaving. Though if you'd given me a mirror, we could've cut to the chase."

Freda exhaled a laugh. "Unfortunately, there are no mirrors on this property, other than pools of water." She reached out an unsteady hand and cupped Elle's face. "*You're the Anima.* I helped bring you into this world. It's now my responsibility to help you fulfill your Task, or at least just keep you alive long enough to try."

Freda's cool hand cradling her jaw made Elle feel both relieved and uncomfortable. She wondered if she'd always be caught between two emotions, two pulls, or if she'd someday find wholeness within herself, or at least comfort in duality. Freda placed her hand back in her lap. Elle knew she had to accept Freda's help. She had to know herself—maybe even accept herself—as this *Anima* thing.

"Where do we begin?" she asked.

Freda swung open the garden gate. Vegetables common and strange sprouted up from the couple dozen rows set out before them. Elle marveled at the flourishing garden. "You made this happen?"

"Of course. It's not hard. Only time consuming. This is where we'll spend a good bulk of our days. Weeding is a never-ending task. In a month, we'll be harvesting not only to eat dinner, but also to preserve. It's the most important time of the year, the harvest. Our survival come winter depends on it."

Elle walked through the garden, observing both the tall stands of corn and the lingering desire to return to town. Not in her wildest imaginations would she have seen herself, as an adult, living in the woods on a homestead.

Freda watched as Elle's face grew strained and distant. With a loud voice, so to be heard over the creek, she said, "I know how strange and overwhelming this is to you. It sure was to me when I first homesteaded."

Elle heard Freda but didn't respond. They walked to the rustic greenhouse a few yards past the garden. When Freda opened the door, a wave of heat fanned their hair. Tomato vines stretched up along trellises, and pepper plants grew along the glass walls. Beads of sweat gathered along their brow lines.

"Wow," Elle said. "It gets hot in here."

"Thank goodness for that, or my garden would be in a sorry state. I grow the starters in here. I leave the warm weather plants inside, obviously. We won't be doing much in here until next spring. The tomatoes will be ripe in a month, and the peppers before that."

Elle noticed a variety of flowers and herbs growing in the far back. "What are those?"

"I'll tell you another time." Freda opened the greenhouse door.

Elle wanted to press the question, but Freda moved forward with haste. What was she not telling her?

Inside the animal enclosure, chickens gaited about, pecking at the dirt. There were two wooden houses, one much larger than the other. Five goats stared at them as they approached. The animals spoke excitedly of dinner.

*Already?* a hen questioned.

*Who's the stranger?* another hen asked. *Why is she here?*

*I'm a new caretaker,* Elle said.

Silence spread across the pen, and all the animals stilled. Their eyes bore into Elle. Some seemed dumbfounded, while others looked scared.

Freda looked at Elle. "What did you say?"

"I told them I'm a new caretaker. Am I wrong?"

"No." Freda smiled. "But it seems they're confused by your ability to communicate."

The animals burst back into talking. *She can talk with us? She can talk with us!* They kept their distance as Elle and Freda walked through the pen.

"They'll get use to you," Freda said.

Elle pointed to a hen with golden and turquoise feathers. "That's a pretty chicken."

*She's talking about me,* the hen said, seeing Elle point at her. *Oh no! She has singled me out.*

Elle laughed at the absurdity of the hen's reaction. *I'm not here to hurt you,* she said. She turned to Freda. "When I was in town, a muskrat told me there were rumors of my existence. He'd heard that the Anima was born again." How *did* that muskrat know? The only animal she had talked to before the muskrat, other than Luna, had been a mouse. Of course, Elle realized. The mouse must have told the other animals of her existence.

"Why is it," she continued, "the chickens and goats didn't know about me? It seems as if all the animals are aware of my existence, but not these ones."

Freda scratched at her throat. "There's separation between the domesticated and wild animals. This is obvious, even to one without the ability to speak with them."

"Yeah. Obvious," Elle said, her voice distant. She remembered the fox's expression of disgust when he told the raccoons they spent too much time in the human world. He had mentioned something about the Order. The things he had said seemed to be fingers pointing to an explanation. The Order was an answer, possibly, to a question she didn't yet know how to word.

Freda moved forward with the tour despite Elle's lack of concentration. "This is where we clean the coop." She opened the backdoor, and the smell of feces and grass drifted out. They ducked into the four-foot house. "You gather the soiled grasses and replace them with new grasses from the forest. There's a pitchfork and scythe in the shed. As you can smell, it's past time to clean the coop. To collect the eggs we simply lift the side hatches." She pointed to a shelf on the backside of the cabin. "There's a basket over there. Let's gather these eggs now."

Once Elle had finished collecting the eggs, she left the pen, scythe in hand. *Swish, swish, swish.* She created a large pile of grasses, thinking about how she would never discover what the Order had to do with her if she stayed on this homestead. Freda must know much more than she was disclosing. What were they doing, cleaning up chicken shit, when there were more important things she needed to learn?

She stopped slashing the scythe. "Freda, what are we doing? Don't I need to, you know, learn about this Anima stuff? I mean, aren't there, well, more important things we should be doing?"

Freda stabbed her pitchfork into the pile of grasses. "There's an expression I once learned in Baninchi. Go to the temple and worship, but first, hitch your camel to the post."

Elle frowned. "What does that mean?"

Freda pointed to a large, cobblestoned structure beyond the greenhouse and shed. "It means help me put these soiled grasses in the compost."

Elle shook her head as she followed Freda to the compost.

"Grab the shovel from the shed and help me clean the goat pen," Freda said, turning back to the pen.

A hide stretched out on the shed's back wall, strung up in a wooden frame with pieces of thin rope. Many implements hung from pegs, creating a collage of steel and wood on the walls. Maps and small tools, nails, and sandpaper littered a working bench. Faint red stained the bench's wood. Elle found the shovel resting against the wall next to the door.

While they cleaned the goat pen, Elle considered the fact Freda had done these chores alone for over two decades now. Elle wouldn't have believed such a life possible, even with the history classes of her education. A century ago this may have been the norm, but now self-sufficient living was going the way of the mammoth. She forked more soiled grasses. Was this really her life now?

"That'll do," Freda said. They brought the tools back to the shed.

"What are you doing with that?" Elle asked, pointing to the hide.

"That was my most recent kill. I hunt for food, but I also use the hide to make things I sell at stores in town."

"What kind of stuff?"

"Wallets, purses, clothing." Freda stroked the hide. "I'll even make shoes sometimes. The cash helps pay for things I can't make or grow myself. But hunting is becoming harder with age. I—*we*—will need the meat and hide."

Elle's face slackened. "*I'm* going to hunt?" She could learn how to garden, how to milk the goats and churn the compost. But killing an animal?

Freda took down her bow and quiver from their pegs. "Of course. Starting now."

As Freda placed the target against a tree, Elle examined the recurve bow. With red and black snakeskin on one side and silky wood on the other, it was one of the most beautiful things Elle had ever held. It felt ancient and vibrant all at once.

"You're right handed?" Freda asked.

Elle nodded.

"Hand me an arrow from the quiver."

Elle did as asked, and Freda situated her body perpendicular to the target. She drew the sinew with a notched arrow behind her ear. The arrow pierced the bull's-eye.

"See me holding my hand here," Freda said, eyes cast down to her hand resting next to the ear. "After releasing your fingers, you need to hold still so the arrow will fly true. Now look at my body. My feet are angled toward the right of the target, while my shoulders and left arm are in line with it. And now look at my left arm. See the slight bend? You need that to both stabilize the bow and so the sinew won't snap against your forearm."

She held the bow out to Elle. "Your turn."

Elle nocked an arrow between the brass sets and positioned her body as Freda had.

"Use your middle and pointer fingers to draw back the sinew. Inhale as you draw, hold your breath as you steady and aim, and exhale when you release. Simple as that."

As Elle pulled the sinew back, it gave her more resistance than she had anticipated.

Freda could tell the draw weight wasn't enough—not for the Anima.

The arrow sailed ten feet above the target, hissing through the forest beyond. Elle relaxed and grinned at Freda. "Could have been worse."

"Could have," Freda agreed, taking out another arrow. "We'll look for the missed shots later. This time, hold your release longer. You forgot to exhale. Synch the movement with breath. Adjust your feet so they're shoulder width apart."

Elle shuffled her feet again and reiterated Freda's words in her head. She nocked, drew, released. The arrow whizzed by the target again, this time to the left.

Freda placed another arrow in Elle's hand. "You've got a nice bend in your left arm, but now rotate the elbow slightly clockwise. Did you notice how the arrow wiggled as it flew? You're gripping the bow too tight. Remember, you're much stronger than you can imagine. A relaxed but steady grip will do the trick."

The next arrow hit a tree to the right. Elle sighed.

"There's the exhale!" Freda said. "Breath with movement. *Breath with movement.* If that's all you remember today, I'll consider it a success. But careful with your breathing. Don't be too loud. You don't want to form habits in practice that you'll bring with you to the field. Animals have incredible hearing." As if she needed to tell the Anima this.

The lesson lasted an hour. Elle began hitting the target halfway through, though she grew irritated with Freda's stream of feedback after each shot.

"The animals are bigger than that sack! I'll hit them."

"You need to hit the lungs or heart. Depending on the species and size, your aiming point could be a quarter of that target. Also, when animals hear the sinew snap, they can jump the shot. If you're at a distance greater than this—which you most likely will be—you want that arrow to be flying toward the heart. That way you might hit the lungs."

Freda remembered the few times a deer had jumped from her arrow, causing the shot to hit without imminent death. She had only managed to find the animal one of those times. The arrow had penetrated the last place she ever wanted to hit: the stomach. The buck had died a slow, painful death. When Freda had butchered the deer, she had realized the bile had already ruined most of the meat. She didn't hunt again for half a year after that nightmare.

"You need to hit the lungs or heart," she repeated. What if Elle made the same mistakes Freda had? She felt the weight of teaching Elle to take another life, a burden heavier than a pack full of meat. She wondered if Todd had felt the same way teaching her.

Elle held out her hand for another arrow, but Freda reached for the bow. "That's enough for today. We'll practice again tomorrow. You'll need a bow with a greater weight, but that'll have to wait. We've got arrows to find and a sick dog to care for."

*Luna!* "I'm going to check on her now," Elle said, sprinting back to the porch.

Luna remained motionless in a deep sleep. Elle ran a hand through her fur before returning to help Freda find the missed shots. Eventually most of the arrows had been gathered.

On their way to the shed, Elle saw the tree house. "That's where you spend your nights? I used to have a tree house! Can we go up there?"

Elle looked spry with excitement. Freda remembered how young she was, barely an adult. She took the arrows Elle carried. "I'll meet you up there."

"Thank you!" Elle bolted to the ladder.

When Freda climbed into the tree house, Elle was examining the lantern. The drawer containing the scroll was in front of Elle's legs. An impulse to steer Elle away from it overcame her. She went to a window.

"Come look out here," Freda said, trying to veil her unease. Why was she worried Elle would find the scroll? It was Elle's story now. It must be the lingering effects of Laurel's potent Florávo.

Elle joined Freda at the window and saw between pine boughs the homestead as one whole. She remembered hiking up to Yarrow and Mystic Peaks and looking at Bighorn Cirque. Never would she have imagined someone living in the wild woods layering the ravine below. "Have you ever seen anybody near your home?"

Freda thought of the handful of hikers, hunters, and skiers to come within feet of her homestead border. Did she reveal now the invisibility decoction made of witch hazel, birch bark, and snapdragons? She remembered the way Elle had withdrawn the last time she had tried to explain the enduring, though oppressed, existence of magic on the planet.

"A few," Freda said. "Let's finish our chores. It's almost dinnertime."

Elle watched Freda chopped vegetables, fascinated. The blade nearly touched Freda's hand guiding the kohlrabi. "How do you not cut your fingers?"

"Practice. Decades of practice. My mother was an avid cook, and she insisted I learn how to when I was young. She wanted to raise me to be a good wife and caretaker."

"Were you?" Elle asked, her voice tentative. "A good wife?"

Freda stilled. "Excuse me?

"The man in the picture." Elle pointed at the photograph of Freda and the man. "I thought..."

"Oh. That's just a good friend." Freda unwrapped the thawed elk steak.

"You know what," Elle said. "You're amazing. I mean, you hunt and grow and cook all your own food. I can't imagine how much work it's all been."

Blushing, Freda began to scar the steak. She remembered saying something similar to Javiera when she first learned how to garden at the Haven. "I had good teachers."

Elle examined the bookshelf as Freda continued to cook. She crouched down to the bottom level, where a box with carved animals sat next to a clay pot. She picked up the magnifying glass on the shelf above the box and looked at the book titles through the glass. All of the items on the shelves seemed ancient. She wondered where Freda had found them all.

She picked up the picture of Freda and her friend. "How old were you in this picture?" Freda appeared to be maybe five or ten years older now.

"Twenty-six."

Elle set the picture down. "So, are you thirty now? Thirty-five?"

Freda glanced at a pot of sage growing on the windowsill. Did she honestly look twenty years younger than her age? Her Florávo must not be as callow as she thought. "Something like that. I lose track—you know, out here."

They ate dinner. As Elle washed dishes, Freda prepared the fire. Purple clouds flowered up from Crescent Saddle as the sun set. Elle pumped the antiquated handle of the pump and walked the water basin back to the cabin. Luna stirred as Elle's feet thumped past.

Elle halted, splashing water onto the porch. *Luna! Lu!* She knelt and set the basin down. *You're alive!* She was crying.

*Elle.* Luna's voice thin and distant, as if she called to her from the end of a long tunnel.

Freda heard Luna whining and ran to the porch. "Quick, Elle, get some of the yarrow infusion."

Elle filled a cup while Freda pulled a small bottle from a cabinet below the washing basin. "Hold out the cup," Freda said. Elle's hands shook as Freda squeezed brown drops into the infusion.

"What is that?" Elle's voice shook as badly as her hands.

"Essence of juniper berry for her liver." Freda held the bottle up to her eyes. "We'll need to make more of it before she's healed."

Elle's chest swelled. "Healed?"

"*If* she heals. Go on, give your dog her medicine."

Luna's whining quieted to a pitiful whimper. Elle brought the cup to Luna's mouth.

*This will help,* she said. She poured most of the medicine down Luna's throat before Luna coughed, splattering foam and green liquid across Elle's legs.

Freda examined Luna's eyes. One eye looked normal, clear as ever. An opaque sheen veiled the other. "Elle, I'm going to cover Luna's left eye. Ask her if she can see anything."

*What do you see, Luna?*

Luna whined. *Nothing,* she said. *Nothing but the shadows of light.*

Freda placed a hand on Luna's head and the other on Elle's thigh. "Luna lives. That is reason enough to celebrate. Blindness in one eye is a small exchange for her life."

"I wish I knew who left that poison there," Elle said, her voice menacing. She paused. "But what's the point in knowing?" Her shoulders slouched. "I'm the one to blame."

The tinder caught fire. Freda added larger pieces of wood until the flames roared and smoke twirled skyward. She walked back to the porch. "It's time, Anima."

"Time for what?" Elle's voice split. She coughed up snot and spit it off the porch.

"I'm going to explain more about who you are," Freda said, though now she doubted the timing. "I'll meet you by the fire." She retrieved blankets from the futon and two books from the shelves. On the bottom tier of the bookshelf, next to the flute case Orvik had made her, was the box that had changed everything. She grabbed it as well.

Darkness suffused sky and mountains. Shadows leaped about the ground, upon the trees and across Elle's face. The fire and creek harmonized in an ancient, hushed hymn. Freda gave a blanket to Elle and placed more wood in the fire. She sat on a stump. "I found a scroll about the Anima in here," she began, handing Elle the box.

Elle remembered seeing the box on the bookshelf. "Where did you find it?" She examined the creatures carved into the wood: winged and water animals, large and small mammals, too many to count.

"I found it at the base of Yarrow Peak on an excavation." She felt the phantom of the scroll's etched letters upon her fingertips. "This box was presumably made by a Bilawáxan. Many of the peoples' deities are carved into the wood."

Elle nodded. "My dad told me about the gods. He was a Bilawáxan." She wished he could be here now, to see his teachings coming to life.

"I don't think you ever told me that." Elle shared a heritage with the first Anima. What were the odds? There was so much to tell her, so much for her to learn. "We think the first Anima was born in these mountains, some fifteen thousand years ago."

"*Fifteen thousand?*" Elle echoed in wonder.

Freda opened *The Secret Sibling of the Fly Agaric*, and Elle scooted closer to see. On a page with a map of the world, little red dots punctuated seemingly random places across the globe. The dots on the map created the Flower of Life pattern.

"This is where the *Anima metamorphas* have grown in the past," Freda said. "The most recent was on Alimendia." She placed her finger on a dot marking the Wildwood Mountains; its red was a darker hue than the others. "I added this dot, as the person who wrote this book didn't include anything about the Anima before you. The Imperium—it did what it could to obscure her history."

"What do you mean? Why would we want to do that?"

Freda stiffened. "There's no more *we*, Elle, between you and the Imperium. You are now, officially, an enemy of the Imperial Army."

The words slapped Elle. What did that mean? She had grown up pledging allegiance to the Imperium. Her father had fought for the Imperium. She had lived her entire life knowing of no social structure other than that created by the Imperium. "But why? What have I done? I didn't mean to eat the mushroom. I wouldn't have, if I had known what would happen!"

Elle's words felt like slaps in return. Freda clenched her fists. All she had ever wanted for over two decades—but enough. There was no more time for bemoaning her dream's death. "It's not what you've done, but what you've *become*. When we last talked about your Task, I began to explain magic. Remember? The ability to talk to animals is a form of magic. Since the Imperium was established, those who practice magic have been persecuted and murdered. Or worse…"

Elle began to shake, and Freda wrapped an arm around her. "This is why, Elle, I had insisted you stay. The invisibility border around this cabin keeps Commoners, including Imperial soldiers, away. If you were to get caught—"

"Commoners?" Elle interrupted.

"People who don't practice magic."

Elle shrugged Freda's arm from her shoulders. She felt hot and itchy. "So are you a, what, a *witch?*"

Freda ignored the mocking tone of Elle's voice. She remembered her righteous suspicions at the Haven. They both were children of the Imperium, educated under its careful eye. Rational thought not only void of magic, but disdainful toward the idea of it, had been engrained in them since their first day of school.

"I'm technically a Mage, though not a well-trained one. I studied plant magic during my time at a Haven in Taléria. That's where Erie lived. Remember me talking about her? The Imperium was forged between the three kingdoms of Lacuserra shortly after Erie's death."

Elle vaguely remembered the things Freda told her that night. "Erie was burned alive?"

Freda said nothing.

"It seems my fate is to be murdered in some gruesome way," Elle whispered.

"This we do not know. But we *do* need to keep your existence secret, or that could very well be your fate. Did anyone see you while you were in town?"

Elle fidgeted on her seat. "Well, my mother, of course. And her boyfriend."

Freda raised her eyebrows.

"But they wouldn't say anything," Elle added quickly. "I mean they might spread rumors that I'm doing drugs. But what would they say? They had no idea what I am."

"We'll have to hope so, Elle. You just—you just don't understand." Freda tilted her head back and sighed. "Though how could you? The Imperium, Elle, it's more powerful than ever. And then there's the Republic…" She worried her lower lip between her teeth. "Your allies, called Keepers, well, they're scared. They're scared for themselves. They're scared for the planet."

"Scared of what?"

The beginning had been so simple: the first Anima was born and buried here. But from that moment on—layers upon layers. Elle needed to know why her existence as the Anima was more imperative than ever, but was Freda really the right one to tell her? And if so, how?

"They're scared of—of irreversible loss. Of mass extinction…" Freda snapped the book shut. "The scroll. I want to show you the scroll. I'll be right back." She strode off into the dark.

Elle stared into the blue belly of the flames. She saw a woman burning alive. Her father polishing the medals he earned while fighting for the Imperium. A stranger's hand carving her ancestors' gods into wood. The history of this world, more than ever before, felt mysterious and profoundly intertwined to Elle. All the images seemed to connect like stars in a constellation.

Freda cleared her throat on the log next to her, startling Elle. She unfurled a roll of vellum on her lap and traced the caricatures. "It was written by a Keeper, a Salvager named Laurel. Salvagers can see into the past, across space. There are always three Salvagers alive, born in the same places the *Anima metamorpha* grows, though not at the same time. Those places, the ones marked with red dots on the map inside that book, are called Spirit Loci."

Elle looked at the vellum. "What does it say?"

Freda recited the scroll. The foreign words moved high and low, between the punch of consonants and the flow of syllables. Elle felt something unusual—something essential, perhaps—passing between them and didn't know what to say. The melody of water and fire resounded across the canyon.

"What do the words mean?" she asked at last.

Freda spoke the translation.

Elle tilted her head. "Is that all?"

"What do you mean *is that all?*"

"I mean that's all the scroll says? It doesn't tell me what to do, or what my fate is, or anything useful like that?"

Freda wanted to shake Elle awake. She had to be the most ungrateful, ill-chosen Anima of all time. Freda had been the one to find the scroll. *She was the one.* If anyone deserved to receive the ancient language of the earth, it was she. "Do you not *feel* the amazing circumstances of your existence? You are part of a sacred, magical lineage, and all you can do is ask for more?"

"I'm *sorry,*" Elle said, leaning away. "I thought we've already established that you're supposed to be the Anima, not me? Just because I've been thrust into this *sacred, magical lineage* doesn't mean I'm suddenly going to understand what that means. In fact, it seems as if becoming the Anima is one of the worst things that could've happened to me. I'll have to live my life hiding so I don't get burned alive."

Freda recognized the truth in Elle's words. Her expectations for Elle's reaction to the scroll reflected Freda's own knowledge and desires—and the power of Laurel's magic.

"It must be late," Elle said. "Let's go to bed."

Freda agreed with a solemn nod. "Yes, time for sleep. We can continue this talk another time. But I want to give you something first. Wait here." She put the scroll back in her tree house and returned to Elle holding a book.

"I made this for the final Anima," she said, handing Elle the book. She had thought she had been making it for herself.

*Task of the Anima*, the title read. Opening to the middle of the book, Elle recognized Freda's tiny, cursive handwriting. She flipped through the pages, seeing Freda had written extensively about the Order and the Task, with pictures and maps scattered throughout. It looked like answers to many of the questions Elle had would be in this journal.

She stilled. "Wait a minute—what do you mean, the *final* Anima?"

Elle's eyes gleamed iridescent green in the dark like those of a wild animal. Freda realized that in all her talk of Animas, she had yet to tell Elle maybe the most important detail of her existence. She swallowed. "You are the twelfth and final Anima."

"How do you know?"

"This is what I was told." Though that could be a lie, too. Freda hadn't considered this, and she frowned at the possibility. "I do know the first Anima was buried here, so we've come full circle. If what the Salvager said is true, you are our last Anima, Elle. And if what I write in that book also proves true, you are humans' last hope to come back into the greater Life that sustains us."

Elle felt the journal in her hands as a heavy encumbrance. She knew she needed to learn more about the Order and her Task, but she realized she wasn't ready. It was all too much. She wanted to throw the journal into the fire. "Well that sounds fun and totally doable."

"Honestly, Elle, I don't think it will be either. But who knows? Either way, you'll at least live a life of greater meaning than you could've ever dreamed." Freda paused. "If nothing made sense tonight, let me make this one thing clear: the sooner you can release your resistance to being the Anima—the fear of your own power—the sooner you can embrace your life as the precious gift it is. And the sooner you'll live for something much greater than yourself."

Elle searched for a response but found none. She walked back to the cabin, turning once. Freda emptied a bucket of water upon the twinkling embers. Smoke snaked around her.

Part of Elle wished to dismiss the night and the things Freda had said. The deeper part of her, though, knew the knowledge she had received was the truth of her new existence. She couldn't will it away. Hunching down to Luna on her way inside, Elle told her dog she loved her in their shared words of the earth's ancient language.

# RECURVE

The summer days passed quickly for Elle. Luna was nearly back to normal, though it took her a while to adapt to being blind in the right eye. She never complained or blamed Elle. When Elle had continued to apologize, Luna had asked her to stop. *If this hadn't happened to me,* she had told Elle, *we'd still be raiding dumpsters with the raccoons. I'm happy we're back here.* Elle saw the truth in Luna's words, and although she still blamed herself for Luna's half sight, she had agreed to quit apologizing and move on.

*The Task of the Anima* remained beneath the futon, unopened since the bonfire. Freda and Elle hadn't talked about that night again. The urgency of this supposed Task felt far away in the warmth of these summer days. Elle chose not to engage in conversation with creatures other than Luna and Freda. Since she spent the majority of her time outside, the voices encompassing her soon became as commonplace and non-consequential as people talking at the Pizza Parlor had once been while she worked.

Each day Elle learned something new as she helped Freda around the homestead. She learned how to milk a goat and churn butter; how to sew a wallet made of hide and sinew; how to pull weeds so the entire root came up; how to churn compost; how to cut and cook food without burning the meal; how to chop wood; how to start and maintain a fire; how to wash her clothes in the creek. She learned all these things and more. And each day, after finishing the chores and before making dinner, Elle practiced shooting the bow. By the end of summer, she consistently hit the target, though still without creating a cluster.

"Tomorrow, we're going to get you your own bow," Freda announced one morning over a breakfast of goat yogurt and fresh huckleberries. "That's the only way you'll achieve the accuracy you need to kill. There's an expert bow crafter I know. He should have something that will work, though you'll have to come to his place with me to make sure you get the right size."

"Isn't it too dangerous to go into town?"

Freda had already deliberated on the risk. "We'll make sure you're dressed in layers, to hide your muscles and face. Besides, the bow maker's house is right outside Middle Fork. Few people live there. We'll go to the general store for the other things we need."

"And what does that include?"

"More jars and lids for canning. Salt. Metal for arrows. I have a list. We'll hike out with the two largest backpacks. We should be back in less than twenty-four hours."

The stern decisiveness in Freda's tone told Elle the trip to town was not up for debate. "Fine," she said, pouting.

"Luna will stay here. We'll leave before sunrise."

With a shake of her shoulder, Elle startled awake. Freda stood over her with a cup of tea in her hand. "Good morning," she said, holding out the cup.

Elle rubbed the sleep from her eyes and took the cup. Night still blackened sky and land outside the window. She felt like she had slept but ten minutes. "What time is it?" She tried not to sound whiny. Freda chided her whenever she whined.

"About three in the morning." Freda put twice the normal amount of deer scraps in Luna's bowl. The dog looked up to her, inquisitive. "Please let Luna know this food is for both breakfast and dinner."

Elle relayed the message to her dog.

*So you're going to leave me here alone,* Luna said.

*Not by choice. We'll be gone a day. Please look after the chickens and goats.*

"Goats are milked, eggs are gathered, and all creatures fed," Freda announced, as if able to hear the conversation. She picked up a pack resting near the front door and brought it to Elle. "Your pack, my Anima."

Elle slipped on the old, camouflage rucksack. It reminded Elle of a bag her dad had owned. She bent down and wrapped her arms around Luna.

*You know I don't like it when you hug me like this,* Luna said to her, though she nuzzled her head into Elle's neck. *It's an act of aggression, in the dog world.*

*I know,* Elle said. *But it's an expression of love in the human one.* She scratched behind Luna's ears. *We'll see you soon.*

Freda waited at the door with her pack on. "Let's get this over with," Elle said, following Freda outside. "We're leaving the door open for Lu, right?"

Freda stuck her arm in the air with a thumb up as she walked away from the cabin. Elle trotted behind her, thankful her abilities as the Anima gifted her with endurance and speed. Otherwise Freda would have quickly left her in the dust. The two maintained an efficient pace as they walked south, through the aspen grove and toward the ridge above Hidden Passage Falls. They followed a faint game trail past the falls and down to the established trail. Elle smelled deer bedded down canyon.

Dawn arrived as a golden affair. When the trail leveled in Owl Creek Canyon, Freda veered north with Elle close behind. Elle realized she had never ventured this way before, even in all the times she had wandered these mountains. The maintained path went the opposite direction, to Mystic Peak and the trailhead. Freda used a long stick to clear the cobwebs.

"I thought this was private property," Elle said.

"It is."

They continued to swish and stomp their way through the growth. Pine boughs hung low, and the canopy still leafed out large and green, though a bite in the air hinted to fall. Sunlight angled through the verdure. Elle listened as the birds and small mammals spoke of their arrival. They sounded surprised.

*Humans,* a small voice cried out ahead. *Two humans are coming.* Wings and paws scurried away. The animals wanted nothing to do with them. Had it always been this way?

Freda and Elle trekked without talking. Elle had never walked through such thick foliage. It felt as if the forest had swallowed them. She found herself amazed, yet again, by Freda, this time for her ability to navigate without a trail. Apart from fleeing creatures, including a pair of bucks thrashing through the trees, stillness surrounded. Wind set the ponderosas swaying, and their old bodies moaned.

Elle thought of how this route was tripling their travel time, though she knew the faster route risked people—including her mother—seeing her. Elle had come to think of her mother less and less. When she did, it was always with regret. Regret that she hadn't helped her when she had begun to drink more and more. Maybe she could've asked her to go to rehab. Maybe if she had commanded her to quit her job at the bar, she would have. But instead Elle had let her go.

They climbed the foothill. Trees thinned and light thickened. When they reached the top, Freda slowed down, looking side to side. Elle took off her newsboy cap and fanned her face. Her hair pressed flat against her skull, soaked with sweat. She envied Freda's shorts and tank top. Her pants and canvas jacket felt as wet as her hair.

"Can you see anyone, Elle?" Freda whispered.

Elle scanned north, east, and south. "I don't. Whose land are we on?"

"A very rich man who doesn't live here, at least not the last time I checked," Freda said, still whispering. "Although once I hunted back here and nearly encountered someone. Let's go. We'll cut southeast and end up near the bow maker's house."

They picked up the pace again. Elle continued to find herself in awe of Freda's agility. How old *was* she? She almost seemed ageless. Elle wondered what Freda would have been like as the Anima. She seemed to have already cultivated aspects of the Anima within herself after years of living in the mountains.

The Brother River meandered through the tiny town of Middle Fork. Much further to the east, miles beyond the silver ribbon of the Sister River, an abandoned coalmine spread as a giant, gaping hole in the Prism's southern end. Black and red terraces, leading deeper and deeper into the earth, made the mine look like a stadium. It reminded Elle of a picture she once saw of an ancient fighting pit. Old, gray structures surrounded the mine, the wooden buildings collapsed and decaying.

Freda walked toward a brick house with a chain-link fence surrounding it. A sturdy mutt charged at them, shrieking of intruders as he threw himself into the fence. Elle spoke to the dog, and he whimpered away with his tail between his legs. Freda raised her eyebrows at Elle.

"I guess I scared him when I said we come in peace," Elle said.

Freda opened the gate, and Elle edged forward. "Who is this guy?" she asked. "What's he going to think about—this?" She pointed at her face.

Freda tugged Elle's cap further down. "Your clothes are hiding the more telling details," she assured Elle. "And besides, Todd's nearly blind."

They walked up the creaking porch steps. Freda knocked on the door. When Todd opened the door, he was sitting in a wheelchair. He had a bald head, dotted with age spots, and wore a tattered camouflage coat. Elle could tell he was at least part Indigenous by the hint of mahogany to his skin. He reminded Elle of her grandfather. Elle wondered if her father would have looked similar, had he reached old age.

"Freda," he said, squinting his eyes. "It's been far too long."

Freda gave him a hug. They held the embrace for a while. Freda held his shoulders and peered into his eyes. "Far too long," she agreed. "How are you, dear friend?"

"Still on this side of the earth." He shifted his milky white eyes to Elle and stared at her, though not unkindly. Elle crossed her arms in front of her chest.

"I see you have company. I never thought there would be a day when you, Freda Johansson, should have a companion."

Freda laughed. "It's not entirely by choice, for either of us," she said, her voice light. "But we're adjusting." She gave Elle a sideways glance. "We're here today on business. She needs a bow with a greater weight than my own."

Todd coughed. Elle flinched at the phlegm clattering within his lungs.

"Excuse me," he wheezed. "I'm not long for this world. The cancer has spread, Freda, and the doctor says I have until the winter at most."

Tears welled in Freda's eyes. "I had no idea. It *has* been far too long."

"Come, come in. We'll head out back and find your friend a bow. Then let's catch up over a cup of coffee." He spun on his wheels with surprising dexterity. Elle could tell he had been an athletic man. His long limbs and torso remained strong looking. "I hope Rex didn't scare you too much," he said, wheeling down a narrow hallway leading to a door.

Elle and Freda followed behind. "I think we scared him off," Freda said, winking at Elle.

Black and white photographs of people decorated the hallway walls. Elle recognized the younger version of Todd as the same man in the picture on Freda's bookshelf. He had apparently fought in the Imperial Army for many years. There were no photographs telling of a wife or kids, but many showed Todd had been a pilot. In one photo he stood next to a fighter jet with a rainforest closing around him.

"My father also flew for the army," Elle said. "Did you serve in Bielam?"

"I did," Todd replied. He pushed a button and the back door opened to a ramp leading down to the backyard. "Did he as well?"

"Yeah," she said with excitement. Maybe Todd knew him.

Freda whirled around, coming face to face with Elle. "The last thing you want to do right now," she said under her breath, "is tell anyone who your parents are or even your real name."

Elle frowned at Freda. "So I no longer can talk to people about my family?"

"Exactly." Freda turned back around.

"What was your father's name?" Todd asked. "And where was he from?"

Elle walked down the ramp. Freda stood behind Todd with a finger to her mouth.

"Errr," Elle said. "Tyler—Smith. And yeah, he was from Prominence."

"Huh." Todd fingered his chin's wrinkles. "I thought I knew all the bombers from the north-central canton, but I never met a Tyler. My memory's slipping, though, like the rest of me. I recall a John, and an Art—"

"Art!" Elle repeated wildly. He knew her dad. Freda shook her head at Elle, but Elle couldn't help herself. "Art Morgan?"

"That's the one. A real standout flier, and a good guy. I heard he met a tragic end, though. Left a wife and a young kid. Lived through the war but still died in flight. Did your father know him?"

Now it was Elle's eyes welling with tears. She wanted to throw herself at Todd's wheels and beg him to tell her all he knew. "He did," she said, her voice cracking.

"Are you crying?" Todd asked, surprised. "There, there, child." He reached out a hand. Elle placed her hand within his gnarly, veined one. He gave it a kiss. Freda watched on, her face pinched.

"I can see he was a dear friend to your father," he said. "Life is cruel, no? To give us such deep connections with others only to find that we must all leave as we came in. Yet let us not forget: death is but a new beginning. What better way to understand this than the hunt, huh? So come, our time as the living is too short to dwell upon the dead."

Elle wiped away the tears with her sleeve. "Thank you, Todd. I've missed Art for years. He was like a"—she glanced at Freda—"like a father to me."

"And to many, child," Todd said. "We were both forced into boarding school, did you know that? Of course you didn't. It was something that bonded us together, even before we knew what brotherhood meant. That would come in the war..." He trailed off, the cataracts in his eyes becoming even paler. After patting Elle's hand, he released it and wheeled to a shed in the back corner of his yard. Rex hid beneath the shed steps, whimpering.

"What's gotten into him?" Todd asked as the mutt darted away. "He's always been a scaredy cat, though usually his way of expressing fear is by terrifying others with that horrible bark of his."

Freda opened the shed's door. "Maybe Elle and I smell strange."

Todd grunted. He rolled into the shed with Freda and Elle close behind. Hanging from hooks on the wall were dozens of bows, all different colors and sizes. Dust particles drifted in the light. Elle looked with wide eyes. She could see why Freda had brought her here; Todd was an expert craftsman.

"So what are you thinking?" he asked.

"Seventy-five, if you got it."

"Huh?" He narrowed his eyes at Elle. "That can't be right. She's a young woman, not a two-hundred-pound man."

"She has muscles enough," Freda said. "She's been practicing with my bow, and although the technique is there, she's still inconsistent because the draw weight is much too light."

Todd frowned as he considered this, but then he smiled. Half his teeth were missing. "Well, I trust your judgment, Freda."

"Thank you, Todd." Freda beamed. "I'm thinking yew, like mine."

"Juniper." Todd wheeled to the end of the shed. He took down a recurve bow, one much longer than Freda's. "Seventy-five inches long, one and half inch wide, one inch deep." He rolled back with one hand, his other grasping the bow. "Juniper, hedge, and ebony."

It was one of the most beautiful manmade things Elle had ever seen. Shiny and smooth, the woods ran seamlessly together. The tan, brown, and black of the various tree species looked striking against one another. Even without shooting it, Elle knew it was her bow. Her fingers twitched with the desire to draw the sinew back and feel its power within her grasp.

"I can see you are only becoming more talented with age," Freda murmured. "It's stunning, Todd."

"She is a magnificent lady," Todd agreed. "I haven't made a bow in years. The arthritis is too bad now. She was the last. I'll be sad to part with her. It looks like she'll be in good hands, though. A friend to Freda and Art is a friend of mine."

He lifted the bow to Elle, and she wrapped a hand around the grip. It felt as if it had been carved for her fingers.

"It looks like we've found your bow," Freda said, still beaming.

Todd drew a pipe and a thin box of matches from his pocket. "And yet again I must say goodbye," he said. He lit a match and smoked.

*Twang. Thunk. Twang. Thunk.* Elle released arrow after arrow, careful not to split them in two. She hadn't known why her shots had been inconsistent at the homestead, but she now saw Freda had been right, as usual. The larger draw weight gave her enough resistance to steady the shot with greater accuracy. She practiced on a faded, yellow target leaned up against the fence.

Rex remained hidden. She was grateful she could practice shooting without the intrusion of his voice in her head. But there still was Freda's voice. While drawing the sinew back, she heard the things Freda had said at the bonfire two months ago. She wondered if she would ever be ready to be the Anima—to release the fear of her own power and live for something greater than herself. She loosed the sinew, holding still as the arrow sailed into the bull's-eye.

Freda and Todd had watched her shoot three rounds of arrows. Before following Todd into the house, Freda complimented Elle on her precision.

Elle said nothing. She was angry with Freda for denying her the rare opportunity to hear stories of her father from someone who knew him well. On a deeper level, she knew Freda had her best interests in mind, but the refusal felt cruel nonetheless.

Elle plucked the arrows free of the target. Her shadow stretched across the yard. She looked to the bluebird sky, relishing the full light on her face. It was a perfect late summer day. On the homestead, leaves fragmented the sunshine. She had forgotten the openness of this valley and realized she missed the expansive view, the sea of golden grasses, the Prisms rising in the east.

Back inside, Elle moved toward the murmuring voices in the kitchen. "And here she is now," Todd commented on Elle's arrival. He dissolved into another coughing fit.

Freda refilled his water glass. "It pains me to see you hurting, Todd." She began to cry.

"There, there, Freda," he said, reaching out to her and taking her hand within his own as he had done with Elle. Freda knelt and wrapped her arms around him. Her tears wet his white shirt as he patted her back, resting his head upon hers.

Elle frowned at the floor, unsure where to look. She decided to wait in the entryway as the old friends said goodbye, probably forever. If he was going to die, couldn't she ask him more about her dad? Who would he tell, anyways? But when Todd rolled into the hallway with Freda close behind, Elle saw Freda's red, puffy face and decided against causing her more trouble.

Freda blew her nose. "Todd has graciously given you the bow for free."

Todd flicked a wrist. "What need do I have for money? I've offered Freda to deed her my worldly goods, but she's too smart for that. She knows it's best to travel light in life." He rested his cloudy eyes on Elle with his chin lifted up at her. Elle felt him *seeing* her. Returning his stare brought heat to her face. "You, on the other hand," he declared, his voice becoming dark, "will never travel light in this life. You will always carry a burden, though in time, you will no longer suffer beneath its weight."

Even Freda seemed surprised, the tone and extent of his words entirely unexpected, unnatural even. But like a small cloud passes across the sun, the shadow disappeared from his face, and he looked at the bow in Elle's hands. "Treat that lady well, as I adore her."

"I will." Elle hugged the bow to her chest. "Thank you, Todd."

He turned back to Freda. "Please, no more crying on my behalf. It's more painful than this damn cancer to feel you grieve. I'll soon be on a new journey and look forward to seeing you in another life." He took her hand again and gave it a kiss. "Now go, before the day grows any older."

Freda embraced him. "Thank you, Todd, for being my teacher," she whispered.

He took her by the arms and looked her square in the face. "The teaching went both ways. Thank you for being my friend." The two held a fierce gaze, tears falling from one another's eyes. They released their hold simultaneously.

The dirt road into town felt long. Freda trudged behind Elle for the first couple of miles. "We're far behind schedule," she said at last, quickening her pace to walk in front of Elle again. "There will be time to mourn at home,"

A single truck passed, leaving a cloud of dust for the women to walk through. The land felt strangely deserted. They crossed the Brother over an old, wooden bridge. The dirt road ended at a paved street, and they turned right toward the dozen buildings populating Middle Fork's downtown. A handful of people strolled along the sidewalks, entering and leaving the shops. Elle tightened her grip on the bow.

"We'll be in and out of here without time for people to even notice you," Freda said.

Elle followed close behind Freda as she opened the general store's door. She pulled her cap even further down; she could barely see out beneath the brim. There was no one else in there but the two of them and a cashier.

"Wait in this lobby area for now," Freda whispered. "If anyone joins you, meet me back at the bridge. I'll round up all we need." Freda retrieved a shopping cart and placed her pack in it. Elle did the same.

"I'll be back in a few," Freda said, pushing the cart down away.

Elle lifted the cap's brim just enough to peek at the cashier. The young woman didn't seem to notice her. Elle walked into the small lobby and plopped down on a couch in front of a television. Her pants and jacket stuck against her skin. She smelled as sweaty as she felt.

Outside of school, Elle hadn't watched much television. The new technology had been too expensive. She watched models proclaiming the merits of some mascara, kids eating boxed cereal, someone chugging a soft drink. Elle dozed off, heat exhaustion and the stream of meaninglessness lulling her to sleep. The news came on, and an anchorman spoke of local events. Footage of a protest on Twin River's Main Street pulled Elle's attention back to the screen. A few people yelled as they marched in circles with handmade signs held high. *The bear did NOT have to die! Embrace wildlife – stop killing them! We are guests in THEIR home.*

Elle leaned toward the television. "The decision to kill the sow and place her two cubs in a zoo have wildlife enthusiasts up in arms," the anchorman said. "Officials say it was a tough decision. With Hidden Passage being such a popular trail in town, they decided it was best to remove the sow after she attacked and killed a man last week on the ridge above the falls. The man was a local hiker, though he didn't carry protection."

The screen switched to an image of the mother bear, dead, and Elle gasped. It was the same bear she had met on her way back to Freda's when Luna had been poisoned. She knew this for sure when the news revealed footage of her two cubs caged. The dead mother was the one she had spoken with, and those were her children, pacing behind bars, mewling loudly. The news was now onto global issues, but Elle didn't see or hear what was happening.

When Freda walked to the check out with a full cart, the cashier pointed a limp finger at Elle. "Your daughter is having a meltdown," she drawled.

Freda whipped around. Elle stared at the television screen, her face streaked with tears. She clutched her knees to her chest on the couch. Freda walked to the lobby and watched an advertisement for tampons before turning off the television. A man entered the store. Elle continued to cry and rock.

"I don't know what happened," Freda whispered, bending down, "but you need to go outside and wait for me at the bridge. You're drawing far too much attention right now."

"They shot her," Elle wailed. "She's dead. They killed her, and now her kids are stuck in a zoo."

"Shhh." Freda glanced over her shoulder to see the man and clerk goggling at them. "No need to stare," she hissed. The strangers pretended to continue about their business, though Freda knew they were still listening. "Tell me more later. But you need to go wait outside. Now."

Elle grabbed her bow and ran from the store, still crying.

"Whose kids are in a zoo?" the clerk asked, bewildered.

"None of your business," Freda snapped. The clerk gave Freda a nasty look. She calculated the total amount. Freda handed over the exact change from her wallet and muttered a thank you. She felt embarrassed, knowing her patience waned with age. She left the store with the stuffed backpacks stowed in the cart.

Freda looked around to see if anyone was watching. With no one in view, she pushed the cart down the street, the wheels whining and swerving across the pebbled road. Elle was waiting atop the bridge, watching the river amble over a mosaic of stone. Although Freda wished to reprimand her, she stood next to her without saying a word.

Downstream, a flock of starlings rose from aspen branches, moving as if they were a single organism. The murmuration twirled across the sky like a black helix, darkening as it bent, lightening as it twisted.

Freda looked to the west. It was past time to leave. "Elle," she said, her voice gentle. "What happened back there?"

Elle dropped her head, closing her eyes and rubbing her palms against her temples. "Remember when I returned with Luna?" Elle asked. "And I told you about running into a grizzly sow and her two cubs? I had a conversation with that mother bear. She said things I had almost forgotten. Between worrying about Luna and doing all the stuff on the homestead, my encounter with her had slipped my mind. She said that if I don't embrace who I am, I would hurt them."

"And you found out while watching television back there that the mother bear has been euthanized, and her two cubs are now in a zoo?"

"What am I suppose to do, Freda? I know a man died because of her, but how many bears have been killed? Even you kill bears, right? For their fur and meat?"

"I have killed many animals for those reasons," Freda replied. She glanced back at the cart. "But we must go, Elle. This is no place to discuss the Holy Paradox."

A car approached the bridge, slowing as it neared them. Elle kept her face to the river until it passed. Freda took Elle by the wrist and led her back to the cart. She felt limp in Freda's hand. "Here's your pack." Freda labored to hold it up.

Elle took it from her without effort and strapped her bow to it. They walked down the road as bipedal turtles, slow with the weight of things and thought. When they passed Todd's house, Elle said, "Why don't you trust Todd? It seems like you two are close."

Freda saw him through the window. He slept on a chair in front of a television, the blue light flickering across his face. "It's complicated, but Todd doesn't know about the Imperium's oppression of magic. If he knew of you as the Anima, the Imperium might be able to get that information from him. It's not that he's an enemy. It's that he doesn't know the Imperium is an enemy of ours."

Elle winced. Enemy of ours meant enemy of hers. She wore her father's coat, the one he had worn in the war. She couldn't decide why she felt slimy for wearing it: was the coat dirty, or was she? She traced the X of the Imperium's emblem stitched onto the right breast pocket. What would he have done if he knew his daughter's veins pulsed with magic he had sworn to bleed dry?

"We're being stalked," Elle whispered, stating the obvious.

They moved toward Hidden Passage Falls in the midnight. The forest girdled them, black and formidable. They had both heard the creature shadow their movement since the foothills. It sounded large.

Freda trembled. Had the Imperium caught rumors already? Her hand found the pouch on her belt. "Do you think it's a human?" she whispered back.

"No." Elle could smell that much.

They quickened their steps, moving past the falls. The water's roar drowned out sounds of the creature's movement, and Freda thought it might have left at last. But over the ridge, they heard again the snapping of twigs and crunching of leaves. They passed the spot Elle had run into the mother bear and cubs. The memory of her encounter with them looped in her mind as they moved down the mountain. She knew she must talk to this stalker.

The creature crept closer. Though exhausted, the straps chafing her shoulders, her knees complaining about the weight, Freda ran the last mile. She realized Elle no longer followed behind. "Elle?" she whispered.

"Go on without me."

Elle's resolve, free of fear, made Freda feel small.

"I'll be in shortly," Elle said. "Make sure Luna doesn't come over here."

Freda hesitated. She also knew this creature in the night was here for Elle. She was the Anima, the last—and she had a Task to fulfill. Freda's own life seemed diminutive in comparison. She turned without a word and continued home alone.

# ELDERS

I*'m here,* Elle called out. The creature held still. All to be heard was water. *Why do you follow me? What do you need?*

A cougar strutted onto the path. Each step was a shiver of muscle. Its fur gleamed in the moonless night, and its eyes shined the color of lapis. *We've anticipated the Anima's return for many winters.* The cougar's voice was fluid and cool. *I am the Elder of cougars. I see the fox Elder spoke the truth about your potential—both in its existence, and in its unfilled state.*

Elle wrapped her arms around her stomach.

*Don't worry,* the cougar continued. *The moment will come when you will own your power. There is time still, as our plan is only now, with your birth, set in motion. This winter, when the night is the longest of the year, you will come to the Waters of the Elders. We will reveal our Cause to you there.*

*Waters of the Elders—what is that?*

*It is a lake in the tallest peak west of here.*

Elle remembered the mythical map she had studied when she had been bedridden on Freda's futon. The lake appeared to be folded into the Home of the Gods. *Do you mean Moonstone Lake?*

*Is that what your kind call it? Few humans have seen the Waters. Most who do, don't return.* The cougar's voice sounded menacing.

Elle looked over her shoulder at the cabin. *May I bring my dog with me? I can't imagine hiking that far back into the mountains by myself, much less in winter.*

*But you must. You alone are the Anima. You alone will come to the Waters of the Elders on the longest night of the year. Until then, do not leave these mountains again.*

The cougar flowed away through the aspens, leaving a shivering Elle by herself in the copse.

Luna rushed over to Elle when she walked onto the homestead. *What happened back there?*

*I met the cougar Elder. She told me I must talk with all the Elders in a few months.*

Luna's good eye glistened. *Where are we going?*

We *aren't going anywhere,* Elle said, her voice gloomy. *I have to go alone, back there.* She pointed a finger west.

*I can't come? How far must you go? Who are these Elders?* Luna trailed behind Elle as she walked toward the cabin. Pale light pressed against the windows.

Elle held the door open for Luna. *I'm not entirely sure who the Elders are.* What were they, really? *It'll be a long trip,* she continued. *I wish you could come, Luna, but the cougar said I have to go alone.*

Luna whined. *Why must I always be left behind?*

*Please, don't make this harder than it already is.*

Freda had prepared a simple soup of chanterelle mushrooms, onions, and carrots. Elle collapsed on the futon. Luna slunk in, despondent. Freda figured the dog felt cast aside, unimportant. She could relate. "Mushroom soup," she said. "In honor of our Anima."

"Not funny," Elle said, her tone flat. "But thanks."

Freda cleared her throat. "So how was your—meeting?"

Elle knew Freda deserved to hear what had happened, but she wanted only to sleep. She yawned, stretching her arms behind her head. "It was a cougar following us," she said over another yawn. "She told me I must go into the Home of the Gods to talk with the Elders."

"The Elders?" Freda set her soup aside.

"I think they might be the oldest creatures in the Crazies." Elle's words came slow. "They're like timeworn versions of their kind. I've met three of them now. A swallow when I was in town. The fox who told me to come back here when Luna was poisoned. And now that cougar, who said I'll need to be at the Waters of the Elders on the winter solstice. I think that's Moonstone Lake. I saw it in *Maps of the Crazy Mountains.* The cougar said few humans have visited the lake. I think those who've tried to go there have been—well, I think they've been killed."

Comprehension dawned on Freda's face. "Headwaters of the Echo. It's in Ghost Peak."

Elle nodded. "Exactly. I'm terrified to go into those mountains alone, much less in the middle of winter. What if I get lost and freeze to death? What if I get buried in an avalanche?"

Freda wondered how she could help Elle become more comfortable in the mountains. It was one thing to study a map, another entirely to know the land. The bow caught the periphery of her vision. "We'll start hunting this week," she said. "I'll show you what I can. Then, when the snow comes, you'll better know the way."

☾

The aspens reached skyward with bare arms, their leaves piled upon the ground as a golden collage. Overcast skies left the day feeling gray and muted. Freda and Elle tramped south down Echo Canyon, alongside Mirror Lake. The waters reflected the evergreen forest edging the shores. A school of fish hovered beneath deadfall.

Both women had their bows attached to their packs. They had left Luna at home, again, to defend the chickens and goats from predators. Their first few hunts, Luna had protested, becoming sullen and refusing to speak to Elle for hours. But a few weeks ago, Luna had to chase off a bear in the animal pen. Luna now felt empowered by her established responsibility to guard the other animals. Elle missed her dog when it came time to hunt, but at least she no longer carried guilt about leaving her behind. Every animal needs a purpose, Elle had realized. She and Luna were on better terms than ever since this understanding was clarified.

Once a week, for the past eight, Elle and Freda had gone further and further back into the wilderness. The first week Freda and Elle had scrambled to the top of the Cougar's Jaw. They had crouched among the granite pinnacles, clutching the rock for life. A herd of mountain goats had shimmied away, weaving along an indiscernible path in the sheer rock face.

Freda had yelled over the wind, pointing to the Home of the Gods rising before them. "The tallest there in the middle is Ghost," she had hollered, the wind snatching the words away. "The Echo's Headwaters will be in its southwest side."

The following hikes, they had ventured west of the Cougar's Jaw and Bighorn Cirque. They had come across only a handful of hunters on their journeys. As Elle and Freda had veered away from them, they could hear them whisper something about women. Little did they know who they saw, Freda had thought, feeling pride in her companion.

It was their third day into this hunt. Late fall surrounded them with snowcapped peaks and dried up streams. The time to harvest was now. They knew where the herd slept and where it ate. Yesterday they had chosen the kill site. Tomorrow morning, Elle would take the shot.

They followed a thin creek streaming from Mirror Lake. The trees opened to reveal a river. They stopped and removed their packs. "This is the Echo," Freda said. "If you follow this river up the mountain, it will bring you to the cave where it originates."

Elle nodded once and swallowed hard. At least she would know the way, as Freda had promised. They drank their water flasks dry. Freda filled a pot with water as Elle prepared a fire. While waiting for the water to boil, they ate deer jerky and dried fruits. Elle felt the oncoming winter and tightened her jacket down. The elk hide still felt strange on her fingertips; it was smooth and cool, unlike her father's canvas jacket. Freda insisted Elle wear the hide when the weather promised moisture.

Steam from the boiling water drifted south. "We won't need to hike north of the herd today," Freda said, placing the pot on a rock to cool. "The wind shifted overnight. Have you noticed?"

"How can you tell?" Elle asked. The air felt stagnant to her.

"I keep my eyes open and my mind in the moment. You have to be present and aware to be a successful hunter. But your thoughts are in midwinter—are they not?"

Elle bit her lower lip. They filled their flasks with the boiled water.

"You still have time before you must go. We're closing in on the kill, Elle. Stay here, or our days of preparation will be wasted. This isn't a game, like it is for some hunters. Our survival come winter depends on our success."

Though still unsettled, her mind gravitating to Ghost Peak, Elle said, "Okay. Let's go."

They continued down the river before cutting east to the kill site. The trail opened into a brief clearing. "We'll sleep here," Freda said, standing in the marshy opening. "There's a shelter in the talus over there."

Elle followed her to the rock tumbled down from the pinnacles above. Freda built the fire as Elle pulled from her pack a dinner of dehydrated corn, peas, and herb soup. Overcast hid the stars when they slipped into their sleeping bags. Red rings circled out from the waning crescent moon, reminding Freda of her first kill, the blood rippling onto snow. She shivered through the night as Elle slept. In the near distance, the Ghost Pack howled and howled as the night crept past.

"Wake up," Freda murmured, touching Elle's shoulder. She felt warm even in the freezing cold of the morning. A fog veiled the mountains and trees. Dull light embodied the mist, hinting at an imminent dawn. Freda had barely slept. She said nothing about the wolves. A small fire crackled between rocks, and she heated water for tea and a gruel of dried huckleberries and ground timothy grass seeds.

Elle rolled her sleeping bag up, her movements stiff. The day to kill had come at last. Her stomach felt hollow.

Freda poured the steaming water into mugs and bowls. She handed a mug to Elle. "Lemon balm and lavender, for your nerves."

Elle sipped the tea. "Were you nervous for your first kill?"

"Of course." Freda finished her gruel and tea and told Elle to do the same.

They sidled across the talus field and into the timberline below Bighorn Cirque. The slope dipped into the elk's preferred drainage. Mist wove between the pines, wet and cold on their faces. Although they had been here a half dozen times, it felt like a foreign place. They descended further into the trees, and the fogged light of sunrise darkened.

Freda removed her pack and placed it, without a sound, on the forest floor. Elle slipped her bow free. She could hear the elk moving toward them, noises Freda wouldn't detect for a while. They crouched behind a pile of deadfall with Elle in front. Elle slid an arrow's notch onto the sinew as she had done hundreds of times now. She worried her heart, banging against her ribs, would reveal their presence.

"Remember your breathing," Freda whispered into her ear.

The bull emerged first. His giant antlers swayed as he moved toward them. Elle couldn't believe how quiet he was despite his titanic body. The harem followed close behind, stepping from the mist as if they were walking into this world from another. They exhaled out their nostrils with force, their breaths visible in the cold.

One cow, then the next sauntered forth. A couple calves followed close behind their mothers. Their coats were matted thick in anticipation of winter. Elle waited for the cow she and Freda had chosen: average in size, with no calf by her side or in her womb. And there she came, lumbering behind. Elle drew the arrow back. Her elbow quivered.

Freda watched the cow amble by. She was broadside. Quartering away. The shot was now. The shot was now!

*Twang. Thunk.*

The cow groaned and lurched back into the mist. The rest of the harem evaporated as well. Elle dropped her bow into her lap, the arrow limp in her hand.

Freda still held her right hand behind her ear. Had she hit the heart or lungs? It was too soon to tell. She looked at Elle as her shooting arm relaxed. Elle's black hair encircled her face, hiding a grimace. Freda placed a hand on her shoulder. "We need that elk," she murmured, the words meant as an apology. She squeezed her hand.

Elle had tried to bring her attention to her breathing. She had tried to slow her heart. But their voices had filled her mind. Cows had urged their calves along. The bull had ordered the cows to stay close. He had spoken of wolves. Elle pushed the hair from her face. "There are wolves nearby."

"We still need to give her time to slow down," Freda said.

Words felt unnatural so they waited without speaking. After a while, they followed the blood. Freda saw hope in the thick pools intermitting the trickling line of blackish red.

Elle smelled iron. She could hear the cow, her breathing a gurgle. They walked into a clearing and found her, sprawled out on the forest floor. Life flowed away from her heaving body.

"Finish her," Freda said. "Get your bow and finish her."

Elle's bow felt slick in her hand. She dropped the arrow.

Freda watched Elle fumbling. "What's your breath doing?" she asked. "Where's your mind?"

The elk said nothing. There was nothing to say. Like all creatures careening toward death, she wished only for passage. The arrow flew into her heart. All was still.

Movement stirred the fog. A wolf, black as the raven, stared back at Elle. She stepped toward him, and he didn't move. His yellow eyes glinted. He tilted his head back and barked, warning his pack of humans.

*This cow is ours,* Elle said. Wind picked up, swaying the fog. The wolf watched her move closer. She pulled her shoulders back. *You'll need to find another elk to claim.* Her voice rang calm and strong. She almost sounded like Freda.

The wolf was not as big as Elle had always imagined wolves to be. Luna was larger. His muzzle was salted, the tips of his black fur white. The rest of the pack shifted in the forest behind him, their presence blurred by the fog.

*It's the Anima,* he said to the other wolves. They slunk closer, curious and shy. The black wolf looked back at Elle. *Keep your elk. We don't want any more trouble from humans.* His words, cold as the morning, spoke to a lifetime of resentment. He and his pack disappeared as they had materialized, without a noise.

Elle gazed into the mist, confused by the sadness she felt. Freda cleaned the elk, and Elle helped her heave the carcass up into the air. After the blood had drained, they packed the meat and hide into leather bags, moving as quickly as possible. Wolves wouldn't attack—but grizzlies, not yet asleep, could smell a kill from miles away. Sun crossed the apex of sky and slid into twilight. They hiked through snow near Golden Falls Saddle and continued on a muddy trail alongside Owl Creek. No bears contested their trek. The fog lifted as night deepened, and they walked under stars the last stretch to home.

☾

Winter arrived in the canyon before the month's end. Snow covered the garden. Cans upon cans of pickled, jammed, and blanched produce lined the food shelves from end to end. Elk cuts filled a freezer made in the snow, offering fresh meat for at least a couple months. The majority of the meat had been brined or canned. Between the wild edibles and the food they had cultivated, Freda and Elle felt prepared to survive the winter.

A week into the snow storms, Elle found herself restless indoors. She and Freda cared for the chickens and goats, even in the blizzards. With another hand to help, the tasks took Freda half as long as they had in the past. Most of the responsibilities were done before breakfast. Afterward, the day spread out before them.

They spent hours drinking tea and reading. Freda scanned all her books on the Anima, looking for any mention of the Elders. She found none.. She couldn't remember Laurel, Javiera, or any of the Keepers mentioning them. Either her memory was fading, or these Elders had been kept secret from her. It was also possible, though doubtful, that the Keepers didn't know about the Elders, either.

Elle read Freda's old anthropology books, learning about cultures across time and space: the Indigenous nations of Montane before Imperial conquest in the third century of the Modern Era; the ancient Talhümus people of the western steppes, all but extinct following a period of genocide; and curiously, an Indigenous peoples named the Tuttuán Elle hadn't heard about before. They, too, had experienced near genocide, though two millennia earlier than the Talhümus and at the hands of the Lyzivers.

Elle knew from school history courses the Lyzivers allied with the Guâdí Empire of Shénchào, forming the Republic. She had little knowledge of the Lyzivers beyond the fact they were half of the problem her father had fought in the Second World War. Come to think of it, she wasn't quite sure why the Imperium and the Republic warred in the first place, something to do with the protectorates of Suqwas.

She wondered if the Elders knew of all this human drama, or if their plan for Elle was separate from cultural power struggles. The answer to this question might have been in *The Task of the Anima.* But of all the books Elle read, that wasn't one of them. It gathered dust beneath the futon. Even thinking about it overwhelmed her.

Freda now slept on the futon at night while Elle stayed in the tree house. Elle preferred sleeping up there, although she missed Luna against her legs. Sometimes she slept on the floor in the cabin to be near her dog. The two of them spent the days together, Luna napping while Elle read when the storms passed through. On the sunny days they set out into the forest, tromping through snow. With no particular purpose on any given day, they simply wandered within the hushed woods. Elle did everything she could to not think of the approaching solstice, though she knew her restlessness was thinly veiled fear. The disquiet shadowed her. She often found herself looking west.

The day before Elle would leave for Ghost Peak, she and Luna walked along the creek. Snow outlined the waterway. Thin, blue ice reached from both banks into a flowing center, where the waters ran obsidian. Boughs hung heavy with snow, and the aspen trees, limbs black and white, appeared stark as woodcarvings.

"I'm ready," Elle chanted to herself with the cadence of her steps. She had no other option than to believe these words. She and Luna continued upstream, to Golden Falls. All around, the wild creatures left traces of their existence: deer and pheasant tracks, raccoon paw marks near the creek, a squirrel's prints scurrying between trees. Elle noticed a strange set of tracks not far from the trail. She realized snowshoes had left them.

Sometimes Elle forgot entirely about humans other than Freda. The snowshoe tracks pulled her mind back to Twin Rivers. She followed the hikers' prints as she continued to the falls, thinking of her mother, Walter, Todd, her dad. She thought of her coworkers at the restaurant, her crush on Nox, her teachers, her former classmates, even her old councilor, Mr. Simmons—people from a lifetime ago. They all moved through her mind, and Elle realized with a shudder these fellow humans were not unlike the animals in this wild world, leaving their marks upon the snow. Their presence on this planet was perhaps nothing more than the bounding paw prints of a raccoon, the delicate indentation of a pheasant foot. This speculation filled her with a curious fusion of sorrow and liberation.

They reached the falls and rested near the pool beneath the cascading waters. In previous trips here this winter, the icicles hanging from the rock face had caught light in a glimmering show, hence Golden Falls. Today, the gray skies left the icicles white. Elle ate a strip of jerky. She remembered the dead cow, and of course, as the two were inseparable now, she remembered the black wolf. Following the hunt, Elle had thought more and more about wolves in general. She felt as if the wolf had arrived to help her cope with the kill. After all, he must kill to survive as well. Of humans and wolves, were they not more alike than different?

Mist gathered upon the pool, and Elle reflected on the magic of her new life. It was not solely her ability to communicate with other creatures making her reality as the Anima feel enchanted. It was the wildness of this world she lived within. She could hear the mysterious humming of a life force, pulsating in the trees, rippling within the frozen and flowing waters, ever changing as light and wind around her. This beauty, created by its own will, spoke of something much greater than any singular existence, human or other.

Though she couldn't name the changes within her, she felt them crystallizing. She crouched down to the water's edge and refused to turn away from her reflection. Though her eyes and face had morphed, she still had her father's nose and hair. Would he be proud of the woman she was becoming? Tears fractured the reflection. She took his knife out of her pocket and flicked the blade out. Running a finger along its spine, she decided she could make him proud. She *would* make him proud.

Elle left in the dark, with Freda and Luna fast asleep. She had prepared the night before, in the tree house, stuffing her pack with her sleeping bag, a small shovel, cooking equipment, and food to last for a week, just in case. As she crested Golden Falls Saddle, the sun rose. Hoar frost shimmered. Alone, as promised, she trudged across the white land, the snow coming up past her knees.

The mountains had pulled all the clouds from the sky around their colossal bodies, as if for warmth. White peaks reared up from the clouds. Elle stood atop the saddle for a long moment, absorbing the spectacle. She walked down into the clouds and the world shrunk to white nothingness. One step at a time brought her out of the clouds again. The rocky slope transitioned into timber.

A herd of elk, perhaps the one they had stalked this fall, had forged a trail through the snow to Mirror Lake. Ravens and magpies flitted between branches. Elle stilled in her tracks. A creature she had never seen in real life watched her pass. The wolverine hunched upon a fallen pine, taut as a snare. Her lip was curled up to reveal one fang, and her claws, spread out on the bark, looked like ten additional fangs, ivory and pointed.

A white hare dashed across the snow. The wolverine charged forth, her body longer, larger than Elle had first perceived. The kill happened quickly, a matter of power and precision. She disappeared into the forest's depths, the hare dangling from her mouth, still twitching. Elle continued on her way. How could she possibly be so lucky to witness such a thing? The wolverine seemed to her a creature from another time, fierce and unapologetic. She reminded Elle of someone she used to know, though the person eluded her now.

Elle reached the lake and skimmed along its shore to the creek. The water, spotted with ice, reflected the cerulean sky. Once flowing in the narrow creek, the water darkened. She took a moment to eat lunch where the creek and the Echo converged. The pemmican Freda had made of bear fat and wild currants filled her stomach. A muskrat downstream rubbed his tiny hands together on the shore. He noticed her watching and dove under a sheet of ice.

It was time to go up the mountain. The river fell in a fairly straight path with many waterfalls and icicles along the way. Elle trudged through the snow, thankful for the elk pants Freda had crafted from the kill. The river rounded north. Snow deepened, and Elle post-holed every step. She stopped again to eat pemmican and drink water. The sun moved behind the Home of the Gods, casting her and the land into a cold shadow.

The ground leveled into upland. Freda had told Elle about this plateau, showing it to her on a map. The clouds of the morning had evaporated hours ago, and Elle looked up to Ghost Peak. Freda had told Elle she should camp within the peak's moraine the day they had practiced digging snow shelters beneath Bighorn Cirque.

Elle found a spot where the snow piled high between two boulders. She worked with haste beget by fading light, digging free the entrance, boring her way inward, compacting the snow up and to the sides. When she finished, ruby and gold light spilled across the snow around her. It was as if she stood in a pool of liquid fire. She stripped off her under layer and tugged on a dry, wool shirt. As the sunset deepened into red, she sat upon the snow and ate more pemmican. Without movement, her mind fixated on tomorrow, the winter solstice.

Elle entered her snow shelter as twilight swelled across the sky. Despite her exhaustion, she couldn't fall asleep. Full of food, warm in the dark cave and sleeping bag, she knew nerves kept her awake. Her mind spun recklessly, relentlessly with thought. How many Elders would there be? What did they need to tell her? Was the Cause the cougar had mentioned the same as her Task?

She clenched her teeth as she thrashed back and forth. The shelter felt suffocating. She kicked the sleeping bag from her body and wiggled out of the entrance. North, above a silhouetted Ghost Peak, a green light swayed. The aurora borealis pulsed across the sky as three snaking rivers. Elle dropped to her knees. The brilliance rolled over her, wave upon wave. The plateau twinkled beneath the lights, the snow crystals as numberless as the stars.

Why her? What had she done to deserve such beauty? Tears came unbidden and froze on her face. Her whole body froze, transfixed, the only movement within her and upon the sky. Was it possible her father was here with her now? Was it possible he danced in those northern lights? She lifted her arms to the sky.

"It's me," she yelled. "It's me, Elle. The Anima reborn."

With the aurora borealis reflecting upon the earth, she could easily find her way to the cave. Elle packed her sleeping bag and walked to the Echo. She followed it around the plateau's southwest end. The shimmering waters reflected the green light. Rocks on the mountainside became many and large. She treaded carefully across them, crawling in places, the going slippery. The effort shallowed her breathing.

Trickling water guided her along, reminding her of where she was going. Or was it where she had come from? Delirium. Exhaustion. Doubt. She was a black spot upon the expanse of white, inching toward a black yawning above. All around the green lights continued to pour, swirl, act without a knowable pattern—the green lights star dust exploding into nothingness. Rising to her feet before the cave, her body vibrated as a drumming. The time was now. The time was now.

She smelled the calcium carbonate of limestone, skeletons of an ocean. White light radiated from within the cave. She stepped inside and followed a stream trickling through a narrow corridor, its waters shining an iridescent blue. Droplets tinkled down from stalactites. The ceiling lifted and the sides expanded. Elle felt she was in the womb of the mountain.

Moonstone Lake retained the mysterious coloring of its namesake, white shifting into blue shifting into white. It looked as if sky, liquefied, filled the crater. She walked to the water's edge. Movement beyond the lake stilled her. She had almost forgotten why she was here. The beauty had bewitched her. Looking up, she remembered. It was dawn, after all, and the winter solstice arrived with the first, gray rays of morning streaming into the cave.

Staggered, Elle knelt. The ground felt moist as a membrane.

Along the other shore crowded hundreds of animals. There was one for each species, she realized, seeing no two animals were the same. A mule and white tail deer. A bison. Black and grizzly bear. Elk. Wolf. Bobcat. Coyote. Goat and sheep. Cougar—the one she had met in the night. And the same fox she had encountered near the Brother River. She recognized the biggest creatures first. Smaller animals stood on rocks, looking back at her. Squirrel. Beaver. A few different bats. Vole. Chipmunk. Birds poised upon boulders, perched on the backs of larger animals, glided through the glow. Owls. Osprey. Eagles. The raven.

*Welcome, Anima,* a voice resounded.

Elle sat back on her heels. She searched for the one who had spoken.

A pika stood on the eastern shore, towering above the rest atop a boulder. *Twenty millennia ago, the human Elder disappeared,* the pika said. *Humans soon after began to act apart from the Sacred Balance sustaining all Life. We asked the Source for help, and the first Anima was born.*

All the animals looked up at the pika with knowing faces. Elle held both of her hands over her heart. She could feel it palpitating against her palm.

*The Anima's Task has always been singular,* the pika continued. *Bring humans back into Order. Yet over the millennia, the Anima and her allies have failed to fulfill her Task. Humans spread Disorder, taking and taking, disregarding their inherent role in the Sacred Balance. They do not consider their kin, their fellow animals, as they consume for their own needs.*

The cougar slunk forward from the crowd. *Now the earth is forever changed,* the cougar said. *The world is no longer shared by all. We have witnessed in horror as Life dwindles. Many Elders have been murdered at the hands of humans, leaving their species to go extinct.*

Silence as the Elders honored the losses. The animals appeared fierce in their poised demeanors, formidable in their diverse numbers. Even the smaller creatures commanded reverence. Elle felt as tiny and naked as a worm.

*The earth has experienced mass extinction many times,* the cougar said. *The difference, now, is our ability to fight for Life.*

A tremor moved through the creatures as they uttered agreements. There were as many different voices as there were animals.

The wolf Elder stepped next to the cougar. *The final Anima's birth sets forth a new Task, a new Cause,* the wolf said. *Life depends on the end of the human race. You, Anima, will join our quest to find and kill the human Elder.*

The cave throbbed as the animals bellowed in unison. Elle fell back as if the noise pushed her down. She tried to find her balance but kept slipping on the ground. *But—doesn't that mean all humans will then die?* she asked, stumbling to a stand. Her voice sounded as meager as she felt.

*Precisely,* the pika said.

*We haven't participated in the Anima's Task until now,* the cougar added. *As Elders, it's our responsibility to stay alive, for the sake of our species. Yet now we must act before it's too late.*

*We must kill the human Elder before the humans can kill all of Life,* the wolf said, snarling.

Elle ran a hand through her hair, her fingers catching in a tangle. She paced in front of the waters. The Elders waited, their stares an intense heat on her face. Light streaming into the cave shifted from gray to gold. She saw the grizzly Elder sit down next to the whitetail deer. She couldn't deny the suffering her kind caused other animals—but to end the human species?

She stopped pacing and squared to the Elders. *Give me a chance,* she said.

The Elders exchanged glances.

*Give me a chance,* she repeated, standing taller, *to fulfill the original*

*Task. If I fail, I will help you with your Cause.*

Tension rang against the cave walls. Each drop of falling water quickened the dread within her. She looked from the pika to the cougar to the wolf. They revealed nothing in their stern faces.

*Fine,* the pika said at last. *You will have one year to complete the original Task.*

*One year?* Elle asked, her jaw dropping. *How am I to complete something in one year that wasn't completed in millennia? I need—I need my* lifetime.

*Twelve years,* the cougar said. *If humans have not been brought back into Order by the winter solstice in twelve years, we will move forward with the hunt of their Elder.*

She heard the finality in the cougar's words and closed her gaping mouth.

*Go now,* the wolf said. *Go now with your last chance.*

Elle straightened her spine and nodded once. Turning from the Elders and their luminous waters, she walked out of the cave and into the dawn.

# APPENDIX

*"A magic as old as history.*
*A mystery as great as the mystery of earth itself.*
*One mushroom blossoms before a new era, its timing following a golden spiral.*
*One woman will eat of the mushroom and journey the fourth world.*
*When she returns—nothing the same.*
*All the vertebrate, apart from humans, she will hear, and they, her.*
*Together they share the ancient language of the earth."*

- Laurel Levin, the scroll

# ALIGAEA WORLD TIMELINE

## YEARS BEFORE PRESENT

### AVNI'S ERA: YIÚSIANS CONQUER NORTHEAST BANINCHI

2,208: *Avni born as the Fifth Anima* in the Purana Mountains of northern Makalon
2,200-1,375: The Yiúsians rebuild their kingdom

### BAZI'S ERA: YIÚSIANS RETURN TO BANINCHI

1,365: *Bazi born as the Sixth Anima* in the Alidima Mountains of Jafard
1,360: Freed Nyachians form a resistance army; they manage to push the Yiúsian Empire back to Lacuserra
1,200: Laurel establishes the Nafáit Haven
900: Flüschen conquer northern Lacuserra, the Albanian Seaterras, and Grahimland
Tuttuáns confined to the Nunlu and Anilsatok Seaterras and the Nigtok Islands

### OILI'S ERA: RISE OF THE FLÜSCHEN

844: *Oili born as the Seventh Anima* in Drauhöir, Grahimland
775-600: The Flüschen recover in northern Lacuserra
Yiúsians continue to engage in minor wars with Nyachians
600: Desnords adopt the Power as its official religion

Desnordian campaigns in the east: establish New Desnord and Nudom
Ongoing wars between the Desnords and the Lyzivers for Taigas
530: Flüschen reclaim Grahimland

## ERIE'S ERA: ESTABLISHMENT OF THE IMPERIUM

522: *Erie born as the Eighth Anima* in Nafáit, Taléria
518: The Desnords return from victory in Taigas to reclaim Taléria from the Flüschen
507-496: Eleven year *War of the Titans* between the Desnord Kingdom, Flüschen Kingdom, and the Yiúsian Empire
495: The Three Kingdoms Union establishes the Imperium and the Modern Era
Formation of Lacuserra's Palatines
494: The Imperial calendar begins on the winter solstice as Year 1 in the Modern Era
350-345: The Imperium conquers all of Baninchi
343: The Imperium invades the Openlands, losing to the alliance between the Jmu'neböna and the Tatankoy
323: The Imperium returns and conquers the Openlands

## WINTER'S ERA: IMPERIUM COLONIZES MONTANE

323: *Winter born as the Ninth Anima* in the Emerald Mountains of eastern Montane
320: *Clash of the Mages and Thorns*
320-310: The Imperium spreads west, conquering central Montane
Openlands and Springston Reservations established
250: The Guâdí Empire and Lyzivers form the Republic, acknowledging the Imperium as its mutual enemy
210-200: The Imperium invades and conquers northern Suqwas

## HANO'S ERA: FIRST WORLD WAR

200: *Hano born as the Ninth Anima* in the Pachaku Mountains of Tawan
*First World War* between the Imperium and the Republic takes place in the Malana Forest of Tawan
195: The Imperium wins the war and establishes Suqwas as a protectorate
128: Imperial colonists claim Wildwood shores

## FLO'S ERA: IMPERIUM DOMINATION

124: *Flo born as the Eleventh Anima* in the Wildwood Mountains
123: The Imperium colonizes all of Wildwood
105: Freda finds the scroll and travels to Old Makalon
101-98: *Second World War* between the Imperium and Republic takes place in western Montane and southeast Shénchåo
The Imperium wins and establishes the seven cantons, creating four districts within each canton; the Imperium also conquers Bielam and establishes it as a military base

# OVERVIEW OF MAGIC

*The Source*: the nameless, formless force creating, dissipating, and recreating energy into all forms of Life is known simply as the Source.

*First Dimension*: here

*Second Dimension*: now

*Third Dimension*: the past

*Fourth Dimension*: infinity

*Spirit Loci*: Spirit Loci are places of metaphysical fluidity, where two-dimensional reality intersects with the Third and Fourth Dimensions. The Spirit Loci are arranged across the planet in the Flower of Life pattern, though only eleven of the pattern's thirteen points are physically expressed. The *Anima metamorpha* grows and Salvagers are born within a Spirit Locus.

*Spirit Loci of the North*: Alidima Mountains, Ollaoise Forest, Kare Mountain

*Spirit Loci of the Center*: Corbel Forest, Emerald Mountains, Crazy Mountains, Orgo Forest, Zerg Forest

*Spirit Loci of the South*: Pachaku Mountains, Wildwood Mountains, Cáidiq Mountains

*Elders*: Elders are the genderless and ageless "prototype" of species. They do not die unless killed; when an Elder is killed, its species goes extinct.

*Animas*: Also known as Animal Women, Animas have top-predator powers and the ability to talk with other animals. Each Anima is tasked to bring humans back into ecological Order. With the speed of a lion, the strength of a bear, the agility of a leopard, and the hearing, smelling, and sight of a wolf, they are exceptional hunters and warriors.

The Anima's face morphs to have a jawline and cheekbones resembling the cougar. Her eyes grow larger, and the irises change to have bright orange coloring encircling a verdant green. Her wounds heal exceedingly fast and her immune system is immaculate. An Anima embodies her full animal potential and serves as a bridge between humans and their wild kin.

*The Task*: Elders created Animas to help bring humans back into the Sacred Balance preserving all Life, simply called the Order. This reason for the Anima's existence is known as the Task.

*The Anima metamorpha*: The mushroom able to transform a woman into the Anima grows in a cycle determined by the golden ratio. Atop its red cap, the white dots are arranged in the *Flower of Life* pattern.

*The Anima's Birth Cycle*: There are twelve Animas total. The first is born in the Spine of the Earth, about 15,000 years before present. The golden ratio determines when the next will be born, making the time between each rebirth shorter. The final Anima is born 77 years before present.

*Animal Communication*: The ancient language of the earth is communicated via the pineal gland. Animas can talk to all classes of vertebrate, including jawless fishes, cartilaginous fishes, bony fishes, amphibians, reptiles, birds, and mammals. The pineal gland exists only in organisms with backbones, (with the exception of the hagfish, sloth, manatee, dugong, and sugar glider). The pineal gland is about the size of a grain of rice; for the Anima, it is the size of its namesake, a pinecone. With its spines and spirals, the pinecone illustrates the golden ratio; it symbolizes growth and the unifying force underlying all Life.

*Keepers*: Keepers are the natural-born allies of the Anima. The term is later modified to include Mages in service of the Anima's Task.

*Shapeshifters*: Shapeshifters are over nine thousand years old and have the ability to change form into an animal. There is one Shapeshifter per terrestrial vertebrate, (totaling 32,500 at their genesis). They cannot die unless killed or if the Elder of their species is killed. They cannot survive outside their species' natural habitat. Shapeshifters may take many lovers, Commoner or Keeper, and they often do, being exceptionally beautiful and lustful humans. They are sterile and will never produce offspring. Their human attributes reflect those of their animals: the giraffe Shapeshifter, for example, is seven feet tall. Shapeshifters are blood-bonded to the Anima and live beholden to her commands.

*Salvagers*: Salvagers are humans born with the ability to see the past. They reincarnate in Spirit Loci east to west. There are always three alive: one in the south, one in the center, and one in the north. They can live up to 3,500 years old. Though Salvagers can procreate with humans, the fetus made from two Salvagers will always die in the womb. They have white-blue eyes and shockingly white hair. When Disorder is violently spreading, they experience debilitating migraines.

*Hindsight*: Salvager's ability to enter the Third Dimension of the Source and see any historical moment across space is called Hindsight.

*Duals*: As children of Salvagers, Duals can live up to 500 years old. Though they do not have Hindsight, they are exceptionally powerful magic practitioners. They have pure black eyes.

*Warps*: Duals corrupted by Disorder. The name also includes corrupted Mages.

*Plant Magic*: Every plant carries a particular energy, and when accessed through a learned magic practitioner, the plant's energy may be *evoked* and applied to a specific *praxis*. There are hundreds of thousands of magic practitioners across the world; they go by different names, depending on culture and time. Witch, medicine person, and shaman are the most common identities for magic practitioners.

*Florávo*: Florávo is the science and art of plant magic, established 900 years before present by the Salvager Laurel.

*Mages*: As students of Florávo, Mages tend to live a bit longer than Commoners, upward of 150, even 200 years.

*The Sub Rosa Forces*: Also known as the *Army of Thorns*, the Sub Rosa Forces is the Imperium's martial application of plant magic.

*Commoners*: Humans without Keeper blood are known as Commoners. The term is later modified to include humans not trained in Florávo, as well as those entirely ignorant to the existence of magic.

*Taker*: A Taker is a Commoner who actively (and violently) spreads Disorder.

# KEEPERS OF IMPORT

## SALVAGERS OF THE NORTH

*Esha the Crow*: Alidima Mountains; 3,570-741 YBP
Facilitates Oili's birth; dies of old age in the Eldis Forest

*Uki*: Ollaoise Forest, Taigas; 741 YBP
Facilities Erie's birth; helps Laurel facilitate Winter's battle, the *Clash of Mages and Thorns*; disappears to find her daughter, *Ada*

## SALVAGERS OF THE CENTER

*Gaagi*: Crazy Mountains, Montane; 5,763-2,189 YBP
Facilitates Avni's birth and the Makalonian Independence; dies of old age

*Laurel*: Orgo Forest, modern day Lyziver; 2,189 YBP
Sends Hamla to facilitate Bazi's birth and the Nyachian Liberation; mother of Florávo; author of the scroll; forges the Grand Alliance for Winter's demonstration of the Task

## SALVAGERS OF THE SOUTH

*Rua*: Wildwood Mountains: 431 YBP
Facilitates Winter's birth; facilitates Flo's birth; enters Fourth Dimension to find Flo's Death Revelation for Freda

## SHAPESHIFTERS

Born 9,336 YBP

*Sabaa*: the golden eagle; born as an Alidiman woman
*Dailan*: the osprey; born as a Dakúdmin woman
*Hamia*: the cheetah; born as a Nyachian woman
*Stian*: the stoat; born as a Flüschen man
*Neva*: the snowy owl; born as a Flüschen woman
*Keno*: the gray wolf; born as a Desnordian man
*Vítor*: the puma; born as a Sypayos man
*Stor*: the polar bear; born as a Tuttuán man

## MAGES

*Freda:* born 129 YBP in Twin Rivers, Prominence; largely self-taught following a two-year stay at the Nafáit Haven
*Javiera:* born 154 YBP in Hermida, Soleria; High Mage of the Nafáit Haven
*Tillie:* born 126 YBP in Havdel, Flaord; trained at the Nafáit Haven
*Brigid:* born 132 YBP in Violtt, Etavl; trained at the Nafáit Haven
*Orvik:* born 135 YBP in Tark, Anilsatok; trained at the Nafáit Haven
*Damari:* born 140 YBP in Fioritlá, Torerra; trained at the Nafáit Haven
*Aife:* born 525 YBP in Habitagne, Sangerria; dies at the Battle of Hellörf, 519 YBP
*Camden:* born 553 YBP in Havdel, Flaord; dies at the Battle of Hellörf, 519 YBP
*Kelvan:* born 561 YBP in Braedan, Desnord; dies at the Battle of Hellörf, 519 YBP
*Jaco:* born 544 YBP at the Nafáit Haven; Kelvan's son; dies in the War of the Titans, 505 YBP
*Ada:* born 515 YBP at the Nafáit Haven; Uki's daughter

# ACKNOWLEDGEMENTS

While this book took many hours of sitting down alone, creating, it feels as if all of Life kept me company. Then and always. So to this earth: thank you. Thank you for sustaining me. Thank you for your nourishing companionship and relentless generosity.

To my husband, thank you. Thank you, Jarred, for your patience, kindness, encouragement, tough love, soft love, ever-evolving-and-never-faltering love. You alone know what this took: thank you for staying by my side through it *all*. Thank you for offering your honest feedback on version one of the manuscript so it—so I—could grow.

To my family, thank you. Thank you, mom, for telling me to keep going, especially when the going's tough. Thank you, dad, for reading me books as a child and taking me camping for the first time. Thank you, Brett, for reading all seven versions of this manuscript; thank you for asking hard questions and helping me improve the writing. But more so, thank you for being the kind of brother who teaches me how to hunt, calls me just to chat, and laughs at my awkward jokes at the dinner table. Thank you, Emily and Scott, for making my life more joyful.

To my friends: thank you. Thank you for witnessing, for holding space. Thank you for asking how it's going, for your excitement, support, cheers for small and large gains, laughter, and love.

To my teachers: thank you. Thank you to Betty Higgins for your soul work. Thank you to all the authors whose writing reworked my life, helping me think and act with more compassion, curiosity, and gratitude. Thank you to my professors in college who taught me the craft. Thank you, Debra Magpie Earling, for your attentive instruction and for encouraging me to elect Creative Writing as my degree.

Thank you, Greg Pape and Judy Blunt, for showing me how to dig deeper and refine whatever I unearth. Thank you, Dan Spencer, for expanding my intellectual and spiritual relationship to the ecological movement and for your mentorship throughout my studies. Thank you, Robin Saha, for your perception-widening class on environmental justice. Thank you, Melanie Rae Thon, Terry Tempest Williams, Greg Smoak, and Teresa Cohn, for further strengthening my foundation. And thank you to all the teachers I've had, from Kindergarten to Graduate School, who dedicate(d) their lives to improving the world, one mind at a time.

To my beta readers: thank you. Thank you, Brett and Jarred, for all your investments. Thank you, Maggie Slepian, for your eagle-eye edits, wit, and companionship. Thank you, Molly May, for your thoughtful questions and in-between-the-lines feedback. Thank you, Christopher J. Carter, for your professional insights. Thank you, Simone Aliya, for your diligent pen. Thank you, Herman Watson, for your humorous and helpful commentary. Thank you, Caroline Bark, Anderson Bouton, and Michael Ochsner, for gifting me encouragement. And thank you to my friends who read the manuscript and offered support simply by keeping me company in the vast world of Aligaea.

To you, who read this book: thank you. Thank you for being here.

*Thank you.*

# ABOUT THE AUTHOR

KELSEY K. SATHER lives in Montana. Her stories explore the complexities of human-nature interconnections. While an author of nonfiction essays for over a decade, fantasy remains her first and true love.

She received an MA in Environmental Humanities from the University of Utah. At the University of Montana, she received the Davidson Honors College Scholar Distinction in Creative Writing and Environmental Studies.

After teaching at the university level, Kelsey co-managed a writers' collective for four years, where she facilitated creative writing workshops for all ages. She's also worked as a skiing and climbing instructor, as well as a baker. When she's not writing, she enjoys mountain sports and spending time with friends and family.

KELSEYKSATHER.COM

Explore the magical world of Aligaea:

ANCIENTLANGUAGEOFTHEEARTH.COM

Ten percent of net profits from *Birth of the Anima* will be donated to the Biocene Foundation.

Learn more:

BIOCENEFOUNDATION.ORG

The Polar Islands
Iceberg Sea
The Lost Lands
Borealis Sea
Mother Water Glacier
Drevdi Sea
A Thousand Lakes
The Wukopa Ice Fields
Lady/dopady Bay
Northstar Lake
The Divide Mountains
Koldno
Lyziver
The Lesto Plains
Titantic
Spine of the Earth
The Kare Mountains
Kare
The Orgo Forest
The Lug Steppes
The Zerg Forest
The Great Lakes
The Neuls Steppes
Shénchåo
Rose
The Baifū Marshlands
The Dáharüd Desert
The Jeolang Forest
Red Earth Desert
Hwalul
Guadí Bay
The Budeond Highlands
The Crown Mountains
The Cáidiq Mountains
Bay of Rogs
Shiteik Seaterra
The Shénchåo Seaterras
Red Sea
Blue Reef Sea
The Wildwood Mountains
Great Alimendia Sea